MOTIVE CLAUSES IN HEBREW LAW

SOCIETY
OF BIBLICAL
LITERATURE

DISSERTATION SERIES

edited by
Douglas A. Knight

Number 45
MOTIVE CLAUSES IN HEBREW LAW
BIBLICAL FORMS AND NEAR EASTERN PARALLELS
by
Rifat Sonsino

Rifat Sonsino

MOTIVE CLAUSES IN HEBREW LAW
BIBLICAL FORMS AND NEAR EASTERN PARALLELS

Scholars Press

Distributed by
Scholars Press
101 Salem Street
Chico, California 95926

MOTIVE CLAUSES IN HEBREW LAW
BIBLICAL FORMS AND NEAR EASTERN PARALLELS
Rifat Sonsino

Ph.D., 1975
University of Pennsylvania

Advisers:
Barry L. Eichler
Jeffrey H. Tigay

Library of Congress Cataloging in Publication Data

Sonsino, Rifat, 1938–
  Motive clauses in Hebrew law.

  (Dissertation series: no. 45 ISSN 0145-2770)
  Originally presented as the author thesis, University
of Pennsylvania, 1975.
  Bibliography: p.
  Includes index.
  1. Law (Theology) — Biblical teaching. 2. Jewish law.
3. Bible. O.T. Pentateuch — Criticism, interpretation,
etc. Assyro-Babylonian literature — Relation to the Old
Testament. I. Title II. Series: Society of Biblical
Literature. Dissertation series ; no. 45.
BS1199.L3S65   1979   222'.1'06   79-15024
ISBN 0-89130-317-0
ISBN 0-89130-318-9 pbk.

Printed in the United States of America
1 2 3 4 5

Edwards Brothers, Inc.
Ann Arbor, Michigan 48106

TABLE OF CONTENTS

TABLE OF ABBREVIATIONS

AASOR	Annual of the American Schools of Oriental Research
AB	Anchor Bible
ABL	R. F. Harper, *Assyrian and Babylonian Letters Belonging to the Kouyunjik Collection of the British Museum*
AfO	*Archiv für Orientforschung*
AGH	E. Ebeling, *Die akkadische Gebetsserie "Handerhebung"*
AHW	W. von Soden, *Akkadisches Handwörterbuch*
AJA	*American Journal of Archaeology*
AJSL	*American Journal of Semitic Languages and Literature*
AnBib	Analecta biblica
ANET	J. B. Pritchard (ed.), *Ancient Near Eastern Texts Relating to the Old Testament*
AnOr	Analecta orientalia
AnSt	*Anatolian Studies*
AOS	American Oriental Series
ARM	Archives royales de Mari
ArOr	*Archiv orientální*
AS	*Assyriological Studies*
asynd	asyndetic
AT	D. J. Wiseman, *The Alalakh Tablets*
BAR	*Biblical Archaeologist Reader*
BASOR	*Bulletin of the American Schools of Oriental Research*
BBB	Bonner biblische Beiträge
BC	Book of the Covenant
BDB	F. Brown, S. R. Driver, and C. A. Briggs, *A Hebrew and English Lexicon of the Old Testament*

BE	H. V. Hilprecht (ed.), *Babylonian Expedition of the University of Pennsylvania*. Series A: *Cuneiform Texts*
BHK	R. Kittel (ed.), *Biblia hebraica*, 7th ed.
BHT	Beiträge zur historischen Theologie
BibOr	Biblica et orientalia
BiOr	*Bibliotheca Orientalis*
BMS	L. W. King, *Babylonian Magic and Sorcery*
BWANT	Beiträge zur Wissenschaft vom Alten und Neuen Testament
BWL	W. G. Lambert, *Babylonian Wisdom Literature*
BZ	*Biblische Zeitschrift*
BZAW	Beihefte zur Zeitschrift für die alttestamentliche Wissenschaft
CAD	I. J. Gelb et al. (ed.), *The Assyrian Dictionary of the Oriental Institute of the University of Chicago*
CBQ	*Catholic Biblical Quarterly*
CCT	*Cuneiform Texts from Cappadocian Tablets in the British Museum*
CD	Cultic Decalogue
concl	conclusion
com	ad hoc commands
CT	*Cuneiform Texts from Babylonian Tablets etc. in the British Museum*
D	Deuteronomy
Dec	Decalogue
EA	J. A. Knudtzon, *Die El-Amarna Tafeln*
EB	*Estudios Biblicos*
EncJud	*Encyclopaedia judaica*
GAG	W. von Soden, *Grundriss der akkadischen Grammatik*
Ges	*Gesenius' Hebrew and Chaldee Lexicon to the Old Testament Scriptures*

Gilg	Gilgamesh
GKC	*Gesenius' Hebrew Grammar*, ed. E. Kautzsch, tr. A. Cowley
H	Holiness Code
HG	P. Koschaker and A. Ungnad, *Hammurabi's Gesetz*
Hh	Lexical series ḪAR.*ra* = *ḫubullu*
HL	Hittite Laws
HUCA	*Hebrew Union College Annual*
IDB	G. A. Buttrick (ed.), *Interpreter's Dictionary of the Bible*
intrn mc	internal motive clause
intro	introduction
JAOS	*Journal of the American Oriental Society*
JBL	*Journal of Biblical Literature*
JCS	*Journal of Cuneiform Studies*
JEA	*Journal of Egyptian Archaeology*
JEN	E. Chiera and E. Lacheman, *Joint Expedition with Iraq Museum at Nuzi*
JNES	*Journal of Near Eastern Studies*
JPSV	*Jewish Publication Society Version* (1917)
JSS	*Journal of Semitic Studies*
KAI	H. Donner and W. Röllig, *Kanaanäische und aramäische Inschriften*
Kbo	*Keilschrifttexte aus Boghaz-köi*
LE	Laws of Eshnunna
LH	Laws of Hammurabi
LI	Laws of Lipit-Ishtar
LU	Laws of Ur-Nammu
MAL	Middle Assyrian Laws
mc	motive clause
MDP	*Mémoires de la Délégation en Perse*

MIO	*Mitteilungen des Instituts für Orientforschung*
MRS	Mission de Ras Shamra
MT	Masoretic Text
NAB	*New American Bible* (1970)
NBL	Neo-Babylonian Laws
NEB	*New English Bible* (1972)
NJV	*New Jewish Version, The Torah* (1967)
nl	not law
OIP	Oriental Institute Publications
OLZ	*Orientalische Literaturzeitung*
OrNS	*Orientalia*, New Series
OTS	*Oudtestamentische Studiën*
PAPS	*Proceedings of the American Philosophical Society*
par	parenesis, parenetic
PBS	Publications of the Babylonian Section, University of Pennsylvania
PC	Priestly Code
PEQ	*Palestine Exploration Quarterly*
R	Redactor
RA	*Revue d'assyriologie et d'archéologie orientale*
RB	*Revue biblique*
RHR	*Revue de l'histoire des religions*
RIDA	*Revue internationale des droits de l'antiquité*
RSO	*Rivista degli studi orientali*
RSV	*Revised Standard Version*
SANT	Studien zum Alten und Neuen Testament
SBT	Studies in Biblical Theology
StudOr	*Studia orientalia*

sum	summary
TBü	Theologische Bücherei
TCL	Textes cunéiformes (Musée national du Louvre)
TMB	F. Thureau-Dangin, *Textes mathématiques babyloniens*
VAB	Vorderasiatische Bibliothek
VT	*Vetus Testamentum*
VTSup	Vetus Testamentum Supplement
WMANT	Wissenschaftliche Monographien zum Alten und Neuen Testament
WZKM	*Wiener Zeitschrift für die Kunde des Morgenlandes*
YOS	Yale Oriental Series
ZAW	*Zeitschrift für die alttestamentliche Wissenschaft*
ZSS	*Zeitschrift der Savigny-Stiftung*

LIST OF CHARTS

PREFACE

Biblical laws, composed in a variety of forms, sometimes contain dependent clauses or phrases which express a motive for a law or for observing it, i.e., a reason why the law is as it is, or an incentive for obeying it. The present study, undertaken within the scope of form criticism, proposes to analyze the use of motive clauses in the Pentateuchal legal corpora in light of biblical and extra-biblical literature.

B. Gemser was the first scholar who seriously addressed himself to the issue of the motive clauses in his article, "The Importance of the Motive Clause in Old Testament Law" (VTSup 1 [1953] 50-66). In his study he defined the motive clauses, discussed briefly their form and classified them as explanatory, ethical, religious and historico-religious. He also defended the originality of many of them and drew attention to the intrinsic coherence between law and wisdom. Gemser, however, was aware that his study was only introductory in nature, and in his article he clearly stated that he had not exhausted the discussion of the motive clauses.

Following his lead, R. W. Uitti, in his doctoral dissertation, "The Motive Clause in Old Testament Law" (Lutheran School of Theology at Chicago, 1973), attempted to present a fuller analysis of the motive clauses. Whereas Gemser examined only five law collections in the Bible (i.e., the Decalogue, the cultic Decalogue, the Book of the Covenant, the Holiness Code and the Deuteronomic Code), Uitti considered seven collections, by adding the Shechemite dodecalogue and the Priestly Code. Furthermore, he set out to reconstruct the history of the motive phenomenon in biblical law by arguing for an oral and cultic origin of the motive clauses in the earlier law collections and for a literary origin of the motive clauses in the later legal corpora. Finally, by joining others who had pointed to the existence of motive clauses in the laws of Hammurabi, he discounted Gemser's contention that motive clauses were unique to biblical law.

A critical evaluation of Gemser's and Uitti's observations indicates the necessity for a re-examination of the legal motive clauses, based upon a more precise argumentation and within a broader scope, encompassing both biblical and extra-biblical literature.

In order to avoid confusion, some of the basic issues will need to be more clearly defined. Both scholars, for instance, studied the motive clauses together with the independent parenetic statements within the category of motive clauses. However, a closer analysis of these components of the law shows that they ought to be distinguished from one another on the basis of their form as well as presumed function. Similarly, it would be necessary to give up the misleading procedure followed by Gemser and Uitti of computing the percentages of the motivated laws by counting paragraphs of prescriptions dealing with the same subject. In fact only individual prescriptions are motivated, and proper ratios can only be established by counting these. Prior to that undertaking, guidelines must be set up in order to isolate the individual legal prescriptions, whether motivated or not. In an effort toward defining what is law in the Pentateuch, it would also be necessary to draw a contrast between curses and laws, parenetic statements and laws, and ad hoc commands and laws.

Gemser did not undertake a formal investigation of the origin and life setting of the motive clauses, although he did suggest a connection between law and wisdom. Uitti, on his part, based his theory of the cultic origin of the motive clauses on the cultic recitation of the apodictic laws. Yet, there is no evidence in the Bible supporting the existence of such a practice in ancient Israel. An empirical way of searching for clues as to the origin and function of the motivated laws in the Pentateuch would be to study the legal motive clauses in light of motive clauses found in other biblical literary genres. Neither scholar considered this aspect of the legal motive clauses. The matter therefore warrants a special investigation.

Inasmuch as ancient Israel was, to a large extent, part of the common culture of the ancient Near East, it will also be necessary to consider the motive phenomenon in biblical law in light of the ancient Near Eastern legal tradition. Gemser stressed the uniqueness of the biblical motive clauses--a point which has been perpetuated by many a scholar until today. However, a number of Assyriologists and certain biblical scholars, among them Uitti, have already confirmed the existence of motive clauses in the laws of Hammurabi. Now, other ancient Near Eastern legal corpora must be analyzed in order to see whether or not motivation is exclusive to the Bible and the laws of Hammurabi. In addition, it would be instructive to study the motive clauses in the cuneiform material with regard to their form, content and origin for possible illumination of the use of motivation in biblical law.

The matter of originality of the motive clauses must be faced, even though the question is admittedly a difficult one. The tendency in biblical scholarship is to view them as additions by later editors. Gemser attempted to prove their originality by indicating that these occur in ancient strata of biblical law and that the rhythmic and proverbial form of some of them point to an archaic formulation of the laws. Uitti, too, maintained the originality of the motive clauses in the earlier law collections by arguing that these originated in connection with the recitation of the sacred law in Israel's early cultic life. All of these opinions need to be evaluated critically on their own merit and also against the backdrop of certain ancient Near Eastern texts containing motivated statements which have not been subjected to the complex and lengthy process of transmission undergone by their biblical counterparts.

The present study, though taking into account the contributions of both Gemser and Uitti, differs from their work, primarily in that it analyzes the legal motive clauses in light of other biblical literary genres and frequently considers the relevant data provided by extra-biblical documents.

The present investigation will unfold in four chapters. Chapter I will deal with the biblical and cuneiform laws. Since the present study is undertaken within the scope of form criticism, the form-critical assumptions as applied to biblical law will be critically evaluated. Moreover, since motive clauses

constitute part of the formulation of the laws, it will be
necessary to examine first the form and setting of the laws
which incorporate them. Chapter II will concentrate on the
biblical legal motive clauses. Having differentiated them from
explicative notes and independent parenetic statements, the
legal motive clauses will be studied with regard to their form,
content, distribution among the biblical law collections and
their function. So as to widen our understanding of the motive
phenomenon, an investigation will be undertaken, in Chapter III,
of the motive clauses found in extra-biblical laws. The results will then be compared and contrasted with those obtained
within the Bible. Finally, in Chapter IV, the question of the
originality of the motive clauses will be discussed, and the
scholarly opinions on this subject will be critically examined
against the background of ancient Near Eastern texts.

I wish to record my gratitude to my teachers and advisers
at the University of Pennsylvania, Dr. Barry L. Eichler and Dr.
Jeffrey H. Tigay, for guiding me through all the stages of this
investigation. I am indebted to Dr. Roger W. Uitti, who
generously placed at my disposal his unpublished doctoral dissertation, "The Motive Clause in Old Testament Law," only a
short time after it was approved by the Lutheran School of
Theology at Chicago in 1973. I would also like to express my
thanks to Dr. Larry K. Robbins of the University of Pennsylvania and to Dr. Douglas A. Knight, the editor of the Society
of Biblical Literature Dissertation Series, for their valuable
suggestions regarding content, style and format. Finally, I am
very appreciative to KTAV Publishing House, New York, for
allowing me to use the Hebrew text in the Appendix, and to
those members of North Shore Congregation Israel in Glencoe,
Illinois, for their financial support toward the publication
of this thesis.

The author gratefully acknowledges
permission granted by KTAV Publishing House to reprint
sections from their Hebrew Bible.

CHAPTER I

FORM AND SETTING OF BIBLICAL AND CUNEIFORM LAWS

THE COMMON LEGAL TRADITION

The ancient Near East constitutes, more or less, a "cultural continuum"[1] in which interpenetration and crossfertilization took place in a variety of areas, including literature and law. Material remains found at numerous sites in Mesopotamia, Asia Minor, Syria-Palestine and Egypt eloquently testify to this common tradition but also reveal local variations and, at times, unique characteristics confined to particular places and peoples. It is to this milieu that Israel belonged. The existing parallels between certain biblical traditions and those known from the other countries of the ancient Near East, in particular Mesopotamia (especially those dealing with the primeval times), show that Israel shared, to a large extent, the common cultural patrimony of her neighbors, far and near. This was possible not only because of the geographic location of Israel as a corridor between Mesopotamia and Egypt but also by the early peregrinations of the Israelite people within the orbit of the ancient Near East which was permeated primarily by Mesopotamian civilization and culture.[2]

Biblical law reflects one aspect of this influence. As E. A. Speiser wrote:

> There is scarcely a section of the Old Testament,
> especially in its early portions, that fails to
> reflect some form of influence from Abraham's home-
> land....And nowhere is such influence more pronounced
> than in the general field of law.[3]

Yet, though Israel shared the common culture of the ancient Near East, the study of the biblical traditions clearly indicates that whatever Israel incorporated from the wealth of traditions of the surrounding cultures, it did so by means of selectivity, adaptation and, at times, transformation.[4] This is also true of biblical law. Even though it reflects the common legal tradition of the ancient Near East, the theoretical basis of the biblical law displays unique characteristics unparalleled in other law corpora, such as divine authorship, religious cast,

1

inextricable relation between covenant and law, and others.[5]
Therefore, in comparing the biblical law with its cuneiform
counterpart, it is necessary to remember that biblical legislation represents a different legal philosophy and that the util-
ization of similar legal forms does not necessarily indicate a
common origin or identity of their life setting.

THE FORM OF BIBLICAL LAWS

Alt's Classification

Biblical law has been analyzed from different perspectives.
Through studies of a general nature or with a more specialized
interest, notable effort has been exerted to understand its
character and meaning and to discern its institutions, values
and concepts.[6] In addition, numerous studies have been devoted
to the investigation of the formal characteristics of the biblical law. The beginning of this analysis can be traced to
H. Gunkel, the founder of the school of biblical form criticism,
and his student H. Gressmann.[7] Both left only brief discussions
of the Israelite legal formulations. More extensive work was
done by scholars such as A. Jirku, A. Jepsen and S. Mowinckel,
all three in 1927. Jirku, using the stylistic formulation of
the laws as a criterion, divided the laws of the Pentateuch into
ten independent collections.[8] Jepsen distinguished between four
types of laws in the Book of the Covenant,[9] and Mowinckel investigated the setting in life of the Decalogue.[10] But it is A.
Alt's essay, "Die Ursprünge des israelitischen Rechts,"[11] published in 1934, that has had a lasting impact on the field of
biblical law.

Alt was struck by the juxtaposition of various legal forms
in the Book of the Covenant. He therefore set out to categorize
the different forms and then investigated their origin. Using
the tools of the form-critical method, he first differentiated
between "casuistic" and "apodictic" laws.[12]

A casuistic law, Alt pointed out, is built on the sequence
of the protasis and apodosis of a conditional sentence. In its
pure form, all parties with whom the law is concerned are referred to in the third person. Whereas the main case is

introduced by the conjunction כִּי ("granted," or "supposing
that"), subsidiary cases, he stated, are introduced by the
weaker אִם ("if").[13]

According to Alt, casuistic laws deal basically with
secular matters and point to their use in the work of ordinary
courts. "They were presumably composed, then, to fulfill the
needs of these courts."[14] However, he added, their ultimate
origin is not to be found in Israel. The "feeble religious
element in the Israelite casuistic law,"[15] its betrayal of a
"completely neutral attitude both in outlook and intention to
everything that we know to be specifically Israelite"[16] and,
finally, its almost exclusive use in extra-biblical legal corpora[17] imply that its source must be sought outside of Israel.
This, however, does not mean that its origin must be traced to
the peoples of far away Mesopotamia or Asia Minor, for in spite
of many similarities these law collections show too many differences both in form and content to be the direct ancestors of the
casuistic law of Israel.[18] Therefore, Alt inferred, the latter
must have been adopted from the Canaanites, who must have had
legal corpora of their own, presumably written in the Babylonian
language and in cuneiform script.[19] He placed the time of the
adoption "between the entry and the foundation of the Israelite
kingdom in Palestine,"[20] though, he admitted, "we have at present no original sources for the study of the Canaanite law."[21]
He further acknowledged that "the process by which the Israelites adopted this body of law is unfortunately also unknown."[22]

As for laws formulated in the "apodictic style," they can
be identified, according to Alt, on the basis of the following
characteristics: they are generally rhythmic and terse in style,
metrical in form, fundamental, categorical and inclusive in nature; they usually appear in series. Here Alt isolated various
series on the basis of their formulation: (1) laws introduced
by means of an active participle, and followed by the מוֹת יוּמַת
formula (e.g., Exod 21:12, 15-17); (2) a "list of crimes laid
under a curse in Deut. xxvii. 15-26,"[23] where the predicate,
"cursed" (אָרוּר), is placed at the beginning of the statement
and the subject which follows it usually takes the form of a
participle to which an object or a qualifying adverb is added;

(3) four short series: (a) Lev 18:7-17 (לא plus second person
imperfect); (b) and (c) two short fragments of lists, one in
Exod 22:17, 20 (with interpolations), 21, 27a,b,[24] and the other
in Exod 23:1-3, 6-9 (with many interpolations);[25] both of them
consist of prohibitions in the second person singular; and,
finally, (d) the Decalogue, where the "categorical negative is
the strongest unifying element in the whole list."[26]

Apodictic laws, Alt noted, generally deal with subjects
not considered in the casuistic laws. Their main concern is
sacral: "Everything in them is related exclusively to the Israelite nation and the religion of Israel."[27] This excludes
the possibility of a common origin for both apodictic and
casuistic forms. The origin of the apodictic laws must be
sought only within Israel. There is, however, no need to in-
vent a context for these laws, for their setting in the cult of
ancient Israel can be recovered on the basis of Deut 27:15-26
and 31:9f. The first text places the reading of a list of
curses within a sacral ceremony. The second refers to a reading of the law before the assembly of the whole people at the
Feast of Tabernacles every seventh year. Yet, he argued, it is
doubtful whether a book of laws as long and as densely packed
as Deuteronomy could be firmly impressed on the memory of a
whole nation if it were read out to them only every seven
years.[28] Therefore, he concluded, the underlying ceremony must
have been one in which shorter series of laws were proclaimed.
"The casuistic law was by its very nature unsuited for such use,
so that the obvious material for the purpose seems to be the
short lists of apodictic laws."[29] Furthermore, these apodictic
laws must have been proclaimed periodically, for, he reasoned,
only in relation to constantly recurring situations can such a
category catch on.[30] Deuteronomy 31 clearly speaks of a regularly occurring situation in the life of the Israelites. Alt
therefore suggested that Deuteronomy 27, too, must be interpreted along the same lines, even though the text neither refers
to a periodic occurrence nor contains a reference to a particular festival.

According to Alt the ceremony itself had a very special
nature. He maintained that it constituted not only the life

setting for the proclamation of apodictic laws, but also "a
regular renewal of the covenant between Yahweh and Israel,"[31]
though, he admitted, the expression "renewal of covenant" is
nowhere attested in the Bible.[32]

Alt's Presuppositions: A Critical Evaluation

Alt chose a form-critical approach to Israelite law because
he was dissatisfied with the limitations of the methods of literary criticism. They alone, he said,

> do not suffice to lead us directly to the oldest forms,
> for they can only show us older literary versions of
> the laws, and the oldest written forms which we can
> isolate with any degree of probability seem bound in
> any case to be secondary productions, quite distinct
> from the first promulgation of the laws.[33]

Arguing that "the making of the law is basically not a literary
process at all, but part of the life of a community,"[34] Alt attempted to investigate the real origins of the legal forms by
applying the form-critical method to the biblical legal material.

Alt's basic presuppositions were the same as those developed and tested by Gunkel on the sagas of Genesis, prophetic
sayings and the Psalms. Alt began by stressing that full attention must be given to "the possibility that the very oldest
written compilations of laws are separated from the real origins
of the law by a considerable period in which the law was developed and handed down orally."[35] He then argued that at this
oral stage there was an inseparable connection between form and
content in that "each form of expression was appropriate to
some particular circumstance amongst the regular recurring
events and necessities of life."[36] This connection is similarly
carried over into the literary stage, for, as Alt put it, "in
each individual form, as long as it remains in use in its own
context, the ideas it contains are always connected with certain fixed forms of expression."[37] Given these assumptions,
the study of legal forms becomes extremely important, for these
forms contain clues as to their real origin and function in the
life of the people.

Alt recognized that a few such attempts had been made in
the field of biblical law,[38] but lamented that the method had
not as "yet been applied as consistently as it ought to be."[39]
He therefore set out to do just that.

Several decades have passed since Gunkel's introduction of
form criticism as well as Alt's application of this method to
the forms of biblical laws. The impact of their work has been
profound. One of the chief accomplishments of form criticism
is that it enlarged the scope of biblical studies by providing,
next to literary and historical analysis, a new approach for the
understanding and interpretation of biblical literature. It did
so by investigating the literary genres of the Bible, their
function and life settings.[40] Furthermore, it constituted a
needed corrective to literary criticism in many areas and, in
particular, in its method of dating texts. It showed that even
the so-called "younger" texts contain "older" forms, probably
going all the way back to an oral stage of transmission. It
also released the Scriptures from the bonds of parochialism[41]--
an attitude which often characterized literary-critical studies
on the Bible--by stressing that to a large measure, and without
denying Israel's creative role, they still reflect the speech
pattern of the peoples of the ancient Near East as recorded in
their literary and nonliterary documents.

In the years since Gunkel, form-critical method has not
remained stagnant. It was constantly analyzed, re-evaluated
and refined to such an extent that some of its original assumptions have either been abandoned (e.g., its "atomism," i.e.,
"the shorter, the more original") or considerably modified.
Among those modifications we can mention a few that have direct
bearing on the study of biblical legal forms.

(1) One of the shortcomings of form criticism has been its
tendency to generalize.[42] Especially in the early periods, its
concern with what is common to all the examples of a given
genre led many scholars to overlook uniqueness and to consider
any deviation as an aberration of an original and alleged
"pure" genre. Thus, for instance, in connection with the
casuistic laws, Alt maintained that "wherever the lawgiver
uses the subjective 'I...' or addresses one of the persons in

the case as 'thou', this is a secondary variation in which
stylistic elements of other forms have crept in."[43] Similarly,
he considered the laws expressed in the relative form as a de-
cayed form: "But for the most part the subject has lost its
participial form and occurs as a relative clause, so that the
style is beginning to break down."[44]

However, it is now recognized that literary genres must be
considered primarily as abstractions, as "ideal forms."[45] This
new understanding acknowledges both the unique and the characteristic. It denies the existence of any "pure" genre as if it
were grounded in the realities in life. It admits, as it must,
that within a set structure there is room for some variation in
the modes of expression.

(2) Form criticism argues that literary material takes the
form appropriate to its content. In other words, content deter-
mines the specific form. For early form critics, the connection
between the two was absolute and inseparable.[46] This point is
now being challenged. Today scholars agree that the connection
is not always inseparable, for there are many examples in both
biblical and extra-biblical literature where a particular literary genre is used for a purpose other than its primary one.
For instance, G. Fohrer draws attention to the prophets' use of
the dirge as a threat or mock threat.[47] K. A. Kitchen refers
to an Egyptian wisdom work, the "Instruction of Sehetepibrē"
which, he says, is "virtually a loyalist hymn to the king."[48]
W. G. Lambert points out that the author of "Advice to a Prince"
has "imitated the style of omens."[49] One can also add here
Sargon's record of his famous eighth campaign which appears both
as an annal as well as an open letter to the god Ashur.[50]

In reality, literary genres are seldom static.[51] Some fall
into disuse; some are imitated; others are incorporated into
new genres.[52] Whatever their origin, they are able to move from
one setting into another within the same cultural environment.[53]
In this process their function is also altered. One may consider, as an example, the blessings and curses that appear in
wisdom texts. No matter what their original Sitz im Leben,
their "use in the wisdom literature is simply didactic."[54] The
form critic should be aware of this constant move. Unlike his

predecessors, he must not fail to distinguish, as Fohrer puts
it, "between the original Sitz im Leben and the rhetorical
setting"[55] of each genre.

(3) One of the major assumptions of biblical form criticism
is that "every ancient literary type originally belonged to a
quite definite side of the national life of Israel."[56]   Thus,
for instance, as Gunkel stated:

> the Song of Victory was sung by maidens to greet the
> returning war-host; the Lament was chanted by hired
> female mourners by the bier of the dead; the Thora
> [sic] was announced by the priest in the sanctuary;
> the Judgment (mishpat) was given by the judge in his
> seat; the prophet uttered his Oracle in the outer
> court of the Temple, the elders at the gate gave
> forth the Oracle of Wisdom.[57]

It is also maintained that this life setting can be recovered
through a study of the genre itself. This one-to-one relationship, however, cannot always be established with certainty, for
it is now recognized that in many cases "the connection with
life is very often lost"[58] and that "the period of time which
has elapsed and the scarcity of material which has survived
does not always make it possible to determine the actual origins of biblical literary forms."[59]   Instead, scholars presently
acknowledge that "in some cases we can reach only very general
conclusions concerning the setting of certain genres."[60]   Furthermore, it is also recognized that "a setting in life compre-
hends a number of literary types, in near or distant relationship to each other, each fulfilling a particular function."[61]
As an example Koch points to liturgy--with worship as its life
setting--which consists of a number of component genres, such
as song, prayers, blessing and others.[62]

In some cases, such as wisdom literature, the correspondence between the genre and its setting is not exclusive. "What
is the life setting of the OT wisdom saying?" asks Murphy.   "It
is a teaching situation, but this tells us little--that of
parents, clan elder, court instructor, or religious teacher?
The form need not vary from one person to another; 'my son' can
be used as a title of address in all four instances."[63]   This,
too, indicates that a given genre may have a long history and
can move from one setting to another without undergoing real

change in its form. In light of all these considerations a
form critic must act with prudence in his attempt to investigate the origins of the literary genres. He must be constantly
on guard against enthusiastic recreation of social realities
that supposedly underlie them.

At the present time, form-critical studies seem to have
reached, in the words of J. H. Hayes, "something of a plateau
or perhaps what might be called a temporary impasse."[64] Not
only are old achievements being reevaluated, but also efforts
are being made to relate form-critical studies to other disci-
plines. Moreover, new directions, such as Muilenburg's proposed rhetorical criticism,[65] are being seriously considered,
and areas of investigation which for a long time fell within
the orbit of form criticism, such as "tradition criticism"[66]
and "redaction criticism,"[67] are progressively assuming independent status, even in the face of serious opposition on the
part of some form-critical scholars, such as Koch.[68]

One of the problems that still plagues form-critical
studies is the terminology employed to identify the literary
genres. First of all, most of the terms have a modern flavor
(e.g., epic, saga, legend), and it is questionable whether they
describe correctly the literary compositions to which they are
related. Secondly, because form criticism was originally developed in Germany, the original terms are in German and there
is no agreement as to how to translate them into English. For
instance, the word *Gattung* is frequently rendered as "genre,"
"literary type," or "form." The consequence is that writer and
reader do not often have a common means of communication. With
regard to the first problem, it is necessary to consider first
the genre terminology that is sometimes found within the original texts (e.g., the Hebrew מִשְׁל, the Akkadian *zamāru*) and,
where it proves inadequate to discriminate between literary
variations, to warn the reader that its modern counterpart or
the newly devised term does not do complete justice to the literary reality it wishes to describe. In the present study, for
the sake of uniformity, *genre* will be differentiated from *form*:
the first refers to the *Gattung* (e.g., law, blessing, prayer,
love song), the second to the literary formulations of a given
genre (e.g., different kinds of legal formulations).[69]

Here one more point needs clarification. Should the expression "literary genre" be reserved only for the literary
stage, or can it be used to refer as well to its preliterary,
oral stage? Whenever human beings communicate with one another,
whether orally or in written form, they use forms of expression
that are already determined for them by society. Therefore,
there is no reason to limit form criticism to oral expression
and oral transmission as if oral forms were different from
written forms.[70] The only referent at hand is a written text,
and it is within this text that one identifies various and distinct genres which presumably have been preserved ever since
their use in the remote oral stage. It is unwarranted and perhaps misleading to attempt to distinguish the written genres
(or, forms) from the oral ones.[71] It is in line with this
reasoning that the expression "literary genre" will be used
hereafter to cover both stages.

Different Criteria and Classifications of the Legal Forms

The impact of Alt's study of biblical law was considerable.
His distinction between laws expressed in the casuistic and apodictic forms was readily accepted by many scholars,[72] and even
some of those who disagreed with certain points in his analysis
continued to operate with these categories.[73] His classic division, however, did not remain unchallenged. Further investiga-
tions revealed the following shortcomings.

(1) Alt did not recognize "mixed forms" and simply maintained that any deviation from the basic casuistic legal form
was to be taken as "a secondary variation in which stylistic
elements of other forms have crept in."[74] This opinion led
some scholars to contradictory conclusions when it came to the
consideration of the mixed forms. Thus, for instance, while
O. Eissfeldt, who otherwise accepted Alt's categories, included
the law in Exod 21:2, "When you acquire...," among casuistic
laws,[75] J. van der Ploeg, also a follower of Alt, specifically
excluded it from this category.[76]

(2) Alt had considered only one form, namely, the "when/if"
form, as casuistic, and placed all the other forms (i.e., the
participial, the curses in Deuteronomy 27 and the prohibitions

in the second person) under the category of apodictic laws. It
soon became apparent, however, that Alt perhaps too quickly sub-
sumed these latter forms under one category and that it was
necessary to study each form independently.[77] In particular,
the classification of the participial forms presented a problem.
Alt had placed them among the apodictic laws and, in fact, argued that they best exemplified the category itself. This consideration raised serious doubts in the minds of scholars.
Thus, Noth remarked, "the brevity and absolute nature of these
sentences stands close to the apodictic formulation; the explicit and emphatic description of the legal consequences (the con-
demnation to death) is reminiscent of the casuistic formulations."[78]

     In this controversy some sided with Alt.[79] J. G. Williams
maintained that "whether or not the participial formulas be
termed 'apodictic', they are definitely closer to the absolute
prohibitions and commands than to the generally recognized
casuistic laws."[80] He proposed, for instance, that Exod 21:12
be translated as "A striker of a man who dies: he shall be put
to death." He acknowledged that the law does describe a "case,"
but added, it is only "in a very narrow sense, certainly no details of the situation are given, although a consequence is indicated."[81] On the other hand, based on R. A. F. MacKenzie's
work,[82] W. Kornfeld chose to place the participial formulas
within the casuistic category. Apodictic laws, he reasoned,
order or prohibit an act, which the addressee is obliged to
carry out or avoid, while laws in the participial form, like
the other casuistic laws, instruct the judicial authorities as
to the nature of the penalty that must be inflicted once the
deed has been committed.[83] A similar thought was advanced by
R. Kilian who argued that participial formulas cannot be considered apodictic, simply because apodictic laws, unlike the
participial, do not consider a case, nor stipulate a legal
consequence.[84]

     A third group of scholars, recognizing the peculiar struc-
ture of the participial forms, chose to consider them as constituting a category by themselves, outside of the casuistic
and apodictic. The most recent example is provided by

F. L. Horton[85] who outlined the legal forms as follows: (1)
participial; (2) casuistic, including פי אם/ forms (i.e., third
person forms, formulations with apodosis in the second person,
formulations entirely in the second person, formulations with
protasis introduced by אשר) and relative form; (3) apodictic
forms which incorporate prohibitions (לא plus imperfect), wisdom prohibitives (אל plus jussive) and positive requirements.

Prior to Horton, H. Cazelles, working mainly in the Book
of the Covenant, distinguished among four different legal formulations:[86] (1) casuistic; (2) participial; (3) direct style
formula; (4) conditional formula in direct style. S. Loewenstamm went even further when he divided the laws into six categories:[87] (1) casuistic; (2) priestly forms (איש כי/אשר, both
with variations); (3) commands (or, prohibitions) in the third
person; (4) commands (or, prohibitions) in the second person;
(5) participial; (6) mixed forms.

This line of reasoning not only expanded the number of
Alt's categories but also led to the abandonment of his classical division altogether. This is, however, unwarranted. A
perusal of the legal forms mentioned above shows that it is
still possible to group them in two categories on the basis of
their syntactical structure. Whereas some laws describe a case
and then stipulate a legal consequence, others do neither. The
distinguishing feature of those which belong to the first category is their conditionality; that is, the legal consequence is
to be applied only when the act described in the protasis has
taken place. These laws are retrospective, in that they look
back to a potentially committed deed. On the other hand, those
which belong to the second category are prospective as well as
absolute and unconditional. They do not depend on the fulfill-
ment of certain acts. They simply express a command, either
positive or negative. On the basis of their distinguishing
features, the first category of legal forms may be referred to
as "conditional" and the second as "unconditional."

The proposal to use a criterion which is at variance with
Alt's will expectedly result in a different classification and
will make it necessary to devise new terminology in order to
describe the new subcategories of legal forms. In fact, it

would be advisable to abandon Alt's terminology altogether,
thus avoiding confusion. It must be noted here that the term
"apodictic"/"apodeictic," first proposed by Alt, is far from
being adequate to describe even the legal forms which Alt incorporated under this title. The word actually means "of clear
demonstration, established on incontrovertible evidence"[88] and
was used in Aristotelian logic to express certainty and absolute
truth.[89] Furthermore, the term "apodictic" is inappropriate to
describe any legal formulation in the Bible, for biblical laws
do not constitute logical conclusions but are considered products of divine revelation.

Here, then, is the classification to be used in the
present study.

Laws in the Conditional Form

"When/if" Form

These laws are built, as Alt had already recognized, on
the sequence of the protasis and apodosis of a conditional sentence. The protasis records the circumstances of a hypothetical
case and the apodosis stipulates a legal consequence.[90] The
protasis is introduced by the particle כי ("when," or "in the
case that"). At times, the law is expanded by the addition of
secondary or subordinate cases introduced, in turn, mostly by
(ו)אם ("[and] if"),[91] but also by או ("or"),[92] אך אם ("but
if"),[93] or והיה אם ("and if").[94] Within this form, three subgroups can be identified.

1. Legal formulation in the third person: "When he"

This corresponds to Alt's "casuistic" form. The verbs are
usually in the imperfect, singular or plural.[95] For example:
"When a man steals an ox or a sheep, and slaughters it or sells
it, he shall pay five oxen for the ox, and four sheep for the
sheep" (Exod 21:37, *NJV*).

An important variation to this form is found in cases
where the introductory particle כי is preceded by the subject.
Mostly, it begins with איש כי (lit. "a man, when he").[96] For
instance: "If a man kills (ואיש כי יקח) any human being, he
shall be put to death" (Lev 24:17).

2. <u>Legal formulation in the second person: "When you"</u>

In this form, both the protasis and apodosis contain verbs
in the second person singular or plural. For example: "When you
make a loan (כי תשּׁה) of any sort to your neighbor, you must not
enter his house to seize his pledge" (Deut 24:10, *NJV*).[97]

3. <u>Mixed forms</u>

There are a few examples of these forms.

(1) The verb in the protasis is in the third person, while
the apodosis contains a verb in the second person. For instance:
"When a virgin is pledged in marriage to a man and another man
comes upon her in the town and lies with her, you shall bring
both of them out to the gate..." (Deut 22:23-24, *NEB*).

(2) The verb of the protasis is in the second person but
the apodosis has a verb in the third person. For example: "When
you acquire a Hebrew slave, he shall serve six years" (Exod
21:2, *NJV*).

Relative Form

The protasis is here introduced by the subject plus the
particle אשּׁר.[98] In a few cases, the legal statements start
simply with אשּׁר, probably a shorter form of איש אשּׁר.[99] The
main law is sometimes expanded by the addition of secondary
clauses introduced, in turn, by (ו)אם.[100] Two subgroups can
be identified.

1. <u>Legal formulation in the third person</u>[101]

For example: "A man who lies (ואיש אשּׁר ישׁכב) with his
daughter-in-law, both of them shall be put to death," Lev
20:12).

2. <u>Mixed forms</u>

There are very few examples of this form. They are found
in the following cases: whereas the verb in the protasis is in
the third person imperfect, the apodosis contains a verb in the
first person perfect with *waw* consecutive (e.g., "And whatso-
ever man there be of the house of Israel, or of the strangers
that sojourn among them, that eateth any manner of blood, I
will set My face against that soul that eateth blood...," Lev

17:10, *JPSV*; cf. 20:6) or, in the second person perfect with
waw consecutive (e.g., "A woman who approaches any beast to
mate with it, you shall kill the woman and the beast...," Lev
20:16).

Participial Form

In this form, the subject referring to the person who committed the deed stands at the beginning of the law and indicates
a condition the occurrence of which involves a legal consequence,
mostly the death penalty.[102] Generally, this subject is expressed by means of an active participle,[103] sometimes accompanied by the word כֹל, "whoever."[104] The verbs in the law are
formulated in the third person. For example: "He who fatally
strikes a man (מַכֵּה אִישׁ וָמֵת, lit. the striker to death) shall be
put to death" (Exod 21:12) or, "Whoever lies (כָּל שֹׁכֵב, lit. any
lier) with a beast shall be put to death" (Exod 22:18).

Laws in the Unconditional Form

Direct Address

1. Positive commands

These commands are expressed in three different
grammatical forms.

a) Preceptive imperfect, second person singular or plural

Examples: "You shall make (תַּעֲשֶׂה) an altar of earth for
me..." (Exod 20:24, *NEB*); or, "You shall each revere (תִּירָאוּ)
his mother and his father, and keep (תִּשְׁמֹרוּ) My sabbaths: I the
Lord am your God" (Lev 19:3, *NJV*).

b) Imperative[105]

For example: "Honor (כַּבֵּד) your father and your mother..."
(Exod 20:12, Deut 5:16, *NJV*).

c) Infinitive absolute

In a few cases, the directive takes the form of an infini-
tive absolute in the sense of an emphatic imperative:[106] e.g.,
"Remember (זָכוֹר) the sabbath day and keep it holy" (Exod 20:8,
NJV).

2. Negative commands

These are sometimes formulated in the second person jussive
preceded by אַל,[107] and more often by the second person imperfect
preceded by the negative particle לֹא: e.g., "Do not (אַל) degrade
your daughter, making her a harlot..." (Lev 19:29, *NJV*); "You
shall not (לֹא) commit adultery" (Exod 20:14, Deut 5:18).[108]
E. Gerstenberger has called this form "prohibitive."[109] W.
Richter, however, claims that the distinction in the use of the
negative particles indicates two different literary forms. He
refers to the first one as "vetitive" and keeps Gerstenberger's
term "prohibitive" only for לֹא followed by the imperfect.[110]
Although there are differences in nuances between the two
forms,[111] their frequent occurrence within the same legal context[112] and the overlapping between the two forms in nonlegal
texts[113] show that it is difficult to discern a clear difference in force and emphasis that would warrant considering them
as two distinct literary forms.[114]

Third Person Jussive

1. Positive commands

For example: "The guilt offering shall be slaughtered at
the spot where the burnt offering is slaughtered..." (Lev 7:2,
NJV).

2. Negative commands

For example: "They shall not shave smooth any part of
their heads or cut the edges of their beards, or make gashes in
their flesh" (Lev 21:5, *NJV*).

Laws in the unconditional form, whether expressed as direct
address or in the third person jussive, are sometimes expanded
by adding secondary legal statements. The latter are usually
introduced by אִם.[115] At times, positive commands are coupled
with negative commands.[116] Statements containing penalties
are added separately to these laws.[117]

Biblical legal formulations can be summarized as follows:

I. Laws in the conditional form
  A. "When/if" form
    1. Third person
    2. Second person
    3. Mixed forms
  B. Relative form
    1. Third person
    2. Mixed forms
  C. Participial form
II. Laws in the unconditional form
  A. Direct address
    1. Positive commands
      a) Preceptive imperfect, second person
      b) Imperative
      c) Infinitive absolute
    2. Negative commands
  B. Third person jussive
    1. Positive commands
    2. Negative commands

ORIGIN AND SETTING IN LIFE OF THE BIBLICAL LEGAL FORMS

The analysis and classification of the legal forms constitute a much simpler undertaking than the investigation of their origin and setting in life, simply because the data at hand are not sufficient to reach definite conclusions. Yet, this undertaking cannot be altogether avoided, for, as Koch stated, "no biblical text can be adequately understood without a consideration of the setting in life of its literary type."[118] This investigation will attempt to summarize the knowledge to be obtained in this area and to evaluate critically some of the assumptions and solutions that have been put forth on this subject.

Each of the legal forms outlined above needs to be studied separately in order to see whether it is possible to identify it with other literary forms in the Bible so as to obtain clues regarding its origin and setting in the life of the ancient Israelites.

This method of analysis is based on the form-critical assumption that literary forms, as long as they remain in use within their own context, reflect real life situations. It will also be helpful to refer to extra-biblical literature in order to gain perspective on, and possible illumination of, inner-biblical data.

Scholars are not of one mind in the classification of the biblical *Gattungen*, for as N. K. Gottwald writes, "no one system has proved both inclusive enough to deal accurately with the variety of types and detailed enough to make convincing distinctions."[119] The difficulty is compounded by the existence of borderline as well as mixed genres. Furthermore, there is a lack of criteria as to how genres ought to be determined; sometimes content is stressed, sometimes form. In the present study, in our search for literary forms in genres other than law that parallel those of the legal forms, we have adopted the main classification of Eissfeldt who distinguishes between three broad categories, namely prose, poetry and sayings.[120] It must be stressed here that this threefold classification (and the subgroups assigned to each one of them) constitutes an attempt on our part to understand the literary structures of the past.[121] It may not totally represent, however, the classification that might have been drawn up or recognized by those in ancient Israel who engaged in creating and preserving literature. With this in mind, we turn to the investigation of the origin and setting of the biblical legal forms.

Laws in the Conditional Form

"When/if" Form

1. Legal formulation in the third person: "when he"

This form dominates a large section of the Book of the Covenant (henceforth, BC).[122] Elsewhere, it appears only in a few laws within the legal corpus of Deuteronomy (henceforth, D).[123] All of these laws deal with legal questions that come up in the normal course of community life, such as slavery, assault and battery, damages, misappropriation of goods given in trust, marriage and the like. They do not, however, ignore "sacral" matters, inasmuch as they do legislate for procedures to be carried out before the deity.[124] Alt maintained that these laws do not reflect "the Israelite national consciousness."[125] The issue, however, is a matter of dispute.[126]

Outside of law, there are no clear examples of this form in the literary genres of the Bible.

The origin of the form as well as its setting in life
(whether original or secondary) is rather obscure. Alt's assumption that it was taken over from the Canaanites is, as de
Vaux put it, "pure guesswork,"[127] for no Canaanite legal text
has yet been discovered. The legal texts which come from the
ancient Near East are dominated by the "casuistic" form, and it
is plausible that the Israelites of the Patriarchal period were
acquainted with it, inasmuch as they were part of that common
culture. Some scholars have already argued that certain laws
in BC could easily have had a seminomadic background and therefore originated in the presettlement period.[128] However, as a
whole, BC seems to point to the period immediately before and
following the conquest.[129] It should also be noted that if it
were true, as Alt had claimed, that "apodictic" laws have nothing to do with "secular" justice, then the question of the existence of Israel's presettlement "secular" legislation would remain in Alt's system unresolved.[130]

As to the life setting of the form, it is generally assumed
that it is found in the legal assembly at the gate where the
elders gathered to dispense justice. This could mean either
that it originated in the court in the form of court decisions
or that legal decisions were arrived at on the basis of laws
already expressed in this "casuistic" form. J. Morgenstern
seems to admit both possibilities. He states that the "casuistic" laws "clearly represent the decisions of courts or other
responsible legal authority or else the formulation in legal
form of long established deeply-rooted and generally accepted
customs."[131] It is not unlikely, he added, that those called
"recorders" (šoṭ^{e}rim) in D were the ones who from time to time
compiled "corpuses [sic] of mišpaṭim."[132]

Alt, too, considered the court of law as the Sitz im Leben
of the "casuistic" law. Though he stated that it "originates
in the day-to-day work of judges and lawyers,"[133] he probably
meant by it that it was used by these judges during the trials,
for he pictured a situation where laws of this kind "would be
read out to the men gathered in the gate to form a court whenever they had to try and give judgment on cases of the particular kind a given law dealt with."[134]

Alt's point of view was taken over by many other scholars
and probably represents the most widely accepted position on
this subject.[135] However, the assumption, though logical, is
not supported by textual evidence in the Bible. It only stands
on the observation that the gate was a place of assembly where
elders of the local community carried out their responsibility
of administering justice.[136] If the contention is that the
elders issued their verdicts in this form, there is no evidence
to prove it. None of the trials or judgments recorded in the
Bible states a verdict in the "when/he" form.[137] It is also
unknown whether during the court sessions the elders had at
their disposal, or made use of, laws drafted in this form.
Neither 1 Sam 30:21-25 nor Num 27:1-11, to which Köhler
alludes,[138] is in the "when/he" form. In Naboth's case, the
relevant laws preserved in the texts are either in the unconditional form (Exod 22:27) or in the conditional relative form
(Lev 24:15). It would be hazardous to suggest that the court
of Ruth 4 was familiar with the injunctions of Deut 25:5-9
(formulated in the "when/he" form), because there are considerable differences between the two cases and it is not clear
which precedes the other.[139] In sum, the court cannot be considered with certainty as the setting of the "when/he" form.
Because of lack of textual evidence in the Bible, the original
setting of the form remains unknown.

The form אִישׁ כִּי is found in the Holiness Code (henceforth,
H)[140] but is more prevalent in the Priestly Code (henceforth,
PC).[141] It does not appear in the other legal corpora of the
Bible. It is used mostly to express cultic/sacral regulations.

Outside of the legal genre, the form אִישׁ כִּי appears seldom:
in a prayer[142] and in prophetic sayings, with the majority coming from Ezekiel.[143] Its prevalence in PC and its frequent use
by Ezekiel, himself a priest, point to a priestly preference
for the form.[144] In both Lev 24:10-16 and Num 27:8-11, the
legal prescriptions expressed in this אִישׁ כִּי form are presented
not only as oracular decisions but also as a pattern of legislative process generated by the result of test cases, in other
words, as indicative of the growth of case law within the framework of priestly oracular consultation.[145] A more specific
setting is nowhere indicated in the Bible.

2. Legal formulation in the second person: "when you"

This is the predominant form in D,[146] but it is also found
in BC,[147] in H,[148] and in PC.[149] It is used to formulate injunctions covering a wide range of subjects related both to the
cultic/sacral and "civil" laws, but in the majority of cases it
expresses the lawgiver's concern for the well-being of the poor
and the needy.[150] In these cases the legal consequence seems
more like an appeal rather than a categorical order.

Outside of law proper, the closest parallel is found in
wisdom literature,[151] even though most wisdom instructions expressed in this form begin with אם instead of כי. The similarity suggests that in setting down certain norms of humanitarian nature, the legislator adopted a form that is most
suited for it, namely, one of the sages' speech pattern. This
is further indicated by its predominance in D, itself considered
to be heavily influenced by wisdom literature.[152]

3. Mixed forms

There are a few examples of these forms. The use of the
second person in the protasis of Exod 21:2 is probably due to
the second person formulation of Exod 21:1,[153] or Exod 20:
24-26.[154] Those few laws in D which in the apodosis have a
verb in the second person[155] deal with criminal matters and
reflect a similar setting as those expressed in the third person. It is likely that the direct address in the apodosis was
imposed upon them by the sermonic style of D.

Relative Form

The form איש אשר is not widely used in biblical law. It
is found only in certain parts of H, especially in Lev 20:
9-21,[156] and in few cases in PC.[157] There are no examples of
it in BC or D.[158] Legal prescriptions introduced by אשר are
rare. There is one example in BC (Exod 21:13), one in H
(Lev 25:33), one in D (Deut 19:4b-5) and one in PC (Lev 4:22).
Most of the laws in the relative form deal with cultic/sacral
matters.

Outside of law, the relative form is frequently found in
prose sections of the Bible and, in particular, in proclamations or decrees. Some of these offer a reward for specific

military exploits[159] or for the interpretation of a royal
dream;[160] others express a threat of punishment, such as for
failing to heed a military call-up[161] or disobeying a royal
decree.[162]

The relative form, as R. Yaron pointed out, is well suited
for proclamations.[163] The "when/if" form appears too "leisurely,
academic and lacking in urgency"[164] to answer the need of the
hour. The relative form is "employed, addressed to the public
at large, but not in its capacity as an entity, rather to every
individuum in it."[165] On the basis of these observations, Yaron
convincingly argues that the form originally developed in the
sphere of proclamations and was later adopted by the legislator
to express norms of conduct.[166]

Participial Form

This form is seldom used in biblical legislation. A short
list is found in BC.[167] H contains a few examples.[168] The
rest come from PC.[169] All of these laws deal with both cultic/
sacral and "civil/criminal" matters.

Outside of law, the form is found in a few narrative texts
where it introduces stern commands issued by those in authority,[170] sometimes of concessive nature.[171] The command is also
placed in the mouth of God.[172] Elsewhere, the participial form
is widely used in wisdom literature, especially in the book of
Proverbs.[173]

Alt saw a close connection between the participial form
and the curses recorded in Deut 27:15-26.[174] In this so-called
Shechemite dodecalogue, each statement starts with a passive
participle, אָרוּר ("cursed"). This is placed at the very beginning, undoubtedly for the sake of emphasis.[175] The description
of the case then follows, introduced by an active participle
(except in vv. 15, 26 which are in the relative). It must be
noted, however, that even though there are striking similarities
between some examples formulated in the legal and curse forms,
both in terminology and content,[176] there is a basic structural
difference between them. In the legal form, the active participle introduces the statement and is followed by a legal
consequence; in the curses, the formulation is reversed.
Furthermore, curses can hardly be considered legal prescriptions.

As Horton points out, curses do not have legal import in establishing rights and duties.[177] The dodecalogue in Deuteronomy
27 is not a collection of laws but basically a liturgy,[178] a
prayer.[179] It has utilized this particular form precisely because it deals with acts that can be carried out "in secret"
(vv. 15, 24), that is, beyond the control of public opinion[180]
as well as public detection and punishment. Consequently, the
perpetrator is left at the mercy of the curses which are in-
voked by the priests and expected to be brought about by God.
The recognition of these differences undermines Alt's assumption that both are grounded in the same cultic setting. Moreover, even in the case of laws formulated with a participle,
the variety of subject matters covered by these laws (e.g.,
homicide [Exod 21:12], striking parents [Exod 21:15], kidnapping [Exod 21:16], lying with a beast [Exod 22:18], sacrificing
to other gods [Exod 22:19]) shows that its origin is not necessarily a cultic one.

A cultic setting was also proposed by Loewenstamm who
stated that the participial form is employed to express strong
warnings to potential offenders, as exemplified by Gen 26:11
and Exod 19:12.[181] This would indicate, he argued, that its
origin is to be found in a cultic ceremony where prohibitions
of this kind are proclaimed in public. However, not only is
the existence of this alleged cultic ceremony highly doubtful,[182] but also the participle, as noted above, is equally
used, for example, to formulate decrees for the purpose of
offering a reward or for the interpretation of a royal dream.
These observations make Loewenstamm's thesis hardly tenable.

Certain laws in the relative form show great similarity in
content and vocabulary to those formulated in the participial
form (e.g., Exod 21:17 and Lev 20:9). Horton argued that,
whereas the rule in Leviticus 20 ("For every one who [כִּי אִישׁ אִישׁ
אֲשֶׁר יְקַלֵּל] curses[183] his father or his mother shall be put to
death;" *RSV*) envisages a judicial process, namely, the determination of guilt or innocence, the one in Exod 21:17 (lit.
"The insulter [וּמְקַלֵּל] of his father or his mother shall be
put to death") assumes that the determination of the guilt
has already been made.[184] This, however, is a forced interpretation. First, it overlooks the conditionality of the

protasis of the participial laws, both here and elsewhere.[185]
Secondly, it seems to be guided by Horton's prior assumption
that the relative form belongs to the realm of positive law,
whereas the directives formulated by means of a participle are
only "heuristic" in nature. By "heuristic" the author means
"broad principles of law."[186] Rules of this kind, he adds,
have their setting in the area of "instruction."[187] Horton
does not provide the reader with arguments supportive of this
proposed life setting, even though he does allude, in another
context, to the existence of participial formulations in wisdom
material.[188]

A careful reading of Lev 20:9, however, shows that it is
no more than merely a longer formula with the same meaning and
force as that expressed in Exod 21:17.[189] Moreover, there are
other examples in the biblical texts where these forms are
often found in the same context, and frequently interchange.[190]
This further weakens Horton's distinction.

It was noted above that the participial form is often used
in the Bible to express various types of commands. This predominant use may possibly indicate that the form ultimately
derives from pronouncements issued by those in authority.

Laws in the Unconditional Form

Direct Address

Legal prescriptions formulated as direct address are
scattered throughout all the biblical legal corpora. They are
mostly used to express fundamental concepts of law and justice[191] dealing primarily with moral[192] and cultic/sacral
subjects. Often they appear in series. The second person
preceptive imperfect, both in the form of positive or negative
command, is the most prevalent one. The imperative and the
infinitive absolute are used infrequently. The imperative
appears mostly in PC.[193] Elsewhere, it is found only in the
Decalogue.[194] There are a few cases of infinitive absolute
in D,[195] PC,[196] and in the Decalogue.[197]

Outside of law, examples of direct address are found in a
great variety of literary genres--in prose, poetry and sayings.
Positive commands in the second person imperfect appear in

narratives as royal orders[198] or directives coming from a
superior.[199]   The form is also found in different kinds of
psalms[200] and in prophetic sayings.[201]   The imperative appears
in narratives, expressing God's commands,[202] a leader's
orders,[203] a father's directives.[204]   It is also found in a
great variety of psalms,[205] in wisdom sayings,[206] in prophetic
sayings,[207] in cultic oracles.[208]   There are fewer examples of
the infinitive absolute. They appear, for instance, expressing
God's orders,[209] a leader's commands[210] and a sage's
exhortations.[211]

Negative commands appear in narrative passages, mostly as
orders directed from a superior to a subordinate. They may be
formulated by God,[212] a king,[213] a military leader,[214] a
father.[215]   At times, they may be used even to express a plea
to someone who has the upper hand in a given situation.[216]
Among poetic compositions, the form is found in love songs,[217]
and in various kinds of psalms.[218]   It also appears in wisdom
sayings,[219] prophetic sayings,[220] and cultic oracles.[221]

The reason for the frequent use of the direct address is
that it constitutes one of the most common forms of human
speech. It is this widespread use of the form that makes it
almost impossible to establish any given setting as its original Sitz im Leben.

Alt had claimed that "apodictic" laws, expressed in the
participial as well as in the "thou shalt (not)" form, originated in a cultic setting and specifically in a covenant renewal festival. His arguments were summarized at the beginning
of this chapter and need not be repeated here. His theory was
readily accepted by a number of scholars, at times with slight
modifications.[222]   However, there are various difficulties inherent in Alt's reconstruction of the alleged festival. First
of all, no such festival is mentioned by this name in the
Bible.[223]   No such festival is listed among the biblical
calendar of festivals.[224]   Neither the laws nor the historical
books in the Bible show any knowledge of it.[225]   The prophets,
who were familiar with concepts and terms dealing with the
covenant, do not seem to know anything about it. The existence
of the festival, therefore, is argued on the basis of inference

alone, and not on concrete evidence. And these inferences are
far from being conclusive. The narratives show the people, on
occasion, recommitting themselves to observe the laws of God.[226]
Yet, these passages do not prove that a periodic festival of
renewal such as described by Alt and others, at which "apodictic" laws were proclaimed, ever took place in ancient Israel.
Joshua 24 does indeed refer to a covenant ceremony, but it lacks
a report about the recitation of the law. Despite Alt's claim,
the terms חק ומשפט in Josh 24:25 cannot be taken to mean only
"apodictic" laws, nor do they refer to a "recitation" of the
law. Deuteronomy 27, as was argued above, does not embody a
collection of laws, nor does it refer to a periodic recitation
of the curses. Deuteronomy 31, which prescribes the reading of
"this Torah" (v. 11) every seven years on the feast of Tabernacles, does not speak of a "covenant" or its renewal. Furthermore, Alt's assertion that the editors of D substituted the
reading of the Torah, which includes both "apodictic" and
"casuistic" laws, for what must have been the recitation of
shorter series of "apodictic" laws cannot be proved on the
basis of Deuteronomy 31. Finally, the reading of the law in
Nehemiah 8 does not involve a covenant, nor does it take place
exclusively on Tabernacles (v. 18). In fact, on the first day
of the seventh month (8:2) Ezra reads the law to the people at
large, but on the second day (8:13) only the heads of families,
the priests and Levites remain "to gain further insight into
the words of the law" (AB), namely, to read and study the law
of God. Nehemiah 9 refers to a reading of the law on the "24th
day of this (i.e., seventh) month" (v. 3), but does not include
a covenant. Nehemiah 10 specifically mentions a written agreement, a covenant made "in view of all this" (v. 1); however,
the relationship between this and the previous two chapters is
unclear.[227] In any case, even if the reading of the law in
chapter 8 and the covenant of chapter 10 were related, it is
not stated that the celebration of both acts represents a
periodic occurrence. It is also doubtful whether an inference
can be drawn from a postexilic event to a preexilic custom in
ancient Israel.

˅   All of these arguments cast serious doubt on the existence
of the postulated ceremony and its place as the setting for the
"apodictic" laws.[228] Even if we were to admit that the introductory formula of the Decalogue points to a cultic recitation
of the Ten Commandments,[229] the question would still remain as
to whether the clauses themselves originated in this setting;[230]
for a distinction must be made between the origin of a given
form and its subsequent use in a new life situation. As
Gerstenberger argues, it is difficult to accommodate all the
apodictic clauses in one principal cultic festival. The commandments, he points out, "do not express the doings of a community assembled in worship, nor the spirit of religious functionaries."[231] Their setting must therefore be sought in an
area that is outside of and prior to the cultic framework in
which most of them are presently found.

    In the search for a setting in life, a point stressed by
Fohrer must be kept in mind: namely, the difference between
"apodictic style" and "apodictic series."[232] The first one,
"do this" or "do not do that," is a primitive form of directive
and is found everywhere. Consequently it is impossible to find
a single Sitz im Leben for it. It is only when similarly formulated commands or prohibitions constitute a "series"--whether
long or short--that one can speak of a pattern and search for
its original setting in life.

    Among the laws formulated as direct address, Gerstenberger
noted that the prohibitives, appearing usually in series, express a deep concern for correct behavior and the preservation
of the social welfare of society. They are authoritative and
mostly "secular," not unlike the commands of the clan elders
of hoary antiquity. Their life setting is to be found in the
instruction given within the tribal circle (i.e., *Sippenethos*).[233] As an example, the author pointed to the teachings
(the word here is צוה, "he commanded") of Jonadab ben Rechab
(Jer 35:6-7) which are expressed in a short series of prohibitives in the second person.

    Gerstenberger sought to confirm his thesis by referring
to the instructions found in wisdom literature. He noted that
the welfare of society is also the concern of wisdom literature,

and in it are preserved series of maxims and exhortations which
in form and content closely resemble the commandments in the
legal corpora of the Bible, such as the series in Prov 3:27-30.
This similarity shows that "once the congruence in form and
content is acknowledged, a common background for wisdom maxims
and legal commandments can no longer be denied."[234] In the
course of time, he added, some of the prohibitives entered the
"cultic zone," others were collected and incorporated in legal
corpora, while a third group came to be included in wisdom books.

Gerstenberger's thesis is very attractive inasmuch as it
accounts best for the coexistence of prohibitive formulations
in a variety of genres, by pointing to the form's prior setting
and its probable move from one Sitz im Leben into another. It
also represents the most satisfactory answer to those who had
objected to the equation of both wisdom maxims and laws formulated as prohibitives. Cazelles had indicated that, whereas
laws formulated in the second person are imperative and obliga-
tory, wisdom maxims are basically exhortations.[235] In the
words of Kaufmann, "the one speaks in categorical imperatives,
the other appeals to prudence and utilitarian considerations."[236]

Gerstenberger seems to deny the equation between law and
wisdom and only indicates that, by becoming part of the legal
corpora, the directives expressed in the prohibitive form,
though similar in form and content to certain wisdom instructions, take an absolute coloration, for they are now considered
divine commands. However, it must be noted here that, while
the majority of the prohibitives in wisdom literature are formulated by אל plus the second person imperfect, those in the
legal corpora appear often with לא followed by the second person imperfect.[237] Even though, as noted above, the two forms
frequently interchange in the Bible, as Bright indicates, it is
still evident that "the 'al prohibitive was felt to be suitable
for Wisdom instruction, while the lōʾ prohibitive was not."[238]

As for the other forms of direct address, their use among
the various biblical literary genres makes it impossible to
establish a specific setting for each one of them. The most
that can be said is that on the whole they correspond to directives formulated by a superior to an inferior. But even this

is not always the case, for the same form is at times used to
address a superior as well (e.g., imperatives in prayer directed to God).

Third Person Jussive

Laws in the third person jussive and expressing positive
or negative commands are found in most of the biblical legal
corpora, though in small numbers. They appear in CD (in Exod
34:25b), in H,[239] in D[240] and in PC.[241] Often, they are scattered among laws composed in a variety of forms, though in Deut
23:1-4 there is a short series of four injunctions introduced
by לא. Mostly, these laws deal with cultic/sacral matters but
do not totally ignore the "civil/criminal."[242]

Outside of the legal genre, examples of the form are found
within the narrative portions of the Bible, invariably as orders
directed to inferiors. They are introduced either by אל or by
לא. They may derive from God,[243] a king,[244] or a leader.[245]
The form also appears in poetry,[246] among cultic oracles,[247] in
prophetic sayings,[248] and in wisdom sayings.[249]

The biblical text does not contain specific clues regarding the original setting of the form. In connection with the
discussion of the priestly instructions, Budd suggested that
"the impersonal form in the sacrificial rituals probably reflects the formulation of agreed procedures rather than priestly Direction as such."[250] However, he did not offer, nor is
there, any evidence to substantiate it. A command from someone
in authority[251] appears to be the closest form to the legal
prescriptions in the third person.

FORM AND SETTING OF THE LEGAL FORMS
IN THE CUNEIFORM LAW CORPORA

We can now turn to cuneiform legal corpora for possible
illumination of the biblical legal forms and their settings.

Cuneiform Legal Corpora

Our knowledge of ancient Near Eastern law derives primarily from law collections[252] of Mesopotamia and Asia Minor
but also from other legal texts that have been discovered
throughout the ancient Near East, such as official documents

(e.g., royal edicts), private documents (e.g., contracts, court proceedings) and scholastic texts (e.g., lexical lists, scribal handbooks).

No formal body of laws has ever been found in ancient Egypt,[253] even though a few royal decrees are known.[254] Canaan has not yet yielded a law corpus. However, there are texts of legal character which are ultimately of Canaanite origin, i.e., the Marseilles Tariff[255] and the Carthage Tariff,[256] both dated about the third century or the early part of the second century B.C.E.

Mesopotamian laws were written in Sumerian and Akkadian. The major Sumerian law collections are: the laws of Ur-Nammu (LU),[257] the laws of Lipit-Ishtar (LI),[258] a text numbered YBC 2177[259] and certain law fragments in AS 16.[260]

There are more extensive legal corpora in Akkadian: the laws of Eshnunna (LE),[261] the laws of Hammurabi (LH),[262] Middle Assyrian laws (MAL)[263] and Neo-Babylonian laws (NBL).[264]

Many fragments of clay tablets inscribed with laws in Hittite have been found in Boghazköy, but only two of them seem to form a continuous series. They are referred to as the Hittite laws (HL).[265]

Among these law collections, LH and HL appear to be the most comprehensive and systematic. Except for LE which displays a variety of legal forms,[266] the collections of laws in the ancient Near East contain an almost uniform mode of expression. An extreme position is exemplified by LH which seems to have levelled all the stylistic variations of previous laws by converting them into a unified form that dominates the collection.[267]

Cuneiform Legal Formulations

A survey of the legal forms found in the legal corpora of the ancient Near East,[268] in comparison with those in the Bible, yields the following data.

Laws in the Conditional Form

"If he" Form

The description of the case is found in the protasis introduced by TUKUM.BI in Sumerian, *šumma*[269] (at times

accompanied by *awīlum*, "a man") in Akkadian, and *takku* in
Hittite (later on, by *mān*). The legal consequence is recorded
in the apodosis. The verbs are in the third person. For ex-
ample: *šum-ma* DUMU *a-ba-šu im-ta-ha-aṣ* KIŠIB.LÁ-*šu i-na-ak-ki-su*
("If a son has struck his father, they shall cut off his hand,"
LH 195).

A form closely related to this *šumma* (*awīlum*) form but
found exclusively in LE is one which Yaron calls "split protasis."[270] The law starts with an introductory passage providing
background information, and the "if" section is postponed until that occurrence for which a remedy is being sought. For
example: LÚ 1 GÍN KÙ.BABBAR *a-na e-ṣe-di a-na* LÚ.HUN.GÁ
[*li*]-*di-in-ma šum-ma re-su la ú-ki-il-ma* [*e*]-*ṣe-dam e-ṣe-dam
la e-ṣi-su* 10 GÍN KÙ.BABBAR (Ì.LAL)-E ("Should a man give 1
shekel of silver to a hired man for harvesting--if he (the
hired man) has not held himself available and has not done the
harvesting for him--he shall pay 10 shekels of silver," LE 9 A_
i 30-33).

Relative Form

In Akkadian laws, the protasis is usually introduced by
awīlum ša ("the man who"); in Hittite, by LÚ *ku-iš* ("the man
who"). This form has also a shortened form, *ša* in Akkadian and
kuiš in Hittite. The legal consequence is recorded in the apodosis. The verbs are in the third person. For example: LÚ *ša
i-na* A.ŠÀ MAŠ.KAK.EN *i-na ku-ru-lim i-na mu-uṣ-la-lim
iṣ-ṣa-ba-tu* 10 GÍN KÙ.BABBAR Ì.LAL.E ("A man who is caught in
the field of a *muškēnum*,[271] in the crop,[272] in broad daylight,
shall weigh out 10 shekels of silver," LE 12 A i 37-39).

Laws in the Unconditional Form

Third Person Commands

Laws are here formulated without a legal consequence.[273]
For example: DUMU.LÚ *la zi-zu ù* SAG.ÌR *ú-ul iq-qi-a-ap* ("To a
coparcener or a slave a loan requiring security shall not be
furnished," LE 16 B i 12).[274]

Prices and Wages

Price stipulations actually constitute nominal sentences.
The third person element is either left out or is part of the

pronominal suffix. They are not expressed in a uniform manner.
Yaron points to three varieties in LE:[275] (a) "the hire of X
(is) Y";[276] (b) "Y (is) the hire of X";[277] (c) "X-its hire (is)
Y."[278] At times, these statements are expanded by adding conditional clauses introduced by šumma[279] or third person
commands.[280]

Life Setting of the Cuneiform Legal Forms

Unlike the Hebrew Bible, cuneiform literature has not been
subjected to an extensive form-critical analysis. Indeed, a
comprehensive study of the literary genres of this literature
has yet to be undertaken.[281] At present, there is growing
recognition that "the ancient categories were far more hetero-
geneous than the modern,"[282] and that in attempting to classify
these genres it may be advisable to begin with the literary
material at hand, for sometimes the texts come provided with
their own generic classification and with specific indication
as to their setting in life.[283]

These considerations will be kept in mind when studying
the cuneiform legal forms in light of literary genres other
than law for possible clues as to their origin and life setting.
However, inasmuch as the present study is not concerned with
the issue of classification of the ancient Near Eastern literature per se and, furthermore, in order to keep a basis of comparison with the biblical material, it will be sufficient to
deal with the three broad categories that had been considered
in connection with the biblical genres, namely, prose, poetry
and sayings.

Laws in the Conditional Form

"If he" Form

This is the most common legal form in the ancient Near
Eastern law corpora. In Sumerian laws it is used exclusively.
It predominates in LH, MAL and HL. A large section of LE is
formulated in this manner. It is absent in the known examples
of NBL.

Outside of the law collections, the form appears in a
variety of texts such as letters,[284] treaty stipulations,[285]

private legal documents,[286] court verdicts,[287] edicts,[288]
medical and omen texts,[289] and astrological texts.[290]

Yaron has indicated that "many scholars maintain that it
(the "if he" form) originated in the courts of law, and this
may well be correct, even though incapable of actual proof."[291]
The following considerations show that it is unlikely that the
form has its origins in the law-court. Existing court verdicts
display, in addition to the *šumma awīlum*, a great variety of
formulations: e.g., "PN will do such and such";[292] "PN prevailed in the law suit and took possession of X";[293] "PN_1 prevailed in the case. The judges committed PN_2 (the loser) to
pay/do such and such to PN_1";[294] "From this day on, PN_1 is not
in debt to PN_2";[295] "The judges decided against PN. He will do
such and such";[296] "PN_1 prevailed in the law case...if the
(object of litigation) has a claimant, PN_2 (the loser) will
clear it for him."[297] Furthermore, there is no clear evidence
that, in actual court procedures, judges consulted laws composed in the *šumma awīlum* form as the basis for the formulation
of the court verdicts.[298]

Noting the typological similarity to omen and medical
texts, some have argued that the enumeration of legal prescriptions in the *šumma awīlum* form really belongs to the scholarly
tradition of the ancient Near East, as were the collections of
omens.[299] The original setting of the form is therefore set
in the scribal academy. Underlying this approach is the idea
that the purpose of these law corpora is not legislative.[300]
However, there is no consensus among scholars as to the actual
nature of these law collections or their ultimate purpose.[301]
It is expected that continuous research in cuneiform law and
new discoveries in this field will shed some light upon this
controversy. At present, the incongruity noted between law and
legal practice[302] and the placing of a body of legal prescriptions within stylized prologues and epilogues of historic and
religious import[303] strengthen the position of those who consider these law corpora mainly documents of scholarly concern.[304] However, it is unknown whether the scribal academy
represents an original setting or whether scholars took over
the form from yet another genre and life setting. The form's

predominant use in texts of legal nature shows that it may well
have emerged from the legal sphere, though it is unclear which
specific life situation originally gave rise to it.

Relative Form

     In the known NBL the relative form is used exclusively,
but it also appears in a few prescriptions in LE,[305] MAL[306] and
HL.[307] It is absent in Sumerian laws and LH. THere are a few
examples of the shortened form, *ša*, in LE,[308] MAL,[309] and *kuiš*
in HL.[310]

     Outside of the law corpora, the form is mostly found in
royal edicts,[311] court decisions[312] and private legal documents.[313]

     Yaron suggested the sphere of proclamation as the original
setting of the form.[314] He supports his assumption with an
example of a proclamation made by a common citizen and formulated by *ša*.[315] The form seems to have met the needs of those
who wished to formulate a message in order to express threats
of punishment as well as to establish norms of conduct. The
examples above show that it was adopted by rulers, military
commanders, judges and legislators.

Laws in the Unconditional Form

Third Person Command

     Ancient Near Eastern law collections contain a small num-
ber of laws formulated in the third person. They are found in
LE,[316] LH,[317] MAL[318] and in HL.[319] Elsewhere, the form appears
in a variety of texts such as in royal edicts,[320] treaty stipulations,[321] court decisions,[322] private legal documents[323] and
royal instructions.[324]

     MacKenzie suggested that the laws in LH expressed in the
third person were "originally royal decrees issued by Hammurabi."[325] Similarly, Yaron stated, "The very peremptoriness
of the apodictic form, its tone of 'no nonsense' show that it
comes from the ruler himself, or from some subordinate authority to whom he has seen fit to delegate his powers."[326] Gerstenberger, who considers the form as a secondary development
in relation to the second person prohibitive, finds its setting

in the instruction of the tribal leaders.[327] Admittedly, there
is no way to prove the accuracy of these contentions. The
above examples indicate that the form does serve as a means of
expressing directives formulated by someone who is in a superior
position and whose authority is recognized by the other party
or parties.

Prices and Wages

Lists of prices and wages are found in LE[328] and HL.[329]
They cover a variety of subjects, such as the hire of boats and
animals, wage of harvesters, various interest rates, sale of
foodstuff, price of animals, garments and real estate. Though
they seem to indicate some kind of economic control, it is not
known whether the intention was to freeze them at their level
or reduce them to an acceptable level.[330]

Elsewhere, price lists also appear in the text dealing
with the reforms of Urukagina.[331] Whether or not the formulation of the price and wages originated with these legal texts
is not known. It is likely that the form itself was taken over
from the realities of the actual life of the market place.[332]

BIBLICAL AND CUNEIFORM LEGAL FORMS: A COMPARISON

Common Forms

"When he" Form

Whereas the *šumma awīlum* form, together with its parallels
in Sumerian and Hittite laws, constitutes the most prevalent
legal form in the law corpora of the ancient Near East, the
corresponding biblical פי/אם form is found, apart from a few
cases in D, only within BC which represents one of the oldest
legal corpora in the Bible and dated to ca. 1300 B.C.E.[333]

The Bible does not contain any clue as to the original
setting of this form. Extra-biblical texts point to the
scribal academy as a possible setting for the form in Mesopotamia. However, it is possible that this, too, represents a
secondary setting and that the form was adapted from another,
as yet undetermined, Sitz im Leben.

Relative Form

This form is characteristic of NBL but is not absent in
the previous law corpora, both Akkadian and Hittite. The
corresponding אֲשֶׁר אִישׁ is found in the Bible, primarily in
certain parts of H.

Both biblical and extra-biblical texts appear to point to
this form's original setting within the sphere of public
proclamations.

Third Person Command

The form is seldom used in extra-biblical laws and infrequently found in biblical law collections. Its form and categorical tone show that it derives from someone in authority.
No one definite setting can be posited.

Legal Forms Found Only in Cuneiform Laws

Split Protasis

It appears exclusively in certain parts of LE. There are
no indications that it comes from a setting different from that
of *šumma awīlum*.[334]

Prices and Wages

They are found, as we saw, only in LE and HL. Their
original Sitz im Leben is probably the actual life in the
market. Their absence in the biblical laws is perhaps indicative of the fact that biblical legislation is not pervaded by
an economic concern as is the case with cuneiform legal
corpora.[335]

Legal Forms Found Only in Biblical Laws

"When you" Form

It is prevalent in biblical legislation, especially in D.
Similar formulations are found in extra-biblical texts, such as
treaty stipulations,[336] private legal documents[337] and
letters.[338] It is predominantly used in wisdom texts,[339] both
Akkadian[340] and Egyptian.[341] This adds weight to the contention that the biblical legal form, which is also frequently

employed in biblical wisdom maxims,[342] ultimately stems from
one of the speech patterns of the sages of the ancient Near
East. Furthermore, it should be noted that D, which was
heavily influenced by wisdom literature and which seems to have
stemmed from wisdom circles in ancient Israel, follows the
classical pattern of treaties in the ancient Near East.[343]

Participial Form

It is seldom used in biblical laws. The form probably
derives from pronouncements issued by those who are in high
positions of authority. In extra-biblical texts, it appears in
imprecations[344] and has been taken as an expression of the
curse genre.[345] This is unlikely, for it also occurs in various wisdom maxims[346] and in what appears to be a cultic inscription.[347] Its original setting in extra-biblical literature remains undetermined.

Direct Address

The direct address, both in its positive and negative
forms, constitutes one of the characteristic expressions of
biblical legislation. According to Alt, the "apodictic" legal
form, which includes the second person command, represents "a
specifically Israelite legal form."[348] This categorical claim
excited the curiosity of scholars who began to search for
similar formulations among the ancient Near Eastern law collections. Meek pointed to the existence of "apodictic" laws in
LH, MAL and NBL and therefore stated: "Hence those scholars
are clearly wrong who say that apodictic law was unique and
original with the Hebrews."[349] However, all of the examples
cited by Meek are formulated in the third person, none in the
second.[350]

The lack of the second person command in the ancient Near
Eastern law corpora does not signify that the form was not
known or used in extra-biblical texts. One is here reminded
of Fohrer's remark that the order, "Do this" and "Do not do
that," is very common and is found almost everywhere.[351] Indeed, there are examples of this form and especially of the
easily recognizable "You shall not" in a variety of texts, such

as in treaty stipulations, both Hittite[352] and Syrian,[353] in
wisdom instructions,[354] in disciplinary warnings,[355] in royal
instructions,[356] in sepulchral inscriptions[357] and others.[358]

The form, therefore, was not unknown outside of the Bible.
Yet, and this must be emphasized, whereas in extra-biblical
texts examples of the form are found scattered among other
modes of expression, in biblical legislation it usually appears
as part of a series. The closest parallel to this pattern is
found in wisdom literature, both biblical and extra-biblical.
Biblical examples were mentioned before.[359] The following are
taken from extra-biblical wisdom texts.

Egyptian
Do not confuse a man with a pen upon papyrus—
              The abomination of the god.
Do not bear witness with false words,
Nor *support* another person (*thus*) with thy tongue.
Do not take an accounting of him who has nothing,
Nor falsify thy pen. (From "The Instruction of
Amen-em-opet," *ANET* 13. 423 [lns. 15:20-16:1-4].)[360]

Akkadian
Do not frequent a law court,
Do not loiter where there is a dispute.
(From "Counsels of Wisdom," *BWL*, 100-101 [lns. 31-32].)

Sumerian
Do not steal anything, do not kill yourself!
Do not break into a house, do not demand the sieve!
(From "The Instructions of Šuruppak," lns. 32-33.)[361]

Whether it ultimately derives from Gerstenberger's
"Sippenethos" or Richter's "Gruppenethos," the direct address
was seen fit to express moral and ethical exhortations (as in
wisdom texts), warnings (as in inscriptional curses), demands
of loyalty (as in treaty stipulations) and outright commands[362]
which, when formulated by rulers in edicts and royal instructions to subordinates, were tantamount to law[363] inasmuch as
the authorship of the laws in the ancient Near East was similarly attributed to the kings.

The question of why the form was given prominence in
biblical legislation, while being absent in cuneiform law
corpora, needs to be raised within the wider context of the
nature of biblical law. It was already pointed out that
biblical legal forms are more numerous than those found in

extra-biblical law collections. The combination within a given
law corpus of variously expressed legal prescriptions can possibly be explained by indicating that biblical law incorporates
moral and cultic injunctions, whereas in cuneiform sources
these are relegated to different realms.[364]

The Bible conceives of God as One who formulated His demands in a covenant law proclaimed to the people at large. His
will is considered to be authoritative and therefore binding.
And it is to this divine will that the legislators in the Bible
attributed various civil ordinances, moral and religious commandments, norms which were products of diverse settings, and
gave them all a categorical and normative coloration.

Legal forms seem to have traversed a long way until reach-
ing their present place in the individual law corpora. At
times, the study of these forms enables us to recapture a
glimpse of their original Sitz im Leben. Mostly, however, the
background is blurred, and we are given evidence only of their
use in secondary life situations. The investigation of this
literary phenomenon is not highly rewarding. Yet, it is a
necessary one, for it constitutes a valuable introduction to
the analysis of the components of the laws, including the
occasional use of the motive clauses. It is, in particular,
to the latter that attention will be drawn in the following
chapters.

[1]N. Sarna, *Understanding Genesis* (New York: Schocken, 1970) xxvi.

[2]Y. Kaufmann, *The Religion of Israel* (trans. and abridged by M. Greenberg; Chicago: University of Chicago, 1960) 220.

[3]E. A. Speiser, "Cuneiform Law and the History of Civilization," *PAPS* 107/6 (1963) 539.

[4]Sarna, *Understanding Genesis*, xxvii-xxviii.

[5]On the nature of biblical law vis-à-vis the legal corpora of the ancient Near East, see the discussions by W. Eichrodt (*Theology of the Old Testament* [Philadelphia: Westminster, 1961] 1. 74-97), M. Greenberg ("Some Postulates of Biblical Criminal Law," *Yehezkel Kaufmann Jubilee Volume* [ed. M. Haran; Jerusalem: Magnes, 1960] 5-28), S. Paul (*Studies in the Book of the Covenant in Light of Cuneiform and Biblical Law* [VTSup 18; Leiden: Brill, 1970] 37-42), and R. de Vaux (*Ancient Israel: Its Life and Institutions* [New York: McGraw-Hill, 1961] 147-50).

[6]See, inter alia, D. Daube, *Studies in Biblical Law* (New York: KTAV, 1969); A. Phillips, *Ancient Israel's Criminal Law* (Oxford: Basil Blackwell, 1970); Z. W. Falk, *Hebrew Law in Biblical Times* (Jerusalem: Wahrmann, 1964); T. J. Meek, *Hebrew Origins* (New York: Harper and Brothers, 1960) 49-81; J. M. P. Smith, *The Origin and History of Hebrew Law* (Chicago: Chicago University, 1931); M. Noth, *The Laws in the Pentateuch and Other Studies* (Philadelphia: Fortress, 1967) 1-107; and R. H. Pfeiffer, *Introduction to the Old Testament* (New York: Harper and Brothers, 1948) 210-270.

[7]Their contribution is referred to by W. M. Clark ("Law," *Old Testament Form Criticism* [ed. J. H. Hayes; San Antonio: Trinity University, 1974] 105). Gunkel's remarks appeared first in *Kultur der Gegenwart* (1/7; 1906) and Gressmann's study in *Die älteste Geschichtsschreibung und Prophetie Israels* (SAT 2/1; Göttingen: Vandenhoeck und Ruprecht, 1910). These two studies were not available to me.

[8]A. Jirku, *Das weltliche Recht im Alten Testament* (Gütersloh: Bortelsmann, 1927). The ten forms are: (1) "If-then"; (2) "Thou shalt (not)"--sing.; (3) "He who" (i.e., אֲשֶׁר אִישׁ); (4) Curse formulae of Deuteronomy 27; (5) "You shall (not)"--pl.; (6) "Jussive" (3rd person sing. or pl.); (7) Participle; (8) "If thou"; (9) "If you"--pl.; (10) "Second if" (i.e., אִישׁ כִּי).

[9]A. Jepsen, *Untersuchungen zum Bundesbuch* (BWANT 3/5; Stuttgart: Kohlhammer, 1927). His four basic types are: (1) "Hebrew mišpaṭim" (= Jirku's "If-then" formula); (2) "Israelite

mišpaṭim" (= Jirku's participle formula); (3) Ethical prohibitions (e.g., Exod 22:27; 23:6-9, 13); (4) Cultic commandments
(e.g., Exod 23:13).

[10]S. Mowinckel, *Le Décalogue* (Paris: L. Alcan, 1927).

[11]The article appeared in *Berichte über die Verhandlungen
der Sächsischen Akademie der Wissenschaften zu Leipzig--
Philologisch-historische Klasse* (Band 86, Heft 1 [Leipzig: S.
Hirzel, 1934]), and was later included in his *Kleine Schriften
zur Geschichte des Volkes Israel* ([Munich: C. H. Beck, 1953]
1. 278-332). It is now available in translation as "The
Origins of Israelite Law," in his *Essays on Old Testament
History and Religion* ([New York: Doubleday, 1968] 103-171).

[12]Alt's categories apply to biblical law collections, exclusive of the Priestly Code. He clearly states: "I shall not
discuss the forms of the Levitical Torah, that is, the instruction of the laity in the law by the priest" ("The Origins of
Israelite Law," 112).

[13]Ibid., 114. There appears to be a typographical error
here. Introductory particles are wrongly identified. The text
reads: "the stronger אם, 'granted', or 'supposing that' and the
weaker כי, 'if'." The German original has them in reverse and
correct order; see Alt, *Kleine Schriften*, 1. 287.

[14]Alt, "Origins of Israelite Law," 116.

[15]Ibid., 124.

[16]Ibid., 119.

[17]Ibid., 118.

[18]Ibid., 125.

[19]Ibid., 125-28.

[20]Ibid., 129.

[21]Ibid., 126.

[22]Ibid., 128.

[23]Ibid., 147.

[24]Ibid., 149-50 and n. 92.

[25]Ibid., 150-51 and n. 94.

[26]Ibid., 153.

[27]Ibid., 160.

[28]Ibid., 163.

[29]Ibid., 164.

[30]Ibid., 162.

[31]Ibid., 166-67.

[32]Ibid., 166.

[33]Ibid., 110.

[34]Ibid.

[35]Ibid.

[36]Ibid., 111.

[37]Ibid.

[38]Ibid., 111, n. 13. The author refers to Gunkel and Jirku whose studies were mentioned in our nn. 7 and 8.

[39]Ibid., 111.

[40]On form-critical method, see inter alia, H. F. Hahn (*The Old Testament in Modern Research* [Philadelphia: Fortress, 1966] 119-56), K. Koch (*The Growth of the Biblical Tradition* [New York: Scribner's, 1969]), G. M. Tucker (*Form Criticism of the Old Testament* [Philadelphia: Fortress, 1971]), and, most recently, J. H. Hayes (editor; *Old Testament Form Criticism* [San Antonio: Trinity University, 1974]).

[41]J. Muilenburg, "Form Criticism and Beyond," *JBL* 88 (1969) 3.

[42]Ibid., 5.

[43]Alt, "Origins of Israelite Law," 114.

[44]Ibid., 145.

[45]See the cogent remarks by M. J. Buss ("The Study of Form," *Old Testament Form Criticism*, 53).

[46]See, for instance, H. Gunkel, "Fundamental Problems of Hebrew Literary History," *What Remains of the Old Testament, and Other Essays* (New York: Macmillan, 1928) 60; Alt, "Origins of Israelite Law," 111.

[47]G. Fohrer, *Introduction to the Old Testament* (Nashville/ New York: Abingdon, 1968) 28.

[48]K. A. Kitchen, *Ancient Orient and Old Testament* (Chicago: Inner-Varsity, 1968) 132.

[49]W. G. Lambert, *Babylonian Wisdom Literature* (Oxford: Clarendon, 1960) 110; hereafter cited as *BWL*.

[50]F. Thureau-Dangin, *Une relation de la huitième campagne de Sargon* (TCL 3; Paris: Geuthner, 1912); D. D. Luckenbill, *Ancient Records of Assyria and Babylonia* (Chicago: University of Chicago, 1927) 2. 73-99. On letters written to the gods, see A. L. Oppenheim (*Ancient Mesopotamia* [Chicago: University of Chicago, 1968] 279). For prayers in letter form, see W. W. Hallo ("Individual Prayer in Sumerian: The Continuity of a Tradition," *JAOS* 88 [1968] 75).

[51]Koch, *Biblical Tradition*, 23.

[52]Muilenburg, "Form Criticism and Beyond," 7; H. E. von Waldow, "Some Thoughts on Old Testament Form Criticism," *Society of Biblical Literature 1971 Seminar Papers* (Missoula: Scholars Press) 2. 593.

[53]Koch, *Biblical Tradition*, 36-37; Kitchen, *Ancient Orient*, 135; see also the remarks by D. Greenwood ("Rhetorical Criticism and Formgeschichte: Some Methodological Considerations," *JBL* 89 [1970] 418), D. A. Knight ("The Understanding of 'Sitz im Leben' in Form Criticism," *Society of Biblical Literature 1974 Seminar Papers* [ed. G. MacRae; Missoula: Scholars Press, 1974] 1. 105-25).

[54]R. E. Murphy, "Form Criticism and Wisdom Literature," *CBQ* 31 (1969) 482.

[55]Fohrer, *Introduction*, 29.

[56]Gunkel, "Fundamental Problems," 61.

[57]Ibid.

[58]Von Waldow, "Some Thoughts on Old Testament Form Criticism," 589.

[59]Koch, *Biblical Tradition*, 33.

[60]Tucker, *Form Criticism of the Old Testament*, 9. For a discussion of different levels of life setting, see D. Knight ("The Understanding of 'Sitz im Leben'").

[61]Koch, *Biblical Tradition*, 28.

[62]Ibid.

[63]Murphy, "Form Criticism and Wisdom Literature," 481.

[64]J. H. Hayes, "Preface," *Old Testament Form Criticism*, xvii. See also the remarks by B. S. Childs in *JBL* 87 (1968) 462.

[65]Muilenburg, "Form Criticism and Beyond," 8. See also Greenwood, "Rhetorical Criticism and Formgeschichte."

[66]See, for instance, W. E. Rast, *Tradition History and the Old Testament* (Philadelphia: Fortress, 1972).

[67]See, for instance, N. Perrin, *What is Redaction Criticism?* (Philadelphia: Fortress, 1973); H. Stein, "What is Redaktionsgeschichte?" *JBL* 88 (1969) 45-56. Although these studies deal with the Gospels, the method is equally applicable to the Hebrew Bible.

[68]Koch, *Biblical Tradition*, 53.

[69]Greenwood, "Rhetorical Criticism and Formgeschichte," 420.

[70]Buss, "Study of Form," *Old Testament Form Criticism*, 54.

[71]See the remarks by H. Cazelles and P. Grelot in the *Introduction à la Bible* (ed. A. Robert and A. Feuillet; Tournai: Desclée et Companie, 1957) 1. 132.

[72]We can cite, among others, W. F. Albright's review of "Die Ursprünge" in *JBL* 55 (1936) 164-69, and *From the Stone Age to Christianity* (New York: Doubleday, 1957) and U. Cassuto, *A Commentary on the Book of Exodus* (Jerusalem: Magnes, 1967) 183; W. J. Harrelson, "Law in the OT," *IDB* 3, 82; R. A. F. MacKenzie, "The Formal Aspect of Ancient Near Eastern Law," *The Seed of Wisdom: Essays in Honour of T. J. Meek* (ed. W. S. McCullough; Toronto: University of Toronto, 1964) 31-44; Pfeiffer, *Introduction*, 211; M. Noth, *Exodus* (Philadelphia: Westminster, 1962) 174-75; G. von Rad, *Deuteronomy* (Philadelphia: Westminster, 1966) 217-18; de Vaux, *Ancient Israel*, 146.

[73]Not even E. Gerstenberger, author of *Wesen und Herkunft des "Apodiktischen Rechts"* (WMANT 20; Neukirchen: Neukirchener Verlag, 1965) and one of Alt's serious critics, denies the validity of the distinction between apodictic and casuistic laws. This point is elaborated in R. A. F. MacKenzie's review of *Wesen und Herkunft* in *CBQ* 28 (1966) 500. See also G. Liedke, *Gestalt und Bezeichnung alttestamentlicher Rechtssätze* (WMANT 39; Neukirchen: Neukirchener Verlag, 1971).

[74]Alt, "Origins of Israelite Law," 114.

[75]O. Eissfeldt, *The Old Testament* (New York: Harper, 1965) 27. Similarly, de Vaux cites Exod 22:25 among the casuistic laws (*Ancient Israel*, 146).

[76]J. van der Ploeg, "Studies in Hebrew Law," Part 2, *CBQ* 1 (1950) 425.

[77]See the remarks by Koch, *Biblical Tradition*, 9 n. 12.

[78]Noth, *Exodus*, 179. Similarly, see J. J. Stamm and M. E. Andrew's remarks in *The Ten Commandments in Recent Research* (SBT 2/2; London: SCM, 1967) 67.

[79]See, for instance, Pfeiffer, *Introduction*, 218; Harrelson, "Law in the Old Testament," 82.

[80]J. G. Williams, "Addenda," *VT* 15 (1965) 113. See also M. Weinfeld, *Deuteronomy and the Deuteronomic School* (Oxford: Clarendon, 1972) 239 n. 3; Liedke, *Gestalt*, 101-53.

[81]Williams, "Addenda," 114.

[82]R. A. F. MacKenzie, "The Forms of Israelite Law" (dissertation; Rome, 1949) 111. This study was not available to me.

[83]W. Kornfeld, *Studien zum Heiligkeitsgesetz* (Wien: Herder, 1952) 49. A. Bentzen, too, considers the participial form as part of the casuistic laws; see his *Introduction to the Old Testament* (Copenhagen: G.E.C. Gad, 1952) 1. 224.

[84]R. Kilian, "Apodiktisches und kasuistisches Recht im Licht ägyptischer Analogien," *BZ* 7 (1963) 189.

[85]F. L. Horton, "A Reassessment of the Legal Forms in the Pentateuch and their Functions," *Society of Biblical Literature 1971 Seminar Papers* (Missoula: Scholars Press, 1971) 2. 359-60.

[86]H. Cazelles, *Etudes sur le code de l'alliance* (Paris: Letouzey et Ané, 1946) 109-16. C. Feucht, too, recognizes four types of legal formulation: (1) Conditional; (2) Metric conditional including the partc.; (3) Apodictic; (4) Mixed. See his *Untersuchungen zum Heiligkeitsgesetz* (Berlin: Evangelische Verlagsanstalt, 1964) 22-30.

[87]S. Loewenstamm, "מִשְׁפָּט, מִשְׁפָּט הַמִּקְרָא," *Encyclopedia Biblica* (Jerusalem: Bialik Institute, 1968) 5. 625-28.

[88]*The Oxford English Dictionary* (Oxford: Clarendon, 1933) 1. 387.

[89]Ibid. See also the remarks by E. Nielsen in *The Ten Commandments in New Perspective* (SBT 2/7; London: SCM, 1968) 56.

[90]This legal consequence does not always entail a penalty.

[91]E.g., Exod 21:3, 4, 5, 8, 9, 10, 11.

[92]E.g., Exod 21:31, 36.

[93]E.g., Exod 21:21.

[94]E.g., Deut 25:2. It should be noted here that the particle הֵן, too, introduces a conditional sentence but is not found in the law collections; cf. Jer 3:1 and Deut 24:1.

[95]Variations do occur: e.g., in Exod 21:8; Deut 22:20, the verb in the protasis is in the perfect, 3rd person; in Exod 21:3b, 6, 11, the verb in the apodosis is in the 3rd person perfect with Waw Consecutive.

[96]Other variations also appear, such as וּבַת כֹּהֵן כִּי, אָדָם כִּי, נֶפֶשׁ כִּי etc.

[97]In a few cases, the protasis is introduced by the preposition בְּ followed by an infinitive construct with plural suffix: e.g., בְּבֹאֲכֶם ("When you enter...," Num 15:18, *NJV*); וּבְקֻצְרְכֶם ("When you reap...," Lev 19:9, *NJV*; cf. 23:22).

[98]Mostly אִישׁ אֲשֶׁר, but also נֶפֶשׁ אֲשֶׁר, כָּל אִישׁ אֲשֶׁר, אִישׁ אִישׁ אֲשֶׁר and others.

[99]The use of אֲשֶׁר introducing a conditional sentence is both "rare and peculiar" (BDB, 83, 8d). Horton includes it among the כִּי/אִם forms, for אֲשֶׁר at times has the force of כִּי or אִם (GKC, #159cc). However, אֲשֶׁר can also be taken as a shortened form of אִישׁ אֲשֶׁר: e.g., Num 5:29 has אֲשֶׁר תִּשְׂטֶה אִשָּׁה, but v. 30 has אִישׁ אֲשֶׁר; the first clause in Exod 30:33aα reads אִישׁ אֲשֶׁר, but the second clause (v. 33aβ) has simply וַאֲשֶׁר; in Deut 27:15, the expression הָאִישׁ אֲשֶׁר seems to be shortened to אֲשֶׁר in 27:26. In all of these cases, אֲשֶׁר is followed by a verb. Lev 4:22 (אֲשֶׁר נָשִׂיא יֶחֱטָא) is difficult. Rashbam considers the clause inverted (cf. Ibn Ezra, ad loc) as in Esth 6:8. In Lev 4:22, אֲשֶׁר may be understood in the sense of כַּאֲשֶׁר ("when"). For examples of this possible equation, see BDB, 83e. As will be indicated below, in Akkadian the legal form *awīlum ša* and in Hittite the legal form LÚ *kuiš* have shortened forms, *ša* in Akkadian and *kuiš* in Hittite. The introductory אֲשֶׁר in Exod 21:13 is interpreted in light of this Akkadian parallel by Paul (*Book of the Covenant*, 115 n. 2).

[100]E.g., Lev 17:16, 20:4.

[101]The verbs are usually in the 3rd person imperfect, or in the 3rd person perfect with Waw Consecutive as in Lev 17:8, 15, 16; 20:17; 22:3.

[102]E.g., Exod 21:12, 15, 16, 17. The penalty, מוֹת יוּמָת, indicates a death penalty inflicted by human beings as in Lev 24:16; cf. Lev 20:2, 27. Death is also stipulated, although differently expressed in Gen 9:6, Exod 22:19, Num 35:30. However, not all participial laws require the death penalty, e.g., Lev 24:18a (=21a). On "מוֹת יוּמָת," see the studies by H. Schulz (*Das Todesrecht im Alten Testament* [BZAW 114; Berlin: Töpelmann, 1969]) and V. Wagner (*Rechtssätze in gebundener Sprache und Rechtssatzreihen im israelitischen Recht* [BZAW 127; Berlin/New York: de Gruyter, 1972] 16-31).

[103]E.g., Exod 21:12, 15, 16, 17.

[104]E.g., Exod 22:18, Lev 15:4, Num 19:13, 35:30.

[105]Restricted to positive commands; see GKC, #46 and #110a.

[106]GKC, #113bb; Joüon, #123u. See also J. D. W. Watts, "Infinitive Absolute as Imperative and the Interpretation of Exodus 20:8," *ZAW* 74 (1962) 141-45.

[107]GKC, #109c; #152f. There are a few examples of לֹא with the jussive; see GKC, #109d.

[108]Number of verse is according to *Biblia hebraica* (ed.
R. Kittel; Stuttgart: Württembergische Bibelanstalt, 1966)
(hereafter cited as *BHK*).

[109]Gerstenberger, *Wesen und Herkunft*, 70-73. According to
the author, the negative command in the 2nd person singular is
the true prohibitive, while the 2nd person plural and the 3rd
person negative commands are secondary developments.

[110]W. Richter, *Recht und Ethos* (SANT 15; Munich: Kösel-
Verlag, 1966).

[111]GKC, #107o.

[112]E.g., Exod 12:9; 23:1; Lev 10:9; 19:29, 31; Num 4:18.
Cf. also Lev 11:43; 25:14 (with אל) and v. 17 (with לא).

[113]E.g., Exod 34:3; Judg 22:23-24; 1 Sam 12:20, 21; 1 Kgs
13:9, 22; 20:8; 2 Kgs 2:16-18; Jer 16:2, 5, 8; 25:6; Prov 22:
24. On the "intensity" of the prohibitives (both with אל and
לא), see Gerstenberger (*Wesen und Herkunft*, 50-54).

[114]This is also the opinion of Murphy ("Form Criticism and
Wisdom Literature," 479) and Clark ("Law," 113). Koch prefers
to keep them separate (*Biblical Tradition*, 9 and n. 11). Other
scholars share Koch's opinion but recognize that there are instances of free use and interchange between the two forms; e.g.
A. Marzal ("Mari Clauses in 'Casuistic' and 'Apodictic' Styles,"
Part 2, *CBQ* 33 [1971] 498) and J. Bright ("The Apodictic Prohibition: Some Observations," *JBL* 92 [1973] 185-204).

[115]E.g., Exod 20:25 (an extension of v. 24); 22:24, 25
(extension of v. 21); 34:20a; Num 10:4; cf. Gerstenberger,
Wesen und Herkunft, 30.

[116]E.g., Exod 22:30b; Deut 12:24; 14:19-20; 18:1-2;
22:1, 4.

[117]E.g., Exod 31:15, 35:2, Lev 7:27; at times, in the form
of motivating clauses.

[118]Koch, *Biblical Tradition*, 33.

[119]N. K. Gottwald, *A Light to the Nations* (New York:
Harper, 1959) 22.

[120]Eissfeldt, *Old Testament*, 12-124; cf. Gottwald, *Light
to the Nations*, 23.

[121]On genre considerations before and after Gunkel, see
Buss ("The Study of Forms," 1-56).

[122]I.e., Exod 21:2-22:16; on 21:2, see below.

[123]Deut 19:11-12; 21:15-17, 18-21aα; 22:13-21a, 22a;
24:1-4a, 5, 7a, bα; 25:1-3, 5-9.

[124]E.g., Exod 21:6; 22:7, 8, 10. Alt recognized this
aspect of "casuistic" laws. He cited Exod 21:6 and 22:7 but
then added: "xiii, 8 is probably a secondary addition; in xxii,
10, the divine name Yahweh is a correction" ("Origins of
Israelite Law," 117 n. 24). I. Rapaport challenged Alt and
pointed out that there is no justification for taking these
verses as secondary amplifications ("The Origins of Hebrew Law,"
PEQ 73 [1941] 158-67).

[125]Alt, "Origins of Israelite Law," 119.

[126]The controversy centers on the "Hebrew slave" of Exod
21:2. According to Alt, this does not mean an Israelite but a
Hebrew corresponding to the *ḫab/piru* of the cuneiform texts
("Origins of Israelite Law," 122 and n. 33). Rapaport has
indicated that the term עברי is an ethnic description in the
Bible: e.g., Jonah 1:9, 1 Sam 14:11, Gen 14:13, etc. ("Origins
of Hebrew Law"). Similarly, M. Greenberg stated that "no
scriptural passage gives explicit ground for extending the
scope of *'ivri* beyond Israelites" ("The Ḫab/piru and Hebrews,"
The World History of the Jewish People: II, Patriarchs [ed.
B. Mazar; New Brunswick: Rutgers University, 1970] 198).
Greenberg's comprehensive study on the subject is *The Ḫab/piru*
(AOS 39; New Haven: American Oriental Society, 1955). Others,
however, on the basis of legal terminology and stipulations in
Exodus and the Hapiru slave documents from Nuzi, incline to
take the referent in Exod 21:2 as an appellative rather than
gentilic; see Paul (*Book of the Covenant*, 46) and M. Weippert
(*The Settlement of the Israelite Tribes in Palestine* [SBT 2/21;
London: SCM, 1971] 85-87).

[127]De Vaux, *Ancient Israel*, 146.

[128]See, for instance, F. C. Fensham, "The Possibility of
the Presence of Casuistic Legal Material at the Making of the
Covenant at Sinai," *PEQ* 93 (1961) 143-46. In addition, there
are significant differences between the developed economy of
Canaan and the primitive economy reflected in BC. On this, see
Cazelles, *Le code de l'alliance*, 166-68; G. E. Mendenhall,
"Ancient Oriental and Biblical Law," *BAR* 3 (1970) 15-16; and
Kaufmann, *Religion of Israel*, 170-71.

[129]Paul, *Book of the Covenant*, 45.

[130]Clark, "Law," 107.

[131]J. Morgenstern, "The Book of Covenant," Part 2, *HUCA* 7
(1930) 32.

[132]Ibid., 224.

[133]Alt, "Origins of Israelite Law," 160; cf. 116.

[134]Ibid., 117.

[135]See, for instance, Noth, *Exodus*, 174-75; Nielsen, *Ten Commandments*, 58; L. Köhler, "Justice in the Gate," *Hebrew Man* (Nashville: Abingdon, 1953) 134 (with references to 1 Sam 30: 21-25, Num 27:1-11).

[136]E.g., Ruth 4:1; Gen 23:18; Deut 21:19, 22:15, 25:7. See, in particular, Köhler, "Justice in the Gate," 127-150.

[137]E.g., Lev 24:14-16, Num 15:35, 27:7-8, 2 Sam 12:5-6, 14:8-11, 1 Kgs 3:25-27, Jer 26:16.

[138]See references in n. 135.

[139]See H. H. Rowley, "The Marriage of Ruth," *The Servant of the Lord* (Oxford: B. Blackwell, 1965) 171-94; M. Burrows, "Levirate Marriage in Israel," *JBL* 59 (1940) 22-33; idem, "The Marriage of Boaz and Ruth," *JBL* 59 (1940) 445-54; Morgenstern, "The Book of the Covenant," Part 2, *HUCA* 7 (1930) 178-83; and D. R. G. Beattie, "The Book of Ruth as Evidence for Israelite Legal Practice," *VT* 24 (1974) 251-67.

[140]Lev 19:20; 20:27; 21:9; 22:11, 12, 13a, 14, 21, 27; 24:15, 17, 19-20; 25:26, 29.

[141]Found in Leviticus 2, 4, 5, 12, 13, 15, 27 and Numbers 5, 6, 9, 30.

[142]1 Kgs 8:37.

[143]E.g., Mic 5:4; Isa 28:18; Ezek 14:9, 13; 18:5, 18, 21; 33:6.

[144]Loewenstamm refers to this form (and to אישׁ אשׁר) as "priestly form"; see "מִשְׁפָּט," 626.

[145]On this, see J. Weingreen, "The Case of the Daughters of Zelophechad," *VT* 16 (1966) 518-22, and "The Case of the Woodgatherer," 361-64.

[146]Found in Deuteronomy 12, 13, 14, 15, 17, 18, 19, 20, 21, 22, 23, 24, 26.

[147]Exod 23:4, 5.

[148]E.g., Lev 19:5-6, 23, 33; 22:29-30; 23:10; 25:14-15, 35, 39-40.

[149]E.g., Num 15:2-7, 8-13, 14-16; 18:26; 33:51-54; 34:2; 35:10-15.

[150]E.g., Exod 23:4, 5; Lev 19:33, 25:14 and the majority of cases in D.

[151]Prov 1:10, 2:1, 6:1, 23:1, 24:12, 25:21, 26:25, 27:22.
Cazelles calls them "formulas in wisdom style" (*Le code de
l'alliance*, 114); cf. Kornfeld, *Heiligkeitsgesetz*, 65.   See
also 2 Kgs 4:29.

[152]M. Weinfeld, "The Book of Deuteronomy in Its Relation
to Wisdom" (in Hebrew), *Yehezkel Kaufmann Jubilee Volume* (ed.
M. Haran; Jerusalem: Magnes, 1960) 89-111; idem, "The Origin of the
Humanism in Deuteronomy," *JBL* 80 (1961) 241-47; and idem, *Deuteronomy and the Deuteronomic School*. See also J. Malfroy, "Sagesse
et loi dans le Deuteronome," *VT* 15 (1965) 49-65.   In his study
on *The If-You Form in Israelite Law* (SBLDS 15; Missoula: Scholars
Press, 1975), Harry W. Gilmer argues that the If-You styled
directives are related to the commands and prohibitions in
biblical law and therefore must have originated in the family
ethos suggested by Gerstenberger. The form was then taken over
by many functionaries but was particularly favored by the wise-
men as a vehicle for their instructions. He also adds that the
use of the form in Deuteronomy strongly suggests a royal court
milieu.

[153]Paul, *Book of the Covenant*, 46.

[154]Alt, "Origins of Israelite Law," 119 n. 28.

[155]E.g., Deut 22:23-24, 25:11-12.

[156]Also in Lev 17:3-14; 20:2, 6, 9; 22:4-8, 18-19.

[157]E.g., Lev 13:45-46, 58; 27:29; Num 19:20, 22.   In PC,
the forms אישׁ אשׁר and אישׁ כי are often found in the same context, with no apparent distinction between them. For example:
והנפשׁ אשׁר in Lev 7:20 is followed by והנפשׁ כי (v. 21); ונפשׁ כי
in Lev 5:1 is followed by או נפשׁ אשׁר (v. 2), to be followed
again by או נפשׁ כי (v. 4); cf. והנפשׁ אשׁר in Lev 20:6 and
ואישׁ או אשׁה כי in Lev 20:27, both dealing with the same
subject.

[158]An exception is Deut 17:12 which is part of the law in
vv. 8-13; cf. Kornfeld, *Heiligkeitsgesetz*, 47 n. 119.

[159]E.g., Josh 15:16 (= Judg 1:12), with אשׁר; 1 Sam 17:25
with האישׁ אשׁר.

[160]Dan 5:7 with כל אנשׁ די.

[161]1 Sam 11:7 with אשׁר.

[162]E.g., Dan 3:10 with כל אנשׁ די; 6:8 with כל די; Ezra
6:11 with כל אנשׁ די.

[163]R. Yaron, "Forms in the Laws of Eshnunna," *RIDA* 9
(1962) 150-53.

[164]Ibid., 150.

[165]Ibid.

[166]However, Yaron also includes here proclamations introduced by מי האיש אשר (Deut 20:5; Judg 10:18), by ככה יעשה
לאיש אשר (Deut 25:9; Esth 6:9-11) and curses (with ארור האיש
אשר) (1 Sam 14:24). These forms are different from our legal
prescriptions.

[167]Exod 21:12, 15, 16, 17; 22:18, 19.

[168]Lev 24:16, 18, 21.

[169]E.g., Gen 9:6; Lev 7:29, 33; 11:41; 15:4, 6, 7, 21, 22,
26, 27; Num 19:11-13; 35:30.

[170]E.g., Gen 26:11, 2 Sam 5:8; cf. 1 Chr 11:6; 2 Kgs 11:8,
15.

[171]E.g., Ezra 7:13, 1 Chr 11:6.

[172]E.g., Gen 4:5, Exod 19:12.

[173]Predominantly in Proverbs 10-21.

[174]Alt, "Origins of Israelite Law," 147; also, Cazelles,
Le code de l'alliance, 110; Kornfeld, *Heiligkeitsgesetz*, 51,
and others.

[175]Alt, "Origins of Israelite Law," 147. On ארור-series,
see Wagner, *Rechtssätze*, 32-39.

[176]E.g., Exod 21:17 and Deut 27:16; cf. Exod 22:18, Lev
20:9 and Deut 27:21.

[177]Horton, "Legal Forms in the Pentateuch," 360.

[178]Pfeiffer, *Introduction*, 226. The author here states
that these curses are "not a code of laws but a liturgy in
which the congregation participated by pronouncing 'Amen' after
each curse." S. Sandmel, too, rejects the idea that these
curses embody legislation; see *The Enjoyment of Scripture* (New
York: Oxford University, 1972) 297 n. 1.

[179]Thus H. Brichto, "Blessing and Cursing," *EncJud* 4, 1084.

[180]Von Rad, *Deuteronomy*, 168.

[181]Loewenstamm, "משפט," 628.

[182]See discussion below.

[183]The verb קלל here can better be rendered as "to insult";
cf. *NJV*; H. M. Orlinsky, ed., *Notes on the New Translation of
the Torah* (Philadelphia: JPS, 1969) 178-79, 217; H. C. Brichto,
The Problem of "Curse" in the Hebrew Bible (JBL Monograph Series
13; Philadelphia: Society of Biblical Literature, 1968) 134-35.

[184]Horton, "Legal Forms in the Pentateuch," 355. Horton
does not mention the אִישׁ כִּי form in his study. Yet, there are
also similarities between participial laws and אִישׁ כִּי: e.g.,
Exod 21:12 and Lev 24:17. See discussion below.

[185]E.g., Gen 9:6; cf. GKC, #116w; Exod 21:17.

[186]Horton, "Legal Forms in the Pentateuch," 368.

[187]Ibid.

[188]Ibid., 383.

[189]J. G. Williams, "Concerning one of the Apodictic
Formulas," *VT* 14 (1964) 485; R. Kilian, "Apodiktisches und
kasuistisches Recht," 188; Wagner, *Rechtssätze*, 17.

[190]E.g., Lev 24:16 (participle), v. 17 (אִישׁ כִּי), v. 18
(participle); Lev 24:4 (participle), v. 4 (relative), v. 5
(relative); Lev 15:5 (relative), v. 6 (participle), v. 7
(participle). The participle with an article is equivalent to
a relative clause. See GKC, #166o.

[191]This point is stressed by S. Herrmann, "Das 'apodiktische Recht'--Erwägungen zur Klärung dieses Begriffs," *MIO* 15
(1969) 249-61.

[192]Their primary nonjuridical aspect was recognized by
Cazelles (*Le code de l'alliance*, 125) and other scholars. For
references, see Paul, *Book of the Covenant*, 123 n. 1.

[193]E.g., Exod 13:2, Lev 10:12, Num 10:2.

[194]Exod 20:12 (= Deut 5:16). Lev 19:2 is a parenetic
statement, not a legal prescription. See below, Chapter II,
p. 68 and n. 13.

[195]Deut 15:2, 16:1, 24:9. But 25:17 is the mc of v. 19a.

[196]Gen 17:10b.

[197]Exod 20:8 (with "זְכוֹר") (= Deut 5:12, with "שָׁמוֹר").

[198]E.g., Exod 1:22, Ezra 7:17.

[199]E.g., Ruth 2:15 (accompanied by a negative command).

[200]E.g., Ps 12:8; 23:5; 44:11-13; 91:8, 12; 104:28-30.

[201]E.g., Mal 2:13.

[202]E.g., Gen 12:1, Exod 34:1, Josh 4:3.

[203]E.g., Josh 1:11, 4:17, 18:8, 21:10; Judg 21:20; 2 Sam
13:28; 2 Kgs 11:15.

[204]E.g., Gen 49:29.

[205]E.g., Ps 6:3; 16:1; 24:9; 26:1; 37:27, 34, 37; 39:12, 14; 45:4, 11; 105:1-5.

[206]E.g, Prov 4:5; 5:15; 6:6, 20; 7:1-4; 8:6, 10, 33; 9:5-6, 9; 23:19, 22, 26 and many others.

[207]E.g., 1 Kgs 18:25, Amos 5:14-15, Hos 10:2 and others.

[208]E.g., Judg 18:6, 20:23; 1 Sam 23:24, 30:8; 2 Sam 2:1, 5:19.

[209]E.g., Gen 2:16, Jer 2:2.

[210]E.g., Deut 27:1, 31:26.

[211]E.g., Prov 21:3.

[212]With לא: e.g., Num 22:12, Deut 1:42, 1 Kgs 13:9. With אל: e.g., Gen 26:2, 1 Sam 16:7, 1 Kgs 13:22.

[213]With לא: e.g., Exod 5:7, 1 Kgs 2:6, 22:31. With אל: e.g., 1 Kgs 2:9.

[214]With לא: e.g., Josh 6:10, 1 Sam 12:21, 2 Kgs 17:35. With אל: e.g., Josh 8:4, 1 Sam 12:20.

[215]With לא: e.g., Gen 28:1, Jer 36:7.

[216]With לא: e.g., Judg 19:24, 2 Sam 18:3, 21:17, 1 Kgs 20:8. With אל: e.g., Judg 19:23, 2 Sam 13:12, 1 Kgs 20:8; cf. Bright, "The Apodictic Prohibition," 197.

[217]With לא: e.g., Cant 1:6.

[218]With לא: e.g., Ps 40:12, 81:10, 91:5. With אל: e.g., Ps 22:11; 26:9; 27:9; 28:1, 3; 95:8.

[219]With לא: e.g., Prov 3:23, 22:24. With אל: Prov 3:23, 25; 6:25; 7:25; 9:8; 20:13, 22; 22:22; 23:3, 10, 17 and many others. These usually appear in short series.

[220]With לא: e.g., 2 Kgs 2:16; 6:22; Amos 5:5; 7:13; Jer 16:2, 8; Isa 1:13. With אל: e.g., 2 Kgs 2:18, Jer 16:5, Isa 43:18, Amos 5:5.

[221]With לא: e.g., 2 Sam 5:23.

[222]Among others, Noth, *Exodus*, 161; von Rad, *Deuteronomy*, 18; idem, *Old Testament Theology* (Edinburgh: Oliver & Boyd, 1962) 1. 192-93; Harrelson, "Ten Commandments," *IDB* 4, 572; Eissfeldt, *Old Testament*, 71; H. Ringgren, *Israelite Religion* (Philadelphia: Fortress, 1966) 136; K. Baltzer, *The Covenant Formulary* (Philadelphia: Fortress, 1971); D. R. Hillers, *Covenant: The History of a Biblical Idea* (Baltimore: Johns

Hopkins, 1970) 59, 76; Koch, *Biblical Tradition*, 31-32; H. G.
Reventlow, *Das Heiligkeitsgesetz* (WMANT 6; Neukirchen: Neukirchener Verlag, 1961). It should also be mentioned that
before Alt, Mowinckel in his *Le Décalogue* had argued that the
origin of the Decalogue is to be found in the New Year and
Enthronement festival and, in particular, in the entrance
liturgies with which the festival began.

[223]Acknowledged by Alt, "Origins of Israelite Law," 166.

[224]M. Greenberg, "Decalogue," *EncJud* 5, 1445.

[225]Ringgren, *Israelite Religion*, 192.

[226]E.g., Josh 24:25, 2 Kgs 22:1-3, Neh 10:30.

[227]Cf. J. M. Myers, *Ezra-Nehemiah* (AB 14; New York:
Doubleday, 1965) 174; H. E. Ryle, *The Books of Ezra and Nehe-
miah* (Cambridge: Cambridge University, 1907) 266; F. Michaeli,
Les Livres des Chroniques, d'Esdras et de Néhémie (Neuchâtel:
Delachaux, 1967) 346. Kaufmann stresses that the reading of
the law (chap. 8) was a unique and a noncultic event; see his
Toledot ha-emunah ha-Yisraelit (Jerusalem/Tel Aviv: Bialik,
1969) 8. 325-26; idem, "The Biblical Age," *Great Ages and Ideas
of the Jewish People* (ed. L. W. Schwartz; New York: Modern
Library, 1956) 83.

[228]That the existence of this festival cannot be proved on
the basis of biblical sources was recognized by H.-J. Kraus
(*Worship in Israel* [Richmond: John Knox, 1966] 13). Doubts
were expressed by de Vaux (*Ancient Israel*, 502), M. Weinfeld
("Covenant," *EncJud* 5, 1014), P. J. Budd ("Priestly Instruction
in Pre-Exilic Israel," *VT* 23 [1973] 9), and van der Ploeg
("Studies in Hebrew Law," Part 2, 425).

[229]This was argued by J. J. Stamm and M. E. Andrew in *The
Ten Commandments in Recent Research*, 77. See also von Rad,
Deuteronomy, 56; Noth, *Exodus*, 161; H. G. Reventlow, *Gebot und
Predigt im Dekalog* (Gütersloh: Gerd Mohn, 1962).

[230]See E. Gerstenberger, "Covenant and Commandment," *JBL*
84 (1965) 47.

[231]Ibid., 47-48. The author refers, for example, to
Leviticus 18; Exod 23:1-3, 6-9; Deuteronomy 24 (except for
vv. 8-9, 16).

[232]Fohrer, *Introduction*, 67.

[233]Instead of a "Sippenethos," Richter proposes a "Gruppenethos" for the life setting of the prohibitives; see his
Recht und Ethos, 117. Fohrer sees the origin of the "apodictically" formulated series among the (semi)-nomads ("Das
sogennante apodiktisch formulierte Recht und der Dekalog,"
Kerygma und Dogma 11 [1965] 49-74).

[234]Gerstenberger, "Covenant and Commandment," 50.

[235]Cazelles, *Le code de l'alliance*, 113.

[236]Kaufmann, *Religion of Israel*, 317.

[237]Bright, "The Apodictic Prohibition," 187-88.

[238]Ibid., 187.

[239]E.g., Lev 17:7; 18:23b; 21:2, 4, 5, 7; 22:10, 13b; 23:3; 24:3; 25:32.

[240]E.g., Deut 14:19; 17:6; 18:1, 3; 19:15; 22:5; 23:1, 2, 3, 4, 18; 24:6, 16.

[241]E.g., Exod 12:3, 43; Lev 6:18; 7:2; 27:30.

[242]E.g., Deut 17:6; 19:15; 23:1; 24:6, 16.

[243]E.g., with לא: Exod 19:23, 34:3. With אל: Exod 19:24, 34:3.

[244]With לא: e.g., 1 Sam 11:13. With אל: e.g., 1 Sam 21:3, Jonah 3:7. Positive commands: e.g., 1 Sam 30:24, Ezra 6:3.

[245]With אל: e.g., Exod 16:19, 26; 36:6. Positive commands: e.g., Deut 27:12-13.

[246]E.g., Gen 49:10 (with לא).

[247]Positive commands: e.g., Judg 1:2, 1 Sam 23:11, 12.

[248]With לא: e.g., Ezek 18:20. With אל: e.g., Jer 9:22, 46:6.

[249]With לא: e.g., Prov 12:3, 19:5. With אל: e.g., Prov 10:30b, 31:4.

[250]Budd, "Priestly Instruction in Pre-Exilic Israel," 6.

[251]Gerstenberger considers the 3rd person jussive as a form of prohibitive and belonging to the same setting as the 2nd person negative command. See above, n. 109.

[252]These law collections are not "law codes" in the modern sense of the word; see T. J. Meek, *Hebrew Origins* (New York: Harper, 1960) 54. According to the author, they are merely collections of precedents (i.e., case law). In the opinion of Oppenheim, "such codes represent an interesting formulation of social criticism and should not be taken as normative directions in the manner of post biblical and Roman law" (*Ancient Mesopotamia*, 158). See also the discussion by J. J. Finkelstein, "Ammiṣaduqa's Edict and the Babylonian 'Law Codes,'" *JCS* 15 (1961) 103-104; Paul, *Book of the Covenant*, 23 n. 2.

[253] According to J. A. Wilson, this is because in Egypt the word of the Pharaoh was considered law. "The authority of codified law would have competed with the personal authority of the pharaoh" (*The Burden of Egypt* [Chicago: University of Chicago, 1951] 50). See also his remarks in "Authority and Law in the Ancient Orient," *JAOS* 17 Supplement (1954); and *ANET*, 212. However, there are indications that Egypt did indeed have laws in written form. E. Seidl mentions an inscription of the 8th dynasty which speaks of a vizier sitting in judgment before forty rolls of law ("Egyptian--Law," *The Encyclopaedia of the Social Sciences* 9 [1933] 209). See also the remarks by A. Théodoridès, "La loi dans l'Egypte pharaonique," *RIDA* 12 (1965) 492-93; idem, "A propos de la loi dans l'Egypte pharaonique," *RIDA* 14 (1967) 107-52. He maintains that there were written pharaonic laws expressing general principles.

[254] "A royal decree of Hem-ur," *ANET*, 212. A new translation of this royal decree appears on p. 672 of *ANET*. For references to other royal decrees, see p. 212 n. 1.

[255] H. Donner and W. Röllig, *Kanaanäische und aramäische Inschriften* (Wiesbaden: Harrassowitz, 1962) 1. 15 (#69); 2. 83-87; hereafter cited as *KAI*. F. Rosenthal's translation in *ANET*, 656-57.

[256] *KAI*, 1. 16 (#74-75); 2. 92-93; Rosenthal's translation in *ANET*, 657.

[257] J. J. Finkelstein, "The Laws of Ur-Nammu," *JCS* 22 (1968-69) 66-82; *ANET*, 523-25.

[258] F. R. Steele, "Lipit-Ishtar Law Code," *AJA* 52 (1948) 425-50; E. Szlechter, "Le code de Lipit-Ishtar," *RA* 51 (1957) 57-82, 177-96; and *RA* 52 (1958) 74-90; S. N. Kramer's translation in *ANET*, 159-60.

[259] Finkelstein, *ANET*, 525-26.

[260] M. Civil, "New Sumerian Law Fragments," *AS* 16 (1965) 1-12. This article contains the following material: (1) additions to LI; (2) the tablet UM 55-21-71 (maybe part of LI); (3) laws about rented oxen.

[261] R. Yaron, *The Laws of Eshnunna* (Jerusalem: Magnes, 1969); E. Szlechter, *Les lois d'Ešnunna* (Paris: Sirey, 1954); A. Goetze, "The Laws of Ešnunna," AASOR 31 (1956), and his translation in *ANET*, 161-63.

[262] G. R. Driver and J. C. Miles, *The Babylonian Laws*, Vols. 1 and 2 (Oxford: Clarendon, 1956 and 1955); Meek's translation in *ANET*, 163-80.

[263] G. R. Driver and J. C. Miles, *The Assyrian Laws* (Oxford: Clarendon, 1935); G. Cardascia, *Les lois assyriennes* (Paris: Les Editions du Cerf, 1969); Meek's translation in *ANET*, 180-88.

[264]Driver and Miles, *Babylonian Laws*, 1. 324-47; Meek's translation in *ANET*, 197-98.

[265]H. A. Hoffner, *The Laws of the Hittites* (Ph.D. dissertation in microfilm, Brandeis University, 1963); J. Friedrich, *Die hethitischen Gesetze* (Documenta et Monumenta Orientis Antiqui 7; Leiden: Brill, 1959); Goetze's translation in *ANET*, 188-97.

[266]Yaron, "Forms in the Laws of Eshnunna," 137-53; idem, *Laws of Eshnunna*, 61-66.

[267]Yaron, "Forms in the Laws of Eshnunna," 141; idem, *Laws of Eshnunna*, 59.

[268]On cuneiform legal formulations, see H. Petschow, "Zu den Stilformen antiker Gesetze und Rechtssamlungen," *ZSS* 82 (1965) 24-38.

[269]Very rarely with *kî*. See NBL 6:21-22; cf. *GAG*, #116d, #162d; *CAD*, K, 318, under *kî*.

[270]Yaron, "The Forms in the Laws of Eshnunna," 141; idem, *Laws of Eshnunna*, 61-64.

[271]According to Finkelstein, the term *muškēnum* denotes a variety of people whose economic resources depended on some relationship to the crown ("Ammiṣaduqa's Edict and the Babylonian 'Law Codes'," 99; see also the discussion in Yaron, *Laws of Eshnunna*, 83 and n. 1).

[272]The meaning of *ku-ru-lim* is uncertain. *CAD* translates it as "among the shocks in the field" (K, 572, under *kurullu* [A]); *AHW* renders it as "Getreideschwade, Garbe," (513a); cf. Yaron, *Laws of Eshnunna*, 25 n. on sec. 12:38.

[273]Yaron states that "it would be wrong to assume that the absence of a sanction is a necessary feature of the apodictic formulation: one finds sanctions added to that formulation by means of a conditional sentence (*šumma awīlum*)[37] [n. 37, *CH*, 36/37] or by means of a relative sentence (*awīlum ša*--"the man, who")[38]"; *Laws of Eshnunna*, 64. [N. 38 refers to MAL 40 and the Nuzi edict in AASOR 16, text 51, where the sanction is introduced by *mannumme*--"whoever."] However, Yaron overlooks the fact that LH 37 is a rewording of LH 36 in a conditional form. MAL 40 contains numerous clauses, both conditional and unconditional; here as well as in LH and in the Nuzi text, the sanctions are "added" and are not part of the same legal statements.

[274]Translation by Goetze, *Laws of Ešnunna*, 56; cf. *CAD*, Z, 149 under *zîzu* ("coparcener"). On *mar awīlim*, see Driver and Miles, *Babylonian Laws*, 1. 81; Yaron, *Laws of Eshnunna*, 94. On *mar awīlim la zîzu*, see Yaron, *Laws of Eshnunna*, 99. In *ANET*, 162, Goetze renders the law as, "To a coparcener or a slave a mortgage cannot be furnished."

[275]Yaron, "Forms in the Laws of Eshnunna," 140; idem, *Laws of Eshnunna*, 60.

[276]LE 4, 11, 14.

[277]LE 7, 8, 9A, 10.

[278]LE 3.

[279]LE 3, 7.

[280]LE 4, 10, 11.

[281]S. N. Kramer distinguished between five genres in Sumerian literature; see *Sumerian Literary Texts from Nippur*, AASOR 23 (1944) 11-41. After him, M. Lambert classified the neo-Sumerian literature within fifteen genres; see "La littérature Sumerienne," *RA* 55 (1961) 177-96; and 56 (1962) 81-90. For the classification of wisdom genres, see J. J. A. van Dijk, *La sagesse Sumero-Accadienne* (Leiden: Brill, 1953); E. I. Gordon, "A New Look at the Wisdom of Sumer and Akkad," *BiOr* 17 (1960) 122-50.

[282]J. Tigay, "Literary-Critical Studies in the Gilgamesh Epic: An Assyriological Contribution to Biblical Literary Criticism" (Dissertation, Yale University, 1971) 274 (microfilm).

[283]See the remarks by W. W. Hallo in his "Individual Prayer in Sumerian: The Continuity of a Tradition"; B. Landsberger, "Die babylonischen Termini für Gesetz und Recht," *Symbolae ad iura orientis antiqui pertinentes Paulo Koschaker dedicatae* (Studia et Documenta 2; Leiden: Brill, 1939) 219-34; M. de J. Ellis, "*ṣimdatu* in the Old Babylonian Sources," *JCS* 24 (1972) 75.

[284]E.g., ARM, 1, 32: 16-20; 45: 16-19 (apodosis introduced by the precative); 49: 12-15 (apodosis introduced by the precative).

[285]E.g., *AT*, 2: 33-35 (treaty between Nikmepa of Alalak and Ir-dIM of Tunip; *ANET*, 531); *KBo*, I, 5, col. ii, lines 16-18 (treaty between Sunaššura and Suppiluliuma; E. F. Weidner, *Politische Dokumente aus Kleinasien* (Boghazköi Studien 8-9; Leipzig, 1923) 96-97; A. Goetze, *Kizzuwatna* (YOS Researches 22; New Haven: Yale University, 1940), 36-41.

[286]E.g., *AT*, 56: 35-36; *JEN*, 93: 12-13, 15-16; 56: 11-16; 36: 11-16; 100: 10-16; 208: 12-13.

[287]E.g., *JEN*, 354: 36-38.

[288]E.g., "Edict of Ammiṣaduqa," 5, 7, 11, 20, 21 (number of paragraphs is according to Finkelstein in *ANET* [526-28]). On this text, see F. R. Kraus, *Ein Edikt des Königs Ammi-ṣaduqa von Babylon* (Studia et Documenta 5; Leiden: Brill, 1958); Finkelstein's review in *JCS* 15 (1961) 91-104; idem, "The Edict of Ammiṣaduqa: A New Text," *RA* 63 (1969) 45-64.

[289]For various examples, see E. Leichty, *The Omen Series
Šumma Izbu* (New York: J. J. Augustin, 1970); G. Pettinato, *Die
Ölwahrsagung bei den Babyloniern* (Studi Semitici 22; Rome:
Istituto di Studi del Vicino Oriente, 1966). On omen and
medical texts in general, see Oppenheim, *Ancient Mesopotamia*,
206-227.

[290]For various examples, see C. Viroleaud, *L'Astrologie
chaldéenne* 2 (Paris, 1910).

[291]Yaron, *Laws of Eshnunna*, 66.

[292]E.g., E. Szlechter, *Tablettes juridiques de la 1re
dynastie de Babylone*, Part 2 (Paris: Recueil Sirey, 1958) 131-39.

[293]E.g., *JEN*, 49: 321, 395.

[294]E.g., *JEN*, 334, 342, 343, 353, 359, 369, 387, 389.

[295]E.g., *AT*, 7, 8, 455.

[296]E.g., H. H. Figula, "Lawsuit Concerning a Sacrilegious
Theft at Erech," *Iraq* 13 (1951) 98.

[297]E.g., *JEN*, 354.

[298]Cf. M. de J. Ellis, "*ṣimdatu* in the Old Babylonian
Sources," 76, 82.

[299]The typological similarity was noted by Cazelles (*Le
code de l'alliance*, 110). The significance of this relationship was considered "dubious" by C. J. Gadd (*Ideas of Divine
Rule in the Ancient East* [London: Oxford, 1948] 79). Others
considered the *šumma awīlum* form as stemming from scholarly
circles. See, in particular, F. R. Kraus, "Ein zentrales
Problem des altmesopotamischen Rechtes: Was ist der Codex
Hammu-rabi?" *Genava* 8 (1960) 283-96; and J. J. Finkelstein,
"Ammiṣaduqa's Edict and the Babylonian 'Law Codes'," 104.

[300]Finkelstein, "Ammiṣaduqa's Edict," 103.

[301]For reference to various opinions, see Paul, *Book of
the Covenant*, 23-26 and n. 2, p. 23.

[302]W. F. Leemans, "Some Aspects of Theft and Robbery in
Old Babylonian Documents," *RSO* 32 (1957) 466; Paul, *Book of the
Covenant*, 24 n. 1.

[303]Paul, *Book of the Covenant*, 11-26.

[304]Kraus, "Was ist der Codex Hammu-rabi?"; Finkelstein,
"Ammiṣaduqa's Edict"; Paul, *Book of the Covenant*, 24-26.

[305]LE 12, 13, 19, 51, 52.

[306]MAL, A, 40: 42-45, 58-60, 61-62; 41: 6-10; 47: 7-13.

307HL 50-52.

308LE 12, 13 (both in second place).

309MAL, A, 40: 63-65, 68-76, 89-93.

310HL 185, 186.

311E.g., "Edict of Ammiṣaduqa," 6, 11, 13, 14, 15, 16, 17,
20; in W. F. Edgerton, "The Nauri Decree of Seti I," *JNES* 6
(1947) 219-230; in various *šipṭum*'s from Mari (ARM, 1, 6: 18-
19; 5, 72: 13); with *mannumme* plus *ša* in ARM, 2, 92: 14-18.
On these *šipṭum*'s, see Marzal, "Mari Clauses," 500-502. According to Marzal, a *šipṭum* is "a strong command, an authoritative decree or edict given by a king; it affects the army
(directly the army officers), has religious connotation and
implies a threat of punishment" (335).

312E.g., *AT*, 7: 38-39; ARM, 3, 73: 11-13; cf. Marzal,
"Mari Clauses," 501.

313Usually introduced by *ša ib-ba-la-ak-ka-tu* ("he who
breaks the contract"). For examples, see *AT*, 52: 18-21; 54:
19-22; 55: 26-29.

314Yaron, *Laws of Eshnunna*, 67-68.

315Ibid., 68 n. 1. The reference is to MAL, B: 6.

316LE 15-16. Gerstenberger adds to this list LE 51.
Loewenstamm ("מִשְׁפָּט," 626) and Yaron ("Forms in the Laws of
Eshnunna," 145) add LE 51-52. However, as Petschow ("Stilformen," 29) and Paul (*Book of the Covenant*, 115 n. 1) correctly indicate, these laws belong to the *awīlum ša* form. Yaron
seems to have accepted the criticism; see *Laws of Eshnunna*,
64 n. 34.

317LH 36, 38-40, 187.

318MAL, A, 40 (several clauses); F, 2. Loewenstamm,
("מִשְׁפָּט," 626) adds MAL, A, 57; cf. Meek, *ANET*, 183 n. 24. This
may be possible, but the text is damaged.

319HL 48, 50-51, 56.

320E.g., "Edict of Ammiṣaduqa," 2, 4; in a *ṣimdat šarrim*,
TCL, 7, 56: 9; cf. *CAD*, Ṣ, 195, under *ṣimdatu*. On *ṣimdatu*, see
the article by Ellis (*JCS* 24 [1972] 74-82); see above, n. 298.
The form also appears in various *šipṭum*'s; see Marzal, "Mari
Clauses," 507.

321E.g., *AT*, 3: 6-7; cf. *ANET*, 532; for other examples,
see D. J. McCarthy, *Treaty and Covenant* (AnBib 21; Rome:
Pontifical Biblical Institute, 1963) 181, 184.

322E.g., *AT*, 7: 34-37.

[323]E.g., E. A. Speiser, "New Kirkuk Documents Relating to Family Laws," AASOR 10 (1930) 31-32.

[324]E.g., *ANET*, 210-11; M. Weinfeld, "The Origin of the Apodictic Law," *VT* 23 (1973) 67.

[325]MacKenzie, "The Formal Aspect of the ANE Law," 42.

[326]Yaron, *Laws of Eshnunna*, 67.

[327]See above, n. 109.

[328]LE 1-4, 7-11.

[329]HL 178-87.

[330]Yaron, *Laws of Eshnunna*, 66.

[331]M. Lambert, "Les reformes d'Urukagina," *RA* 50 (1956) 169-84; I. M. Diakonoff, "Some Remarks on the Reforms of Urukagina," *RA* 52 (1958) 1-15.

[332]Yaron, *Laws of Eshnunna*, 65-66.

[333]Paul, *Book of the Covenant*, 45.

[334]Yaron, *Laws of Eshnunna*, 64.

[335]Greenberg, "Postulates," 19.

[336]E.g., treaty between Mursilis and Duppi-Tessub of Amurru, #11; cf. *ANET*, 204; treaty between Niqmepa of Alalak and Ir-dIM of Tunip, *AT*, 2: 17-18 (the apodosis here is expressed as a curse: *šumma la* ["you must"]).

[337]E.g., a marriage contract from Elephantine. See text in A. Cowley, *Aramaic Papyri of the Fifth Century* (Oxford: Clarendon, 1923) 9. 26-27; cf. *ANET*, 222. The apodosis is expressed in the third person.

[338]E.g., ARM, 3, 70: 16-17; 72: r 11-13; *CCT*, 3, 33b: 8; cf. *CAD*, K, 227(1a).

[339]Cazelles, *Le code de l'alliance*, 114.

[340]E.g., "Counsels of Wisdom," *BWL*, 105, lines 150-51.

[341]Many examples in "The Instruction of the Vizier Ptah-Hotep" (*ANET*, 413).

[342]See above, n. 152.

[343]Weinfeld, *Deuteronomy and the Deuteronomic School*, 57-58, 158-78; idem, "Covenant," *EncJud* 5, 1015.

[344]For examples, see Williams, "Concerning One of the Apodictic Formulas," 485; Cazelles, *Le code de l'alliance*, 111.

[345]Cazelles, *Le code de l'alliance*, 111.

[346]E.g., "Counsels of Wisdom," *BWL*, 105, lines 146-47.

[347]E. Puech and H. Rofé, "L'inscription de la citadelle d'Amman," *RB* 80 (1973) 531-46. The text is in Ammonite. Line 2 reads: י. מת ימתן .עלך מסבב .ככל ("   ]que tous ceux qui t'accompagnent seront mis à mort["). The form is reminiscent of Exod 19:22, 22:18, 31:15; cf. Gen 4:15, Lev 14:14, Exod 35:2. Also, pp. 534-35.

[348]Alt, "The Origins of Israelite Law," 139.

[349]Meek, *ANET*, 183 n. 24.

[350]Paul, *Book of the Covenant*, 119.

[351]Fohrer, *Introduction*, 67.

[352]For many examples, see McCarthy, *Treaty and Covenant*, 35-37, 49.

[353]Many examples in the treaty of Sefîre; see J. A. Fitzmyer, *The Aramaic Inscriptions of Sefîre* (Rome: Pontifical Biblical Institute, 1967); cf. *ANET*, 661.

[354]E.g., "Counsels of Wisdom," *BWL*, 100-101, lines 31-32; "The Šamaš Hymn," *BWL*, 134-35, lines 147-48. "The Dialogue of Pessimism," *BWL*, 144-45, line 15; among proverbs, see *BWL*, 240-47; "Amen-em-opet," #13, *ANET*, 423.

[355]The reference is to *šiptu*'s (cf. n. 311 above); e.g., ARM, 1, 13: 27-29; cf. Marzal, "Mari Clauses," 336; ARM, 3, 30: 27-28; cf. Marzal, "Mari Clauses," 339.

[356]E.g., D. J. Wiseman, "The Vassal Treaties of Esarhaddon," *Iraq* 20 (1958) 52; cf. R. Frankena, "The Vassal Treaties of Esarhaddon and the Dating of Deuteronomy," *OTS* 14 (1965) 142. The instructions are found in lines 291-95 of the treaty. See also S. Alp, "Military Instructions of the Hittite King Tuthaliya(?)," *Belleten* 11 (1947) 384-402; cf. Weinfeld, "The Origin of the Apodictic Law," 64; "Instructions for Temple Officials," #9, *ANET*, 209.

[357]E.g., "Tabnit," *ANET*, 662, lines 3-4; cf. *KAI*, #13.

[358]The Amman Citadel Inscription, referred to above in n. 347, contains a negative command expressed in the second person singular. Line 5 reads as follows: אל ל. חדלת.בדלת.בטן כבה ("]tu [ne] passeras *pas* par la porte de l'intérieur *car* l'effroi..." [Puech]; or, as Rofé reads it, "par la porte de Beton parce que là [line 6] [a passé] sa [pré]sence").

[359]See above, n. 219.

[360]The verbs here are expressed in the vetitive (i.e.,
negative imperative), second person singular. On the vetitive
in Egyptian, see A. H. Gardiner, *Egyptian Grammar* (London,
1957) #340:2. I owe this information to Mr. Lanny Bell of the
Oriental Studies Department, University of Pennsylvania.

[361]B. Alster, *The Instructions of Suruppak: A Sumerian
Proverb Collection* (Mesopotamia-Copenhagen Studies in
Assyriology 2; Copenhagen: Akademisk Forlag, 1974) 36-37.

[362]Paul, *Book of the Covenant*, 122.

[363]Gevirtz states that royal decrees are "tantamount to
law" ("West Semitic Curses and the Problem of the Origin of
Hebrew Law," *VT* 11 [1961] 153). Similarly, Weinfeld argues
that royal instructions constitute "legal ordinances" ("The
Origin of the Apodictic Law," 64).

[364]B. Landsberger, "Die babylonischen Termini für Gesetz
und Recht," 222-23; Kaufmann, *Religion of Israel*, 171; Paul,
Book of the Covenant, 8, 34.

CHAPTER II

MOTIVE CLAUSES IN BIBLICAL LAW

DEFINITION OF THE MOTIVE CLAUSES

In the biblical law collections, laws are sometimes accompanied by clauses or phrases that express the rationale behind them or a motive for obeying them. B. Gemser studied these "motive clauses" in an introductory, yet very incisive, article entitled "The Importance of the Motive Clause in Old Testament Law,"[1] and defined them as follows: "They are grammatically subordinate sentences in which the motivation for the commandment is given."[2]

This definition can be used as a starting point in an attempt to discuss the motive clauses in a comprehensive manner. At the outset, it should be pointed out that Gemser's use of the term "commandment" could be misleading. It may give the impression that motive clauses are found only in laws formulated in the unconditional form. In the course of the present analysis it will become clear that this is not so. Motive clauses are found in laws expressed both in the conditional as well as in the unconditional form. Consequently, rather than use the term "commandment" it would be more accurate to speak of "law" or "legal prescription." In line with this observation, a legal motive clause can be defined as "a dependent clause or phrase which expresses the motive behind the legal prescription or an incentive for obeying it."

R. W. Uitti, who wrote a doctoral dissertation on this subject with the title "The Motive Clause in Old Testament Law,"[3] found Gemser's definition too simple to account for all the intricacies of the motive clauses. Abandoning a general definition, he chose to describe these clauses by spelling out their formal characteristics.[4] However, it must be admitted that, even though general definitions are restrictive, they still constitute valuable guidelines in determining the scope of a given subject. Undoubtedly, they need to be followed by a comprehensive study of the phenomenon under consideration. This detailed analysis will be the subject of the following chapters.

Before undertaking this investigation, it is necessary to
distinguish the legal motive clauses from other clauses or
phrases that frequently appear within the formulation of the
law, particularly explicative notes and parenetic statements.

Motive Clauses and Explicative Notes

Motive clauses essentially attempt to answer questions
such as, "Why is the law thus?," "Why observe this law?," by
providing either a justification or an incentive for observing
the particular legal prescription. They do not add new provisions to the law at hand.

Explicative notes are basically used to interpret or
clarify specific words or clauses within the law, or even to
specify the scope of the particular legal prescription. For
instance, in Lev 19:19 and Deut 22:11, the otherwise unknown
word שַׁעַטְנֵז is explained by means of another phrase. According
to Lev 19:19 this refers to a cloth of two kinds of material,
and in Deut 22:11 it denotes a combination of wool and linen.
Similarly, the so-called "*shekel* of the sanctuary" is often
said to equal twenty *gerah*s.[5] In Lev 18:9, the legislator
seems to have felt the need to define the kinship term "sister"
who is the subject of the law by adding the phrase "your
father's daughter or your mother's daughter, whether born into
the household or outside," in order to clarify the scope of
this particular law. The law of adultery in Deut 22:22 contains an additional phrase, "the man who slept with the woman
and the woman" (v. 22aβ), which clearly identifies each *parti-
ceps criminis* that is to be punished by the death penalty.

These and similar explicative notes remain outside the
scope of the present investigation inasmuch as they do not express the rationale behind the law.

Motive Clauses and Legal Parenesis

Parenesis is defined as "exhortation, advice, counsel, a
hortatory composition."[6] Parenetic clauses are extensive in
the Bible and by no means limited to the legal corpora.

Exhortations often appear within the framework of the biblical law collections,[7] sometimes even taking the form of a parenetic envelope.[8] They are also found within the laws proper, interspersed among individual legal prescriptions. In Deuteronomy, where the rhetorical technique is fully developed, the legal corpus is so saturated with hortatory material that von Rad conveniently speaks of the laws therein as "parenetic laws,"[9] for in many cases it becomes difficult to ascertain where the law ends and where the exhortation begins, or vice versa. The same situation exists in the Holiness Code and to a much lesser degree in the Book of Covenant and in the Priestly Code.

The use of parenesis in biblical legal texts has been the subject of a few studies, none as yet comprehensive. Consequently the delineation of the scope of legal parenesis varies from scholar to scholar. N. Lohfink, who has dealt with the issue more extensively than others, points out that the pattern of these exhortations often reveals a two-part structure.[10] In the first part there is an appeal of general nature, formulated frequently by the imperative of שׁמֹר ("observe") and, to a lesser extent, by עֲשֵׂה ("do"), לְמַד ("learn"), or שְׁמַע ("hear"). The second part contains a blessing which usually refers to long life, inheritance of the land or general well-being. As such, these parenetic statements constitute a variation on the theme: "Observe the law so that it may be well with you." The following example from Deuteronomy is illustrative of a full-fledged parenetic statement: "Be careful to heed all the commandments which I enjoin upon you; thus it will go well with you and with your descendants after you forever, for you will be doing what is good and right in the sight of the Lord your God" (Deut 12:28, *NJV*).

Legal parenesis, however, cannot be restricted to those which use the imperatives of שׁמֹר, עֲשֵׂה, לְמַד and שְׁמַע. There are many other statements which, because of their form and content, can well be included in this category. In fact, many scholars recognize as parenetic a greater number of biblical passages than those identified as such by Lohfink.[11]

In line with this wider understanding of the term parenesis, expressions such as the following will be taken in this
study as introducing legal parenetic statements: "observe the
law,"[12] "be holy,"[13] "be careful to,"[14] "you shall rejoice,"[15]
"you shall fear the Lord,"[16] "follow the Lord,"[17] "do not show
pity,"[18], "do not forget,"[19] "seek not their welfare,"[20] "fulfill what has crossed your lips,"[21] "be wholehearted,"[22] "you
shall not learn to,"[23] "love your neighbor,"[24] "do not bring
sin upon,"[25] "do not pollute,"[26] "do not defile,"[27] "do not
bring abomination,"[28] the instruction to establish one law for
citizen and stranger alike,[29] and the formula "an everlasting
statute."[30]

Gemser did not distinguish between parenesis and motive
clauses. For him, both constituted motive clauses. Thus,
among his examples, one finds motive clauses such as "for the
slave is his money" (Exod 21:21), or "because she was not (yet)
free" (Lev 19:20)[31] as well as parenetic statements such as
"your eye shall not pity" (Deut 19:21)[32] and "be careful to
heed" (Deut 12:28).[33] The same lack of distinction characterizes Uitti's study.[34]

On the other hand, W. Beyerlin, in his article on parenesis in the Book of the Covenant,[35] chose to consider both types
of clauses as being parenetic. His argument is that neither is
of a strict legal nature.[36] Consequently, he placed the motive
clauses in Exod 20:25, 26; 22:20, 22-23, 26; 23:7b, 8, 9, 15 in
the same category of parenetic statements found in Exod 22:30a,
23:13a. Yet, when confronted with the motive clauses in Exod
21:8, 21, he specifically excluded them from consideration on
the ground that "they are, unquestionably, not parenesis."[37]

A comparison of the motive clauses with the parenetic
statements reveals a difference both in purpose and form.

(1) The primary object of a parenetic statement is to
summon people to obedience. This is achieved by means of
appeals formulated in broad terms such as those mentioned previously. The main purpose of a motive clause, however, is to
provide a raison d'être for the law, to justify the appropriateness of the particular legal prescription, to show that the law
is just because of the specific reason or purpose formulated

therein. Here the element of exhortation is only secondary and implicit, inasmuch as a law that proves to be just may be expected to receive assent. Motive clauses do not embody direct appeals of general import, nor exhortations couched in broad, indefinite terminology. Quite the contrary, they tend to be specific, pertaining closely to the law at hand.

(2) There is also a formal difference between the two: a parenetic statement frequently appears as an independent unit even when it is connected with a given law. For example, "Follow none but the Lord your God, and revere none but Him; observe His commandments alone, and heed only His orders; worship none but Him, and hold fast to Him" (Deut 13:5, *NJV*), or, "show no pity" (Deut 25:12, *NJV*). On occasion, it contains its own motive clause.[38] Contrary to this, a motive clause is never an independent entity; in fact, it always constitutes a subordinate clause or phrase.

At times, the motive clause of a parenetic statement—which in Lohfink's two-part structure of parenesis corresponds to the second half—is attached to legal prescriptions. These dependent parenetic statements often stress the idea that heeding the divine command results in well-being. They are indeed formulated as a variation of the theme, "that it may be well with you." Most of these clauses are introduced as follows: "so that your/his days be long,"[39] "so that it may be well,"[40] "for/so that He will/may bless,"[41] "so that you/he may learn,"[42] "so that he may rest."[43]

To these must be added other examples which appear only once, though displaying all the characteristics of a dependent parenetic clause: "so that He may turn away (from anger)" (Deut 13:18), and "so that you may live" (Deut 16:20).

On the basis of these formal and contextual differences, the independent parenetic statements will not be studied along with the legal motive clauses; nor will the motive clauses that on occasion accompany these parenetic statements, since they are not attached to legal prescriptions. The dependent parenetic clauses, however, will be analyzed together with the rest of the motive clauses, inasmuch as they provide a motive for observing the legal prescriptions and thus fall within the scope of the definition of the legal motive clauses.

FORM OF THE MOTIVE CLAUSES

Motive clauses in biblical law display a variety of formal
characteristics with regard to their introductory formulary
and syntactical arrangement.

While some of the motive clauses are introduced by means
of grammatical particles, others are formulated asyndetically.
Each of these will be studied below in greater detail.

I. Grammatical particles
  A. Conjunctions
    1. Simple
      a) כִּי
      b) לְמַעַן
      c) וְ
      d) פֶּן
      e) לְבִלְתִּי
      f) אֲשֶׁר
    2. Composite
      a) אַחֲרֵי אֲשֶׁר
      b) תַּחַת אֲשֶׁר
      c) עַל דְּבַר אֲשֶׁר
      d) לְמַעַן אֲשֶׁר
  B. Prepositions
    1. בְּ
    2. תַּחַת
    3. בִּגְלַל(וּ)
    4. לְ
II. Asyndetic motive clauses

Grammatical Particles

Most motive clauses are introduced by conjunctions, either
simple or composite. Others are introduced by prepositions.
Each of the grammatical particles will be discussed below.

Conjunctions

1. Simple

a) כִּי

The particle כִּי, described as the most comprehensive of
all Hebrew particles,[44] fulfills a variety of functions and,
in particular, serves as a causal conjunction introducing motive clauses. Most often, it expresses the reason behind the
law. For example, "You shall not wrong a stranger or oppress
him, for (כִּי) you were strangers in the land of Egypt" (Exod

22:20, *NJV*). On occasion, it may also introduce a dependent
parenetic clause. For instance, "You shall hold festival for
the Lord your God seven days, in the place that the Lord will
choose; for (כִּי) the Lord your God will bless all your crops
and all your undertakings, and you shall have nothing but joy"
(Deut 16:15, *NJV*).

b) לְמַעַן

This conjunction introduces motive clauses which indicate
the purpose behind the law. For example, "Every daughter among
the Israelite tribes who inherits a share must marry someone
from the clan of her father's tribe, in order that (לְמַעַן) every
Israelite may keep his ancestral share" (Num 36:8, *NJV*). Often,
these motive clauses are of parenetic nature. For instance,
"Honour your father and your mother, that (לְמַעַן) you may live
long in the land which the Lord your God is giving you" (Exod
20:12, *NEB*).

c) <u>Simple *waw* copulative</u>

This *waw*, used as a conjunction, can express causality.[45]
For instance, "You shall not oppress a stranger, for you (וְאַתֶּם)
know the feelings of the stranger," etc. (Exod 23:9, *NJV*). It
can also express purpose,[46] both in the positive sense (e.g.,
"But the seventh year you shall let the land be untilled and
unharvested, that the poor among you may eat [וְאָכְלוּ] of it,"
etc. [Exod 23:11, *NAB*]), and, when coupled with the negative
particle לֹא, in the negative sense (e.g., "Do not degrade your
daughter and make her a harlot, lest [וְלֹא] the land fall into
harlotry," etc. [Lev 19:29, *NJV*]).

There are three recurrent motive clauses which are introduced in combination with the particle *waw*: they all express
purpose: (1) וּבִעַרְתָּ "so that you may sweep away the evil";[47]
(2) וְזָכַרְתָּ "so that you may remember";[48] (3) וְ...יִשְׁמְעוּ וְיִרָאוּ "so
that (they) may hear and fear."[49]

d) פֶּן

This conjunction is of "dehortative, dissuasive character,"[50] and introduces negative final (i.e., purpose) clauses.
For example, "You shall not sow your vineyard with a second

kind of seed, else (פֶּן) the crop--from the seed you have sown--
and the yield of the vineyard may not be used" (Deut 22:9, *NJV*).

e) לְבִלְתִּי

This conjunction serves to introduce negative dependent
clauses (i.e., "so that not") and is used as a motive introduction in Deut 17:20 where it heads a secondary and a tertiary
motive clause: "that his heart may not be lifted up (לְבִלְתִּי רוּם
לְבָבוֹ) above his brethren, and that he may not turn aside
(וּלְבִלְתִּי סוּר) from the commandment," (*RSV*).

f) אֲשֶׁר

This relative conjunction can, at times, have a causal
function[51] of which Deut 16:22 is a possible example: "You
shall not set up a sacred pillar, for (אֲשֶׁר) the Lord your God
hates them" (*NEB*; see also *NJV*). However, the same conjunction
can also introduce a final clause[52] as exemplified by Exod
20:26: "Do not ascend My altar by steps, that (אֲשֶׁר) your
nakedness may not be exposed upon it" (*NJV*).

2. Composite

a) אַחֲרֵי אֲשֶׁר

There exists only one example of this composite causal
conjunction functioning as a primary legal motive clause: "Then
the first husband who divorced her shall not take her to wife
again, since (אַחֲרֵי אֲשֶׁר) she has been defiled," etc. (Deut 24:4,
NJV).[53]

b) תַּחַת אֲשֶׁר

This composite causal conjunction introduces motive
clauses in Deut 21:14: "You shall not treat her as a slave,
since (תַּחַת אֲשֶׁר) you have humiliated her" (*RSV*); and in Deut
22:29: "and she shall be his wife, because (תַּחַת אֲשֶׁר) he has
violated her," etc. (*RSV*).

c) עַל דְּבַר אֲשֶׁר

This composite causal conjunction introduces motive
clauses in Deut 22:24: "You shall take the two of them out to
the gate of that town and stone them to death: the girl because

(על דבר אשר) she did not cry for help in the town, and the man because (על דבר אשר) he violated his neighbor's wife" (*NJV*); and in Deut 23:5: "because (על דבר אשר) they did not meet you with food and water on your journey after you left Egypt, and because (ואשר)[54] they hired Balaam son of Beor, from Pethor of Aram-naharaim, to curse you" (*NJV*).

d) למען אשר

This composite final conjunction introduces a motive clause in Lev 17:5: "This is in order that (למען אשר) the Israelites may bring the sacrifices," etc. (*NJV*); and one in Deut 20:18 that is of parenetic nature: "that they may (למען אשר) not teach you to do according to all their abominable practices," etc. (*RSV*).

Prepositions

There are very few examples of legal motive phrases introduced by means of prepositions. In the text they are followed by nouns or gerunds.

1. ב

This preposition is used only once: בבגדו-בה ("since he broke faith with her," Exod 21:8bβ, *NJV*).

2. תחת

There are two examples of motive phrases introduced by this preposition: תחת עינו ("on account of his eye," Exod 21:26bβ, *NJV*) and תחת שנו ("on account of his tooth," Exod 21:27bβ, *NJV*).[55]

3. (ו)בגלל

This preposition, coupled with *waw*, introduces a secondary motivation in Deut 18:12: "and it is because (ובגלל) of these abhorrent things that the Lord your God is dispossessing them before you" (*NJV*).[56]

4. ל

This preposition followed by an infinitive construct or by a noun is capable of introducing legal motivations. For instance, "These six cities shall serve the Israelites and the

resident aliens among them for refuge, so that (לנוס שמה) anyone who kills a person unintentionally may flee there" (Num
35:15b, NJV); or, "Order the Israelites to bring you clear oil
of crushed olives for the light (למאור), so that you may keep
lamps (להעלת נר) burning regularly" (Exod 24:1, NAB).

Formulated Asyndetically

In Hebrew, causality can be expressed not only by using
particular particles but also by simply juxtaposing the main
clause and the causal clause.[57] This, in turn, enables some of
the asyndetic clauses to function as legal motive clauses. For
instance: "Do not uncover the nakedness of your father's sister,
(for) she is your father's flesh" (Lev 18:12, cf. v. 13; see
NAB ad loc).

The possibility of indicating logical subordination by
means of unconnected grammatical coordination makes it possible
to identify many circumstantial clauses which are formulated
asyndetically as legal motive clauses.[58] For example, in Lev
18:7b, of the two asyndetic clauses, the first is clearly causal
and should be understood as "since she is your mother" (lit.,
she being your mother). This, in turn, constitutes the motivation behind the law in the second clause which prohibits uncovering her nakedness. This half verse must therefore be rendered as in NAB: "Since she is your own mother, you must not
have intercourse with her." As will be shown below, a high
percentage of legal motive clauses are formulated in this
asyndetic manner.

Having discussed the motive introductions,[59] it is now
possible to consider other formal characteristics of the legal
motive clauses. In the majority of cases, a particular law is
motivated by means of a single motive clause. However, on
occasion, some laws are provided with multiple motive clauses
introduced in a variety of ways: by the same grammatical particle (e.g., Deut 15:10b-11, both with כי); by two consecutive
asyndetic clauses (e.g., Lev 20:21); by different particles
(e.g., Deut 16:3b, כי and ו); or by a combination of a grammatical particle and an asyndetic clause (e.g., Lev 23:43, למען

and asyndeton). Often a motive clause contains its own motivation (e.g., Exod 22:26b [end]; Lev 21:15; Deut 12:25, 13:19,
19:6, 21:9).

As a rule, a motive clause follows the legal prescription.
However, at times it may precede the law. For example, in Exod
20:22-23, the statement "You yourselves saw that I spoke to you
from the very heavens" (v. 22b, *NJV*) constitutes the underlying
reason for the prohibition against making images of gods (v.
23).[60] There are also some unusual examples such as the one in
Deut 14:1-2 where two legal prescriptions in verse 1b are motivated by motive clauses that are placed both before (v. 1a) and
after (v. 2).

Finally, it is necessary to point to a handful of cases
where the motive clause is found in the protasis of a law expressed in the conditional form: e.g., Deut 12:20a, 14:24, 29a,
15:16b, 24:1. These do not constitute real motive clauses as
defined in this study, inasmuch as they do not provide a
rationale for the directive(s) found in the apodosis but simply
explain certain elements of the case outlined in the protasis.
Therefore, in the computation of the motive clauses, they will
be listed separately and the laws that contain them will not
be considered motivated legal prescriptions.

The motive clauses themselves usually appear as prose
statements, sometimes short (e.g., "for he is his money," Exod
21:21bβ), sometimes longer (e.g., "for I the Lord your God am
an impassioned God, visiting the guilt of the fathers upon the
children," etc., Exod 20:5-6). There is one example of a motive clause taking the form of a question; the prohibition
against cutting down trees around a besieged city is justified
by stating, "for are trees of the field human that they should
withdraw before you into the besieged city?" (Deut 20:19b).
Very few motive clauses have a poetic structure in their formulation (e.g., Exod 23:8; cf. Deut 16:19b, Gen 9:6, *NJV*).

Whereas in the majority of cases the motive clause expresses the reason or the purpose behind the law, in a few
instances it indicates the adverse consequence, in fact, the
specific penalty that awaits anyone who refuses to obey a given
law, much in the sense of "do not do this, for if you do, such

and such will happen." For example, "For seven days no leaven
shall be found in your houses; for (כִּי) if any one eats what is
leavened, that person shall be cut off from the congregation of
Israel, whether he is a sojourner or a native of the land"
(Exod 12:19, *RSV*).[62]

DISTRIBUTION OF THE MOTIVE CLAUSES

General Considerations

The biblical law collections differ among themselves with
regard to the number and types of motivation found in them.
The study of the distribution of the motive clauses will make
it possible to determine, for each law corpus, the number, percentage and content of the motivated laws, the subject matters
that these motive clauses cover and the kind of legal prescriptions that attract motivation. Such a tabulation will, in
turn, permit a comparison between a given law collection and
others, thus revealing both tendencies and patterns for the
individual collections.

The following will constitute operational guidelines in
the undertaking of this particular investigation.

(1) Each law collection will be studied in its present
form and basically in the order in which it appears in the
Bible. For practical purposes, the two versions of the Decalogue (in Exodus 20 and Deuteronomy 5) will be considered one
after the other. The priestly law corpus will be analyzed at
the end, inasmuch as its legal sections encompass a large number of material, sometimes entire legal complexes, spread
throughout the entire Tetrateuch.

(2) In line with the discussion above, parenetic texts,
whether located within the laws or in their introductory and/or
concluding sections, will not be considered in the computation
of the legal prescriptions.

(3) In each legal corpus, the percentage of the motivated
prescriptions will be determined by following three consecutive
steps: (a) counting separate prescriptions, (b) identifying the
motive clauses, (c) deciding whether a given motive clause
motivates one or more than one legal prescription.

The determination of what is law in the Pentateuch presents some difficulties. Already in our discussion above it
was argued that curses and independent parenetic statements are
not to be considered laws. Yet, even within clearly identified
Pentateuchal legal texts it is difficult to separate the individual legal prescriptions.

One of the characteristics of the biblical legislation in
general and of the Priestly Code in particular, is that its
authoritative instructions are often imbedded in historical
narratives. It therefore becomes necessary first to attempt
to distinguish between an ad hoc command for a given historical
occasion and a legal prescription which has validity for the
future as well.[63] The first one can sometimes be identified by
showing that it was immediately carried out as formulated once
and for all; the second one, by referring to literary references indicative of its binding force for all times.

For instance, in Exod 34:1a (cf. Deut 10:1), the Lord
instructs Moses to "carve two tablets of stone like the first."
According to Exod 34:4 (cf. Deut 10:3), Moses obeyed and
"carved two tablets of stone, like the first." Similarly, in
Num 3:40 God commands Moses to record every first-born male of
the Israelites from the age of one month up. Num 3:42 specifies that this order was duly carried out. Elsewhere, following God's directives, Bezalel builds an ark of acacia wood
(Exod 37:1-5; cf. 25:10-16), a cover (Exod 37:6-9; cf. 25:17-
22), a table (Exod 37:10-16; cf. 25:23-29), a lampstand (Exod
37:17-24; cf. 25:31-40), and other cultic objects. These and
similar instructions can be taken as examples of ad hoc
commands.

On the other hand, some instructions are accompanied by
statements showing that their validity goes beyond the present
time. For example: "It is a law for all time throughout the
ages" (Lev 10:9b); "These are the laws and rules which you must
carefully observe in the land that the Lord, God of your
fathers, is giving you to possess, as long as you live on
earth" (Deut 12:1, NJV). The element of permanence and continuous applicability can also be noted in the very formulation
of the legal prescriptions: e.g., the law in Num 27:8b, "If a

man dies without leaving a son, you shall transfer his property
to his daughter" (*NJV*), is undoubtedly meant to be valid in
every similar situation. At times, instructions of this kind
are followed by statements such as "This shall be the law of
procedure for the Israelites," etc. (Num 27:11b, *NJV*); "Such is
the ritual concerning him who has discharge" (Lev 16:32, *NJV*),
which further point to their character as law rather than ad
hoc commands. The legal saying in Gen 9:6 ("Whoever sheds the
blood of man, by man shall his blood be shed, for in His image
has God created him") similarly indicates that it is valid
whenever a man takes the life of another human being (cf. Exod
20:14, 21:12, Lev 24:17). In addition, instructions to be
applied on a continuous basis after the entry into Canaan (e.g.,
Num 15:1-16, 33:51-56, Deut 26:1-12) are to be viewed as legal
prescriptions.

However, though the formulation of the instruction may be
indicative of its permanent validity, the context, too, sometimes must be taken into account in order to determine whether
or not the instruction is to be regarded as law. Thus, God's
instruction to Moses, "Whoever touches the mountain shall be
put to death" (Exod 19:12b), though formulated in the participial form as Gen 9:6, is only an ad hoc command, inasmuch as
the context in which the instruction is found (i.e., in the
Sinai desert, just before the giving of the Ten Commandments)
makes it clear that we are dealing with an historical situation
at a given time and place and not with a legal prescription
valid for all ages.

At times, an instruction is said to have been properly
carried out, yet it still contains a clause specifying that one
aspect of it is to be observed in the future: e.g., God orders
that an altar for burning incense be built (Exod 30:1-6); so
Bezalel builds it (Exod 37:25-28). However, the text further
indicates (Exod 30:7-10) that the burning of incense as well as
the purification ceremony is to be performed throughout the
ages (vv. 8, 10). In this and similar cases, the order that
was carried out once and for all can be considered an ad hoc
command; and the instruction for the future, a legal
prescription.

Gemser was aware of the difficulties inherent in establishing the ratios of the motivated laws and, in fact, admitted
that

> it is not so easy to determine the proportion of the
> clauses with motive sentences over against those
> without. The difficulty arises out of the question
> how many verses the separate law paragraph comprises,
> and whether the subdivisions of a law statement (e.g.,
> in the casuistic laws the subordinate *'im*-sentences
> after the *kî*-clause which opens the case) must be
> reckoned as a new paragraph.[64]

Similarly, Uitti wrote, "There is certainly involved a measure
of subjectivity in the delineation of the number of paragraphs
and sub-cases as well as the identity and limits of individual
motive clauses."[65]

Gemser's solution was to determine the percentages on the
basis of the number of paragraphs, subjects or cases that he
had counted for every law collection. However, in his foot-
notes, he also gave the ratios reached by taking into account
the sub-cases. Uitti, on the other hand, calculated the proportion of motivated laws solely on the basis of the number of
paragraphs or subjects.

The method of computing percentages on the basis of
separate paragraphs or subjects does not correctly reflect the
situation as evidenced in the biblical texts; for this method
treats each subject or paragraph containing a motive clause as
being a motivated law, even though the motive may apply only
to one of several prescriptions in it. In some cases a "paragraph" or subject may indeed consist of a single motivated
prescription, such as Deut 24:6, considered also by Uitti an
entity by itself.[66] Yet, this is not always the case. For
instance, the law in Exod 21:20-21, taken as a unit by Uitti,[67]
contains a motive clause in verse 21. However, this one does
not motivate the entire unit but only the second prescription
in verse 21. Similarly, the law of the slave-woman in Exod
21:7-11, again taken by Uitti as an entity by itself,[68] includes a motive clause in verse 8. Yet, it is clear that this
motive clause provides a motivation for only one of the several
legal prescriptions that make up the paragraph, namely, for
verse 8. Therefore, it is misleading to use subjects or

paragraphs in the computation of the percentages. Rather, one
should consider individual prescriptions that are found within
a given unit.

In attempting to determine the ratios of the motivated
prescriptions, there is a further need to formulate certain
criteria that will serve as guidelines in identifying the individual legal prescriptions, whether motivated or not. This,
in turn, will help to maintain consistency throughout this
complicated undertaking and provide the basis for dependable
comparative statistics.

The primary goal here is to separate each legal prescription that is capable of attracting a motive clause. For the
purposes of the present study, it will sometimes be possible
to combine certain prescriptive imperatives in order to avoid
an undue division of all the legal material.

This consideration applies to laws formulated in the conditional form just as it applies to those in the unconditional
form, for the delineation of the prescriptions is not made on
the basis of the protasis and by distinguishing the primary
from the secondary cases, but by identifying the separate prescriptions that are found in each apodosis.

The following guidelines have emerged as the result of a
survey of all the law collections in the Bible.

(1) Any command or prohibition that has a distinct subject
matter, whether appearing alone or connected to others by means
of a connective particle, will be considered a separate prescription: e.g., "You shall not murder" (Exod 20:13, *NJV*) constitutes one prescription; "You shall not revile God, nor put
a curse upon a chieftain among your people" (Exod 22:27, *NJV*),
constitutes two separate prescriptions.

(2) Commands or prohibitions referring to the same subject
and constituting steps in a chain of directives will be considered one single prescription: e.g., "Any person, whether
citizen or stranger, who eats what has died or has been torn
by beasts, shall wash his clothes, bathe in water, and remain
unclean until evening; then he shall be clean" (Lev 17:15, *NJV*)
constitutes one prescription.

(3) In passages listing several directives in the form of
a generalization followed by details,

(a) individual directives which could conceivably contain
separate motive clauses will be counted as separate prescriptions with the introductory general instruction considered only
an "introduction," not a prescription at all: e.g., in Deut
16:19, "You shall not judge unfairly" (v. 19aα) is an introduction, while "You shall show no partiality" (v. 19aβ), and
"You shall not take bribes, for bribes blind the eyes," etc.
(v. 19b), constitute two separate prescriptions of which only
the second is motivated.

If a conclusion or a summation is also attached, neither
the introduction nor the conclusion will be counted as a prescription: e.g., in Lev 19:15, "You shall not render an unfair
decision" (v. 15aα) is an introduction, "Do not favor the poor
or show deference to the rich" (v. 15aβ, aγ) are two separate
prescriptions, and "Judge your neighbor fairly" (v. 15b) constitutes a conclusion.

(b) If it is hardly imaginable that the separate directives would contain individual motive clauses, then the introductory directive alone will be considered a separate prescription and the rest only as "illustrations," not as separate
prescriptions: e.g., in Lev 25:2-5, "The land shall observe a
sabbath of the Lord" (v. 2b, *NJV*) will be considered as the
sole prescription; verses 3-5 ("Six years you may sow your
field and six years you may prune your vineyard....You shall
not reap the aftergrowth of your harvest or gather the grapes
of your untrimmed vines....") are simply illustrations. At
times, illustrations may precede the prescription itself (e.g.,
Deut 21:10-13, 24:16).

(4) Positive and negative formulations of the same basic
idea will be counted as one prescription: e.g., "The poles
shall remain in the rings of the ark: they shall not be re-
moved from it" (Exod 25:15, *NJV*).

However, not every positive command followed by a prohibition (or vice versa) can be considered a positive and
negative formulation of the same basic idea. When the second
directive contains a specific instruction that cannot be

derived from the first, then each will be counted as a separate
prescription: e.g., "But you must not partake of the blood; you
shall pour it on the ground like water" (Deut 12:16, *NJV*; cf.
vv. 24-25) constitutes two different prescriptions.

(5) The following will not be counted as separate prescriptions.

(a) Prescriptions duplicated by means of synonymous
terminology: e.g., "Make not mention of the names of other
gods; they shall not be heard on your lips" (Exod 23:13b, *NJV*).

(b) Directives which are explicative of other prescriptions: e.g., in Lev 20:2, "Any man among the Israelites, or
among the strangers residing in Israel, who gives any of his
offspring to Molech, shall be put to death; the people of the
land shall pelt him with stones" (*NJV*); the instruction to pelt
the culprit with stones only comes to explain how the death
penalty is to be carried out and does not constitute a separate
prescription.

(c) Specific instructions which fall within the scope of
another prescription, without appearing as mere illustration
of that prescription: e.g., "Six days you shall work, but on
the seventh day you shall cease from labor; you shall cease
from labor even at plowing time and harvest time" (Exod 34:21,
NJV); or, "He shall not go in where there is any dead body; he
shall not defile himself even for his father or mother" (Lev
21:11, *NJV*). In each case, the second half of the prescription
simply indicates that the application of the law extends even
to that particular area and therefore is not to be considered
a separate prescription on its own.

(6) The treatment of a small number of "permissions" presents a difficulty. These do not embody a prohibition or a
command, but simply allow the individual to act freely in a
given situation (e.g., Deut 12:15a, 20; 14:4-6, 9, 11, 20;
20:14, 20; 23:9). It would therefore appear questionable to
consider them as real legal prescriptions. Yet, it must be
recognized that even these "permissions" delineate the area or
areas of permitted activity, conferring upon the individual
certain rights and privileges. Also, a given permission may,
at times, represent an abrogation of a prior prohibition as,

for instance, in Deut 12:13-19 where slaughtering for secular
use is permitted. According to von Rad, this "seems to assume
that up till then every slaughtering was understood as a ritual
act."[69] In this case, Deuteronomy "deprives this action of any
sacral significance."[70] In light of these considerations, the
few "permissions" that are found in the biblical legal corpora
will be counted as legal prescriptions.

(7) The delineation of the legal prescriptions in PC presents some problems. In the first place, in more than any other
legal corpus in the Bible, narratives frequently accompany the
laws in PC. This makes it difficult, at times, to distinguish
between an ad hoc command and a permanent legal prescription
and requires that each instruction be studied closely in order
to see whether or not it contains clues as to its purpose within the text. Secondly, most of the priestly instructions constitute steps in a chain of directives and it is not always
easy to determine where one legal prescription ends and where
the next one begins. In resolving this question, one possibility is to use the subject matter as a guideline. For
example, burnt offering from the herd (Lev 1:3-9) could be
considered one prescription, burnt offering from the flock
(Lev 1:10-13) another prescription, and burnt offering of
birds (Lev 1:14-17) yet another prescription. However, this
criterion is too general and ignores the presence of numerous
prescriptions, some of them motivated, that are contained
within each unit. For example, Lev 1:3-9 includes the bringing
of the animal to the entrance of the Tent of Meeting (v. 3),
the laying of hands (v. 4), the slaughtering of the animal (v.
5a), the offering of the blood (v. 5b) and others. It is proposed here that each of these acts be taken as constituting a
different legal prescription. In certain instances, it is
possible to consider as single legal prescriptions certain
categories of action which are consistently described by combining a number of verbal imperatives. Thus, for instance,
one can view the treatment of the blood (Lev 4:5-7; cf. vv.
16-18, 25, 30, 34) or the presentation of certain parts of the
dismembered animal (Lev 4:8-9; cf. vv. 19a, 26a, 31aα; 3:3-4,
9-10, 14-15) as compound acts, and therefore as single legal

prescriptions. In each case, the component prescriptions do
not--and it is hardly imaginable that they would--contain
separate motive clauses. It is this latter criterion that
will be used in counting the legal prescriptions in PC.

(8) When a motive clause is directly connected to one
legal prescription but provides a motivation for other prescriptions as well, either preceding or following it, each of
the motivated prescriptions will be counted separately.

At times, the motive clause specifically indicates that
it covers more than one legal prescription. For example, it is
clear from the wording of the motive clause in Deut 22:5b
("for whoever does these things is abhorrent to the Lord your
God," *NJV*) that it applies to both legal prescriptions in verse
5aα ("A woman shall not put on man's apparel," *NJV*) and verse
5aβ ("nor shall a man wear woman's clothing," *NJV*).

This extended use of motivation sometimes appears to be
indicated by attaching the motive clause to two consecutive
legal prescriptions connected by the copula ו ("and"). Thus,
for instance, the motive clause in Lev 19:3b ("I the Lord am
your God," *NJV*) seems to motivate both verse 3aα ("You shall
each revere his mother and his father," *NJV*) and verse 3aβ
("and [ואת] keep My sabbaths," *NJV*). However, the connection
itself cannot always be taken as a dependable guide, for the
content of the motive clause may indicate otherwise. For
example, even though Deut 16:19aβ ("you shall show no partiality," *NJV*) is connected to verse 19bα by means of a *waw*
("and you shall not [ולא] take bribes"), the content of the
motive clause in verse 19bβ-γ ("for bribes blind the eyes,"
etc.) clearly shows that only verse 19b is thus motivated.

Finally, even in cases where legal prescriptions are not
connected with a connective particle, the content of the motive
clause may indicate that the intention is to cover more than
one legal prescription. For example, in Lev 18:17, the clause
in verse 17bβ ("they are kindred; it is depravity," *NJV*) appears to motivate the legal prescription in verse 17a ("Do not
uncover the nakedness of a woman and her daughter," *NJV*) as
well as verse 17bα ("nor shall you marry her son's daughter and
her daughter's daughter," etc.).

Admittedly, there is a subjective element in the evaluation of the scope of the last two kinds of motive clauses.

(9) Only motive clauses which provide a direct motivation
for the legal prescriptions will be considered; motive clauses
which, at times, motivate other motive clauses will not be
counted separately.

The percentages obtained by counting separate legal prescriptions instead of paragraphs or subjects will be considerably lower than those proposed by Gemser and Uitti. Yet, the
result, it is believed, will better reflect the reality as
evidenced in the texts themselves for reasons that were already discussed above.

It must be granted that the delineation of the individual
legal prescriptions will inevitably require some subjective
evaluation of the legal data and the possibility cannot be
altogether excluded that others working with the same method
might choose to combine or separate these legal prescriptions
in a different manner than the one proposed in this study. But
the main point is that the number of prescriptions computed in
this way will be much higher than the figure obtained merely by
counting paragraphs or subjects; that general situation would
not be substantially affected by a slightly different
enumeration.

Before concluding this section, two additional remarks
are in order.

(1) The complete list of the legal prescriptions together
with the text of the motive clauses and related notes will be
given at the end of this work. In this chapter, only the results will be recorded.

(2) In studying the subject matters covered by the motivated prescriptions, an attempt will be made to group these
prescriptions within broad categories in order to get a general
understanding of their content. In doing so, it will be kept
in mind that classifications of this kind are devised purely
from our vantage point and cannot be said to represent necessarily the biblical classification which did not differentiate
between civil, moral and religious obligations.

In his classification of the motivated laws, Uitti chose
as him main division R. de Vaux's four basic institutions in
the social life of ancient Israel; namely, family, civil,
military and religious.[71] In the present study, the survey of
the material has led to a classification which is broader in
scope and will be considered under the following headings: (1)
cultic/sacral legislation,[72] (2) "civil" legislation,[73] (3)
humanitarian admonitions and rules of moral conduct, and (4)
legislation dealing with the political sphere (e.g., kingship,
warfare, foreigners).

Motive Clauses in the Pentateuchal Law Collections

The Decalogue

Exod 20:2-17 (Appendix List, No. 1a)

Gemser identified here only three motive clauses (vv. 5,
7, 11)[74] and set the percentage of the motivated laws between
twenty-five and thirty-three.[75]

Uitti found four motive clauses (vv. 5b-6, 7b, 11, 12b)[76]
and, taking Exod 20:2-6 as a unit, stated that the ratio is
four cases out of nine, or a percentage of 44.4%.[77]

The results of the present study are as follows.

Out of a total of eleven legal prescriptions, five are
motivated by five different motive clauses, bringing the
percentage to ca. 45%.

One of the motive clauses (i.e., v. 2) is asyndetic and
provides a motivation for what follows it (v. 3),[78] three are
formulated by means of כִּי (vv. 5b-6, 7b, 11) and one by לְמַעַן
(v. 12b).

Deut 5:6-18 (Appendix List, No. 1b)

Gemser found here four motive clauses (vv. 9, 11, 14f.,
16)[79] and set the percentage again between twenty-five and
thirty-three.[80]

Uitti listed five motive clauses (vv. 9b-10, 11b, 12b,
14c-15, 16aβ-b)[81] and, taking Deut 5:6-10 as a unit, computed
the percentage as 44.4%, i.e., four out of nine cases.[82]

The following are the results of the present analysis.

Out of a total of eleven legal prescriptions, five are
motivated, this time by seven motive clauses. The extra two
motive clauses represent two secondary motivations found in the
laws dealing with the Sabbath (vv. 12-15) and honoring the
parents (v. 16). The percentage of the motivated prescriptions
is still ca. 45%.

Of the primary motive clauses, one (i.e., v. 6) is asyndetic and provides a motivation for what follows it (v. 7),[83]
two are formulated by means of כי (vv. 9b-10, 11b) and two by
the conjunction למען (vv. 14bβ, 16bα).[84] Of the secondary
motivations, one is introduced by וזכרת, in the sense of "for
you shall remember," etc. (v. 15), and the other by ולמען (v.
16bβ).

In both texts the motive clauses are attached to laws
formulated in the unconditional form and restricted, in the
traditional Jewish counting, to the first five commandments.
With the exception of Exod 20:12 (cf. Deut 5:16), which refers
to honoring the parents, the rest of the motivated laws deal
with cultic/sacral matters such as idolatry, blasphemy[85] and
observance of the Sabbath.

The Book of the Covenant (BC): Exod 20:22-23:33
(Appendix List, No. 2)

The legal corpus proper, found in Exod 20:22-23:19, is
followed by Exod 23:20-33 which functions as a conclusion to
BC because of the blessings and promises found in it.[86]

Gemser considered BC a body of laws surrounded by a
"mantle" (Exod 20:23-26 plus 23:10-19). In this legal "mantle"
he found four cases of motivation, identifying them in a footnote as Exod 20:25, 26; 23:12, 15.[87] Yet, when he discussed
the matter of percentages, he stated that in BC and its legal
mantle there are nine motivated laws, i.e., Exod 20:25; 21:8,
21; 22:20, 25f.; 23:7, 8, 9, 15.[88] The two motive clauses
previously cited in Exod 20:26 and 23:12 are missing from his
second list. He furthermore stated that in BC together with
its legal "mantle" there are fifty-nine paragraphs, giving

a percentage rate of 17%[89] or, including the sub-cases, eighty-
eight cases with a percentage rate of 8%.[90]

Uitti, restricting the designation of BC to Exod 21:1-23:9,
counted thirty-eight paragraphs or subjects, of which he found
only nine motivated.[91] He fixed the percentage rate at 23.6%.[92]
His motive clauses, in order of appearance, are: Exod 21:8bβ,
21b; 22:20b, 22-23, 26, 30a;[93] 23:7c, 8b, c, 9b.[94]

The present study has yielded the following results.

Out of a total of 104 legal prescriptions, only 17 are
motivated. This represents a rate of ca. 16%.

Of the seventeen motivated prescriptions, six (ca. 35%)
are expressed in the conditional form and eleven (ca. 64%) in
the unconditional form.

The seventeen motivated prescriptions are accompanied by
sixteen primary motivations and one secondary motivation: Exod
20:22-23,[95] 25, 26; 21:8, 21, 26, 27; 22:20, 21-23, 25-26 (has
a primary and a secondary motive clause); 23:7b, 8, 9, 10-11a,
12, 15a.

The motive clauses are introduced in a variety of ways.
In the following chart, where their distribution is indicated,
the first number refers to the primary motive clauses; the
second, third and fourth number, to the secondary, tertiary and
quaternary motive clauses.

כִּי: 7/0/0/0	אֲשֶׁר: 1/0/0/0
asynd.: 2/0/0/0	לְמַעַן: 1/0/0/0
תַּחַת: 2/0/0/0	בְּ: 1/0/0/0
וְ: 2/1/0/0	

The areas which these motivated laws cover can be divided
into three broad categories.

(1) Cultic/sacral regulations, seven prescriptions:
idolatry (Exod 20:22-23); laws about the altar (Exod 20:25-26),
the sabbatical year (Exod 23:10-11a),[96] the Sabbath (Exod
23:12) and the feast of Unleavened Bread (Exod 23:15a). This
amounts to ca. 41% of the motivated laws and ca. 27% of all the
cultic/sacral prescriptions in the corpus.

(2) Humanitarian admonitions and rules of moral conduct,
six prescriptions: benevolent treatment of the stranger, widow
and the orphan (Exod 22:20, 21-23; 23:9), kindness to the

debtor (Exod 22:25-26), not bringing death on the innocent and
the righteous (Exod 23:7b) and the prohibition against taking a
bribe (Exod 23:8).[97] These six prescriptions represent ca. 35%
of the motivated laws and ca. 37% of all the prescriptions in
the corpus which are of moral/humanitarian nature.

(3) Finally, in the area of "civil" legislation, there are
four motivated laws dealing with the rights and obligations of
the slave-owner (Exod 21:8, 21, 26, 27). They constitute ca.
23% of the motivated laws but only ca. 6% of all the "civil"
laws in BC.

The Cultic Decalogue (CD): Exod 34:10-26
(Appendix List, No. 3)

The question of how to subdivide Exod 34:10-26 is a matter
of scholarly debate. The general tendency is to consider verses
14-26 as embodying the laws of the "cultic" decalogue, with
verses 10-13 acting as an introduction.[98] However, the legal
prescriptions do not seem to start before verse 17. This was
already noted by Kaufmann who spoke of "the small Covenant Code
34:17-26; with its prologue, verses 10-16."[99] Recently, both
Langlamet[100] and Lestienne[101] have argued that verses 11-16
constitute an ancient parenetic introduction dealing with the
relationship between Israel and the inhabitants of the land
(cf. vv. 12, 15-16).

In this "cultic" decalogue, Gemser cited three motive
clauses (vv. 14, 18, 24).[102] As in the other decalogues, the
percentage is set between 25 and 33.[103]

Uitti, who considers 34:10-16 as a prologue, counted
within verses 17-26 seven paragraphs or subjects of which two
are motivated.[104] The percentage is 28.5%.[105] He identified
two motive clauses:[106] one in verse 18aβ (אֲשֶׁר) followed by a
secondary כִּי (v. 18b) and the other in verse 24 (כִּי).

In the opinion of the present writer, too, verses 10-16
appear to constitute a prologue to the laws contained in verses
17-26. Within this body, it is possible to find fifteen separate prescriptions of which only two are motivated. The percentage rate is ca. 13%.[107]

Both motive clauses are introduced by the particle כִּי (vv.
18b, 24). The motivated prescriptions are expressed in the unconditional form and deal with cultic/sacral matters, i.e., the
festival of Unleavened Bread (v. 18) and the requirement for
every male to appear before God three times a year (vv. 23-24),
most likely during the three pilgrimage festivals.

The Holiness Code (H): Lev 17-26 (Appendix List, No. 4)

The determination of the extent of this collection presents
some difficulties. For, even though Lev 26:3-45 and its sub-
scription in verse 46, with their blessings and curses, constitute a distinct conclusion, it is not at all clear where the
corpus begins, since it lacks a title or a superscription that
would unmistakably mark this beginning. Thus Noth writes, "We
can suppose it to begin with ch. 17, primarily for the simple
reason that we can see elsewhere no other longer collection to
which ch. 17 and the following chapters could have belonged."[108]
It is noteworthy that chapter 17 opens up with instructions regarding the place of sacrifice. This can be considered a
suitable opening for a law collection in light of the fact that
both BC (Exod 20:22-26) and the legal corpus of Deuteronomy
(i.e., chap. 12) begin in similar fashion.[109]

Chapters 17-26 do not constitute an original homogeneous
and self-contained unit. The various repetitions found therein
point to a combination of several individual collections that
were once autonomous.[110] The entire corpus was eventually incorporated into PC. As a whole, H is characterized by its
highly parenetic nature.

In H, Gemser found that "on the 122 subjects or cases
stated in this law-collection there is a total of 77 motive
clauses (made up of 45 times the well-known refrain [כִּי אֲנִי
יהוה אֱלֹהֵיכֶם] plus 32 other forms of motivation), providing a
percentage as high as 65."[111] In a footnote, he added, "by a
less probable counting of 136 items and 95 motivations the
percentage would be almost 70."[112] However, because of the
introductory nature of his article, he did not provide the
reader either a list of the laws or a list of his motive
clauses.

Uitti counted seventy-one separate paragraphs of which
fifty-nine are motivated, resulting in a percentage as high as
83%.[113] He also identified a total of ninety-three motive
clauses.[114]

The following constitute the results of the present study
with regard to H.

Out of a total of 214 legal prescriptions, 110 are provided with motivations. This represents a percentage rate of
ca. 51%.

Of the 110 motivated prescriptions, 84 (ca. 77%) are expressed in the unconditional form and 26 (ca. 23%) in the conditional form, with a heavy concentration on negative commands
in the second person.

A total of ninety-four motive clauses accompany the motivated prescriptions.[115] Of these, seventy-four are primary,
eighteen are secondary, and two are tertiary. The distribution
of these motive clauses can be seen in the chart below.

asynd.: 39/11/0/0	ל: 2/1/0/0
פִי: 25/ 2/0/0	למען: 1/0/0/0
ו: 7/ 3/2/0	למען אֲשֶׁר: 0/1/0/0

The areas covered by these motivated laws can be grouped into
three broad categories.

(1) Cultic/sacral regulations, eighty-five prescriptions:
among these are laws dealing with the place appropriate for
sacrifices as well as related sacrificial acts (Lev 17:3-7a,
10-11, 13-14; 19:7, 8, 30aβ; 22:30; 24:2; 26:2aβ), rights and
duties of the priests (Lev 21:1bβ-6, 7-8, 12, 13-15, 17-23;
22:2, 3, 7, 8, 19, 25; 24:9; 25:33-34), sacred occasions in the
Hebrew calendar, such as the Sabbath (Lev 18:3aβ, 19:30aα,
23:3, 26:2a), the Day of Atonement (Lev 23:27-30), Tabernacles
(Lev 23:36bα, 42-43), the Jubilee year (Lev 25:11-12a). Motive
clauses are also appended to laws concerning matters of idolatry and pagan customs: offering children to Molech (Lev 18:21,
20:2-3), mourning rites (Lev 19:27-28), ghosts and familiar
spirits (Lev 19:31), divination and soothsaying (Lev 19:26b),
making images (Lev 19:4, 26:1). In addition, motive clauses
are found in laws dealing with prohibited sexual acts within
certain degrees of family relationship (Lev 18:6-17, 20:11-21),
prostitution (Lev 19:29, 21:9), homosexuality (Lev 18:22,

20:13) and bestiality (Lev 18:23).[116] Laws about first fruits
(Lev 19:23-25) and the prohibition of selling the land in perpetuity similarly attract motivations (Lev 25:23). These
eighty-five prescriptions represent ca. 75% of the motivated
laws and ca. 55% of all the cultic/sacral regulations in H.

(2) Humanitarian admonitions and rules of moral conduct,
twenty-three prescriptions. Those which show concern for the
fate of the underprivileged in society appear to be in the
majority. They include protection of the poor and the stranger
(Lev 19:9-10, 33-34; 23:22) and kind treatment of the fellow
Israelite in debt (Lev 25:14-16, 35-38, 39-42, 47-55). In
addition, one finds motive clauses in connection with reverence
for parents (Lev 19:3aα, 20:9), general concern for one's
fellow men (Lev 19:16, 17b) and correct weights and measures
(Lev 19:35-36). All of these prescriptions constitute ca. 21%
of the motivated laws and ca. 60% of all the rules of humanitarian nature in the corpus.

(3) To the area of "civil" legislation, it is possible to
ascribe two prescriptions: the prohibition of intercourse with
a slave-girl who is designated for another man but not as yet
redeemed or given her freedom (Lev 19:20) and bearing false
witness (Lev 19:12). These prescriptions make up ca. 2% of the
motivated laws and ca. 10% of all the "civil" laws in the
present law collection.

The Deuteronomic Code (D): (Appendix List, No. 5)

Deuteronomy consists of three long addresses,[117] stated
to have been delivered by Moses to the people of Israel, east
of the Jordan, prior to his death and the conquest of the Land.
The body of laws found in chapters 12-26 purport to be the
regulations that constituted the basis of the covenant in
Moab.[118]

The law corpus begins with instructions regarding the
place of sacrifice (chap. 12) and ends with a parenetic conclusion in 26:16-19, followed by blessings and curses in chapter 28.[119] In addition, among all the instructions found
outside of chapters 12-26, it is possible to consider Deut

1:16-17 and 7:1-6, 25-26 as legal prescriptions, rather than
ad hoc commands, inasmuch as they prescribe continuous
application.

The legal material in D is, as noted before, saturated
with exhortative material.[120]

Within Deuteronomy 12-26, Gemser counted 99 paragraphs and
61 motive clauses, resulting in a high percentage of 60%.[121]
In a footnote, he added, "or when subcases are included and less
certain motivations counted in, a total of 129 cases on which
there are 71 motivations, which means 55 percent."[122] Here,
too, because of the introductory nature of this study, he did
not provide the reader with a list of the laws or the motive
clauses.

By contrast, Uitti counted seventy-two paragraphs of
which, he said, sixty-four are motivated,[123] setting the percentage rate of 88.8%.[124] He also found ninety-nine separate
motive clauses.[125]

The results of the present study are as follows.

Out of a total of 225 prescriptions, 111 are motivated.[126]
This represents a rate of ca. 50%.

Seventy-six (ca. 70%) of the motivated prescriptions are
expressed in the unconditional form, while only thirty-five
(ca. 30%) are formulated in the conditional form.

A total of 111 motive clauses accompany the 111 motivated
prescriptions. Of these motive clauses, 83 are primary, 24 are
secondary, 3 are tertiary and 1 is quaternary. The chart below
shows their distribution.

כִּי:	35/ 5/1/0	תַּחַת אֲשֶׁר:	2/0/0/0
וְ:	21/13/1/0[127]	אֲשֶׁר:	1/0/0/0
לְמַעַן:	9/ 1/0/1	לְמַעַן אֲשֶׁר:	1/0/0/0
asynd.:	7/ 0/0/0	אַחֲרֵי אֲשֶׁר:	0/1/1/0
פֶּן:	4/ 0/0/0[128]	לְבִלְתִּי:	0/1/1/0
עַל דְּבַר אֲשֶׁר:	2/ 2/0/0	(וְ)בִגְלַל:	0/1/0/0

The motivated laws in D cover a wide range of topics which
can be divided into four broad categories.

(1) Cultic/sacral regulations, fifty-four prescriptions:
the issues of idolatry and imitation of Canaanite practices
head the list with twenty-eight laws dealing with pagan altars
(Deut 12:2-3; 7:5-6, 25), sacred pillars and posts (Deut

16:21-22), idols (Deut 7:26a), worship of astral deities (Deut
17:2-7), all kinds of divination and magic (Deut 18:10-12),
false prophets and dream-diviners (Deut 13:2-4, 6), inciting to
idolatry (Deut 13:7-12), touching anything proscribed because
of idolatry (Deut 13:18-19), pagan mourning rites (Deut 14:1-2),
sowing two kinds of seeds (Deut 22:9) and wearing apparel of
the opposite sex (Deut 22:5). Motive clauses are found in connection with sacred occasions in the Hebrew calendar, Passover
(Deut 16:1, 3) and Tabernacles (Deut 16:13-15). Certain dietary
prescriptions (Deut 14:7-8a, 10, 19, 21) and, in particular, the
prohibition against consuming blood (Deut 12:23-25) attract motivations. A few prescriptions about the priesthood, all dealing with the rights and duties of the Levitical priests, are
also provided with motivation (Deut 18:1-2, 3-5; 21:5; 24:8-9).
In addition, motive clauses are appended to centralization of
worship (Deut 12:8-9), prohibition against the sacrifice of
blemished animals (Deut 17:1), expiation for unknown murderer's
crime (Deut 21:7-9), tithes (Deut 14:22-23), payment of vows
(Deut 23:22), purity of the military camp (Deut 23:11-15),
bringing to the Temple the fee of harlotry (Deut 23:19), conditions for entering the cultic community (Deut 23:2-5), utter
destruction of Canaanite cities (Deut 20:16-18) and prohibition
against intermarriage with foreigners (Deut 7:3-4). The fifty-
four laws referred to above constitute ca. 48% of the motivated
laws and ca. 48% of all the cultic/sacral regulations in the
corpus.

(2) "Civil" legislation, twenty-eight prescriptions: laws
concerning sex and marriage head the list: nonvirginity of the
bride (Deut 22:13-21), adultery (Deut 22:22), seduction and
rape (Deut 22:23-29), marriage with a step-mother (Deut 23:1),
taking back one's divorced wife who has remarried (Deut 24:1-
4a), levirate marriage (Deut 25:6) and captive woman taken in
marriage (Deut 21:14). Some prescriptions which regulated
procedural matters are provided with motive clauses: false
witness (Deut 19:16-20), forty lashes (Deut 25:3), ignoring
the instructions of the high court (Deut 17:12-13). Motive
clauses are also appended to a variety of laws dealing with the
remission of debts (Deut 15:1-2), slavery (Deut 15:12-15),

cities of refuge (Deut 19:3, 4b-7, 8-9), right of the first son
(Deut 21:15-17), rebellious son (Deut 21:18-21), kidnapping
(Deut 24:7), building a parapet for a new house (Deut 22:8),
burial of an impaled criminal (Deut 21:22-23a). These twenty-
eight prescriptions represent ca. 24% of the motivated laws and
ca. 51% of all the "civil" laws in the corpus.

(3) Humanitarian admonitions and rules of moral conduct,
twenty-one prescriptions. Special concern is here shown to
those who are at a disadvantage for being left without, or with
very little, protection. Motivated laws in this category refer
to the stranger, widow, fatherless and Levite (Deut 14:27, 29;
24:17-22). Motivation accompanies legal prescriptions dealing
with the protection of the poor during the year of release
(Deut 15:7-11), with hired servants (Deut 24:14-15) and the
debtor (Deut 23:20-21; 24:6, 12-13). Compassion for the
mother-bird, too, attracts a motive clause (Deut 22:7).
Similarly, correct weights and measures (Deut 25:13-16),
honesty in judgment (Deut 1:17a), and the admonition not to
take a bribe (Deut 16:19b) are motivated. All of these prescriptions amount to ca. 20% of the motivated laws and ca. 68%
of all the humanitarian and moral laws in D.

(4) Finally, certain laws governing the "political" sphere
are accompanied by motivations. Eight prescriptions can be
included in this category: destroying Amalek (Deut 24:17-19a),
cutting down food-trees during a siege (Deut 20:19), exemption
from military duty for a newly married husband (Deut 24:5),
against hating the Edomite (Deut 23:8a) and the Egyptian (Deut
23:8b). In addition, a number of prescriptions dealing with
various aspects of kingship are similarly motivated (Deut
17:16, 17a, 19-20). These eight prescriptions constitute ca.
7% of the motivated laws and ca. 36% of all the laws in the
corpus that regulate the "political" sphere.

The Priestly Code (PC): (Appendix List, No. 6)

The title "Priestly Code" derives from the interest it
displays with regard to cultic institutions and priestly regulations. The PC forms part of a large narrative work (i.e.,

priestly work) which traces the history of the Israelites from
Creation to the Exodus and the wilderness experiences.[129]   It
is easily recognizable by its distinctive formal style and use
of special vocabulary.[130]   It constitutes a "literary
composite"[131] which in the process of its formation has incorporated various complexes of laws.

There is a general agreement among scholars as to the extent of the PC in the Pentateuch.[132] Although the bulk of the
uninterrupted priestly instructions is found within Exodus 25 -
Numbers 10, there is a considerable amount of priestly laws
spread among other material both before and after, extending
on the one hand back to Exodus 12 and a few prescriptions in
Genesis 9 and 17, and, on the other, forward to the end of the
book of Numbers.

Historical narratives often accompany these priestly instructions of which some are ad hoc commands and others legal
prescriptions. It is highly possible that some of these ad hoc
commands were meant or were later understood as paradigmatic.
Similarly, certain narrative passages in the greater priestly
work may have had "a legislative purpose."[133] These, however,
remain outside the scope of the present study which concentrates
on legal prescriptions whose permanent validity can be determined on the basis of formal or contextual grounds.

Gemser did not discuss the laws in PC. Uitti studied the
PC but did not distinguish between ad hoc commands and legal
prescriptions. He counted in it 166 paragraphs of which, he
stated, 99 were motivated. This represents a rate of 59.6%.[134]
He also identified a total of 148 motive clauses.[135]

The results of the present study are as follows.

Out of a total of 669 legal prescriptions, 130 are motivated. The rate is ca. 20%.

Of the 130 motivated prescriptions, 93 (ca. 71%) are expressed in the unconditional form and 37 (ca. 28%) in the
conditional form.

A total of 125 motive clauses accompany the motivated
prescriptions. Of these, 108 are primary, 16 are secondary and
1 is tertiary. The distribution of these motive clauses can be
seen below.

asynd.: 48/4/1/0   ל: 9/6/0/0
    כִּי: 29/3/0/0   לְמַעַן: 1/0/0/0
    ו: 21/3/0/0

The overwhelming majority of the motivated laws in PC deal
with cultic/sacral matters, since these are its main concern.
The largest number of these prescriptions deals with the rights
and duties of the priests (Exod 29:27-28, 29; 30:19-21a; Lev
7:6; 10:8-14; 16:2; Num 3:6; 18:3b, 20, 31), with different
kinds of offerings (e.g., Lev 1:9b, 13b, 17aβ-b; 2:6, 11-12,
14-15; 4:21, 24aβ-b; 5:11-12; 6:9-10, 18b, 22) and cultic objects (Exod 27:20; 30:32-33, 37-38; Num 10:2, 9, 10). Many
dietary prescriptions have attracted motive clauses (Lev 7:
23-25, 26, 27; 11:4-42). Similarly, a few regulations concerning certain rituals and signs have motivation: circumcision
(Gen 17:11-13), purification ceremony upon the horns of the
altar of burning incense (Exod 30:10), placing fringes on the
corner of garments (Num 15:38-41), burning the red cow (Num
19:9), keeping alive the goat designated by lot for Azazel
(Lev 16:10), procedure to be followed in case of suspected
adultery (Num 5:15, 24), status and consecration of the
Nazirite (Num 6:6-7, 12b), diagnosis of "leprosy" and other
skin eruptions (in Leviticus 13, 14). Motive clauses accompany
prescriptions dealing with certain religious festivals: Passover and Unleavened Bread (Exod 12:15, 18-19, 22-23; 13:6-9),
Second Passover (Num 9:13), Day of Atonement (Lev 16:29b-30).
Motive clauses are also found in connection with consecration
of the first born (Exod 13:2), prohibition against redeeming
the firstlings (Num 18:17a), paying a ransom for those who are
polled (Exod 30:12, 16), reviling God (Num 15:30-31). In addition, PC contains only a few motivated laws which are not
directly related to the cultic sphere and could perhaps be
assigned to the area of "civil" law: annulment of women's vows
(Num 30:6, 13), homicide (Gen 9:6), cities of refuge and procedural laws regarding homicide (Num 35:10b-28), obligation of
an inheriting daughter to marry within her father's tribe (Num
36:8) and an injunction to take possession of the Land (Num
33:53).

Conclusions (Charts A and B)

The survey of the law collections yields the following
general overview of the motive phenomenon in biblical
legislation.

(1) Within six law collections of the Pentateuch,[136] there
are a total of 1,238 legal prescriptions of which 375 are motivated. This represents a percentage of ca. 30%. This percentage stands very low in comparison with the one proposed by
Uitti. He had identified 247 motivated paragraphs or subjects
out of a total of 393, including those in the Shechemite
Dodecalogue (Deut 27:15-26),[137] yielding a high percentage of
63.1%.[138] The difference between the two rates is the direct
result of varied methods followed in counting the laws as well
as in the delineation of the motive clauses. As was argued
above,[139] the percentage of the motivated laws must be calculated by counting individual legal prescriptions rather than
entire paragraphs or subjects which may, and often do, contain
more than one prescription capable of attracting motive clauses.

(2) Motive clauses are attached to laws formulated both in
the conditional and unconditional form. The present survey
indicates that the majority are found in legal prescriptions
expressed in the unconditional form: out of 375 motivated legal
prescriptions, 107 are in the conditional form (i.e., ca. 28%)
and 268 in the unconditional form (i.e., ca. 72%). The predominance of the motivated laws in the unconditional form over
against those in the conditional form is noted in every law
collection in the Bible.

(3) The highest percentage of motivated prescriptions is
found in H (ca. 51%, out of 214 prescriptions); the next highest is D (ca. 50%, out of 225 prescriptions). The Decalogue,
with ca. 45% (out of 11 prescriptions), occupies third place.
The rate then drops considerably: PC has 20% (out of 669 prescriptions); BC, ca. 16% (out of 104 prescriptions); and CD,
ca. 13% (out of 15 prescriptions). As noted, in the Decalogue
and CD, the number of legal prescriptions is very small.

Both Gemser and Uitti argued that there is a clear and
considerable increase in frequency of motive clauses from the
older to the most recent law collections. According to Gemser,

this is perceivable by taking note of the use in percentages
from BC (17%) to D (60%) and finally to H (65%).[140] Similarly,
Uitti remarks that the earliest collections, such as the Decalogue (44.4%) and CD (28.5%), have an extensive motive segment
in comparison with BC (23.6%) and the Shechemite Dodecalogue
(8.3%), but that none is a match for the extent of paragraph
motivation in D (88.9%), H (83%) or PC (59.6%).[141]

The present survey corroborates this claim, at least
partly. Indeed, the rate in BC (ca. 16%) is much lower than
the one in D (ca. 50%). H contains the highest percentage of
motivation (ca. 51%), but its date is a matter of scholarly
debate.[142] PC, with ca. 20%, exhibits a considerably lower
percentage than the one proposed by Uitti (i.e., 59.6%).

(4) Most of the motivated laws deal with the cultic/sacral
sphere. Out of 375 motivated legal prescriptions, 271 can be
assigned to this category. This represents ca. 72% of the motivated laws but ca. 27% of the cultic/sacral instructions in
the Pentateuchal legal corpora. The cultic/sacral laws, in
turn, constitute ca. 78% of all the legal prescriptions in the
Bible. Motivated humanitarian admonitions and rules of moral
conduct, with 51 prescriptions, claim ca. 14% of the motivated
laws but ca. 53% of the biblical laws that are of humanitarian/
moral nature. Only ca. 8% of all the prescriptions in the
Pentateuch can be ascribed to this category. Motivated laws
regulating "civil" matters, with 45 laws, claim ca. 12% of the
motivated prescriptions and ca. 29% of the "civil" laws in the
Bible. The "civil" laws constitute ca. 12% of all the Pentateuchal legal prescriptions. To the political sphere are
assigned eight motivated laws, representing ca. 2% of the motivated laws and ca. 45% of the laws in the Bible dealing with
warfare, foreigners and kingship. Less than 2% of all the prescriptions in the Pentateuch can be ascribed to this category.
It is significant that the category of humanitarian admonitions
and rules of moral conduct has the highest percentage of motivation (i.e., ca. 53%), even though laws of humanitarian/moral
nature amount only to ca. 8% of all the prescriptions in the
Pentateuch. This is indicative of the special moral concern
that animated the draftsmen who formulated biblical laws; they

not only formulated moral instructions but, in order to ensure
compliance to them, they also provided a great many of these
instructions with motivations, stressing their importance for
the welfare of the individual as well as society.

(5) The 375 motivated prescriptions are accompanied by 361
motive clauses of which 293 are primary, 61 are secondary, 6
are tertiary and 1 is quaternary.[143] Their distribution among
the biblical legal corpora is largely in proportion to the size
of the law collections. PC has the largest number of motive
clauses (i.e., 108/16/1/0, a total of 125). This is followed
by D with 111 motive clauses (i.e., 83/24/3/1), H with 94 motive
clauses (i.e., 74/18/2/0), BC with 17 motive clauses (i.e.,
16/1/0/0), the Decalogue, Deuteronomy 5, with 7 motive clauses
(i.e., 5/2/0/0), Exodus 20, with 5 motive clauses (i.e.,
5/0/0/0), and finally CD with 2 motive clauses (2/0/0/0).

(6) The largest number of motive clauses are introduced by
כִּי (115, i.e., 103/11/1/0) or formulated asyndetically (114,
i.e., 98/15/1/0)--each out of a total of 361. The asyndetic
motive clauses are present in all of the legal corpora except
CD, but are heavily used in PC (53, i.e., 48/4/1/0, out of a
total of 114 asyndetic motive clauses) and then by H (50, i.e.,
39/11/0/0, out of a total of 114 asyndetic motive clauses). The
The motive introduction כִּי is represented in all of the law
collections and predominantly used in D (42, i.e., 35/6/1/0,
out of a total of 114 motive clauses with כִּי), PC (32, i.e.,
29/3/0/0, out of a total of the 114 motive clauses) and H (26,
i.e., 24/2/0/0, out of the 114 motive clauses). Third in frequency is ו with 75 examples (i.e., 51/21/3/0) out of a total
of 359 motive clauses and, even though it is common to all of
the law collections, it is primarily used in D (35, i.e.,
21/13/1/0, out of the 74 cases) and PC (24, i.e., 21/3/0/0, out
of the 74 cases). The fourth place in the list is occupied by
the motive introduction לְמַעַן which is found in all of the law
corpora except CD, but is mostly used in D (11, i.e., 9/1/0/1,
out of a total of 18 examples). The motive introduction ל is
found primarily in PC (15, i.e., 9/6/0/0, out of a total of 18
cases) and, to a lesser extent, in H (3, i.e., 2/1/0/0, out of
the 18 cases). The rest of the 11 motive introductions appear

in fewer numbers and are often limited to a single legal corpus
(see Chart B).

(7) Of all the biblical legal corpora, D contains the
largest variety of motive introductions, twelve out of fifteen.
This is in line with D's expansive and hortatory style. This
is followed by BC with seven, H with six, PC with five, Decalogue of Deuteronomy 5 with four, Decalogue of Exodus 20 with
three, and CD with one.

CHART A

The Law Collec-tions	GEMSER			UITTI			PRESENT STUDY		
	Number of Paragraphs or Subjects	Number of Motivated Paragraphs or Subjects	%	Number of Paragraphs or Subjects	Number of Motivated Paragraphs or Subjects	%	Number of Legal Pre-scriptions	Number of Motivated Legal Pre-scriptions	%
Dec. Ex. 20	—	3	25-33	9	4	44.4	11	5	ca. 45
Deut. 5	—	4	25-33	9	4	44.4	11	5	ca. 45
BC	59	9	17	38	9	23.6	104	17	ca. 16
CD	—	3	25-33	7	2	28.5	15	2	ca. 13
H	122 or 136	77 or 95	65 or 70	71	59	83	214	110	ca. 51
D	99 or 129	61 or 71	60 or 55	72	64	88.8	225	111	ca. 50
PC	—	—		166	99	59.6	669	130	ca. 20
				Also, "Shechemite Dodecalogue" (Deut 27:15-26)			(see n. 137)		
				12	1	8.3			
Total Number		—		393	247	63.1	1,238	375	ca. 30

C H A R T   B

Motive Introductions	Dec		BC	CD	H	D	PC	Total Number
	Ex. 20	Deut. 5						
1. כִּי	3/0/0/0	2/0/0/0	7/0/0/0	2/0/0/0	25/ 2/0/0	35/ 6/1/0	29/ 3/0/0	103/11/1/0 (=115)
2. לְמַעַן	1/0/0/0	2/1/0/0	1/0/0/0	–	1/ 0/0/0	9/ 1/0/1	1/ 0/0/0	15/ 2/0/1 (=18)
3. וְ	–	0/1/0/0	2/1/0/0	–	7/ 3/2/0	21/13/1/0	21/ 3/0/0	51/21/3/0 (=75)
4. פֶּן	–	–	–	–	–	4/ 0/0/0	–	4/ 0/0/0 (=4)
5. בַּעֲבוּר	–	–	–	–	–	0/ 1/1/0	–	0/ 1/1/0 (=2)
6. אֲשֶׁר	–	–	1/0/0/0	–	–	–	–	2/ 0/0/0 (=2)
7. אֲנִי יהוה	–	–	–	–	–	1/ 0/0/0	–	1/ 0/0/0 (=1)
8. אֲנִי יהוה	–	–	–	–	–	1/ 1/0/0	–	2/ 0/0/0 (=2)
9. עַל כֵּן	–	–	–	–	–	2/ 2/0/0	–	2/ 2/0/0 (=4)
10. לְמַעַן אֲשֶׁר	–	–	–	–	–	2/ 0/0/0	–	1/ 1/0/0 (=2)
11. פְּ	–	–	1/0/0/0	–	0/ 1/0/0	–	–	1/ 0/0/0 (=1)
12. תַּחַת	–	–	2/0/0/0	–	–	–	–	2/ 0/0/0 (=2)
13. בִּגְלַל	–	–	–	–	–	0/ 1/0/0	–	0/ 1/0/0 (=1)
14. לְ	–	–	–	–	2/ 1/0/0	–	9/ 6/0/0	11/ 7/0/0 (=18)
15. asynd.	1/0/0/0	1/0/0/0	2/0/0/0	–	39/11/1/0	7/ 7/0/0	48/ 4/1/0	98/15/1/0 (=114)
Total Number	5/0/0/0*	5/2/0/0	16/1/0/0	2/0/0/0	74/18/2/0	83/24/3/1	108/16/1/0	293/61/6/1
	5	7	17	2	94	111	125	361

* In 5/0/0/0, the number 5 represents the number of primary motive clauses; the second number, 0, refers to secondary motive clauses; the third number, 0, refers to tertiary motive clauses; the fourth number, 0, refers to quaternary motive clauses.

THE CONTENT OF THE MOTIVE CLAUSES

The motive clauses cover a variety of subjects. Their
classification according to content should enable one to discern general patterns and major concerns of the biblical motive
clauses.

In his article, Gemser distinguished between four types of
motive clauses: "1) the motive clauses of a simply explanatory
character, 2) those of ethical contents, 3) those of a religious kind, cultic as well as theological, and 4) those of
religious-historical contents."[144] Explanatory motive clauses,
he said, "are an appeal to the common sense, to the *ratio*,
whereby the sense of justice and the moral sense are neither
excluded nor explicitly brought to the foreground."[145] As an
example, he mentioned, "for the slave is his money" (Exod 21:21),
"because she was not (yet) free" (Lev 19:20), "lest another man
dedicate the new house" (Deut 20:5) and others.[146] The motive
clauses of ethical content, he stated, constitute a "direct
appeal to the ethical sentiments or to the conscience,"[147] such
as, "that your manservant and your maidservant may rest as well
as you" (Deut 5:14), "you shall leave them for the poor and the
stranger" (Lev 23:22), "you know the heart (נֶפֶשׁ) of the
stranger," etc. (Exod 23:9). Among the religious motive
clauses he mentioned the twelve *tô'ēbāh* laws in D, the motive
refrain "I am the Lord" in H, those which express "acknowledg-
ment and confession of a holy God who created and who demands
a holy people,"[148] and others which are formulated on "religious grounds" such as "for the Lord will not clear one who
swears falsely by His name" (Exod 20:7, *NJV*); "for in six days
the Lord made heaven and earth," etc. (Exod 20:11); "for I will
not acquit the wrongdoer" (Exod 23:7, *NJV*). Of the motive
clauses of religious-historical character he said: "They urge
the fulfilling of the commandment by reference to and on the
ground of 'die grossen Heilstaten Jahwes in der Geschichte'
[the great saving acts of Yahweh in history], especially the
deliverance from Egypt and the granting of the land of Canaan
as heritage,"[149] as in Exod 23:15 ("for in it [the month of
Abib] you went forth from Egypt") and Deut 16:3 ("for you de-
parted from the land of Egypt hurriedly," etc., *NJV*).

Gemser's four-part classification has certain shortcomings.
First of all, it is difficult to consider the explanatory motive clauses as a distinct category, for all of the motive
clauses are basically of an explanatory nature. They all provide a rationale for the law at hand, a rationale whose main
role is to express the reason or purpose behind a given law.
Secondly, a question can be raised about Gemser's terminology.
The author refers to his third category as "religious" and to
his fourth category as "religious-historical." The use of
similar terms for two different types of motive clauses is
confusing.

Uitti distinguishes between "the kind of motivation" and
"the area appealed to" in a given motivation. By "the kind of
motivation" he means the major thrust behind the motive
clauses, namely, the desire (1) to warn, (2) to incite/encour-
age, and (3) to explain.[150] Numerous are the areas, Uitti adds,
to which an appeal is made in support of the various motivations. The hearer is confronted on the one hand by the world
of man and on the other by the world of Yahweh. To the first
are assigned: (1) the evidence of logic, reason, *ratio*, common
sense, (2) the instinct and desire for self-preservation,
blessing, and general well-being, and (3) the dictates of conscience, ethical or humanitarian concerns as well as the necessity for ecological responsibility over against the world of
nature. To the second, the authority and witness of tradition
as to (1) Yahweh's person, nature and will, (2) Yahweh's word
and commandment, and (3) Yahweh's saving acts in creation,
election and redemption.[151]

Uitti applies these criteria to each of the legal corpora
in the Bible as he proceeds to study them one after the
other.[152] It must be noted that in Uitti's analysis the part
dealing with "the kind of motivation" does not yield information about the content of the motive clauses. This comes from
what he calls, "the area appealed to." The two categories are
not in conflict: a motive clause which "explains" can appeal to
"reason," just as it can refer to "Yahweh's saving acts." However, Uitti's second category (i.e., "area appealed to") contains subdivisions in which it is difficult to maintain clear

distinctions: e.g., differences between "Yahweh's person,
nature and will" and "Yahweh's word and commandment"; "evidence
from logic" and "humanitarian concerns." It is most likely
that Uitti did not mean to take these as absolute categories
but as representative of major concerns.

Another way of looking at the question of the content of
the motive clauses may be to consider the contextual relationship existing between the motive clauses and the laws to which
they are attached. This consideration, lacking from Uitti's
analysis, will show how the legislator went about providing a
law with a motive clause. This, in turn, will permit grouping
similar motive clauses within specific categories.

A review of biblical clauses indicates that there are two
basic ways in which a given law is motivated: (1) by repeating
a key element within the law and underlining it as the motive
of the law, (2) by supplying the law with a new clause or
phrase that actually spells out the reason or the purpose behind that particular legal prescription. Each of the two will
be studied below.

In the first type, the motive clause does not add anything
new to the law at hand. In other words, it does not provide
additional information as to why the law orders or prohibits
the action(s) prescribed in it. Whatever is stated in the motive clause can already be found in the law itself. By underlining the key element in the law, the motive clause seems to
indicate that the given law is justified precisely because of
this matter. This is motivation by means of emphasis.

In most cases, the motive clause repeats amost verbatim
a phrase found within the same prescription. For instance,
sexual relations with a slave girl designated for another man
but not yet ransomed or given her freedom (חפשה לא נתן לה) are
not punished by death, because as the motive clause stresses,
"she had not been freed" (כי לא חפשה, Lev 19:20); the death
penalty imposed upon one who insults his parents (איש אשר יקלל
את אביו ואת אמו) is motivated by a clause which simply states,
"he has insulted his father and his mother" (אביו ואמו קלל,
Lev 20:9, NJV); vows or obligations assumed by a daughter are
made void by a father who restrains her (הניא אביה אתה), as the

motive clause points out, "for her father restrained her"
(כי הניא אביה אתה, Num 30:6); defamation (הוציא שם רע) of a
wife by her husband is punished by fine because, the motive
clause indicates, "the man defamed (הוציא שם רע) a virgin in
Israel" (Deut 22:19).[153]

At times, the motive clause underlines an element that is
part of the same overall subject though not found in the prescription to which it is attached: e.g., a Nazirite whose consecrated hair is defiled (text has וטמא ראש נזרו, Num 6:9a) on
account of the fact that a person died near him, undergoes a
ritual of consecration that lasts eight days. On the eighth
day he is consecrated anew, and the previous period of uncleanness is voided. The last instruction (in v. 12b) is motivated
by a clause which reads "since his consecrated hair was defiled" (כי טמא נזרו, Num 6:12bβ) thus alluding to verse 9a.[154]

In all of these examples, a key element of the case is
repeated in the motive clause. However, there are other instances where the motive clause is only a reformulation of a
basic rule stated previously. A good illustration of this is
found in the dietary laws of Leviticus 11 and Deuteronomy 14.
Here the law prohibits the consumption of animals which do not
chew the cud and have true hoofs (Lev 11:4; Deut 14:7). However, the examples mentioned by this law, such as the eating
of the camel, daman, hare and swine (Lev 11:4b-7; Deut 14:7b-
8a), are motivated only by reference to the basic rule formulated before. Although these motive clauses do provide a
separate rationale for each example and even specify the different reasons for not eating swine and other named animals, they
do not give us new knowledge that would reveal the justification
behind the prohibition formulated as a basic rule. Here, too,
the intention seems to be one of emphasis.

In the second type, the motive clause adds the reason or
purpose behind the legal prescription. It enlarges our understanding of the commands or prohibitions by actually providing
new information which the law assumed but did not express.

Sometimes, for example, the motive clause stresses human
dignity: the guilty person may be administered up to forty
lashes but not more, as the motive clause indicates, "lest

being flogged further, to excess, your brother be degraded
before your eyes" (Deut 25:3, *NJV*). At times, there is an
appeal made to human compassion: a garment taken in pledge must
be returned before the sun sets, for as the motive clause
points out, "it is his only clothing, the sole covering for his
skin. In what else shall he sleep?" etc. (Exod 22:26, *NJV*).
Imitatio dei can be the thrust of a motive clause: the Sabbath
law in Exod 20:11 is motivated by stating that God created the
universe in six days and rested on the seventh. It is implied
that in observing the Sabbath day humans should follow God's
example. A motive clause may emphasize an accepted social
value: a priest's daughter who engages in prostitution is
punished by death, for by this act "she degrades her father"
(Lev 21:9).

Very often, recourse is made to motivation by a type of
classification whereby the motive clause identifies the actor,
the action or the object of the action.

At times, the motive clause stresses the special status of
the actor referred to in the law: e.g., the reason why priests
are forbidden from marrying nonvirgins is "because they [the
priests] are holy to their God" (Lev 21:7); the prohibition
against eating anything that has died a natural death is justified by saying "for you are a people consecrated to the Lord
your God" (Deut 14:21a; see also 7:6, 16:2). In addition to
these examples in which the motive clause refers to that which
precedes and precludes the act, there are examples where the
motive clause refers to a person's status as it results from
the act: e.g., in connection with the cities of refuge, the law
prescribes the death penalty for criminals who commit murder in
a variety of situations described therein, justifying it as "he
is a murderer" (Num 35:16; see also vv. 17, 18, 21).

The motive clause may constitute a value judgment on the
action described by the law; this is usually expressed by means
of a short declarative nominal sentence: e.g., uncovering the
nakedness of a mother and her daughter is prohibited on the
ground that "it is depravity" (זמה הוא, Lev 18:17); bestiality
is prohibited because "it is perversion" (תבל הוא, Lev 18:23b);
a man who marries his sister, whether she be the daughter of

his father or mother, suffers penalty, since this act is considered "a disgrace" (חסד הוא, Lev 20:17a); marrying the wife
of one's brother" is an indecency" (נדה הוא, Lev 20:21a).

In another group of motive clauses, the object of the
action as delineated by the law is variously characterized by
a short declarative statement: e.g., the prohibition against
eating all winged swarming things is motivated by stating "they
are unclean for you" (טמא הוא לכם, Deut 14:19; see also Lev
11:8, 26, 27, 28, 35; Deut 14:10); whatever swarms upon the
earth is not to be eaten for, as the motive clause indicates,
"it is loathsome" (שקץ הוא, Lev 11:41; see also Lev 11:10-11a,
13, 42 [with פי]); sacrificial meat that is eaten on the third
day is considered "an offensive thing" (פגול הוא, Lev 19:7;
see also 7:18); the sin offering is to be slaughtered at the
spot where the burnt offering is slaughtered, for "it is most
holy" (קדש קדשים הוא, Lev 6:18). Furthermore, only males of
the priestly line are allowed to eat it, again because "it is
most holy" (קדש קדשים הוא, Lev 6:22; see also Lev 7:6). Similarly, priests are commanded to take the meal offering that is
left over from the Lord's offering by fire and eat it unleavened beside the altar, "for it is most holy" (כי קדש קדשים הוא,
Lev 10:12; for other examples, see Exod 30:10, 32; Lev 6:10b,
24:9; Num 19:17).

Motivations that accompany certain prescriptions dealing
with the issue of "leprosy"[155] are variously expressed by diagnostic terms: "it is a rash" (מספחת הוא, Lev 13:6), "it is
leprosy" (צרעת הוא, Lev 13:8, 15; also vv. 20, 25, 27, 52),
"for it is the scar of the burn" (כי צרבת המכוה הוא, Lev 13:28),
"it is a scall" (נתק הוא, Lev 13:30), "it is an affection"
(נגע הוא, Lev 13:22), "it is a fret" (פחחת הוא, Lev 13:55).

In addition to these patterns, it is possible to identify
four different categories of motive clauses which are characterized by their general orientation: (1) motive clauses which
express God's authority, (2) motive clauses which allude to
historical experiences of the people, (3) motive clauses which
instill a fear of punishment, (4) motive clauses which promise
well-being to the compliant. Within these four categories of
motive clauses, there are many instances where the same motive

clause is used for several laws, sometimes even laws dealing
with unrelated matters.

(1) God's authority. In biblical legislation certain laws
are, either alone or in conjunction with other motive clauses,
predicated upon God's commanding will: "I am the Lord," or
"(for) I the Lord, am your God."[156] The majority of these
motive clauses, more than twenty in number, are concentrated
in H.

A variety of laws are motivated in this manner: e.g., not
uncovering the nakedness of a close relative (Lev 18:6), not
offering children to Molech (Lev 18:21, second mc), revering
the parents (Lev 19:3), observing the Sabbath (Lev 19:3, 30;
26:2), not turning to idols and making molten images (Lev 19:4,
26:1), leaving some of the harvest to the poor and the stranger
(Lev 19:10, 23:22), not swearing falsely (Lev 19:12, second mc),
not dealing basely with or profiting by the blood of one's
neighbor (Lev 19:16), eating the first fruits only in the fifth
year of their harvest (Lev 19:25, second mc), not practicing
pagan mourning customs (Lev 19:28), revering the sanctuary (Lev
19:30, 26:2), not turning to ghosts and familiar spirits (Lev
19:31), not oppressing the stranger (Lev 19:33-34, second mc),
prohibiting the high priest from leaving the sanctuary (Lev
21:12, third mc), requiring that the priests be scrupulous
about the sacred donations of the Israelites (Lev 22:2, second
mc), punishing the priests who partake of the sacred donations
while being in a state of uncleanness (Lev 22:3), forbidding
the priests from eating anything that died or was torn by beast
(Lev 22:8), eating the meat of the thanksgiving offering on the
same day (Lev 22:30), dwelling in booths for seven days (Lev
23:43, second mc), blowing the trumpets on festive occasions
over sacrifices (Num 10:10, second mc).

In some of the motive clauses, God speaks in the first
person. Here are some examples: the consecration of the first-
born is demanded on the ground that, "man and beast, the first
issue of every womb among the Israelites is Mine" (Exod 13:2,
NJV); the selling of the land in perpetuity is prohibited because "the land is Mine" (Lev 25:23); the Aaronide priests will
have no territorial share among the people, for "I am your

portion and your share among the Israelites" (Num 18:20);
circumcision is prescribed "so that it may be a sign of the
covenant between Me and you" (Gen 17:11; cf. v. 13).[157]

Sometimes the motive clause indicates that the action
specified in the law constitutes an affront to God or is
clearly against His will.

Within this type of motive clauses there are some which
are formulated using the expression תועבת יהוה ("abomination
to the Lord") or simply תועבה הוא ("it is an abomination") in
Lev 18:22 and תועבה עשו ("they have done an abhorrent thing")
in Lev 20:13.

The תועבת יהוה motive clause is found among the legal
corpora of the Bible only in D.[158] It is attached to laws
dealing basically with cultic matters: coveting or appropriat-
ing the silver and gold found on idols (7:25b, second mc),
imitation of Canaanite idolatrous practices (Deut 12:31),
offering blemished animals (Deut 17:1), child sacrifice and all
kinds of divination (Deut 18:12), wearing apparel of opposite
sex (Deut 22:5), bringing to the temple as payment of vows the
hire of a male and female prostitute (Deut 23:19). The motive
clause is also found in connection with taking back one's
divorced wife who has remarried (Deut 24:4, second mc)[159] and
honest weights and measures (Deut 25:16, second mc). In H,
homosexuality is prohibited on the ground that "this is an
abomination" (Lev 18:22; cf. 20:13).

Included in this type of motive clauses are some which
motivate their respective laws by reference to profanation of
matters connected with God. In three motive clauses the acts
described in the law constitute a profanation of the name of
God: offering children to Molech (Lev 18:21), swearing falsely
in His name (Lev 19:12), not being scrupulous about the sacred
donations of the Israelites (Lev 22:2). In the event that the
high priest leaves the precinct of the sanctuary, it is the
sanctuary of God which is profaned (Lev 21:12). An unclean
person who fails to cleanse himself suffers punishment on account of the fact that he has defiled the sanctuary of the Lord
(Num 19:13; cf. v. 20). In one case, that which is sacred to
the Lord is considered to have been profaned: eating of the

sacrificial meat on the third day (Lev 19:8). Offering children to Molech represents a defilement of God's sanctuary and
profanation of God's holy name (Lev 20:2-3).

Finally, there are a few examples where the motive clause
expresses the idea that the deed is against God's will: setting
up stone pillars is something that God detests (Deut 16:22),
keeping an impaled body overnight is "an affront to God"
(קללת אלהים, Deut 21:23, *NJV*),[160] acting defiantly against God
is to despise the word of the Lord and violate His commandment
(Num 15:31).

(2) Historical experiences. Scattered among almost all of
the biblical law collections are some laws which are motivated
by reference to historical experiences of the Israelites. The
predominant theme of these motive clauses is the sojourn in
Egypt and redemption from Egyptian enslavement. It is found in
the following laws: prohibition against oppressing the stranger
("for you were strangers in the land of Egypt," Exod 22:20;
also in Exod 23:9 and Lev 19:33-34), not abhoring the Egyptian
("for you were a stranger in his land," Deut 23:8b), observing
the festival of Passover/Unleavened Bread ("for in the month of
Abib you came out of Egypt," Exod 34:18; also in Exod 12:17,
23:15; Deut 16:1, 3).

A few laws in D protecting the poor and the needy are
motivated by a similar clause which states "so that you may
remember (וזכרת) that you were slaves in the land of Egypt":
manumission of the slave (15:15), prohibition against subvert-
ing the rights of the stranger and the orphan together with the
prohibition against taking the widow's garment as a pawn (24:
18), leaving part of the harvest of the olive tree and grapes
of the vineyard for the poor (24:22), and also resting on the
Sabbath day (5:15, second mc).[161]

There are references to the redemption from Egypt in motive clauses where God identifies Himself as being the one who
brought the Israelites out of the Egyptian bondage: e.g., not
worshiping other gods (Exod 20:2, Deut 5:6; cf. Hos 13:4), not
taking interest from a fellow Israelite (Lev 25:38), making
fringes (Num 15:41, third mc), executing false prophets and
dream-diviners (Deut 13:6), inciting to idolatry (Deut 13:11).

A similar motivation is also found in two prescriptions dealing
with debt-slavery during the Jubilee year (Lev 25:42, 55).

In addition to the above, the law prohibiting the king from
sending his people to Egypt to buy more horses is motivated by
"for the Lord has warned you: 'do not go back that way again,'"
(Deut 17:16).

Reference to the wilderness experiences is made in the
motive clause attached to the law concerning the festival of
Tabernacles (Lev 23:43) and the law against admitting the
Ammonites and the Moabites into the congregation of the Lord
(Deut 25:5). An historical allusion is also present in the
motive clause "for he is your brother" attached to the prohibition against abhorring an Edomite (Deut 23:8a; cf. Gen 25:24-
26, 36:1-43).

(3) Fear of punishment. Certain motive clauses instill a
fear of punishment and thus attempt to keep the potential trans-
gressors from violating the legal prescriptions.

Of these, some are formulated as a variation of "lest he
die" (ולא ימות). They all appear in PC: e.g., priests must
wash when they come to the Tent of Meeting or when they offi-
ciate at the altar (Exod 30:20-21), priests are prohibited from
drinking liquor when entering the Tent of Meeting (Lev 10:9),
priests are prohibited from entering into the Shrine at any
time (Lev 16:2), priests are enjoined to put incense on the
fire before the Lord (Lev 16:13, second mc), the Levites are
prohibited from approaching the altar (Num 18:3).

Other motive clauses indicate that he who violates the law
will be cut off (ונכרתה) from among the people:[162] e.g., consuming leaven on the feast of Unleavened Bread (Exod 12:15),
keeping at home leaven during the seven days of the festival
(Exod 12:19), making anointing oil or incense (similar to that
used in cultic services) for personal use (Exod 30:33, 38),
eating the sacrificial meat in a state of uncleanness (Lev 7:
20), consuming the fat of animals from which offerings by fire
may be offered to the Lord (Lev 7:25), consuming blood (Lev
7:26), doing any kind of work on the Day of Atonement (Lev 23:
29, second mc; cf. v. 30).

In one instance, the motive clause warns obedience "so that no plague may come upon" the Israelites: paying a ransom for those who are polled (Exod 30:12). Reproving one's fellow-man is motivated by stating "so that you may not incur guilt because of him" (Lev 19:17);[163] the command to proscribe the Canaanite nations is motivated by "lest they lead you into doing the abhorrent things that they have done for their gods and you stand guilty before the Lord your God" (Deut 20:18, *NJV*). Some motive clauses warn the potential transgressor against blood-guilt: establishing cities of refuge (Deut 19:10), building a roof with a parapet (Deut 22:8). Adverse consequence is indicated in the motive clause attached to a law which enjoins not to turn one's daughter into a harlot, "lest the land fall into harlotry and the land be filled with depravity" (Lev 19:29, *NJV*). Making fringes is motivated by "so that you do not follow your heart and eyes in your lustful urge" (Num 15:39, *NJV*).

In some of the motive clauses the warning and its implied punishment are placed in the mouth of God. The prohibition of worshiping other gods is accompanied by a motive clause which in essence says: for I the Lord am an impassioned God (אל קנא) who visits the guilt of the fathers who reject Me upon their children, but shows kindness to the future generation of those who love Me and keep My commandments (Exod 20:5-6; cf. Deut 5:9-10, *NJV*); the motivation of the law against oppressing the widow and the orphan has: "I will heed their cry and punish you severely" (Exod 22:22-23); the motive clause attached to the prohibition against bringing death to the innocent and the righteous reads: "for I will not acquit the wrongdoer"[164] (Exod 23:7). In Exod 20:7 and Deut 5:11, the warning is formulated in the third person: the Lord will not clear the one who "swears falsely by His name."[165]

The motif "to learn the fear of God" serves as a motive clause in Deuteronomic laws: eating the tithe in the presence of God is required "so that you may learn to fear the Lord your God forever" (14:23); the king is urged to read the book of the Torah "so that he may learn to fear the Lord his God," etc. (17:19).

Four laws in D are motivated by a secondary motive clause which states, with some variation, "so that they (i.e., the rest of the Israelites) may hear and fear and not do again such evil things": inciting to idolatry (13:12), ignoring the directives of a high court (17:13), punishing the false witness (19:20), stoning the rebellious son (21:21).

Finally, ten legal prescriptions in D are accompanied by the motive formula, "so that you may sweep away (ובערת) the evil from your midst/from Israel":[166] execution of false prophets and dream-diviners (13:6, second mc), worship of astral deities (17:7), ignoring the directives of the high court (17:12), punishing the false witness (19:19), inquest for an unsolved murder (21:9, second mc),[167] rebellious son (21:21), nonvirginity of the bride (22:21, second mc), adultery of a married woman (22:22), seduction (22:24, third mc), kidnapping (24:7).

(4) Promise of well-being. Motive clauses which promise general well-being as a reward for obedience are predominantly found in D.

"Long life" is the motivation for: honoring parents (Exod 20:12, Deut 5:16), the king's reading the book of the Torah (Deut 17:20b, fourth mc), sending the mother bird away (Deut 22:7, second mc), and honest weights and measures (Deut 25:15).

"God's blessing" is promised in connection with: making the tithe of the third year available to the poor (Deut 14:29); generous lending to the poor despite and advent of the year of release (Deut 15:10); celebrating Tabernacles for seven days (Deut 16:15); not taking interest from a fellow countryman (Deut 23:21); leaving the forgotten sheaves for the stranger, orphan and the widow (Deut 24:19); and consideration for the debtor (Deut 24:13). In the law requiring the creditor to return the pledge of a poor person at sundown, it is the debtor who will bless his creditor (Deut 24:12-13).

In a few prescriptions, the motivation is that the compliant will be remembered by God for blessings: giving the expiation money during the census (Exod 30:16), sounding the trumpets during a military attack (Num 10:9), sounding the trumpet on festive occasions over sacrifices (Num 10:10).

Two prescriptions are motivated simply by "so that it may be well with you": prohibition against consuming blood (Deut 12:25), sending the mother bird away (Deut 22:7).

The present survey has shown that, except for a few examples where motivation is achieved by reinforcing the key element(s) of the legal prescriptions, the motive clauses actually specify the reason or purpose behind the laws, thus disclosing some of the presuppositions on which these laws are based. It has further revealed various patterns of motivation and, in particular, four broad categories in which motive clauses either stress God's authority and will, allude to the historical experiences of the people, instill a sense of fear of punishment, or promise well-being to the compliant.

The study of the content has made apparent certain motive preferences among the biblical law collections. For instance, the motive clauses, "abomination to the Lord," "to learn the fear of God," "so that they may hear and fear," "sweeping out the evil" and "so that you may remember," are exclusively found in Deuteronomic laws. Also in D there is a high concentration of motive clauses which promise general well-being. H is characterized by the motive clause "I am the Lord (your God)" and the one that stresses the profanation of the name and sanctuary of the Lord. PC has a preference for classificatory motive clauses where the motivation is expressed by an asyndetic declarative statement. Most of the motive clauses which warn that the transgressor will be cut off are again found in PC.

A perusal of the content of the motive clauses leads one to recognize that for the most part the motivations are not the only possible ones; nor do they seem to be comprehensive in their exposition. The same law could very well have been motivated by another kind of motive clause (e.g., Exod 20:8-11 and Deut 5:12-15) or, if it does not already have it, by a multiple motive clause. Probably the intention was not to provide a motivation that would justify the law from all perspectives but to select from among all the possible rationales the one that would denote best the law's appropriateness in the eyes of the people to whom it was addressed. And it is in choosing among

the alternatives that the lawgiver/draftsman reveals his mode
of thinking.

In the majority of cases, the meaning of the motive
clauses is clear. Only in few instances is the exact sense
presently obscure (e.g., Deut 21:23, 22:9; many diagnostic
terms in Leviticus 13; also Deut 24:1).[168] There are examples
where the motive clause reflects a view which is assumed but
not clearly stated. The motivated prescriptions dealing with
prohibited sexual relations in Leviticus 18 constitute a case
in point. Here, for the most part, the motive clauses restate
in different words the prohibited relationship. But, as Horton
remarked in connection with Lev 18:14, "It is circular to for-
bid marriage with one's aunt and then justify that prohibition
on the ground that she is one's aunt."[169] In other cases, the
motive clauses justify the law by specifying the nature of this
relationship. For example, the nakedness of the father's wife
is said to be that of the father (Lev 18:8), the nakedness of
the brother's wife is that of one's brother (Lev 18:16), the
nakedness of the mother's sister is also that of one's mother's
flesh (Lev 18:3). However, none of these motive clauses specifies why the sexual relation is forbidden in the first place.
They all reflect a common set of values which is assumed to be
known and shared by everyone in society and thus requires no
further explanation.

In sum, motive clauses as a whole constitute, in the words
of Gemser, "an instructive compendium of the religion, theology,
ethics, and democratic, humanitarian outlook of the people of
Israel as represented in the Old Testament laws."[170]

THE FUNCTION OF THE MOTIVE CLAUSES

The use of motivation is by no means exclusive to legal
literature. In fact, motive clauses constitute a common element of speech and thus can be found in many literary genres
with varying frequency. In light of this variation, legal
motive clauses need to be studied within the framework of biblical literary genres other than law, in an attempt to isolate
the literary pattern that appears to be their closest parallel.

Motive Clauses in Non-Legal Genres

Introduced by Means of Grammatical Particles

Conjunctions

1. Simple

a) כִּי

The conjunction כִּי appears as an introduction to motive clauses in a greater number of literary genres than the rest of the motive introductions. In prose texts, there are examples of causal clauses introduced by כִּי within components built into complex literary genres:[171] e.g., narratives,[172] prayers,[173] speeches,[174] naming of children,[175] naming of cities.[176] In poetic compositions, כִּי often appears in wisdom and didactic poetry[177] but also in hymns,[178] laments,[179] songs of thanksgiving[180] and, with less frequency, among songs of everyday life, such as in love songs,[181] in a drinking song,[182] in a taunt song,[183] in a dirge.[184] Among sayings, it is found in certain blessings[185] and curses,[186] in priestly *torot*,[187] in a great variety of prophetic sayings[188] and, in particular, in wisdom sayings where it is heavily used.[189]

b) לְמַעַן

Introducing a final clause, this motivating conjunction is found, for instance, in certain narrative texts,[190] prayers,[191] prophetic sayings,[192] songs of thanksgiving,[193] wisdom and didactic poetry[194] and wisdom sayings.[195]

c) וְ

Introducing either a causal or a final clause, the motive introduction וְ is found, for example, in narrative passages,[196] pilgrim songs,[197] prayers,[198] laments[199] and wisdom sayings.[200]

d) פֶּן

The conjunction פֶּן, introducing negative final clauses, appears as a motive introduction, for instance, in narratives,[201] prayers,[202] dirges[203] and individual laments.[204] There are also many examples among wisdom sayings.[205]

e) לְבִלְתִּי

   This conjunction is used to introduce negative dependent
clauses in some narrative texts[206] and in a few prophetic
sayings.[207]

f) אֲשֶׁר

   Introducing either a causal or a final clause, this motive
introduction appears in narratives,[208] prophetic sayings,[209]
blessings,[210] curses[211] and wisdom sayings.[212]

2. Composite

   A few composite conjunctions introduce nonlegal motive
clauses: אֲשֶׁר אַחֲרֵי and עַל דְּבַר אֲשֶׁר appear in certain narrative
passages (e.g., the former in Judg 11:36 [NAB], 19:23 [NAB],
2 Sam 19:31 [RSV]; the latter in 2 Sam 13:22 [mc of a mc]);
תַּחַת אֲשֶׁר is found in narrative texts (e.g., Num 23:13, 1 Sam
26:21), in prophetic sayings (e.g., 2 Kgs 22:17, Isa 53:12,
Jer 29:19, 50:7, 2 Chr 21:12) and in a curse (Deut 28:47);
לְמַעַן אֲשֶׁר has a motivating function in certain narratives (e.g.,
Gen 18:19, Deut 27:3, Josh 3:4) and in a few prophetic sayings
(e.g., Ezek 36:30, 46:18).

Prepositions

   As in legal texts, prepositions rarely function as motive
introductions. There are, however, a few examples: בְּ appears
in narrative texts (e.g., Deut 9:4, 2 Sam 3:27[?],[213] 1 Chr
10:13 [NAB]); תַּחַת appears in a blessing (1 Sam 2:20 [NAB])--it
is possibly a motive introduction in a wisdom text (Job
34:26);[214] וּבִגְלַל appears in prophetic sayings (e.g., 1 Kgs
14:16, Jer 11:17, 15:4); לְ appears in narratives (e.g., Gen
1:17, 2:15), in prophetic sayings (e.g., Isa 49:5).

Formulated Asyndetically

   Outside of law, asyndetic motive clauses are concentrated
in wisdom sayings (e.g., Prov 3:8; 22:27; 23:5a, 8, 13b, 14,
28; 24:12).

   This brief survey demonstrates that motivation is a normal
part of speech and is used, whenever needed, in a number of

genres throughout the Bible. It also makes it evident that,
among all of the biblical literary genres outside of law, wisdom
has the highest concentration of number and kind of motive
clauses. A closer look at the use of motivation in wisdom literature is therefore now in order.

*Legal Motive Clauses and Motive Clauses
in Wisdom Instructions*

Wisdom literature incorporates a variety of genres such as
popular proverbs, riddles, numerical sayings, parables, fables
and maxims.[215] It is among the maxims that motive clauses appear in substantial numbers.

Maxims, unlike popular proverbs, constitute a "work of
art"[216] and are the product of the literary activity of the
sages in ancient Israel. However, not all of them are expressed in the same manner. On the basis of their form and
content, "sentences" can be differentiated from "instructions."[217] Indeed, it is possible to speak of each as a
separate genre.[218]

A wisdom "sentence" is "an observation with an impersonal
form which states a truth."[219] It is built as a two-limbed
verse with the verbs in the indicative. Its purpose is to
register simply how things are. It does not command or exhort.
It seldom contains motive clauses.[220] Examples:

> The man who tills his land will have plenty to eat,
> But the stupid spends his time chasing rainbows.
> (Prov 12:11, AB)

> A mild answer calms wrath,
> but a harsh word stirs up anger.
> (Prov 15:1, *NAB*)

> He who is a friend is always a friend,
> and a brother is born for the time of stress.
> (Prov 17:17, *NAB*)

"Instructions" constitute authoritative regulations for
behavior, "based on the imperatives of social order and values
or on religious belief."[221] Their purpose is indoctrination.
They are built as a two-limbed verse, but here the verbs are
always in the imperative, and motive clauses, which constitute
an important formal element of the genre,[222] now accompany the

sayings. In addressing his student, the teacher not only
formulates his directive, but also attempts to persuade him of
its validity by spelling out the reason why it should be carried out.[223] The following are random examples of wisdom
instructions.

> Do not take advantage of the helpless poor man,
> Nor crush the needy in the public court,
> For the Lord will take up their cause,
> And will rob those who rob them of life.
> (Prov 22:22-23, AB)

> Do not feel envious of evil men,
> nor have longings to be with them;
> for their minds meditate destruction,
> and their lips speak about misery.
> (Prov 24:1-2, McKane)

> Do not give yourself airs at a royal court
> Or take your position where the great belong;
> It is better to be told, "Come up here,"
> than to be humiliated before a noble.
> (Prov 25:6-7, AB)

In the book of Proverbs, the "sentences" are concentrated
in chapters 10-22:16; 25-29 and the "instructions" are mostly
found in chapters 1-9; 22:17-24:22; 24:23-24. The book of
Ecclesiastes contains examples of both types.[224]

The formulation of the motive clauses in legal prescriptions is in many respects similar to the motivations found in
wisdom instructions. In both, a directive, expressed in the
conditional or in the unconditional form, is then motivated by
a dependent clause wherein the directive's reasonableness is
established and its apparent categorical tenor softened. The
similarity between the legal motive clauses and those found in
wisdom instructions has already been recognized by von Rad who
remarked, "such interpretative motivations are also appended
to legal statements."[225] The likeness between the two becomes
more significant in light of the following points.

(1) As in the case of legal motive clauses, the motivations found in wisdom instructions are introduced by a variety
of motive particles. In fact, both share a large number of
motive introductions used in biblical literary genres, namely,
כי, פן, למען, and ו. Also, the use of asyndetic motive clauses
is virtually exclusive to law and wisdom instruction.

(2) Some of the motivations which accompany the wisdom
instructions are in themselves wisdom sayings (e.g., Prov 1:17;
27:1, 24; Eccl 5:1-2).[226] Similarly, the law about not taking
a bribe is motivated by quoting a proverb (Exod 23:8 and its
parallel in Deut 16:19b).

(3) Just as a number of legal prescriptions are motivated
with clauses stating the specific reasons that lie behind the
law, and others are predicated upon God's commanding will, so
in wisdom instructions certain motive clauses are purely explanatory, prudential and based on daily experiences (e.g.,
Prov 22:25, 27; 23:21; 24:16; 25:8, 17; 27:1, 24), and others
refer to God, to His judgment and to His rule (e.g., Prov
22:23; 23:11; 24:12, 18, 22; 25:22).[227]

(4) In recent years, scholars have become increasingly
aware of wisdom's influence on a number of biblical texts,[228]
and especially on law.[229] A manifestation of this influence
can also be detected in the content of certain motive clauses
in the legal corpora which embody expressions characteristic of
wisdom literature. For example, the expression תועבת יהוה,
appearing in a number of motive clauses,[230] is unique to both
Proverbs and Deuteronomy.[231] The verb נקה, which in its *piel*
form is used in a motive clause in Exod 20:7 (= Deut 5:11), is
found in a distinctive way, namely in its *nifal* form, only in
Proverbs (6:29; 11:21; 16:5; 17:5; 19:5, 9; 28:20). The *piel*
of the same verb, with God as the subject, occurs (with the
exception of the motive clauses in Exod 20:7 [= Deut 5:11] and
the passages dependent upon Exod 34:6-7) only in Job 9:28,
10:14, in a wisdom psalm (19:13) and in Jer 30:11 (= 46:28).
As Dentan points out, the affinities of the expression in the
legal motive clause with wisdom literature are overwhelming.[232]
The verb סלף used in the motive clause in Exod 23:8 (= Deut
16:19b) is found elsewhere only in Prov 13:6, 19:3, 21:12,
22:12 and in Job 12:19. The expression אצדיק רשע in the motive
clause of Exod 23:7 can be compared with מצדיק רשע in Prov
17:15 (cf. also Job 9:20, 40:8 and Isa 5:23).

All of these considerations strongly suggest that the
legislators responsible for the formulation of the legal motive
clauses adopted as their basic model, possibly under the direct

influence of wisdom literature, the type of motivations that
are found in wisdom instructions where motive clauses constitute a formal element of the genre itself. Their main objec-
tive seems to have been to provide the laws, as in wisdom instructions, with acceptable rationales so as to justify the
laws' appropriateness in the eyes of the people. In pursuit
of this goal they emphasized, on occasion, a key element within
the law and used it as its motive, but more often and in the
manner characteristic of wisdom instruction, they predicated
the law upon God's commanding will or actually spelled out the
raison d'être that stood behind the particular legal prescription. They did not, however, limit their motivations to those
which are basically prudential in nature and reflective of the
daily experiences of the people, but also made frequent references to the historic events of the past and used them as the
motivation for a number of laws. In other cases, especially in
priestly laws, they also chose to justify many legal prescriptions by means of formula-type motivations (e.g., "lest he die,"
"it is leprosy") which are unlike the motive clauses found in
wisdom instructions.[233] The variety of motivations indicates
that, although the legislators were influenced by the basic
forms of motivation in wisdom instructions, they seem to have
adopted other motive forms from other literary genres known to
them (perhaps, medical, omen, etc.) in response to a wider
concern of the law which covers more than the scope of wisdom
literature.

     In formulating its own type of motivations, each law
collection in the Bible represents a special effort. D, for
example, with its hortatory style and its heavy use of wisdom
vocabulary, appears to be the closest to wisdom literature and
its use of motive clauses. On the other hand, PC tends to express its own rationales in a rather formulaic pattern in line
with the stereotyped and prosaic style that pervades the corpus
itself. In H, one finds a mixture of styles. In some chapters
(e.g., parts of Leviticus 18-21, 24) motive clauses are rigid,
repetitive and formulaic, in others (e.g., parts of Leviticus
17, 23, 25) they are freely expressed. This is in accordance
with the composite nature of this legal corpus.[234] BC contains

a large variety of motive introductions formulated very much
after the pattern of wisdom instructions, and even though most
of the motive clauses of BC are found outside of Exod 21:1-
22:19, that section, too, is not without its own share of
motivations (e.g., Exod 21:8, 21, 26, 27).

Motive clauses, it must be kept in mind, do not constitute
a genre by themselves. They are only components of the legal
genre. Therefore it is not proper to speak of the Sitz im
Leben of individual motive clauses. However, the use of motivation as a pattern of literary style, it has been argued, can
point to a specific setting in life. Is it possible to recapture this setting?

Morgenstern seems to suggest that the formulation of the
motive clauses constitutes only a literary production and does
not reflect a specific setting in the life of the community.
In his discussion of the "casuistic" laws (= *mišpaṭim*) in D,
he states,

> ...these Deuteronomic editors did not feel all too sure
> of themselves and of their legislative authority and
> therefore felt constrained to justify the *mišpaṭ* by
> exhibiting its internal merit and reasonableness, or,
> second, that, conscious of a definite antiquity of
> these older *mišpaṭim*, they felt that they must justify
> their application to the conditions of a later and
> presumably a more modern day by specifying the par-
> ticular underlying principle which gave these *mišpaṭim*
> validity still in their comparatively late day.[235]

On the other hand, in his article on parenesis in the BC,
Beyerlin[236] maintains that the setting of the laws accompanied
by parenetic statements[237] is to be located in the cultic celebration of the pilgrimage festivals in the early periods of the
amphictyony. He substantiates his point of view by indicating
that parenetic statements--which in his opinion are original in
their formulation--are found only in Exod 20:22-26 and 22:20-
23:19, and that the "apodictic" tone, the concise and rhythmic
style of the commands and prohibitions which incorporate them,
together with their basic cultic concern, point to a recitation
of the law within a cultic setting. He also states that this
cultic background is similarly reflected in the second person
address of these laws as well as in the use of the divine "I"
of the parenetic statements.[238]

Beyerlin's explanations, however, rest on dubious assumptions. The existence of the amphictyony, propounded by scholars such as Alt, Noth and Albright, is rendered doubtful today
after Orlinsky's challenge.[239] The contention that the "apodictic" tone of the commands and prohibitions reflects a cultic
setting--originally put forth by Alt[240] with whom Beyerlin
agrees--can be disproved by texts pointing to various settings,
either original or secondary, in which this form of address is
frequently employed.[241] Beyerlin, in fact, recognizes the
difficulty of assigning the laws in Exod 22:20-25 and 23:1-9,
which deal with the poor, stranger and the administration of
justice, to a cultic setting.[242]

Inspired by Beyerlin and based upon the studies of Alt and
von Rad, Uitti placed the setting of the motivated laws specifically in the so-called "covenant renewal ceremony."[243] As
indicated previously, it was Alt who in his classic essay on
biblical law had argued that, unlike the "casuistic" laws which
originated in the day-to-day work of the courts, the "apodictic"
laws had their setting in the cult of ancient Israel. Having
identified numerous series of "apodictically" formulated law
collections in the Bible, he postulated that they were recited
every seventh year on the Feast of Tabernacles during a covenant renewal ceremony.[244] Pursuing Alt's analysis, von Rad
advanced his reconstruction of the liturgical sequence of this
alleged Shechemite festival: (a) parenetic introduction, (b)
proclamation of the commandments, (c) making of the covenant,
(d) blessings and curses.[245]

According to Uitti, it is at this cultic ceremony that the
motive clauses have their setting in life. In his opinion,
"the motive clauses are tantamount to a kind of 'cultic preaching' as the clauses seek to warn, exhort, and explain on the
basis of the sacred tradition."[246] However, he distinguishes
between the earlier and later law collections. In the earlier
collections (which according to Uitti include the classic
Decalogue of Exodus 20, the Cultic Decalogue in Exod 20:23-26
plus 23:10-33 [R$_1$] and Exod 34:10-26 [R$_2$], the BC [Exodus 21-23]
and the Shechemite Dodecalogue [Deuteronomy 27]), the motive
clauses "were once part of the oral recitation of sacred

(apodictic) law in Israel's early worship."[247] Those found in
later collections (according to Uitti, D, H, PC and Exod 34:24
in the Cultic Decalogue) are "in the main a secondary literary
production."[248]

Uitti advances two additional specific arguments in order
to substantiate his point of view. First, he states that in
the earlier collections it is exclusively the "apodictic" law
or its extensions[249] which are motivated. This suggests to
Uitti a close link between "apodictic" law and the motive phenomenon in the early period.[250] Secondly, the fact that the
motive clauses are able to perpetuate the rhythmic pattern of
the parent law argues "for an original oral and cultic function
connection between the two."[251]

Uitti takes the existence of the "covenant renewal ceremony" and the cultic recitation that assumedly took place in it
as "given," and makes use of the arguments put forth by Alt and
von Rad in support of his thesis. He refers to the covenant of
Joshua 24, to the recitation of the law in Deut 31:9-13 and
also to the cultic ceremony described in Nehemiah 8 as an in-
direct support for the recitation of sacred law in Israel's
early cultic life. The law that was read to the people, he
adds following Alt, must have been of "apodictic" nature, involving recitation of poetic lines, rhythmic and terse in their
formulation, with no superfluous words in them, while the so-
called "casuistic" laws would necessitate the reading of "extensive, often ponderous prose."[252]

Uitti's analysis, based on the assumption that a ceremony
of covenant renewal did indeed exist in ancient Israel, stands
on shaky grounds. It was already pointed out in Chapter I[253]
that the theory is of dubious validity. The arguments enu-
merated there not only cast serious doubt about the very existence of the postulated ceremony, but now also on Uitti's interpretation which is solely based on this background.[254]
Furthermore, it is not correct that in the earlier collections
only "apodictic" laws were motivated, for this overlooks the
fact that in Exod 21:8, 21 there are "casuistically" formulated
legal prescriptions which are accompanied by motive clauses.

In searching for the setting in life of any given genre, one must, following Gunkel, ask the following questions: Who is speaking? Who are the listeners? What is the *mise en scène* at the time? What effect is aimed at?[255] Even if we were to agree with Uitti when he states that the rhetorical style and the direct address of the laws and their motivations "are much better explained upon the background of the give and take between a speaker and his audience than between our editor and his reader,"[256] the question still remains as to whether the interchange must be understood as taking place exclusively between a cultic official and his audience.

It was argued above that legal motive clauses are to a large extent formulated in the manner of motivations found in wisdom instructions. This similarity points to the adoption not only of the form of the motive clauses but also of the function which accompanies the form itself.

The central concern of wisdom literature is pedagogic. This is nowhere better exemplified than in the case of wisdom instructions where the teacher addresses his pupil and, by means of reasonable persuasion expressed in particular through motivating clauses, urges him to carry out his directives in a diligent fashion. An analogous didactic purpose can perhaps be seen behind the use of the legal motive clauses. This invests the lawgiver with the additional role of a teacher. By providing certain legal prescriptions with motivating clauses, he, too, attempts to show that laws do not issue from a capricious mind but that there are compelling reasons for them. His goal is to present the laws in such a way that the people to whom they are addressed will soon come to "accept them inwardly."[257] This is certainly the best way of cultivating assent to a law.

Both Budd and Gerstenberger have already found evidence of the didactic purpose behind particular types of biblical laws precisely in the use of the legal motive clauses. In his article on priestly instruction in pre-exilic Israel, Budd remarks that "it is possible that the motive clauses within the priestly laws point to a genuine teaching role for the priests in so far as they are aimed at fostering particular beliefs and attitudes."[258] Prior to him, Gerstenberger attributed a

pedagogic function to the motive clauses attached to the prohibitives in the legal corpora of the Bible on the basis of a
similar use of motivation both in wisdom and in these prohibitives.[259] However, this didactic purpose should not be limited
to the motivated prohibitives alone, inasmuch as motive clauses
are also found in laws and wisdom sayings formulated in the
conditional form.[260] Furthermore, in light of the fact that
every type of law in the Bible attracts motive clauses, the
pedagogic function can be extended to all types of laws which
are accompanied by motivations. This does not mean that only
the motivated laws were read and explained, for, as stated,
whole units of laws were proclaimed to the people at large
(e.g., Exod 21:1, Deut 33:11, Neh 8:3).[261] Besides, even in
the book of Proverbs there are a few instructions which are not
provided with motive clauses (e.g., 3:5-6, 27, 28, 29, 30;
24:27, 29; 27:2). Yet, no one would deny that these unmotivated
instructions, too, have an educational purpose. The pedagogic
role of the legal corpora is particularly accentuated when the
law embodies a motive clause. It is in these cases, as in motivated wisdom instructions, that the teaching function appears
in its greatest clarity. On the other hand, there is no apparent reason why one law is motivated while the other is not,[262]
although it was pointed out above[263] that, among all the laws
in the Bible, the highest percentage of motivation is found in
humanitarian admonitions and rules of moral conduct, thus revealing the legislator's strong concern with moral issues.

The setting in life of the motivated laws, therefore, cannot be located exclusively in cultic preaching but must be
sought in a wider socio-historical context. Yet, it is here
where we are confronted with serious problems, for the wider
use of motivation in various literary genres in the Bible makes
it very difficult to identify the original life setting which
gave rise to legal motivation.[264] At most, on the basis of
formal and contextual similarities between the legal motive
clauses and wisdom motivations, one can argue, as we did
above,[265] that not only did the motive clauses in wisdom instructions constitute the basic models in the formulation of
the legal motive clauses, but--and this is our point here--there

is also a didactic purpose or function behind the motivated
laws in general. This teaching function is broader in scope.
It accommodates both the wise men and the priests to whom the
primary responsibility of teaching the Law to student priests
and the laity is assigned. The probability is that, while the
latter concentrated on cultic questions, the former dealt primarily with wisdom doctrine as well as noncultic legal matters.
Available information about how they carried out this responsibility is meager, but enough can be gleaned from the Bible
to get a general idea of their teaching function.

The sages (חכמים),[266] who stand behind the wisdom sayings,
not only store up knowledge (דעת; see Prov 10:14, Job 34:2),
but also dispense and teach it (Prov 15:7, Eccl 12:9; cf. Sir
39:1-11). Their teaching includes counsel (עצה; see Jer 18:18),
commandments (מצות; see Prov 4:4, in parallel with דברים; cf.
3:1, 7:2), תורה (Prov 4:2, 13:4), both in the sense of the wise
man's own instructions (Prov 3:1, 4:2) as well as "law" in general (cf. Ps 1:2, 19:8; Prov 28:4).[267] In Jer 8:8, they appear
as legal scholars.[268]

There is almost no clear information about how the sages
imparted their teaching or how they formulated their counsels
in real-life situations. According to McKane, the prophetic
allegation that the scribes' pen has falsified the *torah* (Jer
8:8) may indeed refer to the use made by these *ḥakamim* or
soferim of wisdom terminology and of explanatory expansions
after the manner of wisdom.[269] Our knowledge primarily comes
from the book of Proverbs which appears to be "a manual of
instruction,"[270] and Ecclesiastes which contains a series of
soliloquies and instructions dealing with human life and society, formulated by a wisdom teacher and attributed to the
wise Solomon. Both books faithfully reflect the wisdom genres
of the ancient Near Eastern literature.[271]

As in the other ancient Near Eastern countries, the biblical wisdom teacher models himself after the father's way of
instructing his son.[272] He addresses his pupil as "my son" and
transmits his knowledge primarily by word of mouth, asking him
to "listen" to his words (e.g., Prov 4:1, 10; 5:7; 7:24; 8:16,
32; 19:20, 22, 23; Ps 34:12).[273] In pursuit of his pedagogic

goal, he also makes use of a variety of teaching devices. He
may recite a parable, utter a proverb, resort to a riddle. When
he formulates a maxim of conduct and specifically an "instruction," he frequently accompanies it with a motivating clause in
order to facilitate the acceptance of the directive.

Whether or not the wise men conducted formal classes within a structure of an organized school is hard to tell. There
is no clear reference in the Bible about the existence of
schools in ancient Israel. The first mention of a school is
found in Sirach who speaks of "my school" (בית מדרשי, 51:23).
Yet it is hard to imagine that schools did not exist before
this time. Scribal academies were well known both in Egypt[274]
and in Mesopotamia.[275] Numerous school texts have been un-
earthed in both places. There is also a reference to organized
instruction in pre-Israelite Canaan in a letter written in
Akkadian and discovered in Shechem where a teacher, conducting
a regular class for a number of children, writes the father of
one of his students asking that he pay his son's tuition.[276]

Therefore, when in the wisdom books of the Bible there
appear references to the wise who spread knowledge (Prov 15:7),
to the student who is remorseful for not having paid attention
to the voice of his teachers (Prov 5:13), to the Lady Wisdom
who as a mistress of the house invites the people in (Proverbs
9), it can safely be inferred that the sages, in line with the
ancient Near Eastern tradition, did in fact impart their teaching in a school[277] and that the substance of their instruction
probably constituted the wisdom sayings which they created,
preserved and to which they also added (Prov 22:17, 24:23,
25:1).

The responsibility of teaching the law was also entrusted
to the priests (e.g., Lev 10:11; Deut 24:8-9, 31:11-12; 33:10;
Mic 3:11; Ezek 22:26, 44:23; 2 Chr 15:3, 17:8-9),[278] although
this instruction must be understood in a rather limited way.
Oracular consultation cannot properly be called a teaching
situation.[279] Priestly instruction seems to be basically
directed to that which is bound with cult and ritual,[280] i.e.,
differences between "holy" and "profane," "clean" and "unclean"
(e.g., Lev 10:10-11, 14:57; Deut 24:8; Ezek 44:23).

In Neh 8:7, the Levites are called those who מבינים את העם
לתורה (lit., make the people understand the *torah*; cf. Ezra
8:16, 2 Chr 35:3). As Cody points out, this most likely refers
to "a function as liturgical readers of the sacred text, reading to the people in Aramaic, or reading an interpretation constituting an early form of *targum*, thereby 'causing the people
to understand' the Hebrew text of the sacred writings."[281]

It is highly possible that priests imparted their *torah*
primarily in the Temple. However, they do not seem to have
been limited to this place. According to 2 Chr 17:8-9, at the
time of Jehoshaphat the priests travelled with other officials
throughout the cities of Judah in order to teach the people,
using the book of the Law as a text.[282] However, the material
they covered and the way in which they transmitted their knowledge are not specified. The passage in Hag 2:11-13 (cf. Zech-
ariah 7 and 8) in which priests answer questions concerning
cultic and ethical matters is very brief and insufficient for
drawing significant conclusions about their teaching methods.

In addition to the sages and priests, prophets, too, are
known as imparters of *torah* (e.g., Ezek 43:11, Zech 7:12, Isa
1:10, 8:16),[283] dealing with ethico-religious questions (e.g.,
Isa 1:10-17, Hag 2:11-13) and perhaps with cultic matters (e.g.,
Isa 56:1-7), although they seem to have transmitted this *torah*
after the manner of the priests and sages.[284] It has also been
claimed by scholars such as Alt and Noth that at the alleged
amphictyonic assemblies the "minor judges" who supposedly were
custodians of the law instructed the people as to its meaning
and application.[285] It has already been noted that there is a
lack of evidence to prove the existence of an institution such
as the amphictyony in ancient Israel.[286] Furthermore, the
biblical texts do not yield any information about the presumed
teaching activities of these minor judges. Kaufmann has convincingly pointed out that these were "saviors" like any other
"judges" of this period (cf. Judg 10:1).[287] Moreover, the term
שפט in this context can best be rendered as "ruler" (cf. Exod
2:14, 1 Sam 8:5-6) and not as "judge."[288]

NOTES

CHAPTER II

[1] B. Gemser, "The Importance of the Motive Clause in Old Testament Law," VTSup 1 (1953) 50-66; reprinted in *Adhuc Loquitur-Collected Essays by Dr. B. Gemser* (ed. A. van Selms and A. S. van Woude; Pretoria Oriental Series 7; Leiden: Brill, 1968) 96-115.

[2] Ibid., 50.

[3] R. W. Uitti, "The Motive Clause in Old Testament Law" (dissertation; Chicago: Lutheran School of Theology, 1973) (henceforth, *The Motive Clause*).

[4] Ibid., 6-8.

[5] E.g., Exod 30:13, Lev 27:25, Num 3:47, 18:16. See also "Weights and Measures," *IDB* 4, 833.

[6] *The Oxford English Dictionary* (Oxford, 1961) 7. 451.

[7] E.g., Exod 23:20-33; Lev 11:43-47, 20:22-26, 22:31-33; Num 35:33-34; Deuteronomy 1-11.

[8] E.g., Lev 18:1-5, 26-30; 19:2, 37.

[9] G. von Rad, *Studies in Deuteronomy* (SBT 9; Chicago: Regnery, 1953) 22.

[10] N. Lohfink, *Das Hauptgebot* (AnBib 20; Rome: Pontifical Biblical Institute, 1963) 90-97.

[11] See, for instance, von Rad, "Deuteronomy," *IDB* 1, 834-35; idem, *Studies in Deuteronomy*, 1-36; idem, *Old Testament Theology*, 1. 226; J. L'Hour, "Une legislation criminelle dans le Deutéronome," *Biblica* 44 (1963) 1-28; idem, "Les interdits to'eba dans le Deutéronome," *RB* 71 (1964) 481-503; R. Merendino, *Das deuteronomische Gesetz* (BBB 31; Bonn: Peter Hanstein, 1969); G. Seitz, *Redaktionsgeschichtliche Studien zum Deuteronomium* (BWANT 13; Stuttgart: Kohlhammer, 1971) 101-108.

[12] E.g., Lev 19:19, 37; 20:8, 22; 22:31; 25:18; Deut 12:28; 13:1. Also, Exod 23:13a, 34:11; Lev 22:9; Num 4:19.

[13] E.g., Exod 22:30a; Lev 19:2, 20:7.

[14] E.g., Exod 34:12; Deut 12:13, 19, 30; 15:9; 24:8.

[15] E.g., Deut 12:12, 18; 16:11, 14.

[16] E.g., Lev 19:14b, 32b; 25:17, 36, 43b.

[17] Deut 13:5.

[18] E.g., Deut 19:13, 21; 25:12.

[19] Deut 25:19b.

[20] Deut 23:7.

[21] Deut 23:24.

[22] Deut 18:13.

[23] Deut 18:9.

[24] Lev 19:18, 34.

[25] Deut 24:4b.

[26] Num 35:33.

[27] E.g., Lev 18:24, Num 35:34, Deut 21:23.

[28] Lev 11:43.

[29] E.g., Exod 12:49; Lev 24:22; Num 9:14b; 15:15-16, 29

[30] E.g., Exod 12:17bβ; 27:21b; 28:43b; Lev 3:17a; 10:9b; 16:29a; 17:7b; 23:31b; Num 10:8b; 19:10b, 21a.

[31] Gemser, "The Importance of the Motive Clause," 56.

[32] Ibid., 57.

[33] Ibid., 54 n. 4.

[34] For examples, see his lists of the motive clauses cited below in nn. 114, 125 and 135.

[35] W. Beyerlin, "Die Paränese im Bundesbuch und ihre Herkunft," *Gottes Wort und Gottes Land* (ed. H. G. Reventlow; Göttingen: Vandenhoeck und Ruprecht, 1965) 9-29.

[36] Ibid., 10-11.

[37] Ibid., 19 n. 39.

[38] E.g., Lev 9:2, 20:7; Deut 12:28.

[39] E.g., Exod 20:12b; Deut 5:16b, 17:20b, 25:15b.

[40] E.g., Deut 12:25b, 22:7b.

[41] E.g., Deut 14:29b, 15:10b, 16:15b, 23:21b, 24:19b.

[42] E.g., Deut 14:23b, 17:19b; also 20:18b.

[43] E.g., Exod 23:12b, Deut 5:14bβ.

[44] J. Pedersen, *Israel: Its Life and Culture* (London: Oxford University, 1959) 1-2. 118-119. See also, J. Muilenburg, "The Linguistic and Rhetoric Usages of the Particle כי in the Old Testament," *HUCA* 32 (1961) 135-60; and the Talmudic passages, *Roš. Haš.* 3a and *Giṭ.* 90a (with Rashi, ad loc).

[45] GKC, #158a; Joüon, #170c.

[46] GKC, #109g, #165a.

[47] E.g., Deut 17:7b, 12bβ; 19:19b; 24:7bβ.

[48] E.g., Deut 5:15; 15:15; 24:18, 22.

[49] E.g., Deut 13:12, 17:13, 19:20, 21:21b.

[50] Gemser, "The Importance of the Motive Clause," 54. On this particle, see also I. Eitan, "Hebrew and Semitic Particles," *AJSL* 44 (1927-28) 199.

[51] GKC, #158b; BDB, 83c.

[52] GKC, #165b; BDB, 83b.

[53] See also the remarks by J. Morgenstern ("The Book of the Covenant," 2. 209 n. 266).

[54] An abbreviation for עַל דְּבַר אֲשֶׁר.

[55] תַּחַת עֵינוֹ and תַּחַת שִׁנּוֹ are not clearly identified as legal motive clauses; yet it can be argued that the laws which contain them would be complete even without them. The clauses seem to add a motivation for the laws, i.e., the slave owner is required to free his slave precisely because of the injury he has inflicted upon him.

[56] The motive clause really provides a justification for the Lord's driving out the nations before Israel.

[57] GKC, #158; Joüon, #170b.

[58] In this connection, see T. J. Meek, "Lapses of Old Testament Translators," *JAOS* 58 (1938) 124; idem, "The Coordinate Adverbial Clause in Hebrew," *JAOS* 49 (1929) 156-59; idem, "Syntax of the Sentence in Hebrew," *JBL* 64 (1945) 159.

[59] This list does not totally coincide with those of Gemser or Uitti. Neither, for example, includes the preposition תַּחַת or the composite conjunction אַחֲרֵי אֲשֶׁר. Gemser does not even refer to בגלל(ו), לְמַעַן אֲשֶׁר, לְבִלְתִּי and ל. On the other hand, both consider עַל כֵּן as a motive introduction even though it only comes to indicate a consequence (e.g., Exod 20:11b; cf. Deut 5:15b; 15:15b; 24:22b). Uitti extends his list by adding כַּאֲשֶׁר (Deut 20:17b-18 and elsewhere), אֲשֶׁר in the sense of "as" (Deut 15:14b-15, p. 68), מֵאָשֵׁר (Num 6:11, p. 78) and כִּי אֲשֶׁר (probably a typographical error for כִּי כַּאֲשֶׁר in Deut 22:26b) whereas in

our lists the conjunction אֲשֶׁר is taken as a motive introduction
only when it means "because" or "so that." Uitti also takes
the particle אִם in Exod 22:22 as a motive introduction (p. 63).
In reality, the verse is an asyndetic motive clause, i.e.,
"(for) if you...."

[60]Noth, *Exodus*, 175.

[61]Gemser, "The Importance of the Motive Clause," 64.

[62]Similarly in Exod 12:15, Lev 7:25, 23:29, etc.

[63]J. Heinemann alludes to this distinction in his *Ta'amei
ha-Mitsvot be-Sifrut Yisrael* (5th ed.; Jerusalem: Magnes, 1966)
1. 14. The difference between the two kinds of instructions is
also reflected in the Rabbinic distinction between the rules
governing Passover of Egypt and Passover of the subsequent
generations; see *M. Pesaḥ.* 9:5, *Mekilta Bo* 4, Ibn Ezra on Exod
12:3.

[64]Gemser, "The Importance of the Motive Clause," 51.

[65]Uitti, *The Motive Clause*, 42.

[66]Ibid., 114 n. 30.

[67]Ibid., 105 n. 23.

[68]Ibid.

[69]Von Rad, *Deuteronomy*, 93.

[70]Ibid.

[71]Uitti, *The Motive Clause*, 91. R. de Vaux discusses
these institutions in his *Ancient Israel*.

[72]The term "cultic/sacral" is, in a broad sense, taken
here as "the expression of religious experience in concrete
external actions performed within the congregation or community, preferably by officially appointed exponents and in
set forms" (Eichrodt, *Theology*, 1. 98). To this category are
assigned laws dealing with sacrifices, priests, sacred occasions in the Hebrew calendar, idolatry, dietary matters, etc.

[73]Admittedly, in a legal system where laws are ascribed to
the deity (as is the case in the Bible), there is no room for
"civil" legislation as a separate legal realm. The category
is here considered clearly from a modern point of view and
will include matters such as those that would come up in the
daily activities of the courts, namely, selling, buying, slavery, witnesses, marriages, adultery, inheritance, etc.

[74]Gemser, "The Importance of the Motive Clause," 51 n. 1.
For some reason he overlooked the motive clause in verse 12b
but restored its equivalent in the Deuteronomic text. There is
no indication that he considered the verse in Exodus 20 as a
Deuteronomic gloss.

[75]Ibid., 51.

[76]Uitti, *The Motive Clause*, 13.

[77]Ibid., 100.

[78]Exod 20:2 constitutes a motivation for the following command in verse 3 and should be understood as, "Since I the Lord am your God...therefore, do not..."; see Noth, *Exodus*, 161-62; Paul, *Book of the Covenant*, 32.

[79]Gemser, "The Importance of the Motive Clause," 51 n. 2.

[80]Ibid., 51; cf. n. 75 above.

[81]Uitti, *The Motive Clause*, 14.

[82]Ibid., 100.

[83]See n. 78 above.

[84]Unlike Uitti's study, the present study does not consider the clause introduced by כַּאֲשֶׁר in verse 12b a motive clause, since כַּאֲשֶׁר is a comparative conjunction (see GKC, #161b) introducing comparative clauses.

[85]On the subject matter of Exod 20:7 (= Deut 5:11), see below, n. 165.

[86]Exod 23:20-33, made up of two units (vv. 20-25 and 26-33), is probably of late origin; see Noth, *Exodus*, 192-94.

[87]Gemser, "The Importance of the Motive Clause," 51 n. 4.

[88]Ibid., 51 n. 6.

[89]Ibid., 51.

[90]Ibid., 51 nn. 5 and 7.

[91]Uitti, *The Motive Clause*, 105-106.

[92]Ibid., 106.

[93]In the present study, this clause is considered a parenetic clause; see above, n. 13.

[94]Uitti, *The Motive Clause*, 29.

[95]As indicated in the detailed chart at the end of this study, verse 22 motivates two prescriptions in verse 23. This is the reason why there we count sixteen primary motive clauses but seventeen motivated prescriptions.

[96]The cultic aspect of this law is stressed by Noth (*Exodus*, 189) and Weinfeld (*Deuteronomy and the Deuteronomic School*, 223 n. 1).

[97]Bribes and judicial fees/gifts are, at times, closely
related; cf. Prov 21:14, Isa 1:23 (שׁלׁמׁנׁיׁם, Akk. šulmānu). For
details, see M. Greenberg, "Bribery," *IDB* 1, 465.

[98]See, for example, Noth, *Exodus*, 261-62; Eissfeldt, *The
Old Testament*, 215-17; Fohrer, *Introduction*, 69; J. G. Torralba,
"Decalogo Ritual, Ex. 34, 10-26," *EB* 30 (1961) 407-21.

[99]Kaufmann, *The Religion of Israel*, 166 n. 4.

[100]F. Langlamet, "Israel et 'l'habitant du pays,'" *RB* 76
(1969) 326.

[101]M. Lestienne, "Les dix 'paroles' et le décalogue," *RB*
79 (1972) 484-510. According to this author, the addressee in
Exod 34:10 is Moses; in verse 11 it is the people; and it is
with verse 11 that the introduction begins (ibid., 489).

[102]Gemser, "The Importance of the Motive Clause," 51 n. 3.

[103]Ibid., 51; cf. n. 75, above.

[104]Uitti, *The Motive Clause*, 103.

[105]Ibid., 103 n. 22.

[106]Ibid., 24.

[107]Scholars who start the laws with verse 14 (see above,
n. 98) add one more law to the list. For example, according to
Noth, the law in verse 14a continues with verse 17; verses 14b-
16 are additions expressed in deuteronomic style; see Noth,
Exodus, 262. Another possibility is to limit the prologue to
verses 10-12 and start the legal prescriptions with verse 13.
Here it would be necessary to take the introductory כי in verse
13 and verse 14 as meaning "indeed," "surely." For examples of
this meaning of כי, see GKC (#159ee) and BDB (472); see also
NJV, NAB ad loc. This division of the corpus would add four
more prescriptions: three unmotivated prescriptions in verse 13
(v. 13aα, 13aβ, 13b) and one motivated prescription in verse 14
(v. 14a is motivated by a primary motivation in v. 14b and by a
secondary motivation in vv. 15-16). The rate would then go up
to ca. 15%.

[108]M. Noth, *Leviticus* (Philadelphia: Westminster, 1965)
127. On the relationship between Leviticus 17 and the rest of
H, see R. Kilian (*Literarkritische und formgeschichtliche
Untersuchung des Heiligkeitsgesetzes* (Bonn: Peter Hanstein,
1963) 176-79.

[109]S. R. Driver, *An Introduction to the Literature of the
Old Testament* (9th ed.; Cleveland: World Publishing, 1967) 48;
M. Haran, "Holiness Code," *EncJud* 8, 820.

[110]Eissfeldt, *The Old Testament*, 236; Fohrer, *Introduction*,
138; see also the reconstruction by Kilian, *Untersuchung*, 164-
76; Feucht, *Untersuchungen*, 62-73.

[111]Gemser, "The Importance of the Motive Clause," 51.

[112]Ibid., 51 n. 9.

[113]Uitti, *The Motive Clause*, 43, 122.

[114]Ibid., 44. The following is a list of his motive
clauses:
Lev 17:4b, 17:5-7, 17:11-12, 17:14.
Lev 18:2b-5, 18:6b, 18:7bα, 18:8b, 18:10b, 18:11c, 18:12b,
    18:13b, 18:14b, 18:15bα, 18:16b, 18:17b,c, 18:21b, 18:22b,
    18:23b, 18:24-30.
Lev 19:2b, 19:3b, 19:4b, 19:8aβ, 19:10bβ, 19:12b, 19:14b,
    19:16b, 19:17c, 19:18b, 19:20bβ, 19:22, 19:25aβ,b, 19:28b,
    19:29b, 19:30b, 19:31bβ, 19:32b, 19:34b, 19:36b, 19:37b.
Lev 20:3, 20:7b, 20:8b, 20:9bα, 20:12bα, 20:14bγ, 20:17bα,
    20:19aβ, 20:21bα, 20:22-26.
Lev 21:6b,c, 21:7c, 21:8aβ,c, 21:12b, 21:15, 21:18-23.
Lev 22:2b, 22:3b, 22:7bβ, 22:8b, 22:9b,c, 22:16, 22:20b,
    22:25b, 22:30b, 22:31b, 22:32b-33.
Lev 23:3b, 23:14b, 23:21cβ, 23:22bβ, 23:28b-29, 23:31b, 23:36c,
    23:41b, 23:43.
Lev 24:3b, 24:9c, 24:22.
Lev 25:12a, 25:16c, 25:17b, 25:18b-22, 25:23aβ,b, 25:33b,
    25:34b, 25:36b, 25:38, 25:42a, 25:55.
Lev 26:1b, 26:2b.

[115]The difference between Uitti's list and the one proposed in this study can to a large extent be attributed to the
fact that Uitti includes motive clauses found in the parenetic
introductions and conclusions of the individual units that make
up the Holiness Code (e.g., Lev 18:2b-5, 24-30; 19:37b; 20:
22-26; 22:31b, 32b-33), parenetic statements such as the "institutional" formula (e.g., Lev 17:7b, 23:14b) and motive
clauses attached to parenetic statements (e.g., Lev 19:2b, 14b;
20:7b).

[116]These matters belong to the cultic/sacral sphere; see
Kaufmann, *The Religion of Israel*, 319.

[117]Deut 1:6-4:40, 4:44-49 to the end of 28, 29:1-30:20.
To these are added a number of appendices; cf. Driver, *Introduction*, 70-71; Sandmel, *The Hebrew Scriptures*, 403-416.

[118]Fohrer, *Introduction*, 167.

[119]Deuteronomy 27 interrupts the connection between chapters 26 and 28. Driver suggests that it originally occupied a
different position; see *Introduction*, 94.

[120]See above text and n. 9. R. M. Hals even argued in
favor of a literary genre called "Preached Law," particularly
as exemplified by Deuteronomy 12-26, not as a primary genre but
as a secondary genre, that is, "one which employs material and
several other literary types which is then altered either ex-
plicity [sic] or implicitly." For details, see his article,

"Is There a Genre of Preached Law?," *SBL 1973 Seminar Papers*
(ed. G. MacRae; Cambridge: Society of Biblical Literature,
1973) 1. 1-10; the above quote is from p. 10.

[121]Gemser, "The Importance of the Motive Clause," 51.

[122]Ibid., 51 n. 8.

[123]Uitti, *The Motive Clause*, 114-15.

[124]Ibid., 115.

[125]Ibid., 34-35. The following is a list of his motive
clauses:
Deut 12:3c, 12:7b, 12:9, 12:12, 12:18b, 12:23bα, 12:25b,
    12:28b,c, 12:31b,c.
Deut 13:4bH, 13:6bff.H, 13:11b-12H, 13:18b-19H.
Deut 14:1a,2, 14:7c, 14:8b, 14:21c, 14:23b, 14:26b, 14:27b,
    14:29.
Deut 15:2bβ, 15:4b-6, 15:10b-11, 15:14b,15, 15:18bff.
Deut 16:1b, 16:3bβ,γ, 16:11-12, 16:14-15, 16:19cβ-20, 16:22b.
Deut 17:1b, 17:7b, 17:12b-13, 17:15cβ, 17:16c, 17:17aβ,
    17:19bff-20.
Deut 18:2b, 18:5, 18:12-22.
Deut 19:3c, 19:6-7, 19:9a, 19:10, 19:13, 19:19b-21.
Deut 20:1b, 20:4, 20:5bβ, 20:6bβ, 20:7bβ, 20:8bβ, 20:17b-18,
    20:19b-20.
Deut 21:5bff, 21:9, 21:14bγ, 21:17aγ,b, 21:21b,c, 21:23aγ,b.
Deut 22:5b, 22:7b, 22:8b, 22:9b,c, 22:19aγ, 22:21aγ,b, 22:22b,
    22:24aγδ,b, 22:26b-27, 22:29aγ.
Deut 23:5-6H, 23:8aβH, 23:8bβH, 23:15H, 23:19bH, 23:21bH,
    23:22bH, 23:24bH.
Deut 24:4b, 24:5b, 24:6b, 24:7b, 24:9, 24:13aγ,b, 24:15aγ,b,
    24:16b, 24:18, 24:19b, 24:20b, 24:21b-22.
Deut 25:3b, 25:6b, 25:12b, 25:15b-16, 25:17-18.
Deut 26:11, 26:12d.

[126]This number does not include the legal prescriptions
which contain a motive clause in the protasis, as in Deut 12:
20; 14:24, 29a; 15:16; 24:1; nor does it include Deut 20:5-8
which is not motivated even though the officials' statements
in it are provided with motive clauses.

[127]This includes both simple *waw*, as well as motive
clauses introduced by ובערת, וזכרת and ...ושמעו ויראו; see
above, nn. 47, 48, 49.

[128]This does not include the three motive clauses introduced by פן within the legal prescriptions of Deut 20:5-8;
see above, n. 126.

[129]The question as to whether or not P extends into Joshua
is a matter of debate. For a summary of basic points of view,
see P. R. Ackroyd, *Exile and Restoration* (Philadelphia: Westminster, 1968) 97-98; J. G. Vink, "The Date and Origin of the
Priestly Code in the Old Testament," *OTS* 15 (1969) 12-13.

[130]Driver, *Introduction*, 126-59; R. Rendtorff, *Die Gesetze in der Priesterschrift* (Göttingen: Vandenhoeck & Ruprecht, 1954).

[131]Fohrer, *Introduction*, 183.

[132]This becomes evident by comparing the lists drawn by Driver (*Introduction*, 159), Fohrer (*Introduction*, 179-80), and Eissfeldt (*The Old Testament*, 188-89, 204-205).

[133]Pfeiffer, *Introduction*, 250.

[134]Uitti, *The Motive Clause*, 128.

[135]Ibid., 53, 79. The following is a list of his motive clauses (p. 59):
Gen 9:6b, 17:13b, 17:14b.
Exod 12:17aβ,b, 12:49, 27:21b, 28:29, 28:30b, 28:35, 28:38, 28:43aβ,b, 29:14b, 29:18b,c, 29:22f, 29:25b, 29:28, 29:33d, 29:34bβ, 29:42-46, 30:10b,c, 30:16b, 30:21aβ,b, 30:32b, 30:36b, 30:37b, 31:13c,d, 31:14aβ, 31:16-17.
Lev 1:9bβαδ, 1:13c, 1:17c, 2:2cβγ, 2:3b, 2:6b, 2:9b,c, 2:10b, 2:11b, 2:15b, 2:16b, 3:5b, 3:11b, 3:16aβ,b-17, 4:21b, 4:24b, 4:26b, 4:31b, 4:35b, 5:6b, 5:9b, 5:10b, 5:11bγ, 5:12b, 5:13, 5:16b, 5:18c,d,19, 5:26H, 6:10aβ,b,11H, 6:15bH, 6:18cH, 6:22bH, 7:1b, 7:5b, 7:6c, 7:34-36, 11:4bβ, 11:5b, 11:6b, 11:7b, 11:42b, 11:44-45, 12:7a,b, 12:8b, 13:6b, 13:8b, 13:11bβ, 13:13b, 13:15b, 13:17b, 13:20b, 13:22b, 13:25bα,c, 13:27c, 13:28b, 13:30c, 13:36b, 13:39b, 13:44c, 13:46b, 13:51c, 13:52aε, 13:55cβ, 14:13b,c, 14:20b, 14:44c, 14:48d, 14:53b, 15:15b, 15:30b, 16:4b, 16:13b,c, 16:16, 16:29-34a, 27:26b, 27:28b, 27:30b.
Num 5:15bβγδ, 6:7b-8, 6:11aγ, 6:12bβ, 6:20b, 6:27, 9:13aδ, 9:14b, 10:8b, 10:9b, 10:10b, 15:15-16, 15:21, 15:25-26, 15:28-29, 15:31, 15:41, 18:10b, 18:17b, 18:19, 18:20b-24, 18:31b, 18:32aγ,b, 19:9c, 19:10b, 19:13b,c, 19:20aγ,b,21a, 25:18, 27:11bα, 28:6, 28:10, 28:13b, 30:6bH, 30:13bH, 30:15bH, 35:12b, 35:15c, 35:21b, 35:28a, 35:29, 35:33b, 35:34b, 36:7b, 36:8b-9.

[136]Counting the two versions of the Decalogue as one legal corpus, plus BC, CD, H, D and PC.

[137]In the present study, this text has been excluded from consideration since the curses recorded therein do not constitute law but a liturgical composition; see our discussion in Chapter I, p. 23.

[138]Uitti, *The Motive Clause*, 134.

[139]See pp. 79-80.

[140]Gemser, "The Importance of the Motive Clause," 51-52.

[141]Uitti, *The Motive Clause*, 134.

[142]Most scholars assign H to the middle of the sixth century B.C.E. See, for instance, Pfeiffer, *Introduction*, 242; Eissfeldt, *The Old Testament*, 237-39; Fohrer, *Introduction*, 142. Kaufmann, however, argues for a pre-exilic date of PC, of which H is a part; see *Religion of Israel*, 166, 175-208. Also, in the present study, see above, n. 110. Although there are literary affinities between H and Ezekiel (see Driver, *Introduction*, 49-50; Pfeiffer, *Introduction*, 241-46; Kilian, *Untersuchung*, 180-86) to the point that Ezekiel was thought by some (e.g., L. Horst) as being the redactor of H, it is instructive to note that in Ezekiel only ca. 7% of the prescriptions within chapters 40-48 are provided with motivations, while the percentage in H is ca. 51%. This in itself makes it unlikely that Ezekiel was the redactor of H.

[143]Uitti has identified a total of 367 motive clauses distributed as follows: Dec., Exodus 20, 4 motive clauses; Dec., Deuteronomy 5, 5 motive clauses; within Exod 20:22-26 plus 23:10-33, 6 motive clauses; CD, 2 motive clauses; BC, 9 motive clauses; Shechemite dodecalogue, 1 motive clause; D, 99 motive clauses; H, 93 motive clauses and in PC, 148 motive clauses (see *The Motive Clause*, 295).

[144]Gemser, "The Importance of the Motive Clause," 55-56. This classification was adopted by von Rad (*Theology*, 1. 197), Paul (*Book of the Covenant*, 39), and by J. G. Torralba ("Motivación deuteronómica del precepto del Sabat," *EB* 29 [1970] 73-99).

[145]Ibid., 56.

[146]Ibid., for example, Deut 19; 21:17; 22:24, 26. Translation of the motive clause is by Gemser.

[147]Ibid., 57.

[148]Ibid., 59.

[149]Ibid., 60.

[150]Uitti, *The Motive Clause*, 92.

[151]Ibid.

[152]In his final summary (*The Motive Clause*, 113; cf. 298-99), Uitti indicates that 42% of all the motive clauses appeal to the intellect, 35% to the person and activity of Yahweh, 12% to the human longing for personal well-being and blessing; in five passages in D the appeal is to Moses' authority (Deut 15:10b-11, 14b-15; 19:6-7; 24:21b-22), and only 1% reflects a feeling for ecology or the proper stewardship of God's creation.

[153]See also Exod 21:26, 27; Lev 21:18-21, 25:12; Num 30:13.

[154]For other similar examples, see Lev 22:25 (refers to v. 21); Num 35:28 (refers to v. 25b); and, possibly, Lev 1:9

(refers to v. 3); 1:13b   (refers to v. 3); 1:17b (refers to v.
3); 2:6b (refers to v. 5a); 2:15b (refers to v. 14); 4:24b
(refers to v. 22a); 5:9, 12 (refers to v. 11); 7:5b (refers to
v. 1).

[155]The term צרעת is used in the Bible for a number of
diseases that affect the skin. See the notes in *NJV* for Lev
13:3; in *NAB* for Lev 13:2; and the article "Leprosy" by R. K.
Harrison in *IDB* 3, 111-13.

[156]This translation is according to *NJV* and *NAB*. The old
JPSV and *RSV* render it as "I am the Lord your God." There is
no difference between the two *qua* motive clause. On the question as to how to translate this phrase, see A. Poebel, *Das
appositionell bestimmte Pronomen der 1. Pers. Sing. in den
westsemitischen Inschriften und im Alten Testament* (AS 3;
Chicago: University of Chicago, 1932) 53-72; W. Zimmerli, "Ich
bin Jahwe," *Geschichte und Altes Testament*, A. Alt Festschrift
(BHT 16; Tübingen: J. C. B. Mohr, 1953) 179-209; reprinted in
Zimmerli's *Gottes Offenbarung* (TBü 19; München: Chr. Kaiser,
1963) 11-44.

[157]See also Exod 20:22; Lev 6:10; 7:34; 16:2; 17:11-12, 14;
25:42, 54; Num 18:20.

[158]According to M. Weinfeld, "the general feature common
to them all is the two-faced or hypocritical attitude of the
malefactor, the classic example being that of the falsifier of
weights and measures" (*Deuteronomy and the Deuteronomic School*,
268). On *to'ēbāh* laws, see the study by J. L'Hour ("Les interdits").

[159]Here the motive clause reads, כי תועבה הוא לפני יהוה.

[160]For the discussion of this expression, see H. C.
Brichto (*The Problem of "Curse" in the Hebrew Bible*, 191).

[161]The formula in Deut 16:12 constitutes the motivation of
a parenetic statement which starts with verse 11, and therefore
is not included here.

[162]See M. Greenberg's discussion in *IDB* 1, 734-35. The
author points out that many of the transgressions punished by
karet are elsewhere in the priestly laws punished by death (cf.
Lev 18:8, 29 with 20:11; 18:17 with 20:14; 18:23 with 20:15).
In Exod 31:14-15, the two penalties are found together as the
punishment for the violation of the Sabbath law. In Lev 20:
4-5, it is God who "cuts off." When *karet* appears alone, Greenberg suggests a kind of penalty *in terrorem*. In Rabbinic law,
karet refers to punishment at the hand of heaven. For details,
see "Karet" by Israel Moses Ta-Shma in *EncJud* 10, 788-89.

[163]However, the exact force of the ו in ולא is not clear;
see *NJV*, note to Lev 19:17.

[164]*NAB*, following the LXX, translates: "nor shall you
acquit the guilty."

[165]So according to *NJV*. However, this translation is disputed. Others, such as *JPS*, *NAB*, render it as "take His name in vain." It is not clear whether the law refers here to perjury ("swear falsely") or to profanity ("utter God's name in vain"). For a discussion of this matter, see Orlinsky, *Notes on the New Translation of the Torah*, 175-76.

[166]A similar formula is also found in Deut 19:13, but here it constitutes the motivation of a parenetic statement. On בער laws, see the study by J. L'Hour ("Une legislation criminelle"). See also the remarks by Morgenstern ("The Book of the Covenant," 2. 145).

[167]Here the motive clause read, ואתה תבער הדם הנקי מקרבך.

[168]The meaning of this internal motive clause was already a matter of debate during the Rabbinic period; see *Mishna Giṭṭin* 9:10.

[169]F. L. Horton, "Form and Structure in Laws Relating to Women: Leviticus 18:6-18," *SBL 1973 Seminar Papers* (ed. G. MacRae; Cambridge: Society of Biblical Literature, 1973) 1. 27.

[170]Gemser, "The Importance of the Motive Clause," 63.

[171]For a discussion of components built into complex literary genres, see Koch (*Biblical Tradition*, 23-24). Here the author stresses that "component" literary genres are to be distinguished from the sub-varieties of a given literary genre, as for instance different forms of individual songs of laments (p. 24 n. 19).

[172]E.g., Gen 5:24, 12:10, 26:7, 28:11.

[173]E.g., Gen 32:12, 1 Kgs 8:39, 2 Chr 20:12.

[174]E.g., Josh 23:3, 10; 2 Kgs 18:29, 32.

[175]E.g., Gen 4:25; 17:5; 29:32, 34; 30:20.

[176]E.g., Gen 21:31.

[177]E.g., Ps 1:6; 34:10; 37:2; 49:18; 119:32, 35, 39; Prov 31:21.

[178]E.g., Ps 33:4, 96:4, 147:1.

[179]E.g., Ps 57:2; 59:3-4; 61:4; 71:3; 86:1, 2.

[180]E.g., Ps 67:5, 107:1, 116:2.

[181]E.g., Cant 1:2; 2:5, 10-11, 14; 8:6.

[182]Isa 22:13.

[183]Num 21:27-28.

[184] 2 Sam 1:21.

[185] E.g., Gen 13:17, 17:16, 26:3; Ps 28:6, 31:22; Prov 8:34.

[186] E.g., Gen 3:14, 17; 49:7; Deut 28:38, 39, 40, 41, 45, 62.

[187] E.g., 1 Sam 23:4; 30:8; 2 Sam 5:19, 23-24.

[188] E.g., in oracles of assurance (e.g., Jer 1:8, 14-19; 11:23; 15:19-20), in oracles of judgment (e.g., 2 Sam 12:10; Isa 2:11, 12; 13:6; Joel 2:1; Zeph 1:7), in summons to lamentations (e.g., Isa 23:14, Jer 4:8, Joel 1:5-7, Mic 1:20-22). For more examples, see Muilenberg, "The Linguistic and Rhetoric Usages of the Particle כי in the Old Testament," 135-60. On motivation in prophetic writings, see H. W. Wolff, "Die Begründungen der prophetischen Heils- und Unheilssprüche," *ZAW* 52 (1934) 1-21.

[189] E.g., Prov 1:9, 16, 32; 2:5, 10, 18, 21; 3:1, 12, 14, 26, 32 and many others.

[190] E.g., Gen 12:13, 27:25, 37:22; Josh 4:24.

[191] E.g., 1 Kgs 8:40, 43.

[192] E.g., Isa 45:3; Ezek 11:20, 25:10; Amos 5:14.

[193] E.g., Ps 9:15, 30:13.

[194] E.g., Ps 119:71, 80.

[195] E.g., Prov 2:20, 19:20.

[196] E.g., Gen 20:3, Exod 9:1, 1 Kgs 11:21.

[197] E.g., Isa 2:3.

[198] E.g., Josh 7:9, Judg 16:28.

[199] E.g., Ps 60:13.

[200] E.g., Prov 3:4, 10.

[201] E.g., Gen 11:4; 19:15, 19; Num 20:18 and frequently after the expression "for he thought," as in Gen 26:9, 38:11, Num 16:34; cf. GKC, #152w.

[202] E.g., Gen 32:12, Prov 30:9.

[203] E.g., 2 Sam 1:20.

[204] E.g., Ps 7:3, 13:4, 28:1.

[205] E.g., Prov 5:9, 10; 9:8; 20:13; 22:25; 24:18; 25:8, 10, 16, 17; 26:4, 5; 30:6, 10; 31:5.

[206] E.g., Gen 4:15, 38:9; Exod 20:20; 2 Sam 14:13.

[207]E.g., Jer 7:8, 17:23; cf. BDB, 166; GKC, #152x.

[208]E.g., Gen 11:7; 34:13, 27; 42:21.

[209]E.g., 2 Kgs 9:37, Jer 16:13, Hos 14:4, Mal 3:19.

[210]E.g., 1 Kgs 3:12, 13.

[211]E.g., Deut 28:27, 51.

[212]E.g., Eccl 4:9, 8:11; Job 34:27 (*RSV*).

[213]BDB, 90.

[214]Ges, 862.

[215]For a discussion of these genres, see Fohrer (*Introduction*, 311-15) and J. L. Crenshaw ("Wisdom," *Old Testament Form Criticism*, 229-62).

[216]A. Bentzen, *Introduction to the Old Testament* (Copenhagen, 1952) 1. 127.

[217]These expressions are W. McKane's; see his *Proverbs* (Philadelphia: Westminster, 1970) 3. Gerstenberger, too, uses similar terms: "Sentenz" and "Weisung"; see *Wesen und Herkunft*, 117. However, there is no unanimity among scholars as to terminology. R. E. Murphy speaks of "sayings" and "admonitions" (see his "Form Criticism and Wisdom Literature," 478-79); and R. B. Y. Scott, of "proverbs" and "precepts" (see *The Way of Wisdom in the Old Testament* [New York: Macmillan, 1971] 48-71). On the general problem of genre terminology in wisdom literature, see Murphy, "Form Criticism," 476. Wisdom "instructions" must be distinguished from (royal) instructions discussed by M. Weinfeld in his article "The Origin of the Apodictic Law" (*VT* 23 [1973] 63-75).

[218]McKane, *Proverbs*, 5.

[219]Ibid., 3.

[220]They appear only in Prov 16:12, 26; 19:19; 21:7, 25; 25:6-7, 22; 26:25; 27:1, 24.

[221]Scott, *The Way of Wisdom*, 52.

[222]McKane, *Proverbs*, 370.

[223]Discussing the didactic role of motivations in wisdom instructions, Crenshaw writes: "The didactic character of the proverb is heightened in the admonition....To accomplish this end the admonition makes use of motive clauses, positive commands, and grounds for conduct" ("Wisdom," 235). And similarly, "This pedagogic function of the aphorism was abetted by the addition of motivation clauses" (ibid., 231).

[224] For "sentences," see, for instance, Eccl 4:10, 14,
15-16, 17; 6:7-8, 9a; 7:1, 2, 3, 5, 8, 11-12 (some of these are
motivated, others not); for "instructions," see, for example,
4:17; 5:1, 3, 5-6, 7; 7:9, 10, 13, 16, 17, 18 (all of these are
motivated).

[225] G. von Rad, *Wisdom in Israel* (London: SCM, 1972) 88 n.
24. Similarly, H. Cazelles characterizes the motive clauses in
the Decalogue as "motivations et additions de type sapiental"
("Les origines du Décalogue," *Eretz Israel* 9 [1969] 16).

[226] On quoting wisdom sayings in order to buttress an argument in biblical and ancient Near Eastern literature, see R.
Gordis, *Koheleth: The Man and His World* (New York: Schocken,
1968), 101-103; and his article, "Quotations as Literary Usage
in Biblical, Oriental and Rabbinic Literature," *HUCA* 22 (1949)
157-219. See also the remarks by R. B. Y. Scott in *Proverbs
and Ecclesiastes* (New York: Doubleday, 1965) 38 n. 17; E. A.
Speiser, "The Case of Obliging Servant," *JCS* 8 (1954) 98-105;
reprinted in *Oriental and Biblical Studies: Collected Writings
of E. A. Speiser* (eds. J. J. Finkelstein and M. Greenberg;
Philadelphia: University of Pennsylvania, 1967) 344-66.

[227] On these two types of motivation in Proverbs, see von
Rad (*Wisdom in Israel*, 89-93).

[228] On methodology in this area, see, among others, J. L.
Crenshaw, "Method of Determining Wisdom Influence upon 'His-
torical' Literature," *JBL* 88 (1969) 129-42; R. N. Whybray, *The
Intellectual Tradition in the Old Testament* (BZAW 135; Berlin/
New York: de Gruyter, 1974) 71-156.

[229] See, among others, J. P. Audet, "Origines comparées de
la double tradition de la loi et de la sagesse dans le Proche-
Orient ancien," *International Congress of Orientalists* 25
(1960) 1. 352-57; Gerstenberger, *Wesen und Herkunft*, and his
article, "Covenant and Commandment," *JBL* 84 (1965) 38-51; W.
McKane, *Prophets and Wise Men* (SBT 44; London: SCM, 1965).
See also above, Chapter I, n. 153.

[230] For examples, see text above and n. 158.

[231] McKane, *Proverbs*, 301. J. L'Hour, in his article "Les
interdits to'eba dans le Deuteronome," has already pointed to
its sapiental background. Both McKane and Weinfeld (*Deuteronomy and the Deuteronomic School*, 267) convincingly argue in favor
of D's dependence on Proverbs. The expression seems to depend
ultimately on Amenemope. See the discussions of McKane and
Weinfeld. In extra-biblical literature, the term תועבה is
found in the sepulchral inscription of Tabnit in the form of
תועבת עסתרת ("an abomination to Astarte"). For the text, see
Donner-Röllig, *KAI*, 1, no. 16:6. The term "abomination" is
also found in Mesopotamian wisdom texts in the form of *ik-kib*
dNammu ("abomination to the god Nammu") and *ik-kib ilānimeš*
("an abomination to all gods"). See Lambert, *BWL*, 117 and 215.
Also, the word "*ḫurkel*," which occurs in the Hittite Laws

(#187-91, 195, 196) is translated by E. Neufeld in Hebrew as
‏תועבה‎ and in English as "abomination"; see his *The Hittite Laws*
(London: Luzae, 1951). According to H. A. Hoffner, if an
English word has to be used to render "*ḫurkel*," it would be
either "abomination" or "depravity," adding, "not unlike the
Hebrew '‏תועבה‎'"; *The Laws of Hittites*, 336-37.

[232]R. C. Dentan, "The Literary Affinities of Exodus
XXXIV:6f," *VT* 13 (1963) 46.

[233]The motive clauses in wisdom instructions and wisdom
literature in general do not refer to the historic experiences
of Israel. This can be explained by the universalistic and
humanistic nature of wisdom; see Kaufmann, *Religion of Israel*,
325; O. S. Rankin, *Israel's Wisdom Literature* (New York:
Schocken, 1969) 12. Moreover, cultic regulations and cultic
matters are not predominant in wisdom sayings and in their motive clauses. See discussion of this issue in McKane (*Proverbs*,
293) and Kaufmann (*Religion of Israel*, 326); cf. L. G. Perdue,
Wisdom and Cult (SBLDS 30; Missoula: Scholars Press, 1977).

[234]See references above in n. 110.

[235]Morgenstern, "The Book of the Covenant," 2. 210.

[236]Beyerlin, "Die Paränese im Bundesbuch," 19-29.

[237]Most of Beyerlin's parenetic statements are considered
in the present study as motive clauses; see discussion above
on p. 68.

[238]E.g., Exod 20:22, 24; 22:22, 23, 26, 30; 23:13.

[239]H. M. Orlinsky, "The Tribal System of Israel and
Related Groups in the Period of the Judges," *Studies and Essays
in Honor of A. A. Neuman* (ed. M. Ben-Horin; Leiden: Brill,
1962) 375-87; also in *Oriens Antiquus* 1 (1962) 11-20, reprinted
in the author's *Essays in Biblical Culture and Bible Translation* (New York: Ktav, 1974) 66-77. A number of scholars have
now rejected the theory of the amphictyony; see Orlinsky's
Essays (77) for a list. See also the criticism by A. D. H.
Hayes ("Israel Before the Monarchy") as recorded in the *Bulletin of the Society of Old Testament Study* (Summer Meeting,
1973, p. 7). From the very beginning, an outspoken opponent of
the amphictyony in ancient Israel was Y. Kaufmann; see his remarks in his *Religion of Israel* (256).

[240]Alt, "The Origins of Israelite Law," 164-68.

[241]See discussion above in Chapter I, 24-25.

[242]Beyerlin, "Die Paränese im Bundesbuch," 21.

[243]Uitti, *The Motive Clause*, 135-36. Concerning the form
and structure of this ceremony, see his bibliography on p. 143
n. 18, to which one should add, in particular, A. Weiser (*The
Psalms* [Philadelphia: Westminster, 1962] 23-52).

[244]Alt, "The Origins of Israelite Law," 164-65.

[245]G. von Rad, "The Form-Critical Problem of the Hexateuch," *The Problem of the Hexateuch and Other Essays* (Edinburgh: Oliver & Boyd, 1965) 38-39; see also his *Theology*, 1.
192-93.

[246]Uitti, *The Motive Clause*, 136.

[247]Ibid.

[248]Ibid.

[249]By "extensions" he means legal prescriptions which,
following an "apodictic" law, are introduced by אם instead of
the usual כי, e.g., Exod 22:24, 25. For this, Uitti relies on
Beyerlin ("Die Paränese im Bundesbuch," 19) and Gerstenberger
(*Wesen und Herkunft*, 30); see also Chapter I, p. 16, in the
present study.

[250]Uitti, *The Motive Clause*, 133.

[251]Ibid., 139.

[252]Ibid., 141.

[253]See pp. 25-26.

[254]It is worth noting that E. Jacob rejects altogether the
idea that Israelite cult ever included a preaching element. He
writes: "The literary type of preaching is represented in the
O.T. by the Deuteronomic exhortation, certain speeches in
Chronicles which are put in the mouths of the prophets and by
certain passages in the prophetic books themselves, but everything leads to the belief that preaching lay mainly outside the
truly cultic realm"; *Theology of the Old Testament* (New York:
Harper & Bros., 1958) 270 n. 1. The above text is also quoted
by Uitti (*The Motive Clause*, 135).

[255]Gunkel, "Fundamental Problems of Hebrew Literary
History," 62.

[256]Uitti, *The Motive Clause*, 190.

[257]Von Rad, *Theology*, 1. 198.

[258]P. J. Budd, "Priestly Instruction in Pre-Exilic Israel,"
VT 23 (1973) 6.

[259]Gerstenberger, *Wesen und Herkunft*, 49.

[260]E.g., Prov 1:11-17; 2:1-6, 7-10; 6:1-3; 23:1-3; 25:
21-22; 26:25.

[261]On the didactic aim of biblical legislation, see Paul
(*Book of the Covenant*, 39 and references in n. 1).

[262]In his book *The Laws of Deuteronomy* (Ithaca: Cornell
University, 1974), C. M. Carmichael states that "frequently
they [motive clauses] are attached to unenforceable laws, that
is, laws whose observance cannot be compelled under threat of a
stated penalty, either for lack of an enforcing agency or because such compulsion is not in question" (38). As examples
he refers to Deut 12:23, 16:3, 24:6. However, in light of the
existence of motivated laws in Deuteronomy 22, which, he states,
"are intended to be legislation in the narrow, precise sense,"
he is forced to admit that some motive clauses are attached "to
laws that are enforceable" (39). On the Rabbinic understanding
of the reasons of the commandments, see Heinemann, *Ta'amei
ha-Mitsvot be-Sifrut Yisrael*; M. Scholem, "Commandments,
Reasons for," *EncJud* 5, 783-92.

[263]See above, this chapter, p. 99.

[264]On the difficulty of establishing the precise setting
in life of literary genres, see above, Chapter I, p. 8.

[265]See 121-23.

[266]The term חכם is applied at different periods to different people. See, for example, the list in BDB, 314-15; the
discussion in Fohrer, *Introduction*, 309; and McKane, *Prophets
and Wise Men*, 15-22. Here we are interested in wise men only
as teachers.

[267]G. Östborn, *Tora in the Old Testament* (Lund: Ohlssons,
1945) 119. On the reinterpretation of "*torah*" in Proverbs
from parental or scholastic instructions to God's law, see
McKane (*Proverbs*, 623).

[268]McKane, *Prophets and Wise Men*, 102 n. 1; cf. J. Bright,
Jeremiah (New York: Doubleday Anchor, 1965) 65.

[269]McKane, *Prophets and Wise Men*, 111.

[270]J. Kaster, "Education, O.T.," *IDB* 2, 29. Similarly,
Scott refers to it as "a source book of wisdom materials assembled and edited by a teacher for use in his school" (*The Way
of Wisdom*, 52-53).

[271]For the international context of biblical wisdom literature, see Scott (*The Way of Wisdom*, 23-48; *Proverbs and
Ecclesiastes*, xl-liii) and McKane (*Proverbs*, 51-208).

[272]McKane, *Proverbs*, 303; Weinfeld, *Deuteronomy and the
Deuteronomic School*, 305 n. 3; Östborn, *Tora in the Old Testament*, 114.

[273]Ecclesiastes, however, seems to have a reader in mind
and not a listening pupil; see Gordis, *Koheleth*, 109. The
expressions "my son" and "listen" do not occur here.

[274]On scribal schools in Egypt, see R. J. Williams,
"Scribal Training in Ancient Egypt," *JAOS* 92 (1972) 214-21;
J. A. Wilson, *The Burden of Egypt*, 261-62; F. Dumas, *La civili-
sation de l'Egypt pharaonique* (Paris: Arthaud, 1965) 381-32.

[275]On schools in ancient Mesopotamia, see S. N. Kramer,
The Sumerians (Chicago: University of Chicago, 1963) 229-48;
C. J. Gadd, *Teachers and Students in the Oldest Schools* (School
of Oriental and African Studies, University of London, 1956);
G. R. Driver, *Semitic Writing* (London: Oxford University, 1948)
64-65; W. W. Hallo and W. K. Simpson, *The Ancient Near East:
A History* (New York: Harcourt Brace Jovanovich, 1971) 154-58.

[276]W. F. Albright, "A Teacher to a Man of Shechem About
1600 B.C.," *BASOR* 86 (1942) 30-31; *ANET*, 490. Albright's
interpretation is challenged by B. Landsberger in *JCS* 8 (1956)
59 n. 121. Albright's rejoinder is found in *BASOR* 139 (1955)
22-23. Gezer calendar is taken by some as a tablet written by
a student. See, for example, W. F. Albright, "The Gezer
Calendar," *BASOR* 92 (1943) 21; cf. *ANET*, 320; H. Michaud, *Sur
la pierre et l'argile* (Neuchâtel: Delachaux, 1958) 21.

[277]Eissfeldt, *The Old Testament*, 86. On the possibility
of the existence of schools in the biblical period, see also
W. Chomsky, "The Dawn of Jewish Education," *Gratz College Annual
of Jewish Studies* 3 (1974) 19-27. On the other hand, Whybray
expresses doubts regarding the existence of schools with professional teachers in ancient Israel; see his *The Intellectual
Tradition*, 15-54.

[278]On priests as imparters of *torah*, see Östborn, *Tora in
the Old Testament*, 89-112.

[279]A. Cody, *A History of Old Testament Priesthood* (AnBib
35; Rome: Pontifical Biblical Institute, 1969) 118.

[280]Ibid.; Östborn, *Tora in the Old Testament*, 99.

[281]Cody, *Old Testament Priesthood*, 189. When the Chronicler writes of the "teaching" activity of the priests handing
down *torah*, he does not use the term מבין but the participle
מורה, as in 2 Chr 15:3, כהן מורה. The term מפרש in Neh 8:8 is
problematic. See discussion in von Rad, *Studies in Deuteronomy*,
13. It most likely means "in translation"; cf. Ezra 4:18. See
b. Meg. 3a, *b. Ned.* 37b, *y. Meg.* 4:1(74d), *Gen. Rab.* 36; cf.
"Masorah," *EncJud* 16, 1410-11, 1479; J. M. Myers, *Ezra-Nehemiah*
(New York: Doubleday Anchor, 1965) 151 and n. 8; Cody, *Old
Testament Priesthood*, 150 n. 42. However, on this point, von
Rad disagrees and says that it is possible that the Chronicler
was anticipating a custom of his own time; see *Theology*, 1. 89.

[282]Cody, however, argues that in the original text the
שרים, lay officials of verse 7, were the ones who were sent out
to do the teaching, not the Levites. The Chronicler's contribution was to add the priests and the Levites to the mission,

probably under the influence of the book of the law mentioned
in verse 9; see *Old Testament Priesthood*, 187. According to
Albright, 2 Chr 17:7-9 may well be a misunderstood doublet of
the tradition of Jehoshaphat's judicial reform as recorded in
chapter 19; see "The Judicial Reform of Jehoshaphat," *Alexander
Marx Jubilee Volume* (New York: JPS, 1950) 61-82.

[283] Östborn, *Tora in the Old Testament*, 127-71.

[284] Ibid., 143.

[285] Alt, "The Origins of Israelite Law," 131; M. Noth, *The
History of Israel* (New York: Harper & Row, 1960) 103 and refer-
ences in n. 1; also, idem, "Das Amt des 'Richters Israels,'"
Festschrift A. Bertholet (Tübingen: J. C. B. Mohr, 1950) 404-17.

[286] See above, n. 239.

[287] Y. Kaufmann, *Sepher Shophetim* (Jerusalem: Kiryat
Sepher, 1964) 47-48.

[288] In the Akkadian of Mari, the term *šāpiṭum* means "ruler";
see A. Marzal, "The Provincial Governor at Mari: His Title and
Appointment," *JNES* 30 (1971) 186-217. See also M. S. Rozenberg,
"The Stem *ŠPṬ*: An Investigation of Biblical and Extra-Biblical
Sources," dissertation, University of Pennsylvania, 1963. For
further comments, see A. Malamat, "The Period of the Judges,"
The World History of the Jewish People, III: *Judges* (ed. B.
Mazar; New Brunswick: Rutgers University, 1971) 129-63. On the
terms שׁפט and משׁפט, see E. A. Speiser ("The Manner of the King,"
ibid., 280-87), T. Ishida ("The Leaders of the Tribal Leagues
'Israel' in the Pre-Monarchic Period," *RB* 80 [1973] 514-30);
see also Liedke, *Gestalt*, 62-100.

CHAPTER III

MOTIVE CLAUSES IN EXTRA-BIBLICAL LAW COLLECTIONS

ARE LEGAL MOTIVE CLAUSES UNIQUE TO THE BIBLE?

In light of the recognized common legal tradition of the
ancient Near East, which also includes Israel, it is appropriate to inquire whether or not extra-biblical law collections
feature motive clauses similar to those found in the legal
corpora of the Bible.

In his article of 1953, Gemser claimed that biblical legal
motive clauses were without any parallel. Referring to the law
collections of the ancient Near East, he wrote,

> In absolutely none of these lawbooks or--codes or--
> collections can one single instance of motive clauses
> be discovered. The motive clause is clearly and
> definitely a peculiarity of Israel's or Old Testament
> law.[1]

He argued that the reason for the use of legal motivation in
the Bible must be sought in the very nature of the biblical law
collections. These collections, he said, are rooted in the
cultic gathering of the people,[2] and "direct themselves not so
much to the official instances, the judges and the jurists, as
to the people, collectively and individually."[3] Above all, he
stressed,

> it is the spirit imbued by the leaders and lawgivers
> of Israel, ultimately by its divine Leader and Law-
> giver, which provides the best explanation for this
> remarkable phenomenon of motivated law in Israel, and
> in Israel alone among all the peoples of the Ancient
> Orient as far as we can see at present.[4]

Gemser was not alone in asserting the uniqueness of the
biblical legal motive clauses. Cassuto, in 1951, had already
maintained that "sometimes the Torah adds the reason for the
law, from the religious or ethical point of view, unlike the
codes mentioned above [i.e., extra-biblical law collections],
which give no reasons."[5]

A number of biblical scholars accepted the uniqueness of
the biblical legal motive clauses, and many, either explicitly

or implicitly, based their opinion on Gemser's categorical remarks on this matter. Among them one can cite, in particular,
von Rad,[6] Muilenburg,[7] Koch,[8] and de Vaux.[9]

Some Assyriologists, however, knew of the presence of
motive clauses in the ancient Near Eastern law collections.
About the time of Gemser's article, their existence had been
confirmed at least in LH. Thus, for instance, in 1952 (one
year before the publication of Gemser's article), Driver and
Miles had already identified them in LH 107, 136, 194 and 232.[10]
In 1969, Yaron added LH 146 to the list.[11]

Some biblical scholars, too, appear to have been aware of
the existence of motive clauses in extra-biblical law collections. For example, in the first edition of his *Einleitung in
das Alte Testament* (1949), A. Weiser wrote:

> The greater strength of Israel's characteristic way
> of life made itself felt by its penetration also into
> the casuistic law and its forms; as regards the con-
> tent, this trend can be observed in the combined
> religious and ethical motivation which in comparison
> with early oriental legal codes, is more far-reaching
> and in certain matters more strict.[12]

Here, Weiser seems to be aware of the existence of extra-
biblical legal motive clauses, and simply points to the larger
number and wider range of the biblical examples.

Among the followers of Gemser, there are some who are not
categorical in denying the existence of motive clauses in
extra-biblical laws. For example, Torralba, who agreed with
Gemser in every other respect, still wrote in this connection
that "outside of the Israelite legislation it is difficult to
find motive clauses."[13] Similarly, Paul, who appears to have
accepted Gemser's four-part classification of the motive
clauses, modified Gemser's opinion concerning the uniqueness of
biblical motive clauses by stating that "unlike most other
ancient legal corpora, motive clauses are occasionally appended
to both apodictic and casuistic injunctions,"[14] and he referred
the reader to the writings of Beyerlin[15] and Yaron.[16] Finally,
Uitti totally rejected Gemser's claim of uniqueness but maintained that "the explanatory motive clause is present in only
one Ancient Near Eastern lawcode, the Hammurabi Code."[17] He

referred solely to examples in LH 78 ("E"), 107, 136, 146, 194
and 232.[18]

A perusal of the ancient Near Eastern law collections
indicates that, even though motive clauses do not appear in
Sumerian laws, LE, NBL or HL, they are indeed found in LH and
also in MAL. In LH, motive clauses can be identified in the
following laws: 7, 9, 10, 11, 13, 29, (47), 78 ("E"), 107, 136,
137, 146, 162, 163, 171, 178, 194, and 232. In MAL A, they can
be identified in 23, 24, 29, 36, 38, 45 and 49. These examples, analyzed below, disprove Gemser's claim of uniqueness.

FORM AND CONTENT OF THE MOTIVE CLAUSES

The motive clauses in LH and MAL are introduced either by
grammatical particles or formulated asyndetically.

Grammatical Particles

In Akkadian, *aššum* functions both as a conjunction and as
a preposition.[19] As a conunction it may mean "because," "so
that," or "that."[20] As a preposition it may signify "concerning," "on behalf of," "on account of," "because of," "with
respect to" or "related to."[21] In the law collections, *aššum*,
when used as a conjunction, has a causal meaning and introduces
causal clauses.[22]

The enclitic *-ma* followed by the present tense is capable
of introducing final motive clauses.[23] In LH, there are a few
examples of this kind.

The conjunction *kî* has, among others, a causal function.[24]
A possible example of *kî* introducing a causal clause is found
in MAL A 45:64.

Formulated Asyndetically

Meek has drawn attention to the unusually large number of
asyndetic clauses in LH.[25] While some of these are explicative,
adverbial, temporal, or consequential, others are simply circumstantial. Among the latter, some can well be taken as constituting motive clauses. At times, these asyndetic motive
clauses are expressed by stative verbs, usually preceding the

clauses to which they are circumstantial;[26] in other cases, they appear as nominal sentences immediately following the legal consequence.

Whether introduced by a grammatical particle or formulated in asyndetic manner, the motive clause is found in the apodosis of the law. In only one case, namely in LH 47, is the protasis provided with a rationale.

Motive Clauses in LH

Introduced by Grammatical Particles

aššum

1. LH 78 ("E")

This law,[27] dealing with rents, states that the owner of a house who received the year's rent in advance but nevertheless evicted his tenant before the rental period is over (*a-na wa-aš-[ša-bi-im] i-na u₄-mi-[šu] la ma-lu-tim wa-ṣa-[am] iq-ta-b[i]*, lines 11-14) forfeits the money which he had received from the tenant. The law is justified on the basis: *aš-[šum] wa-aš-ša-[ba-am] i-na u₄-m[i-šu] la ma-lu-[tim-ma] i-na É-šu ú-[še-ṣu-ú]* ("bec[ause] he caused the ten[ant] to mo[ve out] of his house before the comple[tion of his] term," lines 15-19). The motive clause here does not provide new information but simply underscores the key issue of the case.

2. LH 107

According to this law, a merchant (DAM.GÀR, Akk. *tamkārum*) who denied (*it-ta-ki-ir-šu*, line 5) the receipt of certain goods given to him by the plaintiff, an agent (ŠAMÁN.LÁ, Akk. *šamallûm*), is forced to pay six-fold.[28] The law is motivated by *aš-šum* ŠAMÁN.LÁ-*šu ik-ki-ru* ("because he has denied[29] [the receipt to] his agent," lines 9-10). Here, too, the motive clause underscores the key issue of the case.

3. LH 136

This law states that a man who has voluntarily abandoned his city and fled (URU-*šu id-di-ma it-ta-bi-it*,[30] lines 58-59), and whose wife has subsequently remarried, cannot, if he returns to the city, reclaim his ex-wife from her second husband. The justification is: *aš-šum* URU-*šu i-ze-ru-ma in-na-bi-tu*, ("because he rejected his city and fled," lines 68-70).

It must be noted that, while the law proper speaks of URU-*šu id-di-ma* (line 58), the motive clause has URU-*šu i-ze-ru-ma* (lines 68-69). The relationship between these two verbs has a bearing on the scope of the motive clause. The question is whether the motive clause here provides new information or whether the two verbs are to be considered synonymous.

Yaron is of the first opinion and maintains that in the motive clause of LH 136, "a new factual element (viz. "hatred") is introduced."[31] Similarly, E. Szlechter claims that by the insertion of *aššum ālšu izēruma* the law obtains a larger field of application, inasmuch as it can also be applied to fugitives who hated the city without wishing to abandon it altogether.[32]

The verb *zêru* does indeed mean "to hate," and *CAD* even contains examples where it appears in opposition to "love" such as, *šumma šarru bēliya la irâmanni u i-zé-i-ra-an-ni* ("if the king, my lord, does not love but dislikes me").[33] However, *CAD* also refers to other texts where *zêru* means "to reject," such as, *[i]-ze-ra būrīšina* ÁB.GAL.MEŠ ("the cows rejected their calves").[34] Dossin, too, cites certain passages where *zêru* conveys the sense of "to reject, abandon," such as a clause in a Mari letter, *šum-ma A-bi-Sa-mar te-zi-i[r] ù a-l[a-n]i-ka te-zi-ir-m[a]* ("if you abandon Abisamar, you also abandon your cities"),[35] and in light of the parallelism between *ālšu iddima* and *ālšu izēruma*, he states, "the redactor of the text considered *zêru* as a synonym of *nadû*, to leave, abandon."[36]

A close parallel to LH 136 is found in LE 30.[37] The protasis of LE 30 has: URU^ki^-*šu ù be-el-šu i-ze-er-ma* (Text B, line 8). In LH 136, it is replaced by URU-*šu id-di-ma* (line 58). This strongly indicates that in the opinion of the redactor of LH, *zêru* and *nadû* conveyed the same meaning. It appears that the verb *zêru* has a semantic range which includes both the sense of "hate" and "reject, abandon."[38] It is the latter that seems to be intended in the motive clause of LH 136. Hence, the motive clause does not introduce something new to the law, but underscores the key element of the case by using synonymous terminology.

4. LH 146

This law considers the case of a priestess (LUKUR, Akk. $nad\bar{\imath}tum$[39]) who has given her husband a slave girl for the purpose of bearing children. The slave girl, having born sons (DUMU.MEŠ it-ta-la-ad, line 47) for her mistress' husband, then attempted to make herself equal to her mistress. The law stipulates that the mistress may put upon her a slave-mark[40] but cannot sell her. This is justified by stating: $a\check{s}$-$\check{s}um$ DUMU.MEŠ ul-du ("because she bore sons," line 52).[41] Here, too, the motive clause underscores the key issue of the case (cf. LH 147).

5. LH 194

This law deals with the death of an infant who was placed in the care of a wet-nurse. The exact circumstances of the case, however, are not clear. Apparently, after the death of the child, the wet-nurse secretly (ba-lum a-bi-$\check{s}u$ $\grave{u}$ um-mi-$\check{s}u$, lines 30-31) made an agreement to adopt another child (DUMU $\check{s}a$-ni-a-am-ma ir-ta-ka-$\hat{a}s$, lines 32-33) with the presumed intention of passing him off as the one who was originally placed in her care.[42] However, the fact was discovered and proved against her. Consequently, her breast(s?)[43] is cut off. The penalty clause is motivated by the statement: $a\check{s}$-$\check{s}um$ ba-lum a-bi[$\check{s}$]u $\grave{u}$ um-mi-[$\check{s}u$] DUMU $\check{s}a$-ni-a-a[m] ir-ku-[s]u ("because she made an agreement for another child without [the consent of] its father and mother," lines 35-38). Again, the motive clause underscores the key issue of the case.

6. LH 232

This law deals with the responsibility of a builder and rules that he is required to rebuild, at his own expense, the house which had collapsed after he built it. It justifies it by: $a\check{s}$-$\check{s}um$ É i-pu-$\check{s}u$ la $\acute{u}$-dan-ni-nu-ma im-$q\acute{u}$-tu ("because he did not make strong the house which he built and it fell down," lines 87-89). As Driver and Miles indicate, the second clause of LH 232 applies to the three preceding sections of the law and, furthermore, the penalties are cumulative, for it would have been anomalous to require a builder to restore the house

if only the furniture in it were damaged, which is exactly what
is found in the first part of LH 232.[44] The motive clause in
this case underscores the main issue of the case by reiterating
different parts of the group of laws dealing with the builder's
responsibility: É *i-pu-šu*, see line 66; *la ú-dan-ni-nu-ma*, see
line 68; *im-qú-tu*, see line 70.

-ma

1. LH 29

According to this law, the wife of a prisoner, who has a
son under age unable to carry out his father's *ilku*-duty,[45]
receives a portion of the fief. This rule is then motivated
by: *-ma um-ma-šu ú-ra-ab-ba-šu* ("so that his mother may rear
him," lines 48-50).[46]

2. LH 137

This law deals with a man who has made up his mind to
divorce a priestess, either a *šugîtu*[47] who bore him children
or a LUKUR (Akk. *nadîtum*)[48] who has provided him with children.
Each woman is entitled to her dowry (*šeriktum*) and half of the
field, orchard and movable property (A.ŠÀ KIRI$_6$ *ù bi-ši-im*,
line 85).[49] The purpose of this provision is explicated by:
-ma DUMU.MEŠ-*ša ú-ra-ab-ba* ("in order that she may rear her
children," lines 1-3).[50]

Formulated Asyndetically

Formulated by a Stative Verb

1. LH 7

This law considers the case of a man who either buys from
a minor or a slave some goods, or receives from them goods in
custody without any witness or contract. The law then states:
a-wi-lum šu-ú šar-ra-aq id-da-ak ("this man, being a thief,
shall be put to death," lines 55-56).[51] The capital punishment
is here justified on the grounds that the culprit was considered a thief.

2. LH 9

The recovery of stolen property is the subject matter of the group of laws in LH 9-13. Each law considers a different situation. LH 9 deals with the rights of both the owner of a lost property and the buyer who purchased this lost property from a third party. It rules that the owner of the lost property, having produced witnesses testifying to his ownership, gets back his property; the buyer, also having produced witnesses to the sale, recovers the money from the estate of the third party. The third party is adjudged to have stolen it from the original owner and is given the death penalty: *na-di-na-nu-um šar-ra-aq id-da-ak* ("the seller, being a thief, shall be put to death," lines 38-39).[52] Here, too, the capital punishment is justified on the grounds that the seller is considered a thief.

3. LH 10

This law stipulates that, if the owner of the lost property produces witnesses attesting to his ownership but the buyer fails to bring the seller who sold it to him or the witnesses before whom the sale took place, *ša-a-a-ma-nu-um šar-ra-aq id-da-ak* ("the buyer, being a thief, shall be put to death," lines 57-58).[53] The death penalty is again justified on the grounds that the buyer is considered a thief.

4. LH 11

This law reverses the situation dealt with in the previous law. Here it is the owner of the lost property who fails to produce witnesses testifying to his claim of ownership. In this case, the alleged owner, *sà-ar tu-uš-ša-am-ma id-di!*[54] *id-da-ak* ("being a liar [and] having uttered a calumny, he shall be put to death," lines 1-3).[55] The death penalty is here justified on the grounds that the professed owner was really a liar and brought a false and malicious accusation of a capital charge.[56]

5. LH 13

According to this law, if that man (*a-wi-lum šu-ú*, line 14)[57] is not able to produce his witnesses within the deadline

set by the judges, then *sà-ar a-ra-an di-nim šu-a-ti
it-ta-na-aš-ši* ("being a liar, he shall bear the penalty
[involved in] that suit," lines 22-24).[58] The base nature of
the culprit constitutes here the justification for the legal
consequence.

Formulated by a Nominal Sentence

1. LH 162

According to this law, when a man marries and has children, at his wife's demise her father may not claim her dowry[59]
(*a-na še-ri-ik-ti-ša a-bu-ša û-ul i-ra-ag-gu-um*, lines 2-4).
The underlying reason seems to be expressed by an asyndetic
clause which immediately follows it: *še-ri-ik-ta-ša ša*
DUMU.MEŠ-*ša-ma* ("her dowry belongs to her sons," lines 5-6).[60]

2. LH 163

This law states that if a woman died without bearing sons
and her father had returned to the husband his *terḫatu*,[61] the
husband can have no claim to his wife's dowry (*a-na še-ri-ik-ti
MÍ šu-a-ti mu-sà û-ul i-ra-ag-gu-um*, lines 22-23). This seems
to be justified by an asyndetic clause that immediately follows
it: *še-ri-ik-ta-ša ša É a-bi-ša-ma* ("her dowry belongs to her
father's house," lines 22-23).[62]

3. LH 171

Among the dispositions of this law, a *ḫīrtum*[63] who has
been widowed is given back her dowry (*še-ri-ik-ta-ša*, line 79).
In addition, she takes the marriage-gift[64] which her husband
bestowed upon her (*nu-du-na-am ša mu-sà id-di-nu-ši-im*, lines
80-82) and, living in the dwelling place of her deceased husband, enjoys its usufruct, *durante viduitate*. She is, however,
prohibited from selling it; the reason stated is: *wa-ar-ka-sà*
DUMU.MEŠ-*ša-ma* ("her estate[65] belongs to her sons," lines
4-5).[66]

4. LH 178

According to this law, if a father gave his daughter, who
is a NIN.DINGIR (Akk. *ēntum*),[67] a LUKUR (Akk. *nadītum*)[68] or a
MÍZI.IK.RU.UM,[69] a dowry (*šeriktum*), but not the authority to

dispose freely of this property, then after the death of her
father, her brothers, or, if they fail to support her, a person
of her choice, here an *errēšum* ("a cultivator"), can manage it.
As long as she lives, she has the right to enjoy both the property and whatever her father gave her. However, she is not
allowed to sell them or give them away in order to pay a debt
(*ú-ul ú-up-pa-al*, line 17),[70] the reason being: *ap-lu-sà ša
ah-hi-ša-ma* ("her inheritance[71] belongs to her brothers," lines
18-19).[72]

     In all of the examples mentioned above, the motive clause
is found in the apodosis of the law. In LH 47, however, a
motive clause appears in its protasis. LH 45-46 deal with the
question of responsibility in case of damages caused by rain or
flooding, and LH 47 rules on the cultivator's right to a renewal of contract in these circumstances. The first part of
LH 47 can be translated as follows: "If a cultivator (*errēšum*),
because in the previous year he has not recovered his invest-
ment (*aš-šum i-na ša-at-tim mah-ri-tim ma-na-ha-ti-šu la
il-qú!-ú*,[73] lines 59-63), states (that) he will (again) culti-
vate the field, the owner of the field shall not object." The
cultivator's request, found in the protasis of the law, is accompanied by a specific motivation.

Motive Clauses in MAL

Introduced by Grammatical Particles

aššum

1. MAL A 36

     This law deals with the case of a deserted wife. A dis-
tinction is here made between the husband's trip, apparently of
a business nature (*mu-us-sà a-na A.ŠÀ i-it-ta-lak*, line 85),[74]
and his departure on a royal mission (LUGAL *a-na ma-a-te
ša-ni-te-em-ma il-ta-pár-šu*, lines 4-5). In the first case, a
wife without any children is given a five-year waiting period
after which and under certain circumstances she is allowed to
remarry. In the second case, the wife cannot remarry even if
her husband is delayed beyond the five-year period.

The last seven lines (8-14) of the law specify that if, before the expiration of the five-year period, she lives with another man and bears him children, her former husband, upon his return, has the right to take her and her children--presumably the ones she bore for the second husband--away from her second husband.[75] This rule is justified on the basis: *aš-šum ri-ik-sa la-a tu-qa-i-ú-ni ù ta-na-hi-zu!-ú-ni* ("because she did not wait [according to the] act of marriage but allowed herself to be taken in marriage," lines 12-13).[76]

2. MAL A 49

This law deals with the disposition of the inheritance of a harlot. The text is damaged. A motive clause appears in lines 58-59: *aš-šum ŠEŠ.MEŠ-ša[i]-qa-ab-bi-ú-ni* ("because her brothers [so?] declared").

kî

1. MAL A 45

A possible example of a motive clause introduced by the conjunction *kî* is found in this law dealing with the wife of a soldier who is taken prisoner. It specifies that if she has no father-in-law or son she is obligated to wait for a period of two years. One of the questions raised in the law is what to do with her husband's fief if during this waiting period she claims that she has nothing to eat. The text then reads:

62. ^{lú}DI. KU$_5$.MEŠ *ha-zi-a-na* GAL.MEŠ *ša-a* URU
63.   *i-ša-'-ú-lu*
64.   *ki-i* A.ŠÀ *i-na* URU *šu-a-tu il-lu-ku-ú-ni*
65.   A.ŠÀ *ù* É *a-na ú-ku-la-i-ša*
66.   *ša* 2 MU.MEŠ *ú-up-pu-šu*
67.   *i-id-du-nu-ne-eš-še*

(62-63) "The judges shall inquire of the mayor (and) the elders of the city.... (66b) they shall assign[77] to her (65) the field and the house for her support (66a) for two years (and) (67) shall give (them) to her."

The problem is how to render line 64: Is it a conditional clause or a motive clause? *CAD* and *AHW* consider the first three lines as a unit. *CAD* translates: "...they inquire whether he (the husband) used to hold (i.e., perform *ilku*-service for) a field in this town."[78] In *AHW*, *kî* is translated as "if" ("ob").[79] Szlechter has: "as much field ('autant de champ') as he (the husband) held as fief in that city."[80]

The rendering of *kî* by "as much as" is rather free. The translations of both *CAD* and *AHW* seem to go against the regular usage of the dependent clause in Akkadian. As Driver and Miles correctly point out, the dependent clauses precede the governing verb in the Laws (cf. 14:32; 23:17, 33 etc.).[81] If *CAD*'s and *AHW*'s translations were correct, then the following structure would have been expected: DI.KU$_5$.MEŠ...*kî*...*i-ša-'-ú-lu*."[82] Therefore, it is preferable to take line 64 as a motivating clause and translate the lines 62-67 as: "The judges shall inquire of the mayor (and) the elders of the city, (and) because he held a field[83] in that city as a fief,[84] they shall assign to her," etc.[85]

Formulated Asyndetically

The following are possible examples of asyndetic motive clauses.[86]

1. MAL A 24

This law deals with harboring a fugitive married woman. One of the situations it considers is where the owner of the house denies knowledge of the fact that the fugitive married woman has been staying in his house with his wife. The matter is submitted to trial by ordeal. The law then stipulates:

72. *šum-ma* LÚ *ša* DAM-*su i-na pa-ni-šu*
73. *ra-ma-an-ša tal-du-du-ú-ni*
74. *i-na* ÍD$^{i.id}$*it-tu-ra za-a-ku*
75. *gi-im-ri ša* ÍD$^{i.id}$ *ú-ma-al-la*

(72-74a) "If the man, whose wife had run away[87] from him, turns away from the river (ordeal), (74b) being guiltless, (75) he shall pay the expenses[88] for the river (ordeal)."

The difficulty in the text is to determine the subject of
the verbs *za-a-ku* (line 74) and *ú-ma-al-la* (line 75). *CAD*
translates, "If he returns innocent from the river (ordeal), he
has to pay in full the expenses for the river (ordeal)."[89]
This translation is not satisfactory for two basic reasons: the
expression *ina* ÍD *turru* occurs in line 70 where it cannot mean
"to return" but rather "to decline," "to turn away" from the
ordeal, inasmuch as the owner of the house is then required to
pay a sum of money as penalty. Furthermore, *CAD*'s translation
implies that the innocent has to pay the expenses as well.
This is unlikely. It is possible that there is a change of
subject in these verbs: while the stative *zāku* refers to the
owner of the house, *ittūra* and *umalla* refer to the husband whose
wife deserted him.[90]   Lines 72-75 can therefore be interpreted
as: "If the man, whose wife had run away from him, turns away
from the river (ordeal, i.e., refuses to take part in it), (the
owner of the house) being guiltless, he (the prosecuting husband) will pay the expenses in full for the river (ordeal)."
The stative *zāku* (line 74) here[91] seems to point to circumstances under which the legal consequence of line 75 is justified, thus constituting a motive clause.

2. MAL A 23

This law deals with the procuration of a married woman for
sexual purposes by another woman and considers, among others,
the following situation: the mistress brings an innocent married woman into her house by using some kind of excuse[92] and
delivers her to a man who sexually assaults her. The law then
states: *šum-ma iš-tu* É *i-na ú-ṣa-i-ša ki-i ni-ku-tu-ú-ni*
taq-ti-bi MÍ *ú-uš-šu-ru za-ku-a-at* ("If, when she left the
house, she declared that she has been ravished, they shall let
the woman go free, she being guiltless," lines 33-34).[93] This
is followed by a verdict of death penalty to be imposed upon
the adulterer and the procuress (lines 35-36). The stative
za-ku-a-at (line 34b), which follows the legal consequence in
line 34a, seems to express the underlying reason for the ac-
quittal of the victimized married woman, thus constituting a
motive clause.

3. <u>MAL A 29</u>

This law regulates the disposition of certain goods after
the husband's death. It specifies that the husband's brothers
have no claim to the wife's dowry, to what she brought from her
father's house and to whatever her father-in-law gave her on
her entry, *a-na* DUMU.MEŠ-*ša za-a-ku* ("they being reserved for
her children," line 16).[94] Line 16 (cf. LH 162) seems to indicate the underlying reason for the law's verdict, thus functioning as a motive clause.[95]

4. <u>MAL A 36</u>

As noted above, this law deals with the case of a deserted
wife. Of the two situations it considers, the law states in
the first that if the husband, who has apparently gone on a
business trip, stays away for five years, his childless wife
can remarry at the beginning of the sixth year. The text then
reads:

> 101.   *mu-us-sà i-na a-la-ki la-a i-qar-ri-ba-še*
> 102.   *a-na mu-ti-ša ur-ke-e za-ku-at*

(101)"Her husband on coming (back) shall not claim her, (102)she
being exclusively her later husband's."[96] Line 102 can be interpreted as justifying the prohibition of line 101, hence
functioning as a motivating sentence.

5. <u>MAL A 38</u>

This law deals with a case of divorce in which the wife is
still living in her father's house. Her husband, upon divorc-
ing her, can take back the jewels (*dumāqi*)[97] which he had bestowed upon her, but *te-er-ḫe-te ša-a ub-lu-ú-ni la i-qar-rib
a-na* MÍ *za-a-ku* ("he shall not claim the *terḫatu*[98] which he had
brought, it being reserved for the woman," lines 23-25).[99]
Here the prohibition to claim the *terḫatu* is followed by an
asyndetic sentence which seems to spell out the reason behind
it.

General Observations

The following general observations can be made on the basis of the study of individual motive clauses in LH and MAL.

(1) In LH, eighteen (nineteen with LH 47) possible motive clauses were identified.[100]   The percentage of the motivated legal prescriptions in the preserved part of the corpus is about 6%.[101]   In MAL, eight possible motive clauses were noted.[102]   The percentage of the motivated legal prescriptions in the preserved part of the corpus is approximately 5%.[103]

(2) In LH and in MAL, motive clauses appear only within laws formulated in the conditional. *šumma awīlum* type. None of the third person commands found in either of the two collections is accompanied by motivations.

(3) Motive clauses are formulated either asyndetically or by means of grammatical particles, i.e., *aššum*, possibly *kî*, or *-ma*.

(4) With the exception of LH 11 where a primary as well as a secondary motive clause appears in lines 1 and 2, neither LH nor MAL features multiple motivation; each motivated law is accompanied by a single rationale, whether formulated by a grammatical particle or asyndetically.

(5) All of the motive clauses are in the third person. They appear as short, terse and positive statements.

(6) Motive clauses introduced by *aššum* always refer to inner-legal matters and, in fact, accomplish their function by underscoring the key element(s) within the case. As such, they do not yield new information that cannot be gleaned from the laws themselves. In the words of Yaron, "they are all repetitive."[104]   As noted above, even LH 136 does not constitute an exception to this general pattern. It is only among the other types of motivations, that is, *kî*, *-ma* and asyndeton, that the reason or purpose behind a given law is specifically expressed.

MOTIVE CLAUSES IN LITERARY GENRES OTHER THAN LAW

In Akkadian literature motive clauses, whether introduced by the grammatical particles *aššum*, *kî*, *-ma* (followed by the present tense) or formulated asyndetically, are found in a number of genres.

Among prose texts, the conjunction *aššum* is featured in
letters,[105] historical documents,[106] contracts and similar
legal documents,[107] law suits,[108] and mathematical texts.[109]
In poetic compositions, it is found in epics,[110] prayers,[111]
and incantations.[112] Among sayings, it appears in edicts[113]
and popular proverbs.[114]

The conjunction *kî* is found as a motive introduction in
letters[115] and in historical texts.[116] There are examples of
-ma introducing final clauses in epics and myths.[117] Asyndetic
motive clauses are heavily concentrated in wisdom instructions.[118]

This survey shows that motivation is a common literary
device found in a large number of literary genres, although
the frequency of its use varies from genre to genre. It is
noteworthy, however, that the only genre where motive clauses
appear profusely is wisdom instruction. A closer look at this
genre is therefore warranted.

In cuneiform literature the number of texts composed in
the wisdom instruction form is rather limited. "The Instructions of Šuruppak,"[119] written in Sumerian, is a fairly long
composition (281 lines) and contains advice given by Šuruppak,
survivor of the Flood, to his son Ziusudra. Asyndetic clauses
frequently motivate those teachings expressed in the wisdom
instruction form.[120]

Another Sumerian text, "Gilgamesh, Enkidu and the Nether-
world,"[121] although not considered wisdom literature per se,
incorporates the instructions of Gilgamesh to Enkidu (lines
185-203)[122] formulated in the wisdom instruction form. These
instructions are often accompanied by asyndetic motive
clauses.[123]

In Akkadian, the major wisdom text composed in the instruction form is a collection of moral exhortations referred
to as "Counsels of Wisdom."[124] Lambert assigns it to the
Cassite period.[125] Only one section, namely lines 81-96, contains strict vocational instruction, while the rest seems to
have general application. All of the motive clauses found
therein are asyndetic.[126]

In addition to Mesopotamian texts, a few instruction texts
in Akkadian have been found at Ugarit. The principal wisdom
text is "Instructions of Šube-Awilum."[127] The instructions are
directed to his son Zur(?)-ranku on the occasion of his departure from his paternal home. J. Nougayrol remarks that the
text reflects the characteristics of western middle-Babylonian,
both in terms of syntax and vocabulary,[128] and displays the
following structure in its composition: advice (formulated
mostly as a prohibitive), a motive clause (expressed asyndetically) and a statement of consequence.[129]

It must be pointed out that the wisdom instruction genre
does not constitute an isolated phenomenon in Mesopotamia but
is indeed part of an "international genre"[130] for the entire
ancient Near East, with representative works, in addition to
those in Sumerian and Akkadian, also in Egyptian, Aramaic and,
as noted above, in Hebrew. Among those, the genre itself is
nowhere more fully represented than in Egypt.

A large number of instruction texts has been recovered in
Egyptian language.[131] Among those, the most important are
Ptahhotep,[132] Kagemni,[133] Merikare,[134] Ani[135] and Amenemopet.[136]
In other texts only a small part is composed in the instruction
form: Amenemhet,[137] Duauf,[138] Lansing,[139] Onchsheshonqy,[140]
The Teachings of King Ammenemes I to his son Sesostris,[141]
Admonitions of an Egyptian Sage,[142] and a text simply called
"A New Moralizing Text."[143]

Although most of the Egyptian instructions are formulated
with a special elite group in mind, constituting texts for
educating young officials who aspire to positions of responsibility (e.g., Ptahhotep, Merikare, Kagemni), there are some
which are more general in scope and directed to a broader
audience (e.g., Ani and Onchsheshonqy).

In most of these instruction texts, the motive clauses are
formulated asyndetically.[144] In others, there is a combination
of asyndetic motive clauses and those introduced by the copula
"$\check{\imath}w$" which is generally placed at the head of clauses that are
essentially subordinate and commonly circumstantial. This
copula is regularly rendered as "for."[145]

The Aramaic version of "The Words of Ahiqar"[146] contains a
variety of wisdom genres such as proverbs, parables, allego-
ries, fables and instructions.[147] It is usually dated to the
fifth or fourth century B.C.E.[148] Only a small part of the
work consists of instruction proper, concentrated in parts of
columns vii, ix and x (partly damaged). Most of the instructions are general in character and are not limited in their
application to a person training for high office. The motive
clauses therein are expressed by כִּי,[149] asyndetically,[150] and,
possibly, by *waw*.[151]

To this list must be added the wisdom instructions in the
Hebrew Bible to which reference was made in the previous
chapter.

The high number of motive clauses contained in wisdom
instruction texts coming from Egypt and Ugarit can be contrasted with the sporadic use of motivation in other literary
genres of the same social and cultural environment.[152] This
comparison as well as the heavy use of motivation already noted
in the wisdom instructions of Mesopotamia and Israel makes it
abundantly clear that among all the known literary genres of
the ancient Near East, motive clauses are "at home" primarily
in wisdom instructions.

The geographic distribution of the wisdom instructions in
the ancient Near East and the varying number of such works recovered at different places--unless attributed to accidents of
discovery or the destruction of the media upon which they were
recorded--point to the great prominence that the genre had in
the West (i.e., primarily in Egypt, but also in Ugarit and
Israel) rather than in Mesopotamia.[153] This observation adds
support to those who argue that Egyptian wisdom literature has
had considerable influence on certain biblical wisdom texts.[154]

Having surveyed the use of motivation in cuneiform literature and, in particular, in wisdom instructions, one can ask
whether it is possible to discover the source of influence
under which the motive clauses in LH and MAL were formulated
and the function which they have within the laws.

The determination of the source of influence presents
serious difficulties, primarily because of the very low percentage of motivation noted both in LH and MAL. Nothing in the

formulation of these few motive clauses points, with relative
assurance, to a specific genre featuring motive clauses, either
occasionally or as part of its literary form. That the legal
motive clauses were formulated in the same manner as those
found in wisdom instructions in Akkadian--and perhaps under
their influence--is rendered doubtful for a variety of reasons:
(1) Whereas motive clauses in Akkadian wisdom instruction texts
are expressed only in asyndetic manner, legal motive clauses
are formulated both by grammatical particles as well as asyndetically; (2) unlike their instruction counterpart, legal
motive clauses are formulated impersonally, totally lacking the
second person address; (3) unlike wisdom instructions, the
legal motive clauses are mostly repetitive.

A similar difficulty arises in searching for the function
of these motive clauses. Although their apparent purpose is to
provide a justification for the verdict of the law, the reason
for doing this is nowhere clearly stated. This can be inferred
only from the texts themselves.

In *mīšarum*-edicts, which have the force of law, the insertion of the regular *mīšarum* clause within a particular provision
of the edict most probably indicates that it is directly affected by the edict and therefore requires an immediate, albeit
temporary implementation, while those sections of the edict
lacking the standard justifying formula constitute permanent
reforms.[155]

What of the motive clauses appearing in LH and MAL? In
the case of LH 136, Driver and Miles said that the motive clause
aššum ālšu izēru "gives the substance of the reply which the
wife and her new husband are entitled to make and thereby rebut
the claim to take her back; it gives the reason, which will be
pleaded, why this claim fails."[156] These scholars are, however,
silent regarding the function of the other motive clauses in LH
and MAL. In any event, their explanation of the use of the
motive clause in LH 136 can only be viewed as conjecture.

It is questionable whether motive clauses here have a
teaching function, not only on account of the differences noted
above between the legal motive clauses and those found in wisdom instructions, but also because it is not known if cuneiform
laws as a whole had, among others, a pedagogic goal or use.[157]

It is most likely that the original Hammurabi stele stood
in the Esagila.[158]   The epilogue explicitly invites any aggrieved
party to come and ascertain the law that applies to his case.[159]
Also, it is known that the LH were constantly copied. This is
clearly attested by the numerous fragments dating from the Old
Babylonian to the Neo-Babylonian periods.[160] This may show
that the LH were known to a certain segment of the population[161]
but does not constitute clear and sufficient evidence for as-
cribing a didactic aim to the corpus.

The prologue and the epilogue of LH speak of the king's
social and political achievements. They stress, in particular,
that Hammurabi established law and justice (*kittam u mīšaram*)[162]
thus promoting the welfare of the people;[163] that he has inscribed his precious words, namely his laws, in order to give
justice to the oppressed;[164] that he is a "king of justice"
(*šar mēšarim*)[165] and a "shepherd of the people";[166] that he
prays his name be spoken in reverence forever in Esagila,[167]
with various gods speaking on his behalf before the great Mar-
duk and Ṣarpanitum.[168] This "autopanegyric,"[169] as Paul calls
it, seems to have been written in order to bring to the attention of the gods the king's deeds and accomplishments.

The cuneiform law collections in general and LH in particular, with their elaborate prologues and epilogues of historic and religious nature,[170] are presently viewed primarily
as "royal apologia and testaments"[171] directed to the gods and
aiming at obtaining their good favors.[172] If this were indeed
the case, then the legal motive clauses take on a special
significance. They can be interpreted as an extra means of
underscoring the fine sense of justice that permeates the prescriptions of a given law corpus and thus deserving additional
consideration on the part of the gods.

BIBLICAL AND CUNEIFORM LEGAL MOTIVE CLAUSES:
A COMPARISON

The following points emerge as a result of a comparison
between the motive clauses in biblical legislation and those
found in cuneiform legal corpora.

(1) The first item to be noted here is the relative scarcity of motive clauses in cuneiform laws and their greater frequency in biblical legislation. Among the ancient Near Eastern law collections, they appear, as we saw, only in LH and MAL, and there in small numbers. Even the BC, which represents the closest parallel to the ancient Near Eastern legal corpora in terms of both context and legal formulation and is considered to be a very early law corpus in the Bible (ca. thirteenth century B.C.E.),[173] has a much higher percentage of motivated laws (ca. 16%) than the LH (ca. 6%), which was compiled probably towards the end of Hammurabi's reign (ca. mid-eighteenth century B.C.E.),[174] and the MAL (ca. 5%), believed to come from about the end of the twelfth century B.C.E.[175] This low rate in LH and MAL shows that legal motivation is not characteristic of cuneiform laws and its appearance is rather "unusual."[176]

(2) Whereas in cuneiform laws motive clauses are found only in laws formulated in the conditional $šumma$ $awīlum$ form, in the Bible legal motive clauses appear in laws formulated both in the conditional as well as unconditional form, with the majority accompanying second person commands or prohibitions.

(3) In both cuneiform and biblical laws, motive clauses are expressed by means of grammatical particles as well as asyndetically. In cuneiform laws, the introductory grammatical particles are limited to the conjunction $aššum$, perhaps $kī$ (both expressing cause) and -ma (expressing purpose). This is noteworthy, for in addition to the first two, Akkadian texts contemporary with LH and MAL were capable of expressing causality in different ways and using a number of other particles, such as $ištu$ (with -ma)[177] and $kīma$.[178] They could also indicate purpose by -ma plus the precative.[179] The restriction of the motive introductions to a few grammatical forms appears like a deliberate effort on the part of the legislators to keep a uniformity of expression in the formulation of these laws, just as there seems to have been a tendency to introduce the laws in LH and MAL almost exclusively with $šumma$ ($awīlum$).[180] In biblical law, on the other hand, there is a greater variety of motive introductions, numbering as many as fifteen kinds. Not all appear in every law collection, but among the larger

ones, even with the lowest number, PC has five, while D, with
the highest number, has twelve.

(4) With one exception in LH 11, LH and MAL do not feature
multiple motivation. In biblical law collections, both early
and late, there are many examples of multiple motivation,
whether formulated by means of grammatical particles, asyndetically, or both.

(5) Unlike the motive clauses in LH and MAL, which are
expressed impersonally, legal motive clauses in the Bible are
formulated either impersonally or using the second person
address and, rarely, the first person. The element of parenesis, which is prevalent in biblical laws, particularly in D,
is totally absent in cuneiform law collections.

(6) In cuneiform laws, motive clauses introduced by *aššum*
always refer to inner-legal matters and, in fact, achieve their
aim by underscoring the key element in the case. Aside from
the possible example of *kî* in MAL 45, the rationale behind a
given law appears to be expressed only by *-ma* and asyndetic
motive clauses. In biblical law, although a few motive clauses
do underscore the key element in the case, the large majority,
whether introduced by a grammatical particle or not, add new
information and actually spell out the presuppositions of the
laws to which they are attached.

It is noteworthy that, unlike biblical laws, no cuneiform
law is ever motivated by reference to an historic event, a
promise of well-being or, for that matter, a divine will. In
fact, in these laws the deity is completely silent,[181] yielding
its place to a human lawgiver whose main concern is economic
rather than religious.[182] Biblical law, on the other hand,
ascribed in its totality to God both in terms of source and
authorship,[183] displays a concern that goes beyond the economic, enveloping all aspects of community life, whether past,
present and future, and incorporating both the strictly cultic/
sacral and that which remains outside of it. God, it is believed, speaks not only through His laws but frequently also
through their motive clauses, at times explicitly so.

(7) Finally, there seems to be a difference regarding the
literary source of influence as well as the function of the

motive clauses in the respective legal systems. The motive
clauses in biblical laws, to a large extent, appear to have
been formulated like the motivations found in wisdom instructions and probably under the influence of wisdom literature in
general. Ultimately, they seem to point to a teaching function. In cuneiform laws, however, the meagre number of motive
clauses makes it difficult to determine their source of influence, although it seems unlikely that they stemmed from wisdom
literature. It is plausible that their primary function was to
curry the favors of the gods by underscoring the lawmaker's
true concern for justice.

In sum, although both biblical and some cuneiform law
collections feature motive clauses, they display differences
in terms of form, content and function.

NOTES

CHAPTER III

[1]Gemser, "The Importance of the Motive Clause," 52; cf. 63.

[2]Ibid., 62.

[3]Ibid.

[4]Ibid., 63. On the same page (n. 1), Gemser states that "the motivations of explanatory and ethical contents in the Hittite Instructions for Temple Officials...hardly come for comparison on account of their very specific destination." The author was referring to #2, 3, 4, 7, 8, 9, 10, 13, 14, 16, 18, 19. See *ANET*, 207-210; also, see below n. 152.

[5]Cassuto, *Exodus*, 263. The same statement has been preserved in the following and latest edition of the book in the Hebrew original (5th, 1969).

[6]Von Rad, *Theology*, 1. 198. The author credits Gemser on p. 197 n. 19.

[7]J. Muilenburg, *The Way of Israel: Biblical Faith and Ethics* (New York: Harper Torchbooks, 1965) 67. See also his article in *HUCA* 32 (1961) 151. Credit to Gemser is given in *The Way of Israel* (67 n. 1) and in *HUCA* 32 (151 n. 49).

[8]Koch, *Biblical Tradition*, 22. Reference to Gemser is found on p. 22 n. 16 and on p. 10 n. 16.

[9]De Vaux, *Ancient Israel*, 149. Though Gemser is not explicitly credited here, the author's acceptance of Gemser's four-part classification of the motive clauses, together with his claim for their uniqueness, clearly indicates that he has been under the influence of Gemser. In fact, in the bibliography (p. 530), Gemser's article is specifically mentioned.

[10]Driver and Miles, *Babylonian Laws*, 1. 286-87 and 287 n. 1.

[11]Yaron, *The LE*, 75 n. 20. In Volume 1, Driver and Miles overlooked LH 146, for they considered the clause as being part of the protasis (304). In Volume 2, however, they connected it with the apodosis (57).

[12]Weiser's statement has been preserved in the latest translation published in 1963 (*The Old Testament: Its Formation and Development* [New York: Association] 55). The quote is taken from the 1963 edition which repeats what was said on p. 48 of the 1949 German edition.

[13]Torralba, *EB* 29 (1970) 84. Translation is mine.

[14]Paul, *Book of the Covenant*, 39. Reference to Gemser is found on the same page (n. 2).

[15]Ibid. Beyerlin refers, by way of example, to LH 136:68 ("Die Paränese im Bundesbuch," 19 n. 39).

[16]Paul, *Book of the Covenant*, 39 n. 2. The reference is to Yaron (*The LE*, 75 n. 20).

[17]Uitti, *The Motive Clause*, 270.

[18]Ibid., 270-71.

[19]ARM, 15, 177 adds, "adv.?, dès lors(?). Cf. 2, 48:19(?); 5, 15:8(?). It also suggests that it be supplemented by *ki-a-am*. However, A. Finet maintains that *aššum* in these cases (and in 6, 35:21) can be considered an adverb by itself (*L'Accadien des letres de Mari* [Bruxelles: Palais des Académies, 1956] #54a). In a letter appearing in YOS (2, 81:13), *aš-šum i-na ki-it-ti-im ta-ra-am-mi-in-<ni>* 1 URUDU.ŠUN *šu-bi-li-im* ("If thou truly dost love me [then] send me one bronze pot"), the particle *aššum* is probably a mistake for *šumma*. See YOS, 2, 22; cf. *CAD*, A/2, 466 under *aššum*.

[20]See *aššum* in *CAD*, A/2, 466-67; *AHW*, 84; ARM, 15, 177. In LH or MAL, *aššum* does not appear with the meaning "so that" or "that."

[21]*CAD*, A/2, 467; ARM, 15, 177; *AHW*, 84.

[22]*GAG*, #176a.

[23]*GAG*, #158.

[24]*GAG*, #176; *CAD*, K, 319; *AHW*, 469; J. Aro, *StudOr* 22, 43.

[25]T. J. Meek, "The Asyndeton Clause in the Code of Hammurabi," *JNES* 5 (1946) 64-72. See also the discussion in Driver and Miles (*Babylonian Laws*, 2. 357-61).

[26]But see below in MAL, A, 23 where it follows.

[27]The first five lines of the law are restored; see Driver and Miles, *Babylonian Laws*, 2. 37. For a different restoration, see R. Borger, *Babylonisch-assyrische Lesestücke*, Heft I (Rome: Pontificum Institutum Biblicum, 1963) 18. Part of the law is translated in *CAD*, A/2, 461 under *aššābu*. The motive clause is here rendered as, "because he (the owner) has evicted the tenant (before the completion of his term)."

[28]On the role of the *tamkārum*, see Driver and Miles, *Babylonian Laws*, 1. 120; on *samallûm*, see ibid., 198. See also W. Leemans, *The Old Babylonian Merchant* (Leiden: Brill, 1950).

[29]Meek renders the verb *nakāru* as "dispute": "because he had a dispute with his trader" (*ANET*, 170). However, the verb basically means "to deny"; see *AHW*, 719.

[30]The derivation of *ittabit* is not very clear. In a parallel law (i.e., LE 30), we find *it-ta-bi-it* in text A, line 46, but *it-ta-ah-bi-it* in text B, line 8. A. Goetze states that the two verbs "cannot derive from the same verb"; *The Laws of Eshnunna*, 85 n. 1. He takes *ittabit* from *nābutum* ("to flee") found only in the N stem. Von Soden is of the same opinion; see *GAG*, #97 *l*, 128. Driver and Miles, however, derive it from the N stem of *abātu*, "to flee"; *Babylonian Laws*, 2. 363 (Glossary). *CAD* considers *habātu* ("to go astray, to move over," etc.) as a variant of *abātu* B (here used in the N stem) meaning "to turn away"; A/1, 47. Yaron suggests that in LE 30, *ittahbit* (instead of *ittabit*) may be a phonetic spelling; *The LE*, 6 n. 22.

[31]Yaron, *The LE*, 75 n. 20.

[32]E. Szlechter, "Effets de l'absence (volontaire) en droit assyro-babylonien," *OrNS* 34 (1965) 296.

[33]*EA* 158:37 (letter of Aziri). For other examples in *CAD*, see *zêru* (97-99) where references are made to *TCL*, 4, 5:10 (OA let.); *BE*, 183 r. 24 (*kudurru*); *BWL*, 240 ii 29 (prov.).

[34]*CAD*, Z, 97-99 (under *zêru*); also *kā[ru li-id]-di-ka nībiru li-zer-ka* ("may the har[bor rej]ect you, the ferry landing refuse you [for ever]"). However, in Vol. 6(H), which appeared in 1956, under *hadû* (p. 27), and in Vol. 8(K), dated 1971, under *kāru*, the text is restored as follows: *ka-a-[ru aj ih]dīka nībiru lizīrka*. In Vol. 6, the translation is, "may the harbor not welcome you, may the (place where the) ferry (lands) hate you!" In Vol. 8 we find, "may the mooring place not welcome you, the embarkation point of the ferry reject you." In *ANET* (96), the verse is rendered as, "May the landing-pl[ace not rejoice in thee], May the place of crossing renounce thee." Thus in *CAD* (except for Vol. 6), in Vols. 8 and 21 and also in *ANET*, *zêru* is understood as "to reject."

[35]*ARM* 1, 2:7-8; G. Dossin, "L'article 142/143 du Code du Hammurabi," *RA* 42 (1948) 121. For other examples, see ad loc.

[36]Ibid. Translation is mine.

[37]Similarity is based on the substance of the law as well as the terminology employed therein, to such extent that Yaron feels that "the draftsmen of Hammurabi had before them either the actual text of LE itself, or a comparable one from a source not available to us"; *The LE*, 74.

[38]Dossin, "L'article 142/143 du CH," 121.

[39]On *nadītum*, see Driver and Miles, *Babylonian Laws*, 1. 364-67; *AHW*, 704.

[40]The term used is *abbuttum*. Its exact meaning is not at all clear, though all agree that it is some sign of slave status. It may indicate a characteristic hair style or the metal clasp around the *abbuttu*-lock. *CAD* (A/1, 48) takes it in the first sense. See also *AHW* (5) under *abbuttu(m)*. According to Szlechter, the term indicates an engraved tattoo; see "Essai d'explication des clauses: *muttatam gullubu*, *abbuttam šakānu* et *abbuttam gullubu*," *ArOr* 17/2 (1949) 402-12.

[41]Meek translates: "...If later that female slave has claimed equality with her mistress because she bore children, her mistress may not sell her,..." (*ANET*, 172). This translation goes against the general usage in Akkadian. The clause starting with *aššum* usually belongs to that which follows and not to what it precedes; see *GAG*, #176a. Furthermore, in conditional sentences starting with *šumma*, consecutive action is indicated by the perfect tense such as in LH 146: *mārī ittalad warkānum...uštamher*; see *GAG*, #161e. This is immediately followed by the clause *aššum* DUMU.MEŠ. *uldu* where the verb is in the preterite and not in the perfect, thus indicating that it does not belong to what it precedes but to what it follows. *CAD* (A/1, under *abbuttu*, 48) correctly translates: "due to the fact that she (the unsubmissive slave girl) has borne sons, her mistress cannot sell her"; see also above, n. 11.

[42]The problem revolves primarily around the meaning of the verb *rakāsu*. V. Scheil ("Les nourices en Babylonie et le #194 du code," *RA* 11 [1914] 179-82) and, following him, Driver and Miles (*Babylonian Laws*, 1. 406, 2. 248) maintain that the verb means literally "to bind (to the breast)." Substitution of the child, they say, is not the law's concern. As Scheil has already indicated, substitution involves theft, and LH 14 has a death penalty for anyone who steals an infant, whereas in LH 194 only the breast(s?) of the nurse is cut off. The law's intention is to impose upon the nurse the obligation to reveal to the parents of any new child the fact that she lost a previous one while nursing it. Failure to do this brings a penalty. Driver and Miles render the key parts of the case as follows: "(if) the nurse then binds another child (to her breast) without (the knowledge of) its father or its mother, they shall convict her" etc. (2. 77). S. Greengus proposes a different interpretation. He translates the verb *rakāsu* as "to bind by agreement" and suggests that the question at hand is indeed one of secret adoption of another child and hence one of substitution ("The Old Babylonian Marriage Contract," *JAOS* 89 [1969] 506 n. 11). He finds support for his interpretation in Ras Shamra texts where the expression *ana marūti/ahhūti rakāsu* (see MRS 6/1, p. 224 with three examples in 16.292:10, 16.344: 5, 19.92:5) actually means "to bind by agreement" and normally defines the act of adoption. Furthermore, he points out that LH 194 follows directly upon #185-193 which deal with adoption.

The verb *rakāsu*, he adds, with the meaning "to bind by agreement," is similarly attested in OA texts. Reference is here
made to H. Lewy, *ArOr* 18/3 (1950) 377 n. 58. Greengus would
therefore translate the key part of the case as follows: "(if)
the nurse then binds by agreement (i.e., adopts) another child
without (the consent of) its father and its mother, they shall
convict her," etc. Greengus' interpretation is very attractive.
It gets around Scheil's objection: the wet-nurse does not steal
a new child but binds a new one by agreement (i.e., adopts),
has linguistic support, and LH 194 becomes an integral part of
the laws dealing with adoption. In addition, it can be pointed
out that the preposition *balum*, when referring to people,
usually means without the knowledge or consent of and not without telling anyone (e.g., see *CAD*, B, 70, under *balu*). The
latter is generally expressed by adding to it the verb *ša'ālu*
("to ask"), such as *balum ša-al abiša u ummiša* ("without asking
her parents," e.g., LE 26:30[A], 27:31-32[A]). On the other
hand, however, the act of adoption is expressed in Ras Shamra
both by *ana/ina marūti/ahhūti rakāsu* and by *ana marūtim leqû*
(e.g., MRS 6,200:2), whereas in LH only by *ana marūtim leqû*
(e.g., LH 185, 186, 190, 191). If Greengus' interpretation
were to be accepted, then it would have to be assumed that only
in LH 194 the lawgiver meant by *rakāsu*, "to make an agreement
(for an adoption)."

[43]The law itself speaks of UBUR-*ša* ("her breast"). The
noun is in the singular, yet it is possible that it is taken
here in the collective sense, i.e., "her breasts," since the
text does not specify "one of her breasts." See Driver and
Miles, *Babylonian Laws*, 1. 406 n. 12; see also their comments
in 2. 248.

[44]Driver and Miles, *Babylonian Laws*, 1. 427.

[45]The term *ilku* basically refers to a certain kind of duty
that a person has to carry out when holding land in tenure from
a higher authority. The nature of this duty varied; see *CAD*,
I, 73-80, under *ilku* A.

[46]Similarly, Meek translates, "in order that his mother
may rear him" (*ANET*, 167).

[47]Perhaps a lay priestess of a lower class (cf. LH 137,
144, 183, 184); see also the discussion in Driver and Miles,
Babylonian Laws, 1. 371-74.

[48]See above, n. 39.

[49]For *bišu* ("movable property"), see *CAD*, B, 271, where
the term is rendered as "personal property."

[50]Thus, Meek in *ANET*, 172.

[51]Similarly, Meek translates, "since that seignior is a
thief, he shall be put to death" (*ANET*, 166). Even if *šarraq*
is taken as a declarative statement ("he is a thief"), it implies motivation.

[52]Similarly, Meek translates, "and since the seller was the thief, he shall be put to death" (*ANET*, 166).

[53]Similarly, Meek translates, "since the (professed) purchaser was the thief, he shall be put to death" (*ANET*, 166).

[54]The expression *sà-ar* is from *sarāru*, meaning "to be a liar"; see *AHW*, 1028(1a). On *tušamma*, see *GAG*, #20i. Instead of *id-ki*, read rather *id-di*! See *CAD*, D, 125, under *dekû*.

[55]Similarly, Meek translates, "since he was a cheat and started a false report, he shall be put to death" (*ANET*, 166).

[56]Driver and Miles, *Babylonian Laws*, 2. 98. They, however, seem to consider only the second half as a motivating clause: "he is a felon since he has uttered a slander: he shall be put to death" (1. 17).

[57]It is very difficult to determine who is the subject of the law. The likelihood is that it is the buyer who was also the subject of the preceding section; see discussion in Driver and Miles, *Babylonian Laws*, 1. 101.

[58]Similarly, Meek translates, "since that seignior was a cheat, he shall bear the penalty of that case" (*ANET*, 166).

[59]On *šeriktum*, dowry given to the bride by the father, see Driver and Miles, *Babylonian Laws*, 1. 271-75.

[60]Meek translates, "since her dowry belongs to her children" (*ANET*, 173). In *Die Gesetze Hammurabis* (Wien: Alfred Hölder, 1903), D. H. Müller offers both a German and a Hebrew translation of LH. Müller renders the clause in LH 162 as, "denn (in the Hebrew, כי) ihre Mitgift gehört dem Hause ihres Vaters" (44).

[61]The nature of *terḫatu* is not clear. Various theories have been advanced in order to explain it. According to Driver and Miles, it is a marriage gift given by the bridegroom to his new father-in-law (*Babylonian Laws*, 1. 261). Others, however, consider it a "bride-money" paid in order to purchase the bride. For a summary of different points-of-view, see Yaron, *The LE*, 111 and references in n. 10, in particular, B. Landsberger, "Jungfräulichkeit: Ein Beitrag zum Thema 'Beilager und Eheschliessung' (mit einem Anhang: Neue Lesungen und Deutungen im Gesetzbuch von Ešnunna)," *Symbolae iuridicae et historicae Martino David dedicatae* (Leiden: Brill, 1968) 2. 93-94.

[62]Meek translates, "since her dowry belongs to her father's house" (*ANET*, 173). Similarly, Müller, as in n. 61.

[63]A *ḫirtum* is a man's first wife; see R. Borger, *Lesestücke* (I), p. lviii (glossary); cf. *CAD*, H, 200.

[64]In Akk. *nudunnu*. On the nature of this gift, see Driver and Miles, *Babylonian Laws*, 1. 265-66; *AHW*, 800; cf. Cardascia, *Lois assyriennes*, 156-57.

[65]The term for "estate" is *(w)arkatu*; see *CAD*, A/2, 277, under *arkatu*(3b).

[66]Meek translates, "since her heritage belongs to her children" (*ANET*, 173). Similarly, Müller renders it as, "denn (in the Hebrew, כִּי) nach ihr[em Tode] gehört es ihren Kindern" (47). Driver and Miles, too, understand the phrase as providing a motivation for the law at hand; see *Babylonian Laws*, 1. 351.

[67]An *ēntum* is a high priestess; see *CAD*, E, 172; cf. Driver and Miles, *Babylonian Laws*, 1. 361-62.

[68]See above, n. 39.

[69]See *AHW*, 1036, sub *sekretu(m)*. The word denotes a social class of woman connected with temple and palace. However, the exact meaning is not known. Meek renders it as "a votary" (*ANET*, 174); Driver and Miles as "an epicene" (*Babylonian Laws*, 2. 71; see also discussion in 1. 367-68). For additional references, see A. Falkenstein, *OLZ* 56 (1961) 372-73 (I owe this last reference to Dr. A. Sjöberg).

[70]See *uppulu* in *CAD*, A/2, 165, under *apālu* A; *AHW*, 57, under *apālu* I(D).

[71]The term for "inheritance" is *aplūtu*; see *CAD*, A/2, 178(2a).

[72]Meek translates, "since her patrimony belongs to her brother" (*ANET*, 174). In fact, Meek starts the motive clause in line 9 and counts two consecutive motive clauses. Müller renders it as, "denn (in the Hebrew, כִּי) ihr Kindesanteil gehört ihren Brüdern" (*Die Gesetze Hammurabis*, 50). Driver and Miles, who do not usually refer to the motivating function of the asyndetic clauses in LH, clearly recognize that lines 18-19 "merely supply the reason for the prohibition" (*Babylonian Laws*, 2. 242; cf. 1. 376). On the other hand, it is unlikely that the asyndetic clauses containing finite verbs in LH 32: 35-38, 71:15-16, 137:11-13 (cf. 156:16-17, 172:39-40), 144: 26-27, 150:19-25, 177:53-60, 180:58, 181:74, 182:93, 191: 92-95--all of which are considered motive clauses by Meek in *ANET*--are really motive clauses. Each appears to constitute a legal consequence, as for instance, in Driver and Miles, ad loc.

[73]The term *mānaḫtu* comes from *anāḫu*, "to toil, exert oneself"; see *CAD*, A/2, 101, under *anāḫu* A. *Mānaḫtu* means both labor as well as the result of labor; see Driver and Miles, *Babylonian Laws*, 2. 175.

[74]*ana* A.ŠÀ is rendered in *CAD* (E, 251) as "abroad." Driver and Miles state that the husband's departure can be explained as going to work in the fields as a harvester (*Assyrian Laws*, 251). However, as Cardascia points out, the long absence can hardly be interpreted in this fashion. He proposes to take *ana eqli* in its general meaning, "away," involving either

agricultural work or a trip of a business nature (*Lois
assyriennes*, 187-88). Similarly, Szlechter renders the phrase
as "son époux est parti pour l'étranger" ("Effets de l'absence
volontaire," 292).

[75]It is not very clear whether the ruling of these last
seven lines (8-14) refers to both sections of the law or only
to the first case. Both Driver and Miles (*Assyrian Laws*, 255-
56) and Cardascia (*Lois assyriennes*, 190) feel that this ruling
cannot apply to the preceding case where the husband goes out
on a royal mission, or for that matter to the woman in the
first case who has children, since in either case the woman has
no right to remarry at all. Breaking this law brings the death
penalty on the basis of adultery (see LH 133b). The lawgiver,
they say, returns in lines 8-14 to the case where remarriage is
permissible beyond the deadline of five years and establishes a
penalty if the rule is broken. However, Szlechter points out
that LH 133b does not constitute a general law on adultery but
deals with a specific case, namely, the remarriage of a woman
during the absence of her husband who is a prisoner of war
("Effets de l'absence volontaire," 301). For more details, see
his article, "Effets de la captivité en droit assyro-
babylonien," *RA* 57 (1963) 183. LH 133b, therefore, cannot be
applied to our situation. He argues, and convincingly so, that
the last seven lines must indeed refer to both cases of MAL 36:
a woman who has not waited for the five year waiting period, as
well as one who got married in spite of the prohibition to do
so, is exposed to the dissolution of her second marriage. Her
former husband, upon his return, is entitled to take her and
her children away from her second husband ("Effets de l'absence volontaire," 301-305).

[76]The word *riksu* here presents a difficulty. Driver and
Miles translate, "because she has not respected the marriage
contract" (*Assyrian Laws*, 405). Similarly, *CAD* (A/1, 183),
under *aḫāzu*, has "because she had not waited (for the period
per) contract" and in A/2 (466-67), under *aššum*, "because she
did not respect the (terms of the) agreement." See also the
translations by Meek (*ANET*, 183) and Greengus ("The Old Babylonian Marriage Contract," 510). Yet, Cardascia seems to be
right when he argues that *riksu* does not have here the meaning
of marriage contract. The obligation to remain faithful is
more likely to be derived from the law itself rather than a
regular contract. The term *riksu*, he adds, should be translated as "the act of marriage," or to take it literally, "the
(marriage) bond" (*Lois assyriennes*, 191). Already V. Scheil
had rendered this line as "parce que selon la loi elle n'a pas
attendu" (*Recueil de lois assyriennes* [Paris: Paul Geuthner,
1921] 47). Similarly, Szlechter has "parce qu'elle n'a pas
attendu (les delais imposées par) l'acte (de mariage)" ("Effets
de la captivité," 294 n. 3). For the verb *qu'ʾû* (cf. col. V,
line 12, but also above in lines 95 and 98 in col. IV, "to
wait"), see *AHW*, 931. In line 13, read *ta-na-ḫi-zuʾ!-û-ni* (from
aḫāzu in the N stem; see *AHW*, 19; Cardascia, *Lois assyriennes*,
191) rather than *ta-na-ḫi-su-û-ni* (from *neḫēsu*, "to go away")
as did Scheil: "et s'est eloignée" (*Recueil*, 47).

[77]In line 66b, *ú-up-pu-šu* does not mean "to acquire" as rendered by Driver and Miles in *Assyrian Laws* (413), but "to assign"; see *CAD*, E, 232, under *epēšu*. As Cardascia remarks, "les fonctionnaires sont et demeurent de simples administrateurs des fiefs: il n'ont pas à acquiérir la tenure ni à en transférer la propriété à la femme, mais à l'attribuer ou à l'assigner (*epēšu*) à la femme" (*Lois assyriennes*, 223). Szlechter renders it as, "on lui attribuera" ("Effets de la captivité," *RA* 58 [1964] 25).

[78]*CAD*, A/1, 313, under *alāku* with *eqlu*. See also *CAD*, K, 318, under *kî*, for a similar rendition.

[79]*AHW*, 32, under *alāku* (III, 13).

[80]*RA* 58, pp. 25, 33 and n. 2. Translation is mine.

[81]Driver and Miles, *Assyrian Laws*, 485.

[82]Ibid. Furthermore, as Driver and Miles point out, if *kî* is taken as introducing a conditional clause, this would mean that the judges, after making inquiries, proceed to act without awaiting an answer.

[83]Here only a field is mentioned, not "field and house" as in line 65, undoubtedly for the sake of brevity; see Cardascia, *Lois assyriennes*, 222. From the LH we know that the fief usually consisted of a field, house and orchard (cf. LH 27, 28, 30, 31, 32, 36, 37, 38, 39).

[84]For "A.ŠÀ...*il-lu-ku-ú-ni*," see *CAD*, A/1, 313, under *alāku* with *eqlu*, meaning to perform *ilku* duty for a field.

[85]The clause is similarly understood by Driver and Miles who translate it as "inasmuch as he held a field in that city," etc. (*Assyrian Laws*, 413); by Meek, "since he held a field," etc. (*ANET*, 184); by Cardascia, "comme il tenait en fief un champ, on attribuera," etc. (*Lois assyriennes*, 218).

[86]In addition to most of these examples, Meek also identified asyndetic motive clauses in MAL, A, 12:17, 17:69, 17:88, 18:76, 25:64-85; C+G 10:18, 11:23; N 2:8. However, these are questionable. In MAL, A, 12, 17, 18, 19, 25 and N 2, the clause can well be taken as part of the description of the case. See Driver and Miles and Cardascia, ad loc. The texts of C+G 10 and 11 are partly damaged. The motive clause in C+G 10 and the motive introduction in C+G 11 are restored. On the other hand, Meek does not consider MAL, A, 36:102 as a motive clause, even though he does consider MAL, A, 38:25 a motive clause which has the same construction.

[87]The root of the verb is *šdd*, meaning "to withdraw, abandon, go away"; see Driver and Miles, *Assyrian Laws*, 525 (glossary); Carl Bezold, *Babylonisch-assyrisches Glossar* (Heidelberg: Carl Winter, 1926) 266. Driver and Miles have "run away" (*Assyrian Laws*, 397; cf. *CAD*, Z, 26; Meek has "deserted" (*ANET*, 182); Cardascia has "a quitté" (*Lois assyriennes*, 145).

[88]Driver and Miles (*Assyrian Laws*, 397) and Meek (*ANET*, 182) render *umalla* as "to fulfill." It really means to pay the expenses in full; see *CAD*, G, 77, under *gimru*; *AHW*, 289; Cardascia, *Lois assyriennes*, 145. Meek considers line 75 as the motive clause: "since he fulfilled the total (requirement) for the river (ordeal)."

[89]*CAD*, G, 77, under *gimru*(3b).

[90]Cardascia, *Lois assyriennes*, 151. This seems to be understood in this way also in *CAD*, Z, 26, under *zakû*(1b).

[91]However, it is also possible that the intention was to stipulate two consecutive legal consequences: the owner of the house is guiltless (*zāku*), first consequence; the prosecuting husband incurs expenses, second consequence. Elsewhere in the laws, *za-a-ku* (A 14:38, 47:17; B 6:47, 12:17) and *za-ku-at* (A 39:35) appear to constitute a legal consequence, not a motive clause.

[92]The meaning of *ki-i pi-i-gi* is not clear. Cardascia translates it as "par des paroles mensongères" (*Lois assyriennes*, 141 and n. 6). *AHW* (862) has for *pīgu*, "Belügen, falsche Angabe." *CAD* (K, 324, under *kî*) renders the expression as "through trickery."

[93]Meek translates, "since she is guiltless" (*ANET*, 182).

[94]*ana* plus *zakû* means, "reserved for," "being exclusive to"; see *CAD*, Z, 27, under *zakû*.

[95]Meek does not consider this as a motive clause; see *ANET*, 182. However, he considers a similar clause in MAL, A, 38:25 as a motive clause.

[96]Meek does not consider line 102 as constituting a motive clause; see *ANET*, 183.

[97]*CAD*, D, 179, under *dumāqu*; *AHW*, 175.

[98]On *terḫatu*, see n. 61 above.

[99]Driver and Miles render the last clause as: "he (then) is quit in respect to the woman" (*Assyrian Laws*, 405). This may possibly resolve the grammatical problem of the relationship between the feminine *terḫatu* and the masculine *zakû*, but it goes against the general usage of *ana* plus *zakû* meaning, "reserved for"; see above, n. 94.

[100]LH 11 features a primary and a secondary motive clause. Each of the other sixteen motivated laws in LH contains a single motive clause.

[101]Out of the 282 paragraphs, 20 are considerably damaged or not preserved at all. Of the remaining 262 paragraphs, some contain subsidiary cases (e.g., LH 8, 32, 141, 151 and others)

bringing the total number of separate legal prescriptions to
ca. 280, of which 17 (or, 18 with LH 47) are motivated (= ca.
6%). (Seventeen motivated prescriptions have 17 separate
motive clauses, for LH 11 features two motive clauses.)   It
should be kept in mind that even 282 does not represent the
total number of paragraphs that were recorded in LH. Because
of the erasure in the stele, a good number of laws have yet to
be recovered; see discussion in Driver and Miles, *Babylonian
Laws*, 1. 34.

[102]MAL, A, 36 contains two separate motive clauses. Each
of the other six motivated laws has a single motive clause.

[103]Of the 121 paragraphs found in tablets A to O (see
Cardascia, *Lois assyriennes*, 19-22), 41 are considerably
damaged or not preserved at all. Within the remaining 80
paragraphs, some have more than one case (e.g., MAL, A, 23, 24,
33, 36), bringing the total number of legal prescriptions to
158, of which only 8 are motivated (= ca. 5%).

[104]Yaron, *The LE*, 75 n. 20.

[105] E.g., F. Thureau-Dangin, "Textes de Mari," *RA* 33 (1936)
171, lines 13-15 (cf. *CAD*, A/2, 466, under *aššum*); ARM, 2, 62 r.
8-10; YOS 2, 117:5; 3,22:6; *CT* 33, 21:7-8; *BE* 17, 35:25; TCL 7,
72:13; *EA* 35:37; *ABL* 477 r. 5; and many others.

[106]For examples, see *CAD*, A/2, 247, under *aššum*.

[107]E.g., *MDP* 24, 379:7 (dealing with a gift); 28, 389:2
(dealing with inheritance); cf. *CAD*, A/2, 466, under *aššum*.

[108]E.g., TCL 1, 157:49; cf. *RA* 7 (1909/10), 121-22 and
CAD, A/2, 298, under *arnu*; PBS 5, 100 ii.1; cf. Ungnad, *HG*,
Vol. 6, No: 1760, p. 145. On both, see *CAD*, A/2, 466, under
aššum.

[109]E.g., *TMB* 190:23, 191:21, 193:25, 214:10, 227:10, 231:13.

[110]E.g., Thompson, *Epic of Gilgamish* 11. 118-19 (with
aš-šu; var. *ša*); 167-68 (with *aš-šu*); *Era* 1.121 (with *aš-šu*).
On both, see also *CAD*, A/2, 467, under *aššum*.

[111]Addressed to Bau, in *BMS* No:6, lines 74-76, p. 31;
cf. *CAD*, B, 58, under *bulluṭu*, and *AGH*, 46. For other examples, see *CAD*, A/2, 467, under *aššum*.

[112]E.g., *Maqlu* 1.18 (with *aš-šu*); cf. *AFO* 2, Beiheft 2
(ad loc), and *CAD*, A/2, 467, under *aššum*.

[113]There are many motive clauses in *mišarum*-edicts. The
most prevalent one is *aš-šum šar-rum mi-ša-ra-am a-na ma-tim
iš-ku-nu* ("because the king established a *mišarum* for the
land"). The formula is found in the Edict of Ammisaduqa eight
times: 1, 2, 10, 12, 13, 14, 17, 18, all according to Kraus'
text. For references on this text, see Chapter I, n. 288.
Outside of the standard *mišarum* formula, the edict contains
other motive clauses:

(1) *aš-šum i-na la si-ma-an ša-ad-du-ut-ti i-si-ru-ma*
u-ša-ad-di-nu ("because he prematurely collected (the
amount due to him) by means of pressure," #3 in Kraus
[#5 and translation in *RA* 63], lines 41-42). For
discussion of this text, see *RA* 63, 56-57.

(2) *aš-šum ka-ni-ik-šu u-wa-û ka-ni-ik-šu ih-he-pê*
("because he had distorted his document, his document
shall be voided," #4 in Kraus [#6 in *RA* 63], line 54;
translation in *ANET*, 527. See also *JCS* 15, 95).

(3) *aš-šum tup-pa-šu u-wu-û û a-wa-tam ik-ki-ru*
("because he distorted his tablet and denied the
[truth of the] matter," #5 in Kraus, lines 40-41;
translation in *JCS* 15, 94); cf. *ANET*, #7, 527.

(4) *aš-šum šar-rum* LÁL^hi.a^*na-ši* GÚ.U[N] *û-wa-aš-še-ru*
("because the king has remitted the arrears
of the palace tributary," #11, *ANET*, 527;
#9 in Kraus, lines 40-41. See also *JCS* 15,
95). On *naši biltim*, see *AHW*, 764.

[114]Proverbs rarely come with motive clauses. See, for
instance, *eqli-ya aššata ša lā muta mašil aššum bali errēšim*
("my field is like a woman without a husband, because it lacks
a cultivator"). This proverb is quoted four times by Rib-Abdi
of Byblos to the Egyptian king (VAB II 74:18-19, 75:15-17,
81:37-38, 90:42-44). It is the only proverb with an explanatory motive clause in Lambert's *BWL*, 233; cf. McKane, *Proverbs*,
185.

[115]E.g., *EA* I:67, 21:29, 38:23, 288:31; *ABL* 280:24, 1108
r. 8; YOS 3, 51:15; cf. *CAD*, K, 319, under *kî*.

[116]E.g., OIP 2, 42:26; cf. *CAD*, K, 319, under *kî*.

[117]E.g., *Enūma Eliš* I:131, 4:65; cf. *GAG*, #158-59; Gilg.
11:36; *Nergal and Ereškigal* 2:36; cf. *AnSt* 10 (1960) 112-13.

[118]See below for examples.

[119]*ANET*, 594-95. For the full text, see now Alster, *The
Instructions of Suruppak*, 34-51.

[120]For example, lines 14, 15, 16, 17, 18, 19, 20, 21, 38,
41, 42, 43 and many others.

[121]For the text and translation, see A. Shaffer, "Sumerian
Sources of Tablet XII of the Epic of Gilgamesh" (Dissertation,
University of Pennsylvania, 1963) 107-108. See also S. N.
Kramer's translation in *The Sumerians* (Chicago: University of
Chicago, 1970) 203.

[122]The text is also preserved in an Akkadian translation.
See Tablet XII, lines 10-30; cf. Shaffer and *ANET*, 97.

[123]See, for instance, lines 186, 188, 190, 192, 199.

[124]For text and translation, see *BWL*, 96-107; translation only in *ANET*, 426-27 (Pfeiffer) and 595-96 (Biggs). For discussion of the text, see McKane, *Proverbs*, 153-56.

[125]*BWL*, 97.

[126]See, for instance, lines 23, 27, 30, 33, 79, 84, 88, 133, 138. The text called "Advice to the Prince" (*BWL*, 110-15) does not have the form of instruction. The element of command is absent, and so are the motive clauses. As Lambert points out (p. 110), the writer, though leaving out the "If" (*šumma*), seems to have imitated the style of omens. The use of specialized omen terminology in the text and characteristic ideograms of omen literature bear this out.

[127]For text and translation, see J. Nougayrol, *Ugaritica V* (1968) text No:163 (RS 22.439) 273-90.

[128]Ibid., 274.

[129]Ibid., 274 n. 3.

[130]McKane, *Proverbs*, 6.

[131]On Egyptian wisdom instructions in general, see G. Posener, "Literature," *The Legacy of Egypt* (ed. J. R. Harris; Oxford: Clarendon, 1971) 220-55.

[132]*ANET*, 412-14; W. K. Simpson, ed., *The Literature of Ancient Egypt* (henceforth, *LAE*) (New Haven: Yale University, 1973) 159-76; McKane, *Proverbs*, 51-65. The date is ca. 2450 B.C.E.

[133]*LAE*, 177-79; McKane, *Proverbs*, 65-67. It comes from the Old Kingdom. Its date is ca. 2600 B.C.E.

[134]*ANET*, 414-18; *LAE*, 180-92; McKane, *Proverbs*, 67-75, 79-82. The date is ca. 2180 B.C.E.

[135]*ANET*, 420-21; McKane, *Proverbs*, 92-102. The date is ca. eleventh century B.C.E.

[136]*ANET*, 421-25; *LAE*, 241-65; McKane, *Proverbs*, 102-17. Its date is debated. Wilson assigns it to the seventh-sixth century B.C.E.; see *ANET*, 421. R. J. Williams states that the work may be as early as the thirteenth century B.C.E. ("Egypt and Israel," *The Legacy of Egypt*, 277). Simpson suggests the years before the Amarna period, perhaps the reign of Amenhotpe III (1402-1363); *LAE*, 241.

[137]*ANET*, 418-19; McKane, *Proverbs*, 82-86. The date is ca. 2000 B.C.E.

[138]*ANET*, 432-34; McKane, *Proverbs*, 86-91. The date is ca. 2150-1750 B.C.E.

[139]A. M. Blackman and T. E. Peet, "Papyrus Lansing: A
Translation with Notes," *JEA* 11 (1925) 284-98; McKane, *Proverbs*,
87-91. The date is ca. 1200-1150 B.C.E.; cf. W. R. Dawson, "New
Literary Works from Ancient Egypt," *Asian Review* 21 (1925) 309.

[140]S. R. Glanville, The Instructions of Onchsheshonqy,
Catalogue of Demotic Papyri in the British Museum (1955); B.
Gemser, "The Instructions of Onchsheshonqy and Biblical Wisdom
Literature," VTSup 7 (1960) 102-28; McKane, *Proverbs*, 117-50.
Its date is fifth or fourth century B.C.E.

[141]*LAE*, 193-97.

[142]Ibid., 210-29.

[143]A. H. Gardiner, "A New Moralizing Text," *Festschrift
H. Junker*, *WZKM* 54 (1957) 44-45.

[144]See the remarks by McKane (*Proverbs*) on Ptahhotep (76),
Duauf (90) and Onchsheshonqy (121).

[145]For this copula, see A. H. Gardiner, *Egyptian Grammar*
(London: Oxford University, 1957), #117 and #347; A. Erman,
Neuaegyptische Grammatik (Leipzig: Engelmann, 1933) ##471-74.
I owe these references to Mr. Lanny Bell of the Oriental
Studies Department, University of Pennsylvania.

[146]A. Cowley, *Aramaic Papyri of the Fifth Century B.C.*
(Oxford: Clarendon, 1923) 212-20; *ANET*, 427-30. For versions
in other languages, see J. R. Harris, F. C. Conybeare and A. S.
Lewis, *Aḥiḳar* (London: C. J. Clay, 1898).

[147]Van Dijk, *La Sagesse*, 100; McKane, *Proverbs*, 156.

[148]H. L. Ginsberg, *ANET*, 427; McKane, *Prophets and Wise
Men*, 32.

[149]7:95, 97, 98, 99, 103 (כי restored); 8:114, 119;
9:132 (a second כי restored); 10:143 (כי restored); 11:168;
12:178; 14:208.

[150]E.g., 7:100, 101.

[151]*Waw* ("so that") restored in 9:141.

[152]This can be noticed by reading the various texts in
ANET that come from Egypt and Ugarit. For the use of motivation in literary genres in the Bible, see above, Chapter II;
for Mesopotamia, see this chapter. Elsewhere, there are scattered examples of motivation in the Hittite text ("Instructions
for Temple Officials," *ANET*, 207-10; cf. n. 4 above) which does
not constitute a law-corpus, although the directives therein
had the force of law, for they are issued by the king. There
are, however, no examples of motivation in other similar texts
(*ANET*, 207 and 210-11). A few motive clauses can be found in
some of the North-Western sepulchral inscriptions (*ANET*, 662);
building inscriptions (*ANET*, 653-54); and cultic inscriptions
(*ANET*, 655-56).

[153] McKane, *Proverbs*, 151.

[154] The dependence of Prov 22:17-24:22 upon Amenemopet is now generally recognized. See the discussions in Weinfeld, *Deuteronomy and the Deuteronomic School*, 267; *LAE*, 241; P. Montet, *Egypt and the Bible* (Philadelphia: Fortress, 1968) 115-31 and n. 27.

[155] Kraus, *Ein Edikt des Königs Ammi-Saduqa*, 184-85; J. J. Finkelstein, "Ammisaduqa's Edict and the Babylonian 'Law Codes,'" *JCS* 15 (1961) 100.

[156] Driver and Miles, *Babylonian Laws*, 1. 287.

[157] The ultimate purpose and function of the ancient Near Eastern law collections are yet undetermined. For a summary of scholarly positions on this subject, see Paul, *Book of the Covenant*, 23 n. 2.

[158] LH, epil. XXIVb:67-75; cf. Driver and Miles, *Babylonian Laws*, 1. 38.

[159] XXVb:3-19.

[160] Driver and Miles, *Babylonian Laws*, 1. 30; cf. Paul, *Book of the Covenant*, 25 n. 1.

[161] Paul, however, doubts that the LH were part of the public domain (*Book of the Covenant*, 22).

[162] On these terms, see E. A. Speiser, "Cuneiform Law and the History of Civilization," *PAPS* 107/6 (1963) 537; idem, "Authority and Law in Mesopotamia," *JAOS* Supplement 17 (1954) 8-15.

[163] Prol., Va:20-24.

[164] Epil., XXXb:59-78.

[165] Epil., XXIVb:77-XXXb:7.

[166] Epil., IVa:45.

[167] Epil., XXIVb:93-XXVb:2.

[168] Epil., XXVb:48-58.

[169] Paul, *Book of the Covenant*, 23.

[170] On the prologues and epilogues of ancient Near Eastern law collections (e.g., LU, LI, LE, LH), see Paul (*Book of the Covenant*, 11-21). Some law collections, however, do not have prologues and epilogues (e.g., MAL, HL, NBL); ibid., 11 n. 5.

[171] Finkelstein, "Ammisaduqa's Edict and the Babylonian 'Law Codes,'" 103.

[172]Paul, *Book of the Covenant*, 23; D. J. Wiseman, "The Laws of Hammurabi Again," *JSS* 7 (1962) 166.

[173]See above, Chapter I, n. 129.

[174]Driver and Miles, *Babylonian Laws*, 36.

[175]Cardascia, *Lois assyriennes*, 22-23.

[176]Driver and Miles, *Babylonian Laws*, 287.

[177]*GAG*, #176c.

[178]*CAD*, K, 365-66, under *kīma*.

[179]*GAG*, #158.

[180]See above, Chapter I, n. 267.

[181]Eichrodt, *Theology*, 1. 75.

[182]Greenberg, "Crimes and Punishment," *IDB*, 1. 737; idem, "Some Postulates of Biblical Criminal Law," *Yehezkel Kaufmann Jubilee Volume*, 15, 19; Paul, *Book of the Covenant*, 39.

[183]In Mesopotamia, although law was conceived as the embodiment of cosmic truths (*kittum*, pl. *kīnātim*), the formulation of the laws is ascribed to kings. In Israel, however, God is not only the source of Law, but the very formulation of the law is also His. For details on this matter, see discussion in Greenberg ("Some Postulates of Biblical Criminal Law," 21-22) with references to the writings of Speiser.

CHAPTER IV

ORIGINALITY OF THE MOTIVE CLAUSES

THE PROBLEM

The identification and study of the origin of the motive
clauses in biblical legal corpora lead to the consideration of
the originality of these motive clauses. Were the motive
clauses part of the original formulation of the laws, or were
they later accretions? If they were added subsequent to the
first formulation of the laws, is it possible to determine
when and by whom they were appended to the bare, unmotivated
laws?

These are difficult questions for which no easy answers
can be found. Today it is widely acknowledged that many parts
of the Bible went through a continual process of redaction,
which included transcription of texts by copyists who quite
often resorted to what Seeligmann called "revision cum adaptation,"[1] sometimes "erroneous"[2] but never in bad faith. As
Koenig stated, "for the scribes of ancient Judaism, and undoubtedly already for their predecessors before the exile, adding to a text, glossing it and even modifying it on this or on
that point were not done with the purpose of betraying it. It
was to deal with it in the most legitimate and most necessary
way. It meant....helping to bring to light the truths that
were hidden within the text."[3]

Scholars who have taken issue with the originality of the
motive clauses have tended to consider them as glosses. Is
this tendency justifiable?

PRESUPPOSITIONS AGAINST ORIGINALITY

When the originality of the motive clauses in the legal
corpora of the Bible is denied, it is usually on the basis of
certain scholarly presuppositions concerning the formulation of
the law. These are generally assumed but rarely spelled out.
Among them, three major presuppositions can be identified.

The Alleged Original Brevity of the Laws

Scholars have generally maintained that originally laws
were formulated with "that sharp clear brevity which every law
ought to possess"[4] and, therefore, without any kind of additions, whether elucidatory, justificatory or, even, hortatory.
This opinion is clearly expressed by Noth when he stated: "We
have to look for the original material only in the brief legal
clauses themselves."[5]

This presupposition is not restricted to laws formulated
in the second person, such as those in the sixth, seventh and
eighth commandments of the Decalogue, but is also extended to
laws expressed in the so-called "casuistic" form. Thus Muilenburg said, "In Israel the casuistic law is expanded by motivations, though it is probable that these represent for the most
part later accretions to the original."[6] Similarly, Morgenstern maintained that the unmotivated casuistic law in BC
"reflects the true, original *mišpaṭ* form."[7] He therefore
claimed that the motive clause in Exod 21:8b (בְּבִגְדוֹ-בָהּ, "since
he broke faith with her," *NJV*) was "a late gloss inserted by
some one who no longer understood fully the implications of the
law which he was attempting to interpret,"[8] and that the clause
כִּי כַסְפּוֹ הוּא ("since he is the other's property," *NJV*) in Exod
21:21b was to be taken as "in all likelihood a late, Deuteronomic, explanatory gloss."[9]

The presupposition that laws did not originally contain
any kind of explanatory clauses was considered to be a reflec-
tion of the divine authority behind biblical law. Thus, von
Rad asserted, "Jahweh's commandments were all-sufficient in the
sense that they did not intrinsically require any substantia-
tion to legitimate them before men, except perhaps the tauto-
logical one that, just because they are commandments of Jahweh,
they therefore bind men to acceptance."[10] Discussing the nature of the "apodictic" law, Ringgren voiced a similar opinion:
"The apodictic laws are by nature sacral laws, i.e., laws proclaimed at sanctuaries by divine authority: they therefore did
not actually need any motivation."[11] Recently Bright, too,
expressed the same opinion: "In the bare apodictic sentence no
motivation is given: you simply will not do it; it is so

ordered! When motivation is supplied in an apodictic context,
it is all but invariably: because Yahweh has forbidden it and
requires it punishment."[12]

The notion that the so-called "original" law was formulated without motivation is basically a scholarly assumption
reflecting in turn the evolutionary ideas regarding the development of literary works. The belief was that Hebrew literature grew from brief to longer compositions and, along this
path, the simple forms of the past were expanded and burdened
with a variety of additions.[13] Today, the shortcomings of this
point of view are well acknowledged. As Kitchen puts it, "the
idea of a unilinear evolution from smaller, 'primitive,' literary units to larger, more complex entities (and of growth of a
work by gradual accretion) is a fallacy from the mid-third-
millennium BC onwards, as far as Ancient Oriental literature
is concerned."[14] This change of scholarly position was caused
by the realization that throughout the ancient world, both
biblical and extra-biblical, the "preliterary stages of culture
are not confined to brief compositions,"[15] and by the actual
discovery in Mesopotamia and Egypt of literary works which vary
in length, even within a given genre, at any one period.[16]

In light of these considerations, it is unwarranted to
argue for the secondary character of the legal motive clauses
in the Bible on the basis of the alleged brevity of the "original" law form.

Grammatical Inconsistencies

In some cases there appear to be grammatical inconsistencies among the laws themselves as well as between a given law
and its motive clause. This has led many scholars to assume
subsequent alteration of the basic text at the hand of later
editors.

In a few instances, the discrepancy arises in the switch
from the first person to the third person: e.g., Exod 20:1-7a
(God is the speaker) and verses 7b, 11, 12b (?) (God is spoken
of in the third person). According to Noth, "this discrepancy
is hard to explain; it arouses the suspicion that the beginning

of the Decalogue is no longer in its original form but has subsequently been altered in connection with the preliminary remark of v. 2, which is also written with the 'I' of God."[17]

More often, however, it is the shift from the singular to
plural address, or vice versa, that is attested. For example,
while the law in Exod 23:9a is formulated in the second person
singular, the motive clause in verse 9b is in the second person
plural. Similarly, the law in Exod 22:20 is in the singular,
but the motive clause in verse 20b is in the plural; in Exod
22:21 the law is in the plural, the motivation in verse 22 is
in the singular, but in verse 23 the motive clause reverses to
a plural address.[18] For many, these grammatical deviations
indicate editorial revision. Thus, commenting on Exod 23:9,
Torralba claims that "the switch from second person singular
to the plural is a clear indication of a later addition to the
apodictic law."[19]

The singular/plural inconsistency is not limited to the
structural relation between the law and its motive clause. It
is also found within the laws themselves. Thus, for example,
while Exod 20:22-23 is formulated in the plural, the following
verses 24-26 are in the singular. Conversely, as noted above,
while Exod 22:20 is in the singular, 22:21 is in the plural.
These changes, too, have been used to distinguish early material from later ones. For instance, Exod 20:22-23 was considered by Fohrer as "a secondary introduction by the hand of
the writer that incorporated C [BC] into the Sinai narrative";[20]
the plural formulation of Exod 22:30, following immediately after a series of prescriptions in the singular (i.e., Exod 22:
27-29), was taken by I. Lewy to represent "a later addition";[21]
the plural verses in Exod 22:20b, 21, 23, 24, were similarly
assigned to a later editor by a number of scholars.[22] This
point of view finds its clearest expression in Noth when he
writes: "...in the Old Testament apodeictic law in general the
singular address was originally the usual one."[23] Above examples show that the so-called "casuistic" laws were not exempt
from this judgment.

The singular/plural inconsistency has been used also to determine literary strata. In 1894, Staerk and Steurnagel, working independently of one another, proposed it as a new criterion for literary analysis within the book of Deuteronomy.[24] In recent times, Noth, advocating a supplementary hypothesis, argued that Ur-D consisted of singular passages surcharged by plural passages.[25] M. de Tillesse, pursuing this lead, actually identified the author of the plural passages in Deut 4:44-30:20 with the Deuteronomist historian.[26]

The theory, however, has never been universally accepted.[27] Among the objections raised is that it is impossible "to remove the plural passages within [Deut.] v-xxvi without damage to the narrative."[28]

Grammatical inconsistencies are, as indicated above, not limited to the structural relationship between a "bare" law and its motive clause. They are found within the same laws (e.g., Exod 22:24a, 24b; Lev 19:9, 15, 27, 33, 34; 23:22; 25:14, 17; Deut 12:5, 16) and, as Uitti observed,[29] even within the motive clauses themselves (e.g., Exod 22:22-23; Lev 21:8; Deut 12:9, 13:6, 23:5-6). Consequently, it is doubtful whether the shift in person can be indicative of divergent authorship in biblical material, both legal and even non-legal.[30]

In his article on BC, Beyerlin suggested that the switch from singular to plural indicates, not an editorial revision, but a practice within a cultic setting; in fact, it is a means of intensifying the admonitions that were directed to every listener.[31] For Weinfeld, this change in style may simply "reflect the urge for literary variation."[32]

Uitti correctly remarked that the problem at hand is one for the modern person, not necessarily for those who lived in the past.[33] Ancient Semites, he added, may have had their own ways of expressing themselves, and therefore "our linguistic ignorance may thus be the real explanation of these stylistic inconsistencies."[34]

It is possible to substantiate Uitti's claim by referring to examples in ancient Near Eastern literature where grammatical fluctuation appears as a normal phenomenon. Thus, for instance, the change from second to third person is well attested in

West-Semitic curses,[35] in treaty curses,[36] as well as in
Hittite royal instructions.[37]   The switch from singular to
plural is common in treaties such as Sefire and others.[38]   As
Hillers indicates, the variations often result from a momentary
shift of the writer's point of view.[39]

These extra-biblical examples show that the particular
grammatical inconsistencies noted in the biblical texts are
really part of the normal literary style of the ancient Near
East and need not be explained by recourse to a theory of editorial reworking.   The secondary character of the motive clauses
cannot therefore be argued on the basis of this criterion.

Stylistic Affinity

Motive clauses are frequently considered editorial expansions on account of their similarity to passages of later origin.   The presupposition involved here can be expressed as
follows: when a given motive clause, found in an earlier law
collection, is similar in form, style, terminology, and content
to those appearing in later collections, the former motive
clause constitutes an editorial addition formulated under the
influence of the later texts and often by their editors.

For example, the motive clause in Exod 20:5b-6 (= Deut 5:
9b-10) is usually assigned to a later editor, often to R^D.
According to Noth, these clauses "recall the Deuteronomic-
deuteronomistic style."[40]   Likewise, Dentan states that Exod
20:5-6 "exhibits the same typically Deuteronomic features and
is presumably of similar, or even later, relative date."[41]
Nielsen argues that verses 5b-6 represent "an extremely ancient
and genuinely Israelite element,"[42] "written under the influence of Ex. 34:7,"[43] "in combination with the sharp cleavage
drawn by the Deuteronomists between those who are sinful and
hate God and those who keep his commandments and love him."[44]
Those who consider verse 6 an editorial expansion but of pre-D
times substantiate their position by arguing that the very idea
of "visiting the guilt of the fathers upon the children" is in
contradiction to Deut 24:16 and therefore must be prior to D.[45]

Within the earlier law collections, Deuteronomic origin
has, in a similar way, often been claimed for motive clauses

such as Exod 20:12b,[46] Exod 22:20b and 23:9b,[47] and Exod
34:24.[48] The priestly origin of Exod 20:11 has frequently been
defended on the same basis.[49]

The criterion of literary affinity, however, is far from
being a dependable one. The main objection against it is that
it cannot always guarantee the direction of the influence.
Secondly, a mechanical application of the criterion would appear to reflect yet another assumption that each law collection
creates its own vocabulary *de novo*, which can hardly be the
case. In this connection, it is instructive to remember Weinfeld's remarks concerning the characteristics of the
Deuteronomic style:

> The main characteristic of Deuteronomic phraseology
> is not the employment of new idioms and expressions,
> because many of these can be found in earlier sources
> and especially in the E source. Indeed, it cannot
> be said that in the seventh century a new vocabulary
> and new expressions were suddenly created. Language
> grows in an organic and natural way and it is not
> created artifically. What constitutes the novelty
> of the Deuteronomic style, therefore, is not new
> idioms and new expressions but a specific jargon
> reflecting the religious upheaval of this time.[50]

Therefore, in applying the criterion of literary affinity,
the probability should also be considered that the motive
clauses, especially those in the earlier law collections, were
subsequently adapted by late writers who in turn made extensive
use of them.[51]

Thus, for instance, in Exod 20:5b-6, the expression אל קנא
("an impassioned God," *NJV*), found also in Exod 34:14, Deut
4:24, 5:9, 6:15, and in the form of אל קנוא in Jos 24:19 and
Nah 1:2, need not be taken as a Deuteronomic expansion. As
many scholars have already recognized, the affinity with the
early Exodus 34 argues for a pre-D origin[52] and its later
adoption into the Deuteronomic work.

Another example is the motive clause in Exod 22:20b and
23:9b: "for you were strangers in the land of Egypt." This
statement is also found in Lev 19:34 and Deut 10:19. However,
this is not sufficient for concluding, as Hyatt does, that the
motive clause derives from R^D.[53] A careful reading of these
verses in the three corpora indicates a difference in content

among the instructions.[54]   In Exodus 22 and 23, oppressing the
stranger is prohibited.   In Leviticus 19, the prohibition of
oppressing the stranger is augmented by the request to grant
him citizen status; in fact, the Israelite is exhorted to love
him.   In Deuteronomy 10, the above motive clause accompanies
only the exhortation to love the stranger.   The change of
subject matter may well indicate an expansion on the part of
Leviticus and Deuteronomy.   In this connection, Cazelles
rightly remarks, "one could ask if D has not taken it [the
motive clause] over from our code" (i.e., BC).[55]

When similar laws contain different kinds of motivations,
editorial reworking is readily suspected.   A case in point is
the motive clauses accompanying the Sabbath law in the Decalogue.   In Exod 20:11, the law is motivated by reference to
God's rest after creation.   In the parallel law of Deut 5:
12-15, there are two consecutive motivations: "so that your
slaves and your slave-girl may rest as you" (v. 14b); and the
remembrance of the Exodus from Egypt (v. 15).   The theme of
God's rest is also mentioned in Gen 2:1-3 and Exod 31:17 (both
PC), while the social motivation figures in Exod 23:12.[56]   This
multiplicity of motivations has been variously explained.   Some
have argued that neither motive clause is original in its
place.[57]   However, most scholars maintain that, although the
motivation in Deuteronomy 5 is in line with Deuteronomic language, the one in Exodus 20 seems to have been inserted subsequently, namely after D and under the influence of priestly
passages such as those in Gen 2:1-3 and Exod 31:17.[58]   However,
this view seems unpersuasive on a number of grounds.

First of all, the assumption of PC's lateness underlies
this view.   The Sabbath, along with the practice of circumcision, is considered to have acquired great importance during
the Babylonian exile as a result of the destruction of the
national cultic center in Jerusalem.[59]   Yet, not only has the
late dating of PC been seriously challenged,[60] but particularly
with regard to the Sabbath, Weinfeld has demonstrated that the
four basic motifs of Genesis 1 (i.e., God's work and rest, the
existence of primordial material, the council of God, the
creation of humanity in God's image) are primitive and

anthropomorphic, and appear to have been rejected already by
Second Isaiah (cf. Isa 40:13-14, 28; 44:5, 24; 45:7).[61]

Furthermore, if the two sets of motive clauses are compared with their respective laws, it can be readily noticed
that the motivation in Exodus 20 follows the pattern of the law
(i.e., Yahweh performs his work in six days, rests in the
seventh and declares it holy), whereas the motivation in Deuteronomy 5 introduces a different subject matter (i.e., slavery
in Egypt and the Exodus) which seems to have been attracted by
the reference to the "man-servant and maid-servant" of Deut
5:14b.[62] Moreover, the closing section of the motive clause
in Exod 20:11 (ויקדשהו, "and hallowed it") clearly refers to
the first clause of the Sabbath law (לקדשו, "to keep it holy,"
v. 8), in an envelope style. This structure is lacking in
Deuteronomy 5. All of this argues for the priority of Exod
20:11 over Deut 5:14b-15.[63]

Finally, although there are striking similarities between
Exod 20:10-11 and the priestly passages Gen 2:1-3 and Exod 31:
13-17, namely the use of עשׂה, בּרך (not in Exodus 31), קדשׁ and
מלאכה, there are also noticeable differences. Exod 20:11 uses
the verb וינח, whereas Gen 2:2 and Exod 31:17 have שׁבת; Exod
20:11 has a long reference to the creation of the heaven, earth
and sea and all that is in them, whereas Gen 2:2 simply states
that "the heaven and earth were finished and all their array"
(NJV). In light of these differences, it is difficult to
maintain the Decalogue's dependence on PC. One could argue
equally well that it is PC which is dependent upon the passage
in Exodus 20.[64]

It is more difficult to account for the differences between the motive of God's rest in Exod 20:11 and the social
motivation attached to the Sabbath law in Exod 23:13, especially because both texts are taken to belong to the oldest
strata of biblical law. Here it is not impossible to assume
that the two motivations co-existed in different contexts and
were preserved by different social milieux. It would be in
line with what is known about PC and D to assume that PC adopted
the sacral motivation from Exodus 20 and developed it in its
own special way, while D chose the social motivation of Exodus
23:13 and gave a humanistic interpretation to the Sabbath law.[65]

In the same way, the possibility of the co-existence of
different motive clauses attached to laws that are similar in
scope and nature can be argued, for instance, for those in Lev
19:36 and Deut 25:16, Lev 22:19, and Deut 17:1. One need
not hastily conclude that one of these motivations is the original while the other is secondary. The co-existence here may
point to various social realms which preserved similar laws
with diverse rationales in line with their own particular theological and institutional perspectives. It is also possible
that each source, without denying the validity of the other,
simply stresses one idea over the other.[66]

It was indicated above that the pre-Deuteronomic date of
Exod 20:5b-6 (= Deut 5:9b-10) was argued on the grounds that it
actually contradicted the norm in Deut 24:16. The underlying
assumption is that if a motive clause (here, Deut 5:9b-10),
although formulated in the style of the law collection in which
it occurs, is found to be in contradiction to a law of the same
collection (i.e., Deut 24:16), the motive clause cannot be
original to that law corpus. While the method here is correct,
the information seems to be wrong. The reference in Exod 20:
5b-6 (= Deut 5:9b-10) is to the divine providence of God, but
Deut 24:16 is a directive prescribed for human action and administration of justice by the state.[67] As Greenberg keenly
pointed out, "A principle which is rejected in the case of
judicial punishment is yet recognized as operative in the
divine realm."[68]

In summary, a critical evaluation of the three major presuppositions that have led many scholars to assume the secondary character of the motive clauses indicates the following:
(a) there is no reason to suppose an originally brief law, (b)
grammatical inconsistencies are not necessarily indicative of
editorial reworking, and (c) the argument of stylistic affinity
cannot be used with certainty to prove the lateness of the
motive clauses found in the earlier law collections.

INTEGRATION OF THE MOTIVE CLAUSES

In contrast to those who assumed the lateness of the motive clauses, Gemser and Uitti argued in favor of the antiquity
and originality of some of the motive clauses.

Gemser observed that motive clauses are found in the most ancient strata of the biblical law, namely, "in the Book of the Covenant, in the so-called Yahwistic Decalogue and perhaps also in the Elohistic Decalogue."[69] He further indicated that the rhythmic and proverbial form of some of the motive clauses (e.g., Gen 9:6, Exod 23:8; cf. Deut 16:19b, Exod 23:7; cf. Prov 17:15) clearly shows them to be an archaic, traditional element in the formulation of the laws.[70] In connection with Gen 9:6, he specifically stated: "I do not even see an insurmountable difficulty in assuming that the motive clause here is an integral part of the stipulation."[71]

Uitti followed Gemser's lead and, on the basis of the work of Alt, Beyerlin and others, argued for a two-level solution. In the early law collections (i.e., E_1 [= the Decalogue in Exodus 20]; R_1 [= the cultic Decalogue in Exod 20:22-26 plus 23:10-19]; C [= Exod 21:1-23:9] and S [= Deut 27:15-26]), writes Uitti, "there was an *oral* motive clause which accompanied the recitation of apodictic law,"[72] a kind of "cultic preaching."[73] Then, "there came a *written* motive clause"[74] which is found in the later law collections (i.e., E_2 [= the Decalogue in Deuteronomy 5]; R_2 [= Exod 34:10-26, D, H and PC]) and formulated "in imitation of earlier oral practice."[75] Furthermore, Uitti identified the potential composers of the secondary motive clauses as follows: behind R_2 stands the JE editor; behind D stands the Deuteronomic/Deuteronomistic school, involving both priestly and prophetic elements; behind H, the Zadokite priesthood; and behind PC, the Aaronide Jerusalem priesthood.[76]

A number of scholars have maintained that the motive clauses in the earlier collections of biblical law belong to the earliest times of Israel's history and that, even if they cannot be proven to be original, they can at least be dated to the period before D. Thus, in connection with the motivations of both Decalogues, Driver wrote:

If the clauses were transferred to Ex. from Dt., it is
not apparent why portions of them were omitted. On
the whole, therefore, the more probable view appears
to be that these clauses are in their original place
in Exodus, and that they are of the same character as

> certain other sections in Ex., chiefly of a parenetic
> or hortatory character (as 13:3-16; 23:20-33), which
> do exhibit an approximation to the style of Dt., and
> which were adopted afterwards by the author of Dt.,
> and became part of his phraseology.[77]

Similarly, Beyerlin remarked that if D were accepted as the
source of influence for the parenetic statements in BC, the
question is why so few laws were motivated in this fashion.[78]
He therefore argued that these parenetic statements were not
the result of Deuteronomic editing but originated in the pre-
monarchic period.[79] In the same vein, Driver assigned the motive clauses in BC to the compiler of JE.[80] Of the motivations
in CD, Exod 34:18b (cf. Exod 23:15) is dated pre-D by Beyerlin[81]
and Uitti;[82] and Exod 34:24, though considered an editorial
addition,[83] is still attributed to R[JE] by Driver[84] and Uitti.[85]

As in the earlier law collections of the Bible, it is also
difficult to determine the originality in loco of the motive
clauses in the later collections. Uitti's examination of the
motivations in H, D and PC shows that they largely reflect the
literary style of their respective law collections.[86] This
argues for their integration and authenticity in the legal corpora. However, if in some cases the motive clauses were not
present from the very beginning, it is impossible to establish
with certainty at what stage they became part of the law. It
is evident that the law collections went through various stages
of editorial reworking, either in the same basic style or under
the influence of other sources (e.g., H by PC). H is considered
to be a combination of several collections,[87] although Fohrer's
reconstruction of the four stages of this law corpus is admittedly a hypothetical one.[88] In the case of D, the composite
nature of the book,[89] as is generally recognized, makes it unlikely that the present text can be equated with the original
form of the book. Yet, because of the thoroughness of the editorial expansion it is difficult to determine both the scope
of the so-called Ur-D as well as the various stages of its
compilation.[90] Similarly, it is now generally accepted that PC
is not an original literary unit but a "literary composite."[91]
Nevertheless, "the stages of its evolution are not easily to be
defined either chronologically or in precise extent."[92] Thus,

for example, while Wellhausen attempted to isolate three strata
in PC, von Rad argued only for two.[93]

Consequently, although Uitti assigns the motive clauses in
these later law collections to their secondary framework and
even suggests certain potential composers of these motivations,
there is no reason not to allow for the possibility that at
least some motive clauses were original in their formulation.

EVIDENCE FROM EXTRA-BIBLICAL LITERATURE AND ITS IMPLICATION FOR THE LEGAL MOTIVE CLAUSES IN THE BIBLE

It has already been pointed out that motive clauses are
used in a variety of genres, both in biblical and extra-
biblical literature. Biblical texts cannot be depended upon in
determining the originality of the motive clauses because the
texts underwent editorial revision. However, it is possible to
get some assitance from certain extra-biblical texts that have
not been subjected to the complex and lengthy process of transmission undergone by their biblical counterparts.

Cuneiform laws, extra-biblical wisdom texts and other
"canonical texts"[94] of the ancient Near East which contain motive clauses cannot be used as evidence, because it is known
that they were copied over and over again and, consequently,
their textual integrity cannot be guaranteed. What is needed
here is to find "virgin" texts which have not undergone editorial reworking, either because they are the only original
example of their kind or are duplicates of the original. Motive clauses found in such original texts would clearly not
constitute secondary expansions, for the very reason that they
are part of the original, unexpanded texts.

Among the extra-biblical literary genres, original formulation of motive clauses can be reasonably assumed in the
following types of "virgin" texts.

Letters

In addition to numerous Akkadian letters containing motive
clauses mentioned above,[95] one can refer here to the concluding
section of one of the Lachish ostraca: "And let (my lord) know
that we are watching for the signals of Lachish, according to

all the indication which my lord hath given, for (כִּי) we cannot
see Azekah."[96]

Popular Proverbs

eqli-ya aššata ša lā muta mašil aššum bali errēsim ("my
field is like a woman without a husband because it lacks a
cultivator"). This proverb, noted before, was repeated verbatim four times by Rib-Abdi of Byblos to the Egyptian king.[97]

Treaties

In the Akkadian version of the treaty between Suppiluliumas
and Mattiwaza (fourteenth century B.C.E.), there is a statement
which reads: "A duplicate of this tablet has been deposited before the Sun-goddess of Arinna, because (*ki-me-e*) the Sun-
goddess of Arinna regulates kingship and queenship."[98]

In the Sefire treaty (ca. 750 B.C.E.) between Bar-ga'yah
of KTK and Matti'el of Arpad, one of the stipulations contains
a motivated directive where the motive clause follows an imperative: "You must not loose your tongue in my house and among my
sons and among (my) bro[thers and among] my offspring and among
my people, saying to them: Kill your Lord, and be in his place,
for (כִּי) he is not better than you!"[99]

Commemorative Building Instructions

The Siloam inscription, which is found on the rock wall
of the lower entrance to Hezekiah's tunnel, south of the temple
area in Jerusalem and dated to ca. 715-687 B.C.E., contains the
following lines: "and while there were still three cubits to be
cut through, [there was heard] the voice of a man calling to
his fellow, for (כִּי) there was an *overlap* in the rock on the
right and on the left."[100]

Northwestern Royal Inscriptions

Among the sepulchral inscriptions, in that of Tabnit of
Sidon (fifth century B.C.E.), a motive clause accompanies a
prohibitive in line six: "don't disturb me, for (כּ) such a
thing would be an abomination to Astarte";[101] in that of

Eshmunazar of Sidon (fifth century B.C.E.) the text has, in
part, "whoever you are, ruler and (ordinary) man, may he not
open this resting place and may he not search in it for anything, for (כ) nothing whatever has been placed in it!"[102]

In a cultic inscription wuch as that of Zakir of Hamat and
Lu'ath (eighth century B.C.E.), there is a motivated prohibitive: "Be'elshamayn [said to me]: do not fear, for (כי) I made
you king, and I shall stand by you."[103] Similarly, in the inscription of Yehawmilk of Byblos (fifth-fourth century B.C.E.)
there is the following blessing: "May the Lady of Byblos bless
and preserve Yehawmilk king of Byblos, and prolong his days and
years in Byblos, for (כ) he is a righteous king."[104]

In the building inscription of Yehimilk of Byblos (ca.
tenth century B.C.E.), there is a blessing which states: "May
Ba'lshamem and the Lord of Byblos and the Assembly of the Holy
Gods of Byblos prolong the days and years of Yehimilk in Byblos, for (he is) a righteous king (פמלך צדיק) and an upright
king before the Holy Gods of Byblos."[105]

In the Moabite stone, erected by Mesha king of Moab (cf.
2 Kgs 3:4-5, ca. 830 B.C.E.), one finds the following statement: "as for Omri, king of Israel, he humbled Moab for many
years (lit. days), for (כי) Chemosh was angry at his land."[106]

Contracts

For examples of motive clauses in contracts introduced by
aššum, see above, Chapter III, n. 107.

Law Suits

For examples of motive clauses in law suits introduced by
aššum, see above, Chapter III, n. 108.

Royal Proclamations and Edicts

From Nuzi (AASOR 16, No. 51)

This proclamation[107] in Akkadian and presumably of royal
origin[108] concerns the personnel of the palace. The section
that is of interest here reads as follows: "Thus [the king]:
No one, whether a servant of the palace or a (member of the)

personnel of the palace, shall cause his daughter to go out as
a homeless girl (*a-na e-[ku]-ti*)[109] or as a prostitute (*a-na
ḫa-ri-mu-ti*) without (the consent of) the king. Whoever
causes his daughter to go out as a homeless girl or as a prostitute without (the consent of) the king, they shall take to
the palace him who ...-ed[110] his daughter as a homeless girl or
as a prostitute, and (*māras-su ša-nu-ú a-na li-iq-ti*[111] *a-na
ēkallim^lim ki-i-ma i-liq-qú-ú ù i-liq-qú-ú*, lines 18-22) they
shall take another daughter of his to the palace for possession,
because[112] he had taken away (the other one)."

Edict of Ammiṣaduqa

It was stated previously[113] that, besides the four different motive clauses of explanatory type, the edict also contains
eight standard *mīšarum* motive formulae. Both Kraus and Finkelstein distinguish between the *mīšarum* text and the *mīšarum* act
and point out that the *mīšarum* text contains provisions of a
general nature which are not related to remission of specific
kinds of debts and obligations. The edict, they add, is retrospective and was most likely drawn up some time after the act
was proclaimed in the first full year of the king's reign.[114]

The *mīšarum* act does not constitute a "reform" intended to
have permanent effect. It only restores an equilibrium in the
economic life of the community by remitting certain debts and
obligations for a limited period. Within the *mīšarum* text, the
distinction between temporary and permanent reforms is indicated, according to Kraus and Finkelstein, by the use of the
mīšarum motive clause: its inclusion within a section shows
that the particular provision was meant to have effect only at
the time of the announcement of the *mīšarum*, whereas the sections of the text lacking the clause are to be kept as permanent reforms.[115] This means that the *mīšarum* motive clause is
original with the *mīšarum* text but not with the act, which was
not necessarily accompanied by the issuing of a formal text
containing all the provisions of the act. The remissive provisions were probably diffused throughout the realm by official
correspondence from the royal chancery.[116]

The motivations in LH and MAL point to the antiquity of
the use of motive clauses in the legal corpora of the ancient
Near East. The question is, were they also original? The examples taken from virgin texts clearly prove that motivations
could be part of the original formulation of a text. Therefore, given the fact that in the ancient Near East the authorship of laws was often claimed by kings (e.g., LH, LI),[117] the
evidence from royal proclamations and edicts[118] (both of which
had the force of law) carrying original motive clauses strongly
suggests that the few motivations found in LH and MAL may well
have been original in their places.

Establishing the textual integrity of virgin texts with
motive clauses has significant implications for the study of
biblical material. It can now be asserted with reasonable
assurance that in many of the biblical genres, too, the motive
clauses might well belong to the original formulation of the
texts themselves. Thus, for instance, the motivations in biblical letters (e.g., Jer 29:7), curses (e.g., Gen 3:14, 17;
Deut 28:38, 39, 40, etc.), royal orders (e.g., Exod 5:8, 2 Kgs
2:13, Jonah 3:9, Ezra 7:14) can likewise be considered original.
For the purposes of the present study, however, the implications
for legal texts are most important. The differences between the
biblical and extra-biblical law collections with regard to their
sources, nature, and, to a certain extent, form have already
been discussed above.[119] In spite of these differences, the
recognition of the common legal tradition of the ancient Near
East which included the biblical law, the noted similarity of
many of the legal forms, and now the possibility of considering
the motive clauses in LH and MAL original add further weight to
the position that legal motive clauses in the Bible, too, need
not be taken *ab initio* as editorial expansions.

It must be admitted that, because of lack of independent
textual evidence, there is no way of proving the originality of
the biblical legal motive clauses *in loco*. However, the present study has indicated that scholarly presuppositions which
see in them a secondary reworking at the hand of later editors
must be re-evaluated. The ancient Near Eastern examples cited

above strongly suggest that a motive clause should not be taken
as secondary just because it is a motive clause. It is always
possible that it is part of the original formulation of the law.

CHAPTER IV

[1]I. L. Seeligmann, "Indications of Editorial Alteration and Adaptation in the Massoretic Text and the Septuagint," *VT* 11 (1961) 205.

[2]Ibid., 213.

[3]J. Koenig, "L'activité hermeneutique des scribes dans la transmission du texte de l'Ancien Testament," *RHR* 161 (1962) 150. Translation of the quote is mine.

[4]H. Ewald, *The History of Israel* (London: Longmans, Green & Co., 1876) 2. 159.

[5]Noth, *Exodus*, 161; cf. S. R. Driver, *Introduction*, 34. See also, for similar comments, his *The Book of Exodus*, Cambridge Bible for Schools and Colleges (Cambridge: University Press, 1953) 192.

[6]Muilenburg, "Usages of the Particle כִּי in the OT," 151.

[7]Morgenstern, "The Book of the Covenant," 2. 209.

[8]Ibid., 49 n. 40; cf. 52 n. 43.

[9]Ibid., 53 n. 43; cf. 209 n. 263a.

[10]Von Rad, *Theology*, 1. 196-97. In n. 19, he refers the reader to Gemser's article, "The Importance of the Motive Clause."

[11]Ringgren, *Israelite Religion*, 135-36.

[12]Bright, "The Apodictic Prohibition," 201. However, this observation is not totally correct. Different types of motive clauses are attached to the so-called "apodictic" laws: e.g., Exod 20:11, 12, 26; 22:20; 23:8, 9, 12, 15; 34:18; Lev 18:7-17; Deut 14:2, 7; 16:1, 19, 20; 22:7, 9; 23:1, 5, 8, 21; 24:6; 25:15.

[13]In this connection, see, for example, H. Gunkel's following remarks: "The oldest types...are always pure and un-unmixed; but in later periods, when men and conditions of life were more complex, when professional writers adopted the type, there occur deviation and mixtures of styles" ("Fundamental Problems of Hebrew Literary History," 65). Or his statement: "the briefer a legend, the greater the probability that we have it in its original form" (*The Legends of Genesis* [New York: Schocken, 1964] 47).

[14]Kitchen, *Ancient Orient and Old Testament*, 131, citing
Albright, "Some Oriental Glosses on the Homeric Problem," *AJA*
54 (1950) 162-64, and Albright, "Canaanite-Phoenician Sources
of Hebrew Wisdom," VTSup 3 (1955) 4.

[15]J. Wilcoxen, "Narrative," *Old Testament Form Criticism*,
64.

[16]See Kitchen, *Ancient Orient*, 131, for many examples.

[17]Noth, *Exodus*, 161; cf. Nielsen, *The Ten Commandments*,
37.

[18]Similarly, see Exod 22:20, 21; Lev 19:10, 34; 23:22;
25:37-38, etc.

[19]Torralba, "Motivación Deuteronómica," 94. Translation
of the quote is mine. Similarly, see Hyatt, *Exodus*, 246.

[20]Fohrer, *Introduction*, 133.

[21]I. Lewy, "Dating of Covenant Code Sections on Humaneness
and Righteousness," *VT* 7 (1957) 322.

[22]Driver, *Exodus*, 231-32; I. Lewy, "Dating of the Covenant
Code," 322; Hyatt, *Exodus*, 218.

[23]Noth, *Leviticus*, 139.

[24]W. Staerk, *Das Deuteronomium, sein Inhalt und seine
literarische Form* (Leipzig: Hinrichs, 1894); C. Steurnagel,
Der Rahmen des Deuteronomiums (Halle a.S.: Wischan & Wettengel,
1894).

[25]M. Noth, *Überlieferungsgeschichtliche Studien* (Tübingen:
Max Niemeyer, 1957) 16.

[26]G. Minette de Tillesse, "Sections 'tu' et sections
'vous' dans le Deutéronome," *VT* 12 (1962) 47-86.

[27]De Tillesse, "Sections tu et vous," 33 n. 4; E. W.
Nicholson, *Deuteronomy and Tradition* (Philadelphia: Fortress,
1967) 33-34; A. Rofé, "The Strata of the Law About the Centralization of Worship in Deuteronomy and the History of the
Deuteronomic Movement," *VT* 22 (1971) 222.

[28]Nicholson, *Deuteronomy and Tradition*, 33.

[29]Uitti, *The Motive Clause*, 83.

[30]S. Lowenstamm, משפט, 627; Rofé, "The Strata of the Law
About the Centralization of Worship in Deuteronomy," 222. The
redactor is capable of harmonizing differences when he combines
sources which differ with regard to 1st, 2nd, or 3rd person,
e.g., Samaritan Exodus 18 combining MT's Exodus 18 and Deuteronomy 1. See J. H. Tigay, "An Empirical Basis for the

Documentary Hypothesis," *JBL* 94 (1975) 329-42. Such differences, therefore, do not likely represent traces of divergent
authorship. Furthermore, a perusal of glosses in works such as
Jewish and Samaritan Version of the Pentateuch (eds. Avraham
and Ratson Sadaqa; Jerusalem: Rubin Mass, 1961-64), *The Dead
Sea Scrolls of St. Mark's Monastery* (Vol. 1; ed. M. Burrows;
New Haven: American School of Oriental Research, 1950), *The
Dead Sea Psalms Scroll* by J. A. Sanders (Ithaca: Cornell University, 1967); *The Septuagint Version of Isaiah* by I. L. Seeligmann (Leiden: E. J. Brill, 1948), and *The Language and Linguistic Background of the Isaiah Scroll* by E. Y. Kutscher (in
Hebrew; Jerusalem: Magnes, 1959) has revealed that later
interpolations in these texts do not display grammatical inconsistencies with the MT. To my knowledge a thorough study of
these glosses has not yet been undertaken.

[31] Beyerlin, "Die Paränese in Bundesbuch," 20.

[32] Weinfeld, "Deuteronomy," *EncJud* 5, 1575.

[33] Uitti, *The Motive Clause*, 86.

[34] Ibid., 87.

[35] Gevirtz, "West-Semitic Curses," 157.

[36] D. R. Hillers, *Treaty-Curses and the Old Testament
Prophets* (BibOr 16; Rome: Pontifical Biblical Institute, 1964)
32-33. The reference is to the curses of Ashurniari's treaty.

[37] Weinfeld, "The Origin of the Apodictic Law," 67-68 n. 4.

[38] Hillers, *Treaty-Curses*, 32.

[39] Ibid., 33. In connection with the switch to the plural
formulation in Deut 28:62-63, Hillers says that "the author
momentarily abandoned the rather artificial habit of addressing
the nation as an individual" (ibid.).

[40] Noth, *Exodus*, 163. Similarly, Hyatt, *Exodus*, 210.

[41] Dentan, "The Literary Affinities of Exodus XXXIV:6f," 38.

[42] Nielsen, *The Ten Commandments*, 99.

[43] Ibid., 36.

[44] Ibid., 99. See also Driver, *Exodus*, 195; Koch, *Biblical
Tradition*, 47.

[45] Stamm and Andrew, *The Ten Commandments in Recent Research*, 17; H. Cazelles, "Les Origines du Décalogue," 15. But
see below, n. 78.

[46] Hyatt, *Exodus*, 213; Koch, *Biblical Tradition*, 48;
Driver, *Exodus*, 195.

[47]Hyatt, *Exodus*, 223, 242, 246; Pfeiffer, *Introduction*, 226.

[48]Hyatt, *Exodus*, 324; Noth, *Exodus*, 264; Morgenstern, "The Book of the Covenant," Part 2, 58; W. Beyerlin, *Origins and History of the Oldest Sinaitic Traditions*, (Oxford: Blackwell, 1965) 85.

[49]Driver, *Exodus*, 192; Hyatt, *Exodus*, 212; Noth, *Exodus*, 164; Beyerlin, *Sinaitic Traditions*, 12; Pfeiffer, *Introduction*, 228; Ringgren, *Israelite Religion*, 201.

[50]Weinfeld, "Deuteronomy," *EncJud* 5, 1581-82.

[51]See the remarks on the Decalogue by M. Greenberg (*EncJud* 5, 1444).

[52]Driver, *Exodus*, 192, 195; Nielsen, *The Ten Commandments*, 89; Langlamet, "Israel et l'habitant du pays," 493; Lestienne, "Les dix paroles," 500.

[53]Hyatt, *Exodus*, 242.

[54]Weinfeld, *Deuteronomy and the Deuteronomic School*, 289.

[55]Cazelles, *Le Code de l'alliance*, 78. Translation of the quote is mine.

[56]A third motivation appears in Ezek 20:12b.

[57]For instance, M. Tsevat, "The Basic Meaning of the Biblical Sabbath," *ZAW* 84 (1972) 449.

[58]For references, see above, n. 49.

[59]J. Wellhausen, *Prolegomena to the History of Ancient Israel* (Cleveland: World Publishing, Meridian Books, 1961) 492.

[60]See, in particular, Kaufmann, *Religion of Israel*, 175-211; cf. Hahn, *The Old Testament in Modern Research*, 33-34 n. 62; A. Hurvitz, "The Evidence of Language in Dating the Priestly Code," *RB* 81 (1974) 24-56.

[61]M. Weinfeld, "God the Creator in Gen. 1 and in the Prophecy of Second Isaiah" (Hebrew), *Tarbiz* 37 (1968) 105-32 (cf. English summary, pp. I-II).

[62]Nielsen, *The Ten Commandments*, 39-40.

[63]Ibid.; Uitti, *The Motive Clause*, 172-75.

[64]Nielsen, *The Ten Commandments*, 40-41; Uitti, *The Motive Clause*, 167.

[65]Weinfeld, *Deuteronomy and the Deuteronomic School*, 222.

[66]Admittedly, there is also a third possibility, namely, an unmotivated stage to which each text added a motive clause in keeping with its own interest and character.

[67]S. R. Driver, *Deuteronomy*, The International Critical Commentary (New York: Scribners, 1909) 277-78.

[68]Greenberg, "Some Postulates of Biblical Criminal Law," 24-25.

[69]Gemser, "The Importance of the Motive Clause," 63-64.

[70]Ibid., 64-65.

[71]Ibid., 64.

[72]Uitti, *The Motive Clause*, 3-4.

[73]Ibid., 4.

[74]Ibid.

[75]Ibid.

[76]Ibid., 300; cf. 236.

[77]Driver, *Introduction*, 35.

[78]Beyerlin, "Die Paränese in Bundesbuch," 18. It should be recalled that most of Beyerlin's parenetic statements in BC were considered above, in Chapter II, as motive clauses.

[79]Ibid., 13-19.

[80]Driver, *Exodus*, 202.

[81]Beyerlin, *Sinaitic Traditions*, 85.

[82]Uitti, *The Motive Clause*, 184, 186.

[83]On the grounds that it is lacking in the parallel corpus Exod 23:17-19. See Morgenstern, "The Book of the Covenant," Part 2, 58. Noth refers to Exod 34:24 as "a deuteronomistic addition" (*Exodus*, 264).

[84]Driver, *Exodus*, 372.

[85]Uitti, *The Motive Clause*, 186.

[86]Ibid., 223-56.

[87]See discussion in Eissfeldt, *The Old Testament*, 236-38. Also, see above, Chapter II, n. 110.

[88]Fohrer, *Introduction*, 142.

[89]Fohrer points to two introductions (i.e., 1:1-4:40, 4:44-11:32), two kinds of blessings and curses (i.e., 27:11-26, 28:1-68), and various appendices (*Introduction*, 169). Similarly, Weinfeld, "Deuteronomy," *EncJud* 5, 1574. With regard to the various strata within the legal materials, see Merendino, *Das deuteronomische Gesetz*; and Rofé, "The Strata of the Law About the Centralization of Worship in Deuteronomy," 221-24.

[90]Fohrer, *Introduction*, 170.

[91]Ibid., 183.

[92]Ackroyd, *Exile and Restoration*, 84.

[93]For the discussion of the various strata in PC, see Fohrer (*Introduction*, 182).

[94]Hallo and Simpson, *The Ancient Near East: A History*, 156.

[95]Chapter III, nn. 105 and 115.

[96]*ANET*, 322. For the text, see Donner and Röllig, *KAI*, No. 194; I, 35; II, 193-96.

[97]See above, Chapter III, n. 114.

[98]I r. 35. See *ANET*, 205; Weidner, *Politische Dokumente aus Kleinasien*, 26-27. See also *CAD*, K, 366, under *kimē*.

[99]*ANET*, 661. The motive clause reads: כי לטב הא מן מך (Sefire III, line 22). Rosenthal apparently reads מ<נ>ך. See remarks by Fitzmyer, *The Aramaic Inscriptions of Sefîre*, 118. D. Sommer has rendered the clause as "car cela ne serait pas bien de ta part"; *Les inscriptions araméennes de Sfiré* (Paris: Imprimerie Nationale, 1958), 131.

[100]*ANET*, 321. For the text, see Donner and Röllig, *KAI*, No. 189:2-3, I, 34; II, 186-88. The motive clause reads: כי.היה.זדה.בצר. מימן. The exact meaning of the word זדה is not known. For various attempts, see Donner and Röllig, *KAI*, II, 187.

[101]Ibid., 662. For the text, see Donner and Röllig, *KAI*, No. 13:6; I, 2-3; II, 17-19. There is another motive clause in line 4, introduced by כ.

[102]Ibid. For the text, see Donner and Röllig, *KAI*, No. 14:5; I, 3; II, 19-23.

[103]Ibid., 655. For the text, see Donner and Röllig, *KAI*, No. 202(A):13; I, 203; II, 204-11.

[104]Ibid., 656. For the text, see Donner and Röllig, *KAI*, No. 10:9; I, 2; II, 11-15.

[105]Ibid., 653. For the text, see Donner and Röllig, *KAI*, No. 4:6; I, 1; II, 6-7.

[106]Ibid., 320. For the text, see Donner and Röllig, *KAI*, No. 181:4-6; I, 33; II, 168-79. There is another motive clause in line 4 introduced by כי.

[107]On this text, see R. H. Pfeiffer and E. A. Speiser, *One Hundred New Selected Nuzi Tablets* (AASOR 16; New Haven: American Schools of Oriental Research, 1936), transliterated on p. 51 and translated on p. 103; H. Lewy, "Gleanings from a New Volume of Nuzi Texts," *OrNS* 10 (1941) 214-15; *CAD*, E, 73, under *ekûtu* (A), and L, 29, under *labîru* (ld); E. Weidner, "Hof- und Harems-Erlasse assyrischer Könige aus dem 2. Jahrtausend v. Chr.," *AfO* 17 (1956) 257-58. This proclamation may be a copy of the original, for it iṣ entitled *ša-du-du an-nu-û ša awēlūtimeš warad ēkallim^(lim) û ša [ni]-iš bīti ša ēkallim^(lim) la-beru-[um]-ma*, "This (is) the proclamation concerning the slaves of the palace and the domestics of the palace, the old one"; Pfeiffer and Speiser, AASOR 16, 31, 103. Similarly, Weidner translates the last word as "ein (seit) alter(sher gültiger)," p. 257. However, *CAD* restores it as *la-be-ru-[tum]-ma* and takes it as an adj. of *[ni]-iš bīti*, "the old personnel of the palace," 9, 29. According to this understanding, the edict applies both to the young slaves as well as the old personnel of the palace. This would mean that we have an original text at hand and not a copy of an old decree. This is highly plausible.

[108]The term LUGAL is restored in line 5: *um-ma*[LUGAL]-*ma*.

[109]On *ekûtu*, see *CAD*, E, 73, under *ekûtu* (A), meaning "status of homeless, destitute and unprotected girl." Also, *AHW*, 196.

[110]The word is *i-lu-ša-aš-še*. Its derivation is obscure. Speiser suggests *i-ki!-ša-aš-še*, from *qâšu*, to dedicate, to give up and therefore translates, "whosoever...his daughter... has given up," p. 103 n. 17. Both Lewy and *CAD* leave the term untranslated.

[111]*liqtu*, instead of *liqûtu*; cf. *AHW*, 555.

[112]On *kīma*, meaning "because," see *CAD*, K, 365.

[113]See above, Chapter III, n. 113.

[114]Kraus, *Ein Edikt des Königs Ammi-Ṣaduqa*, 243-47; Finkelstein, "Ammiṣaduqa's Edict and the Babylonian 'Law Codes,'" 101-102.

[115]Kraus, *Ein Edikt des Königs Ammi-Ṣaduqa*, 243-47; Finkelstein, "Ammiṣaduqa's Edict and the Babylonian 'Law Codes,'" 100.

[116]Finkelstein, "Ammiṣaduqa's Edict," 102.

[117]Speiser, "Authority and Law in the Ancient Orient," 12; Greenberg, "Some Postulates," 21-22; cf. Chapter III, n. 183.

[118]See also the motivations within the "Instructions for Temple Officials" (Hittite), *ANET*, 207-10; cf. Chapter III, n. 102.

[119]See above, Chapter I, pp. 35-39, and Chapter III, p. 174.

SUMMARY AND CONCLUSIONS

The main results obtained in the present study can be
summarized as follows.

Classification and Life Setting of the Pentateuchal and Cuneiform Legal Forms

The laws in the Pentateuch may be classified according to
two major types of legal formulation: conditional and unconditional. Whereas the former describes a case and then stipulates a legal consequence, the latter simply expresses a command, either positive or negative, without indicating a legal
consequence. Laws in the conditional form display varied
styles in their composition: "when/if" form (including "when
he" and "when you"), relative form and participial form. Laws
in the unconditional form appear either as direct address
(positive or negative) or as third person jussive (positive or
negative).

A similar type of classification may be applied to cuneiform law corpora. Here laws in the conditional form are introduced by "if (a man)" (TUKUM.BI in Sumerian, *šumma* [*awīlum*] in
Akkadian, and *takku* in Hittite) or by the relative "a man who"
(*awīlum ša* or simply *ša* in Akkadian, and LÚ *kuiš* or simply *kuiš*
in Hittite); laws in the unconditional form appear as third
person jussive.

Lack of evidence makes the determination of the setting in
life of the legal forms very difficult. Often it is unknown
whether the law's use of the forms reflects an original or a
secondary setting for the particular legal forms. Therefore
the results obtained in this area are at best tentative in
nature.

Within the category of laws in the conditional form, the
court of law has frequently been suggested as the setting for
the "when/if he" form. However, neither in the Bible nor in
the cuneiform material is there textual evidence to prove this
claim. None of the court decisions recorded in the Bible is
expressed in the conditional "if he" form. In the cuneiform
legal texts, court verdicts are formulated in a variety of ways,

219

the "if he" form appearing only as one among many.   Furthermore,
there is no evidence in the Bible or in the cuneiform texts that
laws expressed in the conditional "if he" form constituted the
basis for the formulation of court decisions.   Because of the
similarity in formulation between laws and omens, it has also
been suggested that the form in cuneiform law derived from the
scribal academy, just as omen literature emerged from scholarly
circles.   Underlying this notion is the assumption that cuneiform laws are not "legislative" in nature but constitute literary productions.   However, the question of the ultimate nature
of the ancient Near Eastern legal corpora has not as yet been
settled.   Furthermore, it is not known whether the academy
represents an original or a secondary life setting.

The legal form "when you," found only in the Pentateuchal
legal corpora, appears to reflect an original teaching situation, especially in light of the fact that the form is frequently used in wisdom literature, both biblical and extra-
biblical.

The relative form, found both in biblical and cuneiform
laws, most likely derives from the sphere of proclamations in
view of the predominant use of the relative form in proclamations recorded in biblical and extra-biblical texts.

The participial form, exclusively used in biblical laws,
stems perhaps from pronouncements issued by those in authority,
for the form is very often used in the Bible to express various
types of commands.   In extra-biblical literature, although the
participial form appears in certain curses and wisdom sayings,
there are no clues as to its original life setting.

As for laws in the unconditional form, in spite of the
claims to the contrary, there is no proof that laws formulated
as direct address in the Bible had their setting in the alleged
covenant renewal ceremony.   In fact, it is unlikely that a
festival of this nature ever existed in ancient Israel.   The
most likely setting for the direct address is Gerstenberger's
"*Sippenethos*," i.e., the authoritative teachings given within
the tribal circle.   The second person command, although not
found in cuneiform law corpora, is well attested in a variety
of genres in extra-biblical literature.

The third person jussive, found both in biblical and extra-biblical laws, seems to derive from the instructions given by those in authority. Frequent examples of this form found in the Bible and in cuneiform material appear to justify this claim. A more specific life setting is nowhere indicated.

The formulation of the prices and wages, found only in cuneiform laws, most likely derives from the actual language of the market place.

Percentage of Motivation Within the Legal Corpora

The legal prescriptions in the Pentateuch are very often accompanied by narrative material. In order to identify what is "law" in the Pentateuch, it is therefore necessary to distinguish between laws and curses, laws and parenetic statements, and laws and ad hoc commands.

In the present study, within the six law collections in the Pentateuch (namely, Dec, BC, CD, H, D, PC), 1,238 legal prescriptions were counted; of these, 375 are motivated. This represents a rate of ca. 30%. Compared to Uitti's overall result of 63.1%, the figure of ca. 30% is a very low one. Yet, it better reflects the reality, for in the present study the percentages of the motivated prescriptions were computed not on the basis of paragraphs or subjects, which is Uitti's method, but by considering the individual legal prescriptions that are included within the paragraphs. Thus, a higher number of legal prescriptions, with a different delineation of motive clauses, yielded a lower percentage of motivations.

Biblical law corpora differ among themselves with regard to the percentage of motivated laws. The rate goes up from ca. 13% in CD, ca. 16% in BC, ca. 20% in PC, ca. 45% in the Dec., ca. 50% in D, to the highest figure of ca. 51% in H. Here it is necessary to note that, even though D and H have the highest percentage of motivation, the use of motivation cannot be employed in establishing the relative dating of the legal corpora, for it is difficult to determine at what stage the motive clauses became part of the law, if all or some of them were not present from the very beginning.

The motivated laws may be classified on the basis of their
content into four broad categories: cultic/sacral, humanitarian/
moral, civil, and political. Of the 375 motivated legal prescriptions, 271 deal with cultic/sacral matters. This represents ca. 72% of the motivated laws. The 51 motivated humani-
tarian/moral prescriptions constitute ca. 14% of the motivated
laws. The 45 motivated laws regulating "civil" matters represent ca. 12% of the motivated laws. To the political sphere
are assigned 8 motivated laws, representing ca. 2% of the motivated laws in the Pentateuch. These results can graphically be
seen in the following chart.

CHART C:

Percentage of Motivated Laws in the
Pentateuch (Based on Content)

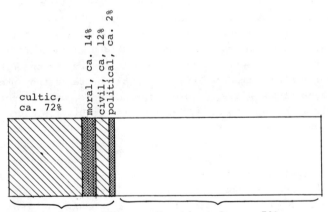

The chart gives the impression that cultic/sacral laws
contain the highest percentage of motivation. However, when
each of the above four categories is seen in light of the
totality of the legal prescriptions in the Bible, a different
picture emerges. Thus, even though ca. 78% of all the laws in
the Pentateuch are of cultic/sacral nature, only ca. 27% of
these are motivated and ca. 73% are not. Similarly, "civil"

laws in the Bible amount to ca. 12% of the legal prescriptions,
but ca. 29% of these are motivated and ca. 71% are not. Laws
of political nature claim ca. 2% of the Pentateuchal laws, but
ca. 45% of these are motivated, and ca. 55% are not. In the
case of humanitarian/moral prescriptions, which constitute only
ca. 8% of all the laws in the Pentateuch, ca. 53% are motivated
and ca. 47% are not. Therefore, it is the last category which
contains the highest percentage of motivation in the biblical
laws. A second chart will bring these results into bolder
relief.

CHART D:

Percentage of Motivated Pentateuchal
Laws in Each Category

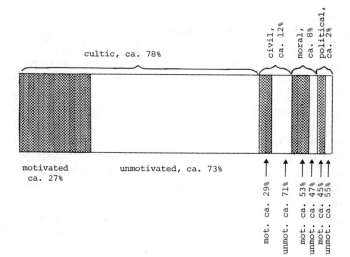

The high percentage of motivation noted in the biblical
humanitarian/moral prescriptions is perhaps indicative of the
special moral concern that animated the legislators who also
wanted to ensure compliance to these laws.

In contrast to the biblical law collections, LH and MAL
contain very few cases of motivation. In LH, the percentage is

ca. 6%; in MAL, ca. 5%. All of these motivated laws regulate
"civil" matters. The low rate shows that motivation is not
characteristic of the ancient Near Eastern law corpora.

The Legal Motive Clauses: Formulation and Function

Motive clauses, defined in this study as dependent clauses
or phrases which express the motive behind the legal prescriptions, must be distinguished from explicative notes and parenetic statements. Explicative notes are basically used to interpret or clarify specific words or clauses within the law. On
the other hand, the primary object of the parenetic statements
is to summon people to obedience by means of appeals formulated
in broad terms; they very often appear as independent units.
Yet, motive clauses where the element of exhortation is only
secondary and at best implicit do not appear as independent
statements; they are always dependent upon the laws which they
motivate.

In the Bible as well as in LH and MAL, the legal motive
clauses are formulated either by means of grammatical particles
or asyndetically. However, there is a difference in the way in
which motivation is achieved in biblical laws on the one hand
and in the cuneiform laws on the other. In the biblical law
collections, while some of the motive clauses simply repeat a
key element within the law and underline it as the motive of
the law, the majority supply the law with a new clause or
phrase that spells out the reason of or the incentive for observing the law. Among the latter, a variety of types is noted:
e.g., motivating by classification, predicating the law upon
God's authority, referring to historical experiences of the
people, instilling fear of punishment, and promising well-being.
The motive clauses themselves are formulated either impersonally or in the second person. In the LH and MAL, however, the
motive clauses always refer to inner-legal matters and achieve
their goal by underlining a key element within the law. In
that sense, they are all "repetitive." Furthermore, they are
formulated impersonally, totally lacking the second person
address.

In searching for the function of the legal motive clauses, it is necessary to view them in light of motive clauses found in other literary genres.

In the Bible, among all the literary genres outside of law, wisdom instructions have the highest concentration of number and kind of motive clauses. These motive clauses are in many respects very similar to those found in laws. This similarity, along with the recognized influence of wisdom upon law, suggests that the motive clauses in wisdom instructions constituted the basic models for the formulation of the legal motive clauses. A teaching function (as in the case of wisdom instruction) rather than an alleged cultic preaching seems to be reflected best in the use of the legal motive clauses.

In the cuneiform laws it is difficult to determine the source of influence upon the use and formulation of the legal motive clauses. This is not only because the motive clauses in LH and MAL are very few in number, but also because they are all "repetitive"--a pattern which is not apparent in any of the known literary genres, including wisdom. Although the ultimate purpose of the cuneiform legal corpora is yet undetermined, the placing of the law collections within elaborate prologues and epilogues of historic and religious nature strongly suggests that they were directed to the gods and aimed at obtaining their good favors. The function of the motive clauses would therefore appear to underscore the lawmaker's true concern for justice.

The Originality of the Legal Motive Clauses

The secondary character of the biblical legal motive clauses has been frequently argued on the basis of certain scholarly assumptions. However, a critical evaluation of these assumptions has yielded the following conclusions. (1) The alleged brevity of the law was maintained primarily on the assumption that in the remote past only small compositions were created and that longer texts were the products of later periods. The discovery of long texts coming from the early periods of the ancient Near East has proven that, in literary

creativity, the idea of unilinear evolution from shorter to
longer compositions is simply a fallacy. Consequently, there
is no reason to suppose an original brief law devoid of motivation.   (2) The acknowledged existence of grammatical fluctua-
tions in ancient Near Eastern texts shows that grammatical inconsistencies occasionally noted between the motive clauses and
their laws cannot necessarily be taken to indicate editorial
reworking.   (3) The argument of stylistic affinity, whereby a
motive clause whose style and content resemble those of later
texts must be considered of late origin, cannot be used with
certainty to prove the lateness of the motive clauses found in
the earlier law collections, since it is difficult to determine
the direction of the influence and also because the argument
would appear to assume that each law collection creates its own
vocabulary *de novo*, which is unlikely.

Motive clauses identified in ancient Near Eastern texts,
both legal and non-legal, which by their nature are not likely
to have undergone editorial reworking clearly indicate that a
motive clause cannot be ascribed to later editors just because
it is a motive clause.

APPENDIX

APPENDIX: LISTS

This appendix contains a detailed list of the laws and motive clauses found in the six Pentateuchal legal collections (i.e., the Dec, BC, CD, H, D and PC) studied in the present work. Each legal collection is analyzed separately and includes the following information.

1. A list of the individual legal prescriptions. A motivated law will be identified by placing "mc" (abbreviation for "motive clause") next to it. When a given mc constitutes a motivation for more than one legal prescription, this will be noted by placing a perpendicular line covering all these laws. Parenetic statements ("par"), introductions ("intro") and conclusions ("concl") will not be counted as laws, and the texts so identified will be placed in parentheses. In the lists, "nl" will stand for "not law," "intrn" for "internal motive clause," and "com" for "ad hoc commands."

2. The Hebrew text of the motivated laws. In each case, motive clauses will be underlined. On the righthand side of the Hebrew text a few selected sources will be added to indicate that these, too, clearly recognize the motive clauses as such. The vocalized Hebrew text is reprinted, with permission, from *Tikkun Lakoreim* (New York: KTAV, 1946).

3. Notes, referring either to the lists of legal prescriptions or to the lists of motive clauses.

1.   THE DECALOGUE

1.1   Exod 20:2-17

(a)   *The Legal Prescriptions*

			Verses
(n. 1)	1.	mc	2-3
	2.		4
(n. 2)	3.	mc	5-6
	4.	mc	7
	5.	mc	8-11
	6.	mc	12
	7.		13
	8.		14
	9.		15
	10.		16
(n. 3)	11.		17

(b)   *The Motive Clauses*

(n.1) ס אָנֹכִי   2

יְהוָה אֱלֹהֶיךָ אֲשֶׁר הוֹצֵאתִיךָ מֵאֶרֶץ מִצְרַיִם מִבֵּית עֲבָדִים׃

לֹא־יִהְיֶה לְךָ אֱלֹהִים אֲחֵרִים עַל־פָּנָי׃ לֹא־תַעֲשֶׂה לְךָ   3
4
פֶסֶל ׀ וְכָל־תְּמוּנָה אֲשֶׁר בַּשָּׁמַיִם ׀ מִמַּעַל וַאֲשֶׁר בָּאָרֶץ

מִתַּחַת וַאֲשֶׁר בַּמַּיִם ׀ מִתַּחַת לָאָרֶץ׃ לֹא־תִשְׁתַּחֲוֶה לָהֶם   5

(n.2) וְלֹא תָעָבְדֵם כִּי אָנֹכִי יְהוָה אֱלֹהֶיךָ אֵל קַנָּא פֹּקֵד עֲוֹן

אָבֹת עַל־בָּנִים עַל־שִׁלֵּשִׁים וְעַל־רִבֵּעִים לְשֹׂנְאָי׃ וְעֹשֶׂה   6

חֶסֶד לַאֲלָפִים לְאֹהֲבַי וּלְשֹׁמְרֵי מִצְוֹתָי׃ ס לֹא תִשָּׂא   7

אֶת־שֵׁם־יְהוָה אֱלֹהֶיךָ לַשָּׁוְא כִּי לֹא יְנַקֶּה יְהוָה אֵת אֲשֶׁר

יִשָּׂא אֶת־שְׁמוֹ לַשָּׁוְא׃
ס

זָכוֹר אֶת־יוֹם הַשַּׁבָּת לְקַדְּשׁוֹ׃ שֵׁשֶׁת יָמִים תַּעֲבֹד וְעָשִׂיתָ   8
9
כָּל־מְלַאכְתֶּךָ׃ וְיוֹם הַשְּׁבִיעִי שַׁבָּת ׀ לַיהוָה אֱלֹהֶיךָ לֹא־

תַעֲשֶׂה כָל־מְלָאכָה אַתָּה ׀ וּבִנְךָ־וּבִתֶּךָ עַבְדְּךָ וַאֲמָתְךָ

וּבְהֶמְתֶּךָ וְגֵרְךָ אֲשֶׁר בִּשְׁעָרֶיךָ׃ כִּי שֵׁשֶׁת־יָמִים עָשָׂה   11

יְהוָה אֶת־הַשָּׁמַיִם וְאֶת־הָאָרֶץ אֶת־הַיָּם וְאֶת־כָּל־אֲשֶׁר־בָּם

וַיָּנַח בַּיּוֹם הַשְּׁבִיעִי עַל־כֵּן בֵּרַךְ יְהוָה אֶת־יוֹם הַשַּׁבָּת

וַיְקַדְּשֵׁהוּ׃ ס כַּבֵּד אֶת־אָבִיךָ וְאֶת־אִמֶּךָ לְמַעַן יַאֲרִכוּן   12

יָמֶיךָ עַל הָאֲדָמָה אֲשֶׁר־יְהוָה אֱלֹהֶיךָ נֹתֵן לָךְ׃ ס לֹא   13
14
תִּרְצָח׃ ס לֹא תִּנְאָף׃ ס לֹא תִּגְנֹב׃ ס לֹא־   15
16
(n.3) תַעֲנֶה בְרֵעֲךָ עֵד שָׁקֶר׃ ס לֹא תַחְמֹד בֵּית רֵעֶךָ   17
ס לֹא תַחְמֹד אֵשֶׁת רֵעֶךָ וְעַבְדּוֹ וַאֲמָתוֹ וְשׁוֹרוֹ וַחֲמֹרוֹ
וְכֹל אֲשֶׁר לְרֵעֶךָ׃

Gemser, Uitti, *NJV*, *NAB*,
RSV (5b-6); *NEB* (5bα)

Gemser, Uitti, *NJV*, *NAB*,
RSV (7b)

Gemser, Uitti, *NJV*, *NEB*,
RSV (11)

Uitti, *NJV*, *NAB*, *NEB*,
RSV (12b)

(c)   *Notes*

1. (20:2) This verse constitutes a motivation for the following command
and should be understood as, "Since I the Lord am your God...therefore, do
not...." See Noth, *Exodus*, 161-62; Paul, *Book of the Covenant*, 32. Cf. this
study, Chapter II, n. 78.

2. (20:5a) The two prohibitives are considered here as one legal prescription. Cf. Deut 4:19, 8:19, 11:16.

3. (20:17) This verse embodies one legal prescription; v. 17b para-
phrases the whole inclusive term "house."

1.2   Deut 5:6-21

(a)   *The Legal Prescriptions*

			Verses
(n. 1)	1.	mc	6-7
	2.		8
(n. 2)	3.	mc	9-10
	4.	mc	11
(n. 3)	5.	mc(2)	12-15
		v.14bβ,15	
	6.	mc(2)	16
		v.16bα,16bβ	
	7.		17
	8.		18
	9.		19
	10.		20
(n. 4)	11.		21

(b)   *The Motive Clauses*

(n.1)

6 אָנֹכִי יְהוָה אֱלֹהֶיךָ אֲשֶׁר הוֹצֵאתִיךָ
7 מֵאֶרֶץ מִצְרַיִם מִבֵּית עֲבָדִים: לֹא־יִהְיֶה לְךָ אֱלֹהִים
8 אֲחֵרִים עַל־פָּנָי: לֹא־תַעֲשֶׂה־לְךָ פֶסֶל ו כָּל־תְּמוּנָה אֲשֶׁר
בַּשָּׁמַיִם ו מִמַּעַל וַאֲשֶׁר בָּאָרֶץ מִתָּחַת וַאֲשֶׁר בַּמַּיִם ו

Gemser, Uitti, *NJV*, *NAB*,
RSV (9b-10); *NEB* (9bα)

Gemser, Uitti, *NJV*, *NAB*,
RSV (11b)

(n.2)

9 מִתַּחַת לָאָרֶץ: לֹא־תִשְׁתַּחֲוֶה לָהֶם וְלֹא תָעָבְדֵם כִּי אָנֹכִי
יְהוָה אֱלֹהֶיךָ אֵל קַנָּא פֹּקֵד עֲוֹן אָבֹת עַל־בָּנִים וְעַל־
10 שִׁלֵּשִׁים וְעַל־רִבֵּעִים לְשֹׂנְאָי: וְעֹשֶׂה חֶסֶד לַאֲלָפִים
11 לְאֹהֲבַי וּלְשֹׁמְרֵי מִצְוֹתוֹ: ס   לֹא תִשָּׂא אֶת־שֵׁם־יְהוָה
אֱלֹהֶיךָ לַשָּׁוְא כִּי לֹא יְנַקֶּה יְהוָה אֵת אֲשֶׁר־יִשָּׂא אֶת־שְׁמוֹ
12 לַשָּׁוְא: ס   שָׁמוֹר אֶת־יוֹם הַשַּׁבָּת לְקַדְּשׁוֹ כַּאֲשֶׁר צִוְּךָ ו
13 יְהוָה אֱלֹהֶיךָ: שֵׁשֶׁת יָמִים תַּעֲבֹד וְעָשִׂיתָ כָּל־מְלַאכְתֶּךָ:
14 וְיוֹם הַשְּׁבִיעִי שַׁבָּת ו לַיהוָה אֱלֹהֶיךָ לֹא תַעֲשֶׂה כָל־
מְלָאכָה אַתָּה וּבִנְךָ־וּבִתֶּךָ וְעַבְדְּךָ־וַאֲמָתֶךָ וְשׁוֹרְךָ וַחֲמֹרְךָ

Gemser (14bβ-15); Uitti
(14c-15); *NJV*, *NEB*, *RSV*
(14bβ); *NAB* (15)

(n.3)

וְכָל־בְּהֶמְתֶּךָ וְגֵרְךָ אֲשֶׁר בִּשְׁעָרֶיךָ לְמַעַן יָנוּחַ עַבְדְּךָ
15 וַאֲמָתְךָ כָּמוֹךָ: וְזָכַרְתָּ כִּי־עֶבֶד הָיִיתָ ו בְּאֶרֶץ מִצְרַיִם
וַיֹּצִאֲךָ יְהוָה אֱלֹהֶיךָ מִשָּׁם בְּיָד חֲזָקָה וּבִזְרֹעַ נְטוּיָה עַל־
16 כֵּן צִוְּךָ יְהוָה אֱלֹהֶיךָ לַעֲשׂוֹת אֶת־יוֹם הַשַּׁבָּת: ס   כַּבֵּד אֶת־
אָבִיךָ וְאֶת־אִמֶּךָ כַּאֲשֶׁר צִוְּךָ יְהוָה אֱלֹהֶיךָ לְמַעַן ו יַאֲרִיכֻן
יָמֶיךָ וּלְמַעַן יִיטַב לָךְ עַל הָאֲדָמָה אֲשֶׁר־יְהוָה אֱלֹהֶיךָ

Gemser, *NAB* (16b); Uitti
(16aβ-b); *NJV*, *NEB*, *RSV*
(16bα,β)

(n.4)

נֹתֵן לָךְ: ס 17 לֹא תִרְצָח: ס 18 וְלֹא תִנְאָף: ס 19 וְלֹא
תִּגְנֹב: ס 20 וְלֹא־תַעֲנֶה בְרֵעֲךָ עֵד שָׁוְא: ס 21 וְלֹא
תַחְמֹד אֵשֶׁת רֵעֶךָ   ס   וְלֹא תִתְאַוֶּה בֵּית רֵעֶךָ שָׂדֵהוּ
וְעַבְדּוֹ וַאֲמָתוֹ שׁוֹרוֹ וַחֲמֹרוֹ וְכֹל אֲשֶׁר לְרֵעֶךָ:

(c)   *Notes*

    1. (5:6-7) See n. 1 in Chart 1.1.

    2. (5:9a) See n. 2 in Chart 1.1.

    3. (5:15) This is a secondary motivation, understood as "for you shall remember that...." Cf. *NAB*.

    4. (5:21) As in Exod 20:17, this verse, too, is taken as embodying one legal prescription. It should be noted, however, that in Deuteronomy, unlike Exodus, the married wife is mentioned first (v. 21a) and then the neighbor's house(hold) (v. 21b). Furthermore, D substitutes תתאוה ("desire") in v. 21b for תחמד in v. 21a. This indicates that D clearly regarded the injunction as banning guilty desires (M. Greenberg, "Decalogue," *EncJud* 5, 1443).

2.   BOOK OF THE COVENANT (Exod 20:22-23:33)

(a)   *The Legal Prescriptions*

	Exodus 20		Verses		Exod. 21 cont.		Verses
	–	intro	(22a)		28.		22
	1.		⌈23a-baא		29.		23-25
	2.		⌊23bβ	(n. 2)	30.	mc	26
(n. 1)		mc	22b	(n. 2)	31.	mc	27
	3.		24a		32.		28a-ba
	–	par	(24b)		33.		28bβ
	4.	mc	25		34.		28bγ
	5.	mc	26		35.		29a-ba
					36.		29bβ
	Exodus 21				37.		30
	–	intro	(1)		38.		31
	6.		2		39.		32a-ba
	7.		3a		40.		32bβ
	8.		3b		41.		33-34a
	9.		4a-ba		42.		34b
	10.		4bβ		43.		35a-ba
	11.		5-6		44.		35bβ
	12.		7		45.		35bγ
	13.	mc	8		46.		36a-ba
	14.		9		47.		36bβ
	15.		10		48.		37
	16.		11				
	17.		12		Exodus 22		
	18.		13	(n. 3)	49.		2b
	19.		14		50.		3
	20.		15		51.		1
	21.		16		52.		2a
	22.		17		53.		4
	23.		18-19a		54.		5
	24		19ba		55.		6
	25.		19bβ		56.		7
	26.		20		57.		8
	27.	mc	21		58.		9-10

	Exodus 22 cont.	Verses
	59.	11
	60.	12
	61.	13
	62.	14a
	63.	14b
	64.	15
	65.	16
	66.	17
	67.	18
	68.	19
	69. mc	20
(n. 4)	70. mc	21-23
	71.	24
	72. mc(2)	25-26
(n. 5)	v.26a-bα,bβ	
	73.	27a
	74.	27b
	75.	28a
	76.	28b
	77.	29
	- par	(30a)
	78.	30bα
	79.	30bβ

	Exodus 23	
	80.	1a
	81.	1b
	82.	2a
	83.	2b
	84.	3
	85.	4
	86.	5
	87.	6
	88.	7a
	89. mc	7b
	90. mc	8
	91. mc	9
	92. mc	10-11a
	93.	11b
	94. mc	12
	- par	(13a)
	95.	13b
	- intro	(14)
	96. mc	15a
	97.	15b
	98.	16a
	99.	16b
	100.	17
	101.	18a
	102.	18b
	103.	19a
	104.	19b
	- concl	(20-33)

(b)   *The Motive Clauses*

Exodus 20

(n. 1) 22 וַיֹּאמֶר יְהֹוָה אֶל־מֹשֶׁה כֹּה תֹאמַר אֶל־בְּנֵי יִשְׂרָאֵל אַתֶּם
        23 רְאִיתֶם כִּי מִן־הַשָּׁמַיִם דִּבַּרְתִּי עִמָּכֶם: לֹא תַעֲשׂוּן אִתִּי
        24 אֱלֹהֵי כֶסֶף וֵאלֹהֵי זָהָב לֹא תַעֲשׂוּ לָכֶם: מִזְבַּח אֲדָמָה
           תַּעֲשֶׂה־לִּי וְזָבַחְתָּ עָלָיו אֶת־עֹלֹתֶיךָ וְאֶת־שְׁלָמֶיךָ אֶת־
           צֹאנְךָ וְאֶת־בְּקָרֶךָ בְּכָל־הַמָּקוֹם אֲשֶׁר אַזְכִּיר אֶת־שְׁמִי
           אָבוֹא אֵלֶיךָ וּבֵרַכְתִּיךָ: 25 וְאִם־מִזְבַּח אֲבָנִים תַּעֲשֶׂה־לִּי
           לֹא־תִבְנֶה אֶתְהֶן גָּזִית כִּי חַרְבְּךָ הֵנַפְתָּ עָלֶיהָ וַתְּחַלְלֶהָ:
        26 וְלֹא־תַעֲלֶה בְמַעֲלֹת עַל־מִזְבְּחִי אֲשֶׁר לֹא־תִגָּלֶה
           עֶרְוָתְךָ עָלָיו:

Gemser, Uitti, *NAB*, *NEB*, *RSV* (25b); *NJV* (22b=25bH)

Gemser, Uitti, *RSV* (26b); *NJV* (23b=26bH)

Exodus 21

        8 אִם־רָעָה בְּעֵינֵי אֲדֹנֶיהָ אֲשֶׁר־
           לוֹ יְעָדָהּ וְהֶפְדָּהּ לְעַם נָכְרִי לֹא־יִמְשֹׁל לְמָכְרָהּ בְּבִגְדוֹ־
           בָהּ:

Gemser, Uitti, *NJV*, *NAB*, *RSV* (8bβ)

Gemser, *NJV*, *NAB*, *NEB*, *RSV* (21bβ); Uitti (21b)

        ב
        21 וְכִי־יַכֶּה אִישׁ אֶת־עַבְדּוֹ
           אוֹ אֶת־אֲמָתוֹ בַּשֵּׁבֶט וּמֵת תַּחַת יָדוֹ נָקֹם יִנָּקֵם: אַךְ אִם־
           יוֹם אוֹ יוֹמַיִם יַעֲמֹד לֹא יֻקַּם כִּי כַסְפּוֹ הוּא:

        26 וְכִי־יַכֶּה אִישׁ
(n. 2)   אֶת־עֵין עַבְדּוֹ אוֹ־אֶת־עֵין אֲמָתוֹ וְשִׁחֲתָהּ לַחָפְשִׁי יְשַׁלְּחֶנּוּ
(n. 3) 27 תַּחַת עֵינוֹ: וְאִם־שֵׁן עַבְדּוֹ אוֹ־שֵׁן אֲמָתוֹ יַפִּיל לַחָפְשִׁי יְשַׁלְּחֶנּוּ
           תַּחַת שִׁנּוֹ:

Exodus 22

        20 וְגֵר לֹא־תוֹנֶה וְלֹא תִלְחָצֶנּוּ כִּי־גֵרִים הֱיִיתֶם בְּאֶרֶץ מִצְרָיִם:
(n. 4) 21 כָּל־אַלְמָנָה וְיָתוֹם לֹא תְעַנּוּן: 22 אִם־עַנֵּה תְעַנֶּה אֹתוֹ כִּי
        23 אִם־צָעֹק יִצְעַק אֵלַי שָׁמֹעַ אֶשְׁמַע צַעֲקָתוֹ: וְחָרָה אַפִּי
           וְהָרַגְתִּי אֶתְכֶם בֶּחָרֶב וְהָיוּ נְשֵׁיכֶם אַלְמָנוֹת וּבְנֵיכֶם יְתֹמִים: פ
        24 אִם־כֶּסֶף | תַּלְוֶה אֶת־עַמִּי אֶת־הֶעָנִי עִמָּךְ לֹא־תִהְיֶה לוֹ
        25 כְּנֹשֶׁה לֹא־תְשִׂימוּן עָלָיו נֶשֶׁךְ: אִם־חָבֹל תַּחְבֹּל שַׂלְמַת
        26 רֵעֶךָ עַד־בֹּא הַשֶּׁמֶשׁ תְּשִׁיבֶנּוּ לוֹ: כִּי הִוא כְסוּתֹה לְבַדָּהּ
           הִוא שִׂמְלָתוֹ לְעֹרוֹ בַּמֶּה יִשְׁכָּב וְהָיָה כִּי־יִצְעַק אֵלַי וְשָׁמַעְתִּי
(n. 5)   כִּי־חַנּוּן אָנִי:

Gemser, Uitti, *NJV*, *NAB* (20b); *RSV* (21b=20bH)

Uitti (22-23)

Gemser (26bα,bβ); Uitti, *NAB* (26); *NEB*, *RSV* (27=26H)

Exodus 23

מִדְּבַר־שֶׁקֶר תִּרְחָק וְנָקִי וְצַדִּיק אַל־תַּהֲרֹג 7

כִּי לֹא־אַצְדִּיק רָשָׁע: וְשֹׁחַד לֹא תִקָּח כִּי הַשֹּׁחַד יְעַוֵּר 8

פִּקְחִים וִיסַלֵּף דִּבְרֵי צַדִּיקִים: וְגֵר לֹא תִלְחָץ וְאַתֶּם 9

יְדַעְתֶּם אֶת־נֶפֶשׁ הַגֵּר כִּי־גֵרִים הֱיִיתֶם בְּאֶרֶץ מִצְרָיִם:

וְשֵׁשׁ שָׁנִים תִּזְרַע אֶת־אַרְצֶךָ וְאָסַפְתָּ אֶת־תְּבוּאָתָהּ: ·

וְהַשְּׁבִיעִת תִּשְׁמְטֶנָּה וּנְטַשְׁתָּהּ וְאָכְלוּ אֶבְיֹנֵי עַמֶּךָ וְיִתְרָם 11

תֹּאכַל חַיַּת הַשָּׂדֶה כֵּן־תַּעֲשֶׂה לְכַרְמְךָ לְזֵיתֶךָ: שֵׁשֶׁת יָמִים 12

תַּעֲשֶׂה מַעֲשֶׂיךָ וּבַיּוֹם הַשְּׁבִיעִי תִּשְׁבֹּת לְמַעַן יָנוּחַ שׁוֹרְךָ

וַחֲמֹרֶךָ וְיִנָּפֵשׁ בֶּן־אֲמָתְךָ וְהַגֵּר: וּבְכֹל אֲשֶׁר־אָמַרְתִּי 13

אֲלֵיכֶם תִּשָּׁמֵרוּ וְשֵׁם אֱלֹהִים אֲחֵרִים לֹא תַזְכִּירוּ לֹא

יִשָּׁמַע עַל־פִּיךָ: שָׁלֹשׁ רְגָלִים תָּחֹג לִי בַּשָּׁנָה: אֶת־חַג 14

הַמַּצּוֹת תִּשְׁמֹר שִׁבְעַת יָמִים תֹּאכַל מַצּוֹת כַּאֲשֶׁר צִוִּיתִךָ

לְמוֹעֵד חֹדֶשׁ הָאָבִיב כִּי־בוֹ יָצָאתָ מִמִּצְרָיִם וְלֹא־יֵרָאוּ

פָנַי רֵיקָם:

Gemser, *NJV*, *NEB*, *RSV*
(7bβ); Uitti (7c)

Gemser, *NJV*, *NAB*, *NEB*, *RSV*
(8b); Uitti (8b,c)

Gemser, Uitti, *NJV*, *NEB*
(9b); *NAB* (9bβ); *RSV*
(9bα,bβ)

Uitti (11aβ,b); *NAB*, *RSV*
(11aα-aβ)

Gemser, Uitti, *NJV*, *NAB*,
NEB, *RSV* (12b)

Gemser, *NJV*, *NAB*, *NEB*, *RSV*
(15aβ); Uitti (15bα,γ)

(c)   *Notes*

1. (20:22) Verse 22b constitutes the underlying reason for the prohibitions against making images of gods (v. 23). See Noth, *Exodus*, 175. Cf.
Deut 4:15ff.

2. (21:26, 27) See Chapter II, n. 55.

3. (22:26) This half verse is to be connected with the law in 21:37,
NJV, ad loc. Cf. Paul, *Book of the Covenant*, 86; Noth, *Exodus*, 183.

4. (22:22-23) The intent of these verses is to indicate what will
happen if the injunction in v. 21 is overlooked: i.e., do not oppress the widow
or the orphan, for if you do, then I, God, will take action against you. Verses
22-23 can therefore be considered motive clauses introduced asyndetically. For
motive clauses embodying threats of punishment, see Chapter II.

5. (22:26) In v. 26, there are two motive clauses (v. 26a-bα, bβ). The
clause אָנִי חַנּוּן כִּי (v. 26-end) is an internal motive clause and motivates the
verb וְשָׁמַעְתִּי, not the law in v. 25.

3.   THE CULTIC DECALOGUE (Exod 34:10-26)

(a)   *The Legal Prescriptions*

			Verses
(n. 1)	-	intro	(10-16)
	1.		17
	2.	mc	18
	3.		19
	4.		20aα
	5.		20aβ
	6.		20bα
	7.		20bβ
(n. 2)	8.		21
(n. 3)	9.		22a
	10.		22b
	11.	mc	23-24
	12.		25a
	13.		25b
	14.		26a
	15.		26b

(b)   *The Motive Clauses*

17
18 אֱלֹהֵי מַסֵּכָה לֹא תַעֲשֶׂה־לָּךְ: אֶת־
חַג הַמַּצּוֹת תִּשְׁמֹר שִׁבְעַת יָמִים תֹּאכַל מַצּוֹת אֲשֶׁר צִוִּיתִךָ
לְמוֹעֵד חֹדֶשׁ הָאָבִיב כִּי בְּחֹדֶשׁ הָאָבִיב יָצָאתָ מִמִּצְרָיִם:
19 כָּל־פֶּטֶר רֶחֶם לִי וְכָל־מִקְנְךָ תִּזָּכָר פֶּטֶר שׁוֹר וָשֶׂה:
וּפֶטֶר חֲמוֹר תִּפְדֶּה בְשֶׂה וְאִם־לֹא תִפְדֶּה וַעֲרַפְתּוֹ כֹל
(n. 2)   21 בְּכוֹר בָּנֶיךָ תִּפְדֶּה וְלֹא־יֵרָאוּ פָנַי רֵיקָם: שֵׁשֶׁת יָמִים
תַּעֲבֹד וּבַיּוֹם הַשְּׁבִיעִי תִּשְׁבֹּת בֶּחָרִישׁ וּבַקָּצִיר תִּשְׁבֹּת:
(n. 3)   22 וְחַג שָׁבֻעֹת תַּעֲשֶׂה לְךָ בִּכּוּרֵי קְצִיר חִטִּים וְחַג הָאָסִיף
23 תְּקוּפַת הַשָּׁנָה: שָׁלֹשׁ פְּעָמִים בַּשָּׁנָה יֵרָאֶה כָּל־זְכוּרְךָ
24 אֶת־פְּנֵי הָאָדֹן | יְהוָה אֱלֹהֵי יִשְׂרָאֵל: כִּי־אוֹרִישׁ גּוֹיִם
מִפָּנֶיךָ וְהִרְחַבְתִּי אֶת־גְּבֻלֶךָ וְלֹא־יַחְמֹד אִישׁ אֶת־אַרְצְךָ
בַּעֲלֹתְךָ לֵרָאוֹת אֶת־פְּנֵי יְהוָה אֱלֹהֶיךָ שָׁלֹשׁ פְּעָמִים בַּשָּׁנָה:
25 לֹא־תִשְׁחַט עַל־חָמֵץ דַּם־זִבְחִי וְלֹא־יָלִין לַבֹּקֶר זֶבַח חַג
26 הַפָּסַח: רֵאשִׁית בִּכּוּרֵי אַדְמָתְךָ תָּבִיא בֵּית יְהוָה אֱלֹהֶיךָ
לֹא־תְבַשֵּׁל גְּדִי בַּחֲלֵב אִמּוֹ:

Gemser, Uitti, *NJV, NAB,*
NEB, RSV (18b)

Gemser, Uitti, *NAB, NEB,*
RSV (24)

(c)   *Notes*

       1. (34:10-16) For a discussion of this introduction, see Chapter II,
p. 89 and n. 107.

       2. (34:21) Verse 21b does not constitute a separate legal prescription;
see Chapter II, p. 82.

       3. (34:22) Verse 22 contains two separate legal prescriptions; cf.
Exod 23:16.

4.   THE HOLINESS CODE (Leviticus 17-26)

(a)   *The Legal Prescriptions*

		Leviticus 17	Verses
	-	intro	(1-2)
(n. 1)	1.	mc(3)	3-7a
		v.4bαⰃ,5-6,7a	
	-	par	(7b)
	-	intro	(8aα)
	2.		8aβ-9
	3.	mc(2)	10-11
		v.11aαℵ,11aⰃ-b	
	-	sum	(12)
	4.		⌐13a-bα
	5.		⌊13bβ
		mc v.14	
	6.		15
	7.		16

		Leviticus 18	Verses
(n. 2)	-	par intro	(1-5)
(n. 3)	8.	mc	6
(n. 4)	9.	mc	7
	10.	mc	8
	11.		9
	12.	mc	10
	13.	mc	11
	14.	mc	12
	15.	mc	13
	16.	mc	14
	17.	mc	15
	18.	mc	16
	19.		⌐17a
	20.		⌊17b
(n. 5)		mc v.17bβ	
	21.		18
	22.		19
	23.		20
(n. 6)	24.	mc(2)	21
		v.21bα,bβ	
(n. 7)	25.	mc	22
	26.		⌐23a
	27.		⌊23b
(n. 8)		mc v.23bβ	
	-	par concl	(24-30)

		Leviticus 19	Verses
	-	par intro	(1-2)
	28.		⌐3aα
	29.		⌊3aβ
		mc v.3b	
	30.		⌐4aα
	31.		⌊4aβ
		mc v.4b	

		Lev. 19 cont.	Verses
	-	intro	(5)
	32.		6aα
	33.		6aβ
(n. 9)	34.	mc	7
	35.	mc	8
	36.		⌐9a
	37.		9b
	38.		10aα
	39.		10aβ
	40.		⌊10bα
		mc v.10bβ	
	41.		11a
	42.		11bα
	43.		11bβ
(n.10)	44.	mc(2)	12
		v.12bα,bβ	
	45.		13aα
	46.		13aβ
	47.		13b
	48.		14aα
	49.		14aβ
	-	par	(14b)
	-	intro	(15aα)
	50.		15aβ
	51.		15aγ
	-	concl	(15b)
	52.		⌐16aα
	53.		⌊16aβ
		mc v.16b	
	54.		17a
	55.	mc	17b
	56.		18aα
	57.		18aβ
	-	par	(18b)
	-	par	(19aα)
	58.		19aβ
	59.		19aγ
	60.		19b
	61.	mc	20
	62.		21
(n.11)	-	concl	(22)
	63.		⌐23
	64.		⌊24
	65.		⌊25aα
		mc(2)	
		v.25aβ,b	
	66.		⌐26a
	67.		⌊26bα
	68.		⌊26bβ
	69.		⌊27a
	70.		⌊27b

Lev. 19 cont.

			Verses
	71.		⎡28aα
	72.		⎣28aβ
		mc v.28b	
	73.	mc	29
	74.		⎡30aα
	75.		⎣30aβ
		mc v.30b	
	76.	mc	31
	77.		32aα
	78.		32aβ
	-	par	(32b)
(n.12)	79.	mc(2)	33-34
		v.34aβ,b	
	80.	mc	35-36
	-	par concl	(37)

Leviticus 20

			Verses
	-	intro	(1-2aα)
	81.	mc	2aβ-3
	82.		4-5
	83.		6
	-	par	(7-8)
(n.13)	84.	mc	9
	85.		10
(n.14)	86.	mc	11
	87.	mc	12
(n.15)	88.	mc	13
(n.16)	89.	mc(2)	14
		v.14aβ,bβ	
	90.		15a
	91.		15b
	92.		16aα
	93.		16aβ
	-	sum	(16b)
(n.17)	94.	mc(2)	17
		v.17aα ,b	
(n.18)	95.	mc	18
	96.	mc	19
(n.19)	97.	mc	20
(n.20)	98.	mc(2)	21
		v.21aα ,bα	
	-	par	(22-26)
	99.		27

Leviticus 21

			Verses
	-	intro	(1a-bα)
	100.		⎡1bβ-3
	101.		4
	102.		5aα
	103.		5aβ
	104.		⎣5b
(n.21)		mc v.6	

Lev. 21 cont.

			Verses
	105.		⎡7aα
	106.		⎣7aβ
		mc(2)	
		v.7b-8a,b	
(n.22)	107.	mc	9
	108.		10a-bα
	109.		10bβ
	110.		11
	111.	mc(2)	12
		v.12aβ-bα,bβ	
(n.23)	112.	mc	13-15
	-	intro	(16-17a)
(n.24)	113.	mc	17b-21
	114.		22
	115.	mc(2)	23
		v.23aβ,b	
	-	concl	(24)

Leviticus 22

			Verses
	-	intro	(1-2aαא)
	116.	mc(2)	2aב-b
		v.2aβ,bβ	
	-	intro	(3aαא)
	117.	mc	3aב-b
	118.		4a
	119.		5b-6
	120.	mc	7
	121.	mc	8
	-	par	(9)
	122.		10a
	123.		10b
	124.		11a
	125.		11b
	126.		12
	127.		13a
	-	sum	(13b)
	128.		14
(n.25)	-	par concl	(15-16)
	-	intro	(17-18a)
	129.		18b-19
	130.	mc	20
	131.		21-22,24a
	132.		23
	133.		24b
	134.	mc(2)	25
		v.25bα,bβ	
	-	intro	(26)
	135.		27
	136.		28
	-	intro	(29)
	137.	mc	30
	-	par concl	(31-33)

Leviticus 23		Verses
	- intro	(1-2)
(n.26) 138.	mc	3
	- intro	(4)
139.		5
140.		6a
141.		6b
142.		7
143.		8a
144.		8b
	- intro	(9-10aα)
145.		10aβ-b
146.		11
147.		12-13
148.		14a
	- par	(14b)
149.		15-16a
150.		16b
151.		17
152.		18
153.		19a
154.		19b
155.		20
156.		21a
	- par	(21b)
157.		⌈22aα
158.		22aβ
159.		22bα
	mc v.22bβ	
	- intro	(23-24a)
160.		24b-25a
161.		25b
	- intro	(26)
162.		⌈27a
163.		27b
164.		28a
	mc(3)	
	v.28b,29,30	
	- par concl	(31-32)
	- intro	(33-34a)
165.		34b
166.		35
167.		36a
(n.27) 168.	mc	36bα
169.		36bβ
	- concl	(37-38)
170.		39
171.		40-41a
	- par concl	(41b)
172.	mc(2)	42-43
	v.43a,b	
	- concl	(44)

Leviticus 24		Verses
	- intro	(1-2aα)
173.	mc(2)	2aβ-b
	v.2aβℶ,b	
174.		3a
	- par	(3b)
175.		4
176.		5-7
177.		8
178.	mc	9
	- nl	(10-14)
	- intro	(15)
179.		16
180.		17
181.		18
182.		19-20
	- sum	(21)
	- par concl	(22)
	- nl	(23)

Leviticus 25		Verses
	- intro	(1-2aα)
(n.28) 183.		2aβ-5
	- sum	(6-7)
184.		8
185.		9
186.		10
187.	mc	11-12a
188.		12b
	- sum	(13)
189.	mc	14-16
	- par sum	(17)
	- par	(18-22)
190.	mc(2)	23aα
	v.23aβ,b	
	- intro	(24)
191.		25
192.		26-27
193.		28
194.		29
195.		30
196.		31
197.		32
198.	mc	33
199.	mc	34
200.	mc	35-38
201.		⌈39-40a
202.		40b-41
	mc v.42	
	- par sum	(43)
203.		44
204.		45a
205.		45b-46a
	- par sum	(46b)

Lev. 25 cont.	Verses
206.	47-49
207.	50-52
208.	53
209.	54
mc(2)	
v.55a,b	

Leviticus 26

210.	1aα
211.	1aβ
212.	1aγ
mc v.1b	
213.	2aα
214.	2aβ
- concl	(3-46)

(b)   *The Motive Clauses*

Leviticus 17

(n. 1)

וַיְדַבֵּ֥ר יְהוָ֖ה אֶל־מֹשֶׁ֥ה לֵּאמֹֽר׃ דַּבֵּ֨ר אֶֽל־אַהֲרֹ֤ן וְאֶל־בָּנָיו֙ 2 ×
וְאֶל֙ כָּל־בְּנֵ֣י יִשְׂרָאֵ֔ל וְאָמַרְתָּ֖ אֲלֵיהֶ֑ם זֶ֣ה הַדָּבָ֔ר אֲשֶׁר־
צִוָּ֥ה יְהוָ֖ה לֵאמֹֽר׃ אִ֥ישׁ אִישׁ֙ מִבֵּ֣ית יִשְׂרָאֵ֔ל אֲשֶׁ֨ר יִשְׁחַ֜ט 3
שׁ֥וֹר אוֹ־כֶ֛שֶׂב אוֹ־עֵ֖ז בַּֽמַּחֲנֶ֑ה א֚וֹ אֲשֶׁ֣ר יִשְׁחַ֔ט מִח֖וּץ
לַֽמַּחֲנֶֽה׃ וְאֶל־פֶּ֜תַח אֹ֤הֶל מוֹעֵד֙ לֹ֣א הֱבִיא֔וֹ לְהַקְרִ֥יב 4
קָרְבָּן֙ לַֽיהוָ֔ה לִפְנֵ֖י מִשְׁכַּ֣ן יְהוָ֑ה דָּ֣ם יֵחָשֵׁ֞ב לָאִ֤ישׁ הַהוּא֙
דָּ֣ם שָׁפָ֔ךְ וְנִכְרַ֛ת הָאִ֥ישׁ הַה֖וּא מִקֶּ֣רֶב עַמּֽוֹ׃ לְמַ֡עַן אֲשֶׁר֩
יָבִ֨יאוּ בְּנֵ֣י יִשְׂרָאֵ֗ל אֶֽת־זִבְחֵיהֶם֮ אֲשֶׁ֣ר הֵ֣ם זֹבְחִים֮ עַל־
פְּנֵ֣י הַשָּׂדֶה֒ וֶֽהֱבִיאֻ֣ם לַֽיהוָ֗ה אֶל־פֶּ֛תַח אֹ֥הֶל מוֹעֵ֖ד אֶל־
הַכֹּהֵ֑ן וְזָ֨בְח֜וּ זִבְחֵ֧י שְׁלָמִ֛ים לַֽיהוָ֖ה אוֹתָֽם׃ וְזָרַ֨ק הַכֹּהֵ֤ן 6
אֶת־הַדָּם֙ עַל־מִזְבַּ֣ח יְהוָ֔ה פֶּ֖תַח אֹ֣הֶל מוֹעֵ֑ד וְהִקְטִ֣יר הַחֵ֔לֶב
לְרֵ֥יחַ נִיחֹ֖חַ לַֽיהוָֽה׃ וְלֹא־יִזְבְּח֥וּ עוֹד֙ אֶת־זִבְחֵיהֶ֔ם לַשְּׂעִירִ֕ם
אֲשֶׁ֛ר הֵ֥ם זֹנִ֖ים אַחֲרֵיהֶ֑ם

וְאִ֣ישׁ אִ֗ישׁ מִבֵּ֣ית יִשְׂרָאֵ֔ל וּמִן־
הַגֵּר֙ הַגָּ֣ר בְּתוֹכָ֔ם אֲשֶׁ֥ר יֹאכַ֖ל כָּל־דָּ֑ם וְנָתַתִּ֣י פָנַ֗י בַּנֶּ֙פֶשׁ֙
הָֽאֹכֶ֣לֶת אֶת־הַדָּ֔ם וְהִכְרַתִּ֥י אֹתָ֖הּ מִקֶּ֥רֶב עַמָּֽהּ׃ כִּ֣י 11
נֶ֣פֶשׁ הַבָּשָׂר֮ בַּדָּ֣ם הִוא֒ וַֽאֲנִ֞י נְתַתִּ֤יו לָכֶם֙ עַל־הַמִּזְבֵּ֔חַ
לְכַפֵּ֖ר עַל־נַפְשֹׁתֵיכֶ֑ם כִּֽי־הַדָּ֥ם ה֖וּא בַּנֶּ֥פֶשׁ יְכַפֵּֽר׃ עַל־כֵּ֤ן 12
אָמַ֙רְתִּי֙ לִבְנֵ֣י יִשְׂרָאֵ֔ל כָּל־נֶ֥פֶשׁ מִכֶּ֖ם לֹא־תֹ֣אכַל דָּ֑ם וְהַגֵּ֛ר
הַגָּ֥ר בְּתֽוֹכְכֶ֖ם לֹא־יֹ֥אכַל דָּֽם׃ וְאִ֣ישׁ אִ֗ישׁ מִבְּנֵ֣י יִשְׂרָאֵ֗ל 13
וּמִן־הַגֵּר֙ הַגָּ֣ר בְּתוֹכָ֔ם אֲשֶׁ֨ר יָצ֜וּד צֵ֥יד חַיָּ֛ה אוֹ־ע֖וֹף אֲשֶׁ֣ר
יֵֽאָכֵ֑ל וְשָׁפַךְ֙ אֶת־דָּמ֔וֹ וְכִסָּ֖הוּ בֶּֽעָפָֽר׃ כִּֽי־נֶ֣פֶשׁ כָּל־בָּשָׂ֗ר 14
דָּמ֤וֹ בְנַפְשׁוֹ֙ ה֔וּא וָֽאֹמַר֙ לִבְנֵ֣י יִשְׂרָאֵ֔ל דַּ֥ם כָּל־בָּשָׂ֖ר לֹ֣א
תֹאכֵ֑לוּ כִּ֣י נֶ֤פֶשׁ כָּל־בָּשָׂר֙ דָּמ֣וֹ הִ֔וא כָּל־אֹכְלָ֖יו יִכָּרֵֽת׃

Uitti (4b)

Uitti (5-7); *NJV* (5-7a);
NEB (5aα); *RSV* (5-6,7a?)

Gemser, *NAB* (11); Uitti,
NJV, *NEB*, *RSV* (11-12)

Gemser, Uitti, *NAB*, *RSV*
(14); *NJV*, *NEB* (14a,bα)

Leviticus 18

אִישׁ אִישׁ

(n. 2)	6 אֶל־כָּל־שְׁאֵר בְּשָׂרוֹ לֹא תִקְרְבוּ לְגַלּוֹת עֶרְוָה אֲנִי יְהוָה׃	Uitti (6b)
(n. 3)	7 ס עֶרְוַת אָבִיךָ וְעֶרְוַת אִמְּךָ לֹא תְגַלֵּה אִמְּךָ הִוא לֹא	Uitti, *NAB* (7bα)
	8 תְגַלֶּה עֶרְוָתָהּ׃ ס עֶרְוַת אֵשֶׁת־אָבִיךָ לֹא תְגַלֵּה	Gemser, Uitti, *NAB* (8b); *NEB* (8b?)
(n. 4)	9 עֶרְוַת אָבִיךָ הִוא׃ ס עֶרְוַת אֲחוֹתְךָ בַת־אָבִיךָ אוֹ	Uitti, *NJV, NAB, RSV* (10b); *NEB* (10b?)
	בַת־אִמֶּךָ מוֹלֶדֶת בַּיִת אוֹ מוֹלֶדֶת חוּץ לֹא תְגַלֶּה עֶרְוָתָן׃	
	10 ס עֶרְוַת בַּת־בִּנְךָ אוֹ בַת־בִּתְּךָ לֹא תְגַלֶּה עֶרְוָתָן כִּי	Uitti (11c); *NAB, RSV* (11aβ)
	11 עֶרְוָתְךָ הֵנָּה׃ ס עֶרְוַת בַּת־אֵשֶׁת מוֹלֶדֶת	Uitti, *NAB* (12b)
	12 אָבִיךָ אֲחוֹתְךָ הִוא לֹא תְגַלֶּה עֶרְוָתָהּ׃ ס עֶרְוַת	Gemser, Uitti, *NJV, NAB, RSV* (13b)
	13 אֲחוֹת־אָבִיךָ לֹא תְגַלֵּה שְׁאֵר אָבִיךָ הִוא׃ ס עֶרְוַת	
	14 אֲחוֹת־אִמְּךָ לֹא תְגַלֵּה כִּי־שְׁאֵר אִמְּךָ הִוא׃ ס עֶרְוַת	Uitti, *NAB* (14b)
	אֲחִי־אָבִיךָ לֹא תְגַלֵּה אֶל־אִשְׁתּוֹ לֹא תִקְרָב דֹּדָתְךָ הִוא׃	Uitti (15bα)
	15 ס ס עֶרְוַת כַּלָּתְךָ לֹא תְגַלֵּה אֵשֶׁת בִּנְךָ הִוא לֹא תְגַלֶּה	
	16 עֶרְוָתָהּ׃ ס עֶרְוַת אֵשֶׁת־אָחִיךָ לֹא תְגַלֵּה עֶרְוַת	Uitti, *NAB* (16b); *NEB* (16b?)
	17 אָחִיךָ הִוא׃ ס עֶרְוַת אִשָּׁה וּבִתָּהּ לֹא תְגַלֵּה אֶת־	Gemser, *NAB* (17bβ); Uitti (17b,c)
(n. 5)	בַּת־בְּנָהּ וְאֶת־בַּת־בִּתָּהּ לֹא תִקַּח לְגַלּוֹת עֶרְוָתָהּ שַׁאֲרָה	
	18 הֵנָּה זִמָּה הִוא׃ וְאִשָּׁה אֶל־אֲחֹתָהּ לֹא תִקָּח לִצְרֹר לְגַלּוֹת	Uitti (21b)
	19 עֶרְוָתָהּ עָלֶיהָ בְּחַיֶּיהָ׃ וְאֶל־אִשָּׁה בְּנִדַּת טֻמְאָתָהּ לֹא תִקְרַב	Gemser, Uitti (22b)
	20 לְגַלּוֹת עֶרְוָתָהּ׃ וְאֶל־אֵשֶׁת עֲמִיתְךָ לֹא־תִתֵּן שְׁכָבְתְּךָ	Gemser, Uitti (23b)
(n. 6)	21 לְזָרַע לְטָמְאָה־בָהּ׃ וּמִזַּרְעֲךָ לֹא־תִתֵּן לְהַעֲבִיר לַמֹּלֶךְ וְלֹא	
(n. 7)	22 תְחַלֵּל אֶת־שֵׁם אֱלֹהֶיךָ אֲנִי יְהוָה׃ וְאֶת־זָכָר לֹא תִשְׁכַּב	
(n. 8)	23 מִשְׁכְּבֵי אִשָּׁה תּוֹעֵבָה הִוא׃ וּבְכָל־בְּהֵמָה לֹא־תִתֵּן שְׁכָבְתְּךָ	
	לְטָמְאָה־בָהּ וְאִשָּׁה לֹא־תַעֲמֹד לִפְנֵי בְהֵמָה לְרִבְעָהּ תֶּבֶל	
	הִוא׃	

Leviticus 19

3 אִישׁ אִמּוֹ וְאָבִיו תִּירָאוּ וְאֶת־שַׁבְּתֹתַי תִּשְׁמֹרוּ
4 אֲנִי יְהוָה אֱלֹהֵיכֶם: אַל־תִּפְנוּ אֶל־הָאֱלִילִם וֵאלֹהֵי מַסֵּכָה
5 לֹא תַעֲשׂוּ לָכֶם אֲנִי יְהוָה אֱלֹהֵיכֶם: וְכִי תִזְבְּחוּ זֶבַח
6 שְׁלָמִים לַיהוָה לִרְצֹנְכֶם תִּזְבָּחֻהוּ: בְּיוֹם זִבְחֲכֶם יֵאָכֵל
7 וּמִמָּחֳרָת וְהַנּוֹתָר עַד־יוֹם הַשְּׁלִישִׁי בָּאֵשׁ יִשָּׂרֵף: וְאִם
8 הֵאָכֹל יֵאָכֵל בַּיּוֹם הַשְּׁלִישִׁי פִּגּוּל הוּא לֹא יֵרָצֶה: וְאֹכְלָיו
עֲוֹנוֹ יִשָּׂא כִּי־אֶת־קֹדֶשׁ יְהוָה חִלֵּל וְנִכְרְתָה הַנֶּפֶשׁ הַהִוא
9 מֵעַמֶּיהָ: וּבְקֻצְרְכֶם אֶת־קְצִיר אַרְצְכֶם לֹא תְכַלֶּה פְּאַת
שָׂדְךָ לִקְצֹר וְלֶקֶט קְצִירְךָ לֹא תְלַקֵּט: וְכַרְמְךָ לֹא תְעוֹלֵל
וּפֶרֶט כַּרְמְךָ לֹא תְלַקֵּט לֶעָנִי וְלַגֵּר תַּעֲזֹב אֹתָם אֲנִי יְהוָה
11 אֱלֹהֵיכֶם: לֹא תִּגְנֹבוּ וְלֹא־תְכַחֲשׁוּ וְלֹא־תְשַׁקְּרוּ אִישׁ
12 בַּעֲמִיתוֹ: וְלֹא־תִשָּׁבְעוּ בִשְׁמִי לַשָּׁקֶר וְחִלַּלְתָּ אֶת־שֵׁם
13 אֱלֹהֶיךָ אֲנִי יְהוָה: לֹא־תַעֲשֹׁק אֶת־רֵעֲךָ וְלֹא תִגְזֹל לֹא־
תָלִין פְּעֻלַּת שָׂכִיר אִתְּךָ עַד־בֹּקֶר: לֹא־תְקַלֵּל חֵרֵשׁ וְלִפְנֵי 14
עִוֵּר לֹא תִתֵּן מִכְשֹׁל וְיָרֵאתָ מֵּאֱלֹהֶיךָ אֲנִי יְהוָה: לֹא־תַעֲשׂוּ טו
עָוֶל בַּמִּשְׁפָּט לֹא־תִשָּׂא פְנֵי־דָל וְלֹא תֶהְדַּר פְּנֵי גָדוֹל
16 בְּצֶדֶק תִּשְׁפֹּט עֲמִיתֶךָ: לֹא־תֵלֵךְ רָכִיל בְּעַמֶּיךָ לֹא תַעֲמֹד
17 עַל־דַּם רֵעֶךָ אֲנִי יְהוָה: לֹא־תִשְׂנָא אֶת־אָחִיךָ בִּלְבָבֶךָ
18 הוֹכֵחַ תּוֹכִיחַ אֶת־עֲמִיתֶךָ וְלֹא־תִשָּׂא עָלָיו חֵטְא: לֹא־
תִקֹּם וְלֹא־תִטֹּר אֶת־בְּנֵי עַמֶּךָ וְאָהַבְתָּ לְרֵעֲךָ כָּמוֹךָ אֲנִי
19 יְהוָה: אֶת־חֻקֹּתַי תִּשְׁמֹרוּ בְּהֶמְתְּךָ לֹא־תַרְבִּיעַ כִּלְאַיִם
שָׂדְךָ לֹא־תִזְרַע כִּלְאָיִם וּבֶגֶד כִּלְאַיִם שַׁעַטְנֵז לֹא יַעֲלֶה
כ עָלֶיךָ: וְאִישׁ כִּי־יִשְׁכַּב אֶת־אִשָּׁה שִׁכְבַת־זֶרַע וְהִוא שִׁפְחָה
נֶחֱרֶפֶת לְאִישׁ וְהָפְדֵּה לֹא נִפְדָּתָה אוֹ חֻפְשָׁה לֹא נִתַּן
לָהּ בִּקֹּרֶת תִּהְיֶה לֹא יוּמְתוּ כִּי־לֹא חֻפָּשָׁה:
23 וְכִי־תָבֹאוּ אֶל־הָאָרֶץ וּנְטַעְתֶּם כָּל־עֵץ וַעֲרַלְתֶּם
עָרְלָתוֹ אֶת־פִּרְיוֹ שָׁלֹשׁ שָׁנִים יִהְיֶה לָכֶם עֲרֵלִים לֹא יֵאָכֵל:
24 וּבַשָּׁנָה הָרְבִיעִת יִהְיֶה כָּל־פִּרְיוֹ קֹדֶשׁ הִלּוּלִים לַיהוָה:
כה וּבַשָּׁנָה הַחֲמִישִׁת תֹּאכְלוּ אֶת־פִּרְיוֹ לְהוֹסִיף לָכֶם תְּבוּאָתוֹ
26 אֲנִי יְהוָה אֱלֹהֵיכֶם: לֹא תֹאכְלוּ עַל־הַדָּם לֹא תְנַחֲשׁוּ
27 וְלֹא תְעוֹנֵנוּ: לֹא תַקִּפוּ פְּאַת רֹאשְׁכֶם וְלֹא תַשְׁחִית אֵת
28 פְּאַת זְקָנֶךָ: וְשֶׂרֶט לָנֶפֶשׁ לֹא תִתְּנוּ בִּבְשַׂרְכֶם וּכְתֹבֶת
29 קַעֲקַע לֹא תִתְּנוּ בָּכֶם אֲנִי יְהוָה: אַל־תְּחַלֵּל אֶת־בִּתְּךָ
ל לְהַזְנוֹתָהּ וְלֹא־תִזְנֶה הָאָרֶץ וּמָלְאָה הָאָרֶץ זִמָּה: אֶת־
31 שַׁבְּתֹתַי תִּשְׁמֹרוּ וּמִקְדָּשִׁי תִּירָאוּ אֲנִי יְהוָה: אַל־תִּפְנוּ
אֶל־הָאֹבֹת וְאֶל־הַיִּדְּעֹנִים אַל־תְּבַקְשׁוּ לְטָמְאָה בָהֶם אֲנִי
32 יְהוָה אֱלֹהֵיכֶם: מִפְּנֵי שֵׂיבָה תָּקוּם וְהָדַרְתָּ פְּנֵי זָקֵן וְיָרֵאתָ
33 מֵּאֱלֹהֶיךָ אֲנִי יְהוָה: ס וְכִי־יָגוּר אִתְּךָ גֵּר בְּאַרְצְכֶם לֹא
34 תוֹנוּ אֹתוֹ: כְּאֶזְרָח מִכֶּם יִהְיֶה לָכֶם הַגֵּר הַגָּר אִתְּכֶם
וְאָהַבְתָּ לוֹ כָּמוֹךָ כִּי־גֵרִים הֱיִיתֶם בְּאֶרֶץ מִצְרָיִם אֲנִי יְהוָה
לה אֱלֹהֵיכֶם: לֹא־תַעֲשׂוּ עָוֶל בַּמִּשְׁפָּט בַּמִּדָּה בַּמִּשְׁקָל
36 וּבַמְּשׂוּרָה: מֹאזְנֵי צֶדֶק אַבְנֵי־צֶדֶק אֵיפַת צֶדֶק וְהִין צֶדֶק
יִהְיֶה לָכֶם אֲנִי יְהוָה אֱלֹהֵיכֶם אֲשֶׁר־הוֹצֵאתִי אֶתְכֶם מֵאֶרֶץ
מִצְרָיִם:

(n. 9)

(n.10)

(n.12)

Uitti (3b)

Uitti (4b)

Uitti, *NJV*, *NEB*, *RSV* (8aβ); *NAB* (8aβ?)

Uitti (10bβ)

Uitti (12b)

Uitti (16b)

Uitti (17c)

Gemser, Uitti, *NJV*, *NAB*, *NEB*, *RSV* (20bβ)

Uitti (25aβ,b); *NJV*, *RSV* (25aβ)

Uitti (28b)

Uitti, *NJV*, *NAB*, *RSV* (29b)

Uitti (30b)

Uitti (31b)

Uitti (34b); *NJV*, *NAB*, *NEB*, *RSV* (34aβ)

Gemser, Uitti (36b)

Leviticus 20

וַיְדַבֵּר יְהוָה אֶל־מֹשֶׁה לֵּאמֹר׃ וְאֶל־בְּנֵי יִשְׂרָאֵל תֹּאמַר ² א
אִישׁ אִישׁ מִבְּנֵי יִשְׂרָאֵל וּמִן־הַגֵּר ׀ הַגָּר בְּיִשְׂרָאֵל אֲשֶׁר
יִתֵּן מִזַּרְעוֹ לַמֹּלֶךְ מוֹת יוּמָת עַם הָאָרֶץ יִרְגְּמֻהוּ בָאָבֶן׃
וַאֲנִי אֶתֵּן אֶת־פָּנַי בָּאִישׁ הַהוּא וְהִכְרַתִּי אֹתוֹ מִקֶּרֶב עַמּוֹ ³
כִּי מִזַּרְעוֹ נָתַן לַמֹּלֶךְ לְמַעַן טַמֵּא אֶת־מִקְדָּשִׁי וּלְחַלֵּל אֶת־
שֵׁם קָדְשִׁי׃

כִּי־אִישׁ אִישׁ אֲשֶׁר יְקַלֵּל אֶת־אָבִיו וְאֶת־אִמּוֹ ⁹
(n.13) מוֹת יוּמָת אָבִיו וְאִמּוֹ קִלֵּל דָּמָיו בּוֹ׃ וְאִישׁ אֲשֶׁר יִנְאַף ·
(n.14) אֶת־אֵשֶׁת אִישׁ אֲשֶׁר יִנְאַף אֶת־אֵשֶׁת רֵעֵהוּ מוֹת־יוּמַת
הַנֹּאֵף וְהַנֹּאָפֶת׃ וְאִישׁ אֲשֶׁר יִשְׁכַּב אֶת־אֵשֶׁת אָבִיו עֶרְוַת ¹¹
אָבִיו גִּלָּה מוֹת־יוּמְתוּ שְׁנֵיהֶם דְּמֵיהֶם בָּם׃ וְאִישׁ אֲשֶׁר ¹²
(n.15) יִשְׁכַּב אֶת־כַּלָּתוֹ מוֹת יוּמְתוּ שְׁנֵיהֶם תֶּבֶל עָשׂוּ דְּמֵיהֶם
בָּם׃ וְאִישׁ אֲשֶׁר יִשְׁכַּב אֶת־זָכָר מִשְׁכְּבֵי אִשָּׁה תּוֹעֵבָה ¹³
(n.16) עָשׂוּ שְׁנֵיהֶם מוֹת יוּמָתוּ דְּמֵיהֶם בָּם׃ וְאִישׁ אֲשֶׁר יִקַּח ¹⁴
אֶת־אִשָּׁה וְאֶת־אִמָּהּ זִמָּה הִוא בָּאֵשׁ יִשְׂרְפוּ אֹתוֹ וְאֶתְהֶן
וְלֹא־תִהְיֶה זִמָּה בְּתוֹכְכֶם׃ וְאִישׁ אֲשֶׁר יִתֵּן שְׁכָבְתּוֹ ¹⁵
בִּבְהֵמָה מוֹת יוּמָת וְאֶת־הַבְּהֵמָה תַּהֲרֹגוּ׃ וְאִשָּׁה אֲשֶׁר ¹⁶
תִּקְרַב אֶל־כָּל־בְּהֵמָה לְרִבְעָה אֹתָהּ וְהָרַגְתָּ אֶת־הָאִשָּׁה
וְאֶת־הַבְּהֵמָה מוֹת יוּמָתוּ דְּמֵיהֶם בָּם׃ וְאִישׁ אֲשֶׁר־יִקַּח ¹⁷
(n.17) אֶת־אֲחֹתוֹ בַּת־אָבִיו אוֹ־בַת־אִמּוֹ וְרָאָה אֶת־עֶרְוָתָהּ וְהִיא
תִרְאֶה אֶת־עֶרְוָתוֹ חֶסֶד הוּא וְנִכְרְתוּ לְעֵינֵי בְּנֵי עַמָּם
(n.18) עֶרְוַת אֲחֹתוֹ גִּלָּה עֲוֹנוֹ יִשָּׂא׃ וְאִישׁ אֲשֶׁר־יִשְׁכַּב אֶת־אִשָּׁה ¹⁸
דָּוָה וְגִלָּה אֶת־עֶרְוָתָהּ אֶת־מְקֹרָהּ הֶעֱרָה וְהִיא גִּלְּתָה אֶת־
מְקוֹר דָּמֶיהָ וְנִכְרְתוּ שְׁנֵיהֶם מִקֶּרֶב עַמָּם׃ וְעֶרְוַת אֲחוֹת ¹⁹
(n.19) אִמְּךָ וַאֲחוֹת אָבִיךָ לֹא תְגַלֵּה כִּי אֶת־שְׁאֵרוֹ הֶעֱרָה עֲוֹנָם
יִשָּׂאוּ׃ וְאִישׁ אֲשֶׁר יִשְׁכַּב אֶת־דֹּדָתוֹ עֶרְוַת דֹּדוֹ גִּלָּה כ
חֶטְאָם יִשָּׂאוּ עֲרִירִים יָמֻתוּ׃ וְאִישׁ אֲשֶׁר יִקַּח אֶת־אֵשֶׁת ²¹
(n.20) אָחִיו נִדָּה הִוא עֶרְוַת אָחִיו גִּלָּה עֲרִירִים יִהְיוּ׃

Uitti (3); *NJV*, *NAB*, *RSV* (3b)

Uitti, *NAB* (9bα)

Gemser, Uitti, *NAB* (12bα)

Gemser (13aα)

Uitti (14bγ); *NJV*, *NAB*, *RSV* (14bβ)

Uitti (17bα)

Uitti (19aβ); *NJV*, *RSV* (19bα)

Uitti, *NAB* (21bα)

Leviticus 21

א וַיֹּאמֶר יְהוָה אֶל־מֹשֶׁה אֱמֹר אֶל־הַכֹּהֲנִים בְּנֵי אַהֲרֹן

2 וְאָמַרְתָּ אֲלֵהֶם לְנֶפֶשׁ לֹא־יִטַּמָּא בְּעַמָּיו: כִּי אִם־לִשְׁאֵרוֹ

3 הַקָּרֹב אֵלָיו לְאִמּוֹ וּלְאָבִיו וְלִבְנוֹ וּלְבִתּוֹ וּלְאָחִיו: וְלַאֲחֹתוֹ

הַבְּתוּלָה הַקְּרוֹבָה אֵלָיו אֲשֶׁר לֹא־הָיְתָה לְאִישׁ לָהּ יִטַּמָּא:

4 לֹא יִטַּמָּא בַּעַל בְּעַמָּיו לְהֵחַלּוֹ: לֹא־יִקְרְחֻה קָרְחָה בְּרֹאשָׁם

5 וּפְאַת זְקָנָם לֹא יְגַלֵּחוּ וּבִבְשָׂרָם לֹא יִשְׂרְטוּ שָׂרָטֶת:

6 קְדֹשִׁים יִהְיוּ לֵאלֹהֵיהֶם וְלֹא יְחַלְּלוּ שֵׁם אֱלֹהֵיהֶם כִּ

אֶת־אִשֵּׁי יְהוָה לֶחֶם אֱלֹהֵיהֶם הֵם מַקְרִיבִם וְהָיוּ קֹדֶשׁ:

7 אִשָּׁה זֹנָה וַחֲלָלָה לֹא יִקָּחוּ וְאִשָּׁה גְּרוּשָׁה מֵאִישָׁהּ לֹא

8 יִקָּחוּ כִּי־קָדֹשׁ הוּא לֵאלֹהָיו: וְקִדַּשְׁתּוֹ כִּי אֶת־לֶחֶם אֱלֹהֶיךָ

הוּא מַקְרִיב קָדֹשׁ יִהְיֶה־לָּךְ כִּי קָדוֹשׁ אֲנִי יְהוָה מְקַדִּשְׁכֶם:

9 וּבַת אִישׁ כֹּהֵן כִּי תֵחֵל לִזְנוֹת אֶת־אָבִיהָ הִיא מְחַלֶּלֶת

בָּאֵשׁ תִּשָּׂרֵף: וְהַכֹּהֵן הַגָּדוֹל מֵאֶחָיו אֲשֶׁר־יוּצַק

10 עַל־רֹאשׁוֹ שֶׁמֶן הַמִּשְׁחָה וּמִלֵּא אֶת־יָדוֹ לִלְבֹּשׁ אֶת־

11 הַבְּגָדִים אֶת־רֹאשׁוֹ לֹא יִפְרָע וּבְגָדָיו לֹא יִפְרֹם: וְעַל

12 כָּל־נַפְשֹׁת מֵת לֹא יָבֹא לְאָבִיו וּלְאִמּוֹ לֹא יִטַּמָּא: וּמִן־

הַמִּקְדָּשׁ לֹא יֵצֵא וְלֹא יְחַלֵּל אֵת מִקְדַּשׁ אֱלֹהָיו כִּי נֵזֶר

13 שֶׁמֶן מִשְׁחַת אֱלֹהָיו עָלָיו אֲנִי יְהוָה: וְהוּא אִשָּׁה בִבְתוּלֶיהָ

14 יִקָּח: אַלְמָנָה וּגְרוּשָׁה וַחֲלָלָה זֹנָה אֶת־אֵלֶּה לֹא יִקָּח

15 כִּי אִם־בְּתוּלָה מֵעַמָּיו יִקַּח אִשָּׁה: וְלֹא־יְחַלֵּל זַרְעוֹ בְּעַמָּיו

16 כִּי אֲנִי יְהוָה מְקַדְּשׁוֹ: ס וַיְדַבֵּר יְהוָה אֶל־מֹשֶׁה

17 לֵּאמֹר: דַּבֵּר אֶל־אַהֲרֹן לֵאמֹר אִישׁ מִזַּרְעֲךָ לְדֹרֹתָם אֲשֶׁר

18 יִהְיֶה בוֹ מוּם לֹא יִקְרַב לְהַקְרִיב לֶחֶם אֱלֹהָיו: כִּי כָל־

אִישׁ אֲשֶׁר־בּוֹ מוּם לֹא יִקְרָב אִישׁ עִוֵּר אוֹ פִסֵּחַ אוֹ חָרֻם אוֹ שָׂרוּעַ:

19 אוֹ אִישׁ אֲשֶׁר־יִהְיֶה בוֹ שֶׁבֶר רָגֶל אוֹ שֶׁבֶר יָד:

20 אוֹ־גִבֵּן אוֹ־דַק אוֹ תְּבַלֻּל בְּעֵינוֹ אוֹ גָרָב אוֹ יַלֶּפֶת

21 אוֹ מְרוֹחַ אָשֶׁךְ: כָּל־אִישׁ אֲשֶׁר־בּוֹ מוּם מִזֶּרַע אַהֲרֹן

הַכֹּהֵן לֹא יִגַּשׁ לְהַקְרִיב אֶת־אִשֵּׁי יְהוָה מוּם בּוֹ אֵת לֶחֶם

22 אֱלֹהָיו לֹא יִגַּשׁ לְהַקְרִיב: לֶחֶם אֱלֹהָיו מִקָּדְשֵׁי הַקֳּדָשִׁים

23 וּמִן־הַקֳּדָשִׁים יֹאכֵל: אַךְ אֶל־הַפָּרֹכֶת לֹא יָבֹא וְאֶל־

הַמִּזְבֵּחַ לֹא יִגַּשׁ כִּי־מוּם בּוֹ וְלֹא יְחַלֵּל אֶת־מִקְדָּשַׁי כִּי

24 אֲנִי יְהוָה מְקַדְּשָׁם: וַיְדַבֵּר מֹשֶׁה אֶל־אַהֲרֹן וְאֶל־בָּנָיו

וְאֶל־כָּל־בְּנֵי יִשְׂרָאֵל:

Left margin notes: (n.21), (n.22), (n.23), (n.24)

Uitti (6b,c); *NJV*, *NEB*, *RSV* (6b)

Uitti (7c); *NJV* (7b-8); *NAB*, *NEB*, *RSV* (7b)

Gemser (8b); Uitti (8aβ,c); *NAB* (8bβ); *NEB*, *RSV* (8aβ,bβ)

Uitti, *NJV*, *NEB*, *RSV* (12b); *NAB* (12aβ,b)

Uitti, *NJV*, *RSV* (15); *NAB* (15a); *NEB* (15b)

Uitti (18-23); *NJV*, *NAB*, *NEB* (21bα); *RSV* (18-21)

Gemser (23c); *NJV*, *NEB* (23aβ); *NAB* (23bβ); *RSV* (23aβ-b)

Leviticus 22

<table>
<tr><td>

א 2 וַיְדַבֵּר יְהוָה אֶל־מֹשֶׁה לֵּאמֹר: דַּבֵּר אֶל־אַהֲרֹן וְאֶל־בָּנָיו
וְיִנָּזְרוּ מִקָּדְשֵׁי בְנֵי־יִשְׂרָאֵל וְלֹא יְחַלְּלוּ אֶת־שֵׁם קָדְשִׁי
3 אֲשֶׁר הֵם מַקְדִּשִׁים לִי אֲנִי יְהוָה: אֱמֹר אֲלֵהֶם לְדֹרֹתֵיכֶם
כָּל־אִישׁ ׀ אֲשֶׁר־יִקְרַב מִכָּל־זַרְעֲכֶם אֶל־הַקֳּדָשִׁים אֲשֶׁר
יַקְדִּישׁוּ בְנֵי־יִשְׂרָאֵל לַיהוָה וְטֻמְאָתוֹ עָלָיו וְנִכְרְתָה הַנֶּפֶשׁ
4 הַהִוא מִלְּפָנַי אֲנִי יְהוָה: אִישׁ אִישׁ מִזֶּרַע אַהֲרֹן וְהוּא
צָרוּעַ אוֹ זָב בַּקֳּדָשִׁים לֹא יֹאכַל עַד אֲשֶׁר יִטְהָר וְהַנֹּגֵעַ
בְּכָל־טְמֵא־נֶפֶשׁ אוֹ אִישׁ אֲשֶׁר־תֵּצֵא מִמֶּנּוּ שִׁכְבַת־זָרַע:
ה 5 אוֹ־אִישׁ אֲשֶׁר יִגַּע בְּכָל־שֶׁרֶץ אֲשֶׁר יִטְמָא־לוֹ אוֹ בְאָדָם
אֲשֶׁר יִטְמָא־לוֹ לְכֹל טֻמְאָתוֹ: נֶפֶשׁ אֲשֶׁר תִּגַּע־בּוֹ וְטָמְאָה
6 עַד־הָעָרֶב וְלֹא יֹאכַל מִן־הַקֳּדָשִׁים כִּי אִם־רָחַץ בְּשָׂרוֹ
7 בַּמָּיִם: וּבָא הַשֶּׁמֶשׁ וְטָהֵר וְאַחַר יֹאכַל מִן־הַקֳּדָשִׁים
8 כִּי לַחְמוֹ הוּא: נְבֵלָה וּטְרֵפָה לֹא יֹאכַל לְטָמְאָה־בָהּ
<u>אֲנִי יְהוָה:</u>

</td><td>

Uitti (2b); *NJV, NAB, NEB,*
RSV (2aβ)

Uitti (3b)

Uitti, *NJV, NEB, RSV* (7bβ)

Uitti (8b)

Uitti, *NJV, NAB, NEB, RSV*
(20b)

Uitti (25b); *NJV, NAB, RSV*
(25bα)

Uitti (30b)

</td></tr>
</table>

17
18 וַיְדַבֵּר יְהוָה אֶל־מֹשֶׁה לֵּאמֹר: דַּבֵּר אֶל־אַהֲרֹן וְאֶל־בָּנָיו
וְאֶל כָּל־בְּנֵי יִשְׂרָאֵל וְאָמַרְתָּ אֲלֵהֶם אִישׁ אִישׁ מִבֵּית
יִשְׂרָאֵל וּמִן־הַגֵּר בְּיִשְׂרָאֵל אֲשֶׁר יַקְרִיב קָרְבָּנוֹ לְכָל־
נִדְרֵיהֶם וּלְכָל־נִדְבוֹתָם אֲשֶׁר־יַקְרִיבוּ לַיהוָה לְעֹלָה:
19
ב 20 לִרְצֹנְכֶם תָּמִים זָכָר בַּבָּקָר בַּכְּשָׂבִים וּבָעִזִּים: כֹּל אֲשֶׁר־
21 בּוֹ מוּם לֹא תַקְרִיבוּ כִּי־לֹא לְרָצוֹן יִהְיֶה לָכֶם: וְאִישׁ כִּי־
יַקְרִיב זֶבַח־שְׁלָמִים לַיהוָה לְפַלֵּא־נֶדֶר אוֹ לִנְדָבָה בַּבָּקָר
22 אוֹ בַצֹּאן תָּמִים יִהְיֶה לְרָצוֹן כָּל־מוּם לֹא יִהְיֶה־בּוֹ: עַוֶּרֶת
אוֹ שָׁבוּר אוֹ־חָרוּץ אוֹ־יַבֶּלֶת אוֹ גָרָב אוֹ יַלֶּפֶת לֹא־
תַקְרִיבוּ אֵלֶּה לַיהוָה וְאִשֶּׁה לֹא־תִתְּנוּ מֵהֶם עַל־הַמִּזְבֵּחַ
23 לַיהוָה: וְשׁוֹר וָשֶׂה שָׂרוּעַ וְקָלוּט נְדָבָה תַּעֲשֶׂה אֹתוֹ וּלְנֵדֶר
24 לֹא יֵרָצֶה: וּמָעוּךְ וְכָתוּת וְנָתוּק וְכָרוּת לֹא תַקְרִיבוּ לַיהוָה
25 וּבְאַרְצְכֶם לֹא תַעֲשׂוּ: וּמִיַּד בֶּן־נֵכָר לֹא תַקְרִיבוּ אֶת־לֶחֶם
אֱלֹהֵיכֶם מִכָּל־אֵלֶּה <u>כִּי מָשְׁחָתָם בָּהֶם מוּם בָּם לֹא יֵרָצוּ</u>
<u>לָכֶם:</u>

<u>וְכִי־תִזְבְּחוּ</u>
29
ל זֶבַח־תּוֹדָה לַיהוָה לִרְצֹנְכֶם תִּזְבָּחוּ: בַּיּוֹם הַהוּא יֵאָכֵל
לֹא־תוֹתִירוּ מִמֶּנּוּ עַד־בֹּקֶר <u>אֲנִי יְהוָה:</u>

Leviticus 23

א ²וַיְדַבֵּ֥ר יְהוָ֖ה אֶל־מֹשֶׁ֥ה לֵּאמֹֽר׃ דַּבֵּ֞ר אֶל־בְּנֵ֤י יִשְׂרָאֵל֙
וְאָמַרְתָּ֣ אֲלֵהֶ֔ם מוֹעֲדֵ֣י יְהוָ֗ה אֲשֶׁר־תִּקְרְא֥וּ אֹתָ֖ם מִקְרָאֵ֣י
3 קֹ֑דֶשׁ אֵ֥לֶּה הֵ֖ם מוֹעֲדָֽי׃ שֵׁ֣שֶׁת יָמִים֮ תֵּעָשֶׂ֣ה מְלָאכָה֒ וּבַיּ֣וֹם
הַשְּׁבִיעִ֗י שַׁבַּ֤ת שַׁבָּתוֹן֙ מִקְרָא־קֹ֔דֶשׁ כָּל־מְלָאכָ֖ה לֹ֣א תַעֲשׂ֑וּ
(n.26)   שַׁבָּ֥ת הִוא֙ לַֽיהוָ֔ה בְּכֹ֖ל מוֹשְׁבֹתֵיכֶֽם׃

22 וּֽבְקֻצְרְכֶם֮ אֶת־קְצִ֣יר אַרְצְכֶם֒
לֹֽא־תְכַלֶּ֞ה פְּאַ֤ת שָׂדְךָ֙ בְּקֻצְרֶ֔ךָ וְלֶ֥קֶט קְצִירְךָ֖ לֹ֣א תְלַקֵּ֑ט
לֶֽעָנִ֤י וְלַגֵּר֙ תַּעֲזֹ֣ב אֹתָ֔ם אֲנִ֖י יְהוָ֥ה אֱלֹהֵיכֶֽם׃

26 וַיְדַבֵּ֥ר יְהוָ֖ה אֶל־מֹשֶׁ֥ה

27 לֵּאמֹֽר׃ אַ֡ךְ בֶּעָשׂ֣וֹר לַחֹ֩דֶשׁ֩ הַשְּׁבִיעִ֨י הַזֶּ֜ה י֧וֹם הַכִּפֻּרִ֣ים
ה֗וּא מִֽקְרָא־קֹ֙דֶשׁ֙ יִהְיֶ֣ה לָכֶ֔ם וְעִנִּיתֶ֖ם אֶת־נַפְשֹׁתֵיכֶ֑ם
28 וְהִקְרַבְתֶּ֥ם אִשֶּׁ֖ה לַֽיהוָֽה׃ וְכָל־מְלָאכָה֙ לֹ֣א תַעֲשׂ֔וּ בְּעֶ֖צֶם
הַיּ֣וֹם הַזֶּ֑ה כִּ֣י י֤וֹם כִּפֻּרִים֙ ה֔וּא לְכַפֵּ֣ר עֲלֵיכֶ֔ם לִפְנֵ֖י יְהוָ֥ה
29 אֱלֹהֵיכֶֽם׃ כִּ֤י כָל־הַנֶּ֙פֶשׁ֙ אֲשֶׁ֣ר לֹֽא־תְעֻנֶּ֔ה בְּעֶ֖צֶם הַיּ֣וֹם
הַזֶּ֑ה וְנִכְרְתָ֖ה מֵֽעַמֶּֽיהָ׃ וְכָל־הַנֶּ֗פֶשׁ אֲשֶׁ֤ר תַּעֲשֶׂה֙ כָּל־ ל
מְלָאכָ֔ה בְּעֶ֖צֶם הַיּ֣וֹם הַזֶּ֑ה וְהַֽאֲבַדְתִּ֛י אֶת־הַנֶּ֥פֶשׁ הַהִ֖וא
מִקֶּ֥רֶב עַמָּֽהּ׃

36 שִׁבְעַ֣ת יָמִ֔ים תַּקְרִ֥יבוּ אִשֶּׁ֖ה
לַֽיהוָ֑ה בַּיּ֣וֹם הַשְּׁמִינִ֡י מִקְרָא־קֹדֶשׁ֩ יִהְיֶ֨ה לָכֶ֜ם וְהִקְרַבְתֶּ֥ם
אִשֶּׁ֤ה לַֽיהוָה֙ עֲצֶ֣רֶת הִ֔וא כָּל־מְלֶ֥אכֶת עֲבֹדָ֖ה לֹ֥א תַעֲשֽׂוּ׃
(n.27)

42 בַּסֻּכֹּ֥ת תֵּשְׁב֖וּ שִׁבְעַ֣ת יָמִ֑ים
43 כָּל־הָֽאֶזְרָח֙ בְּיִשְׂרָאֵ֔ל יֵשְׁב֖וּ בַּסֻּכֹּֽת׃ לְמַ֙עַן֙ יֵדְע֣וּ דֹרֹֽתֵיכֶ֔ם
כִּ֣י בַסֻּכּ֗וֹת הוֹשַׁ֙בְתִּי֙ אֶת־בְּנֵ֣י יִשְׂרָאֵ֔ל בְּהוֹצִיאִ֥י אוֹתָ֖ם
מֵאֶ֣רֶץ מִצְרָ֑יִם אֲנִ֖י יְהוָ֥ה אֱלֹהֵיכֶֽם׃

Leviticus 24

א ²וַיְדַבֵּ֥ר יְהוָ֖ה אֶל־מֹשֶׁ֥ה לֵּאמֹֽר׃ צַ֞ו אֶת־בְּנֵ֣י יִשְׂרָאֵ֗ל וְיִקְח֙וּ
אֵלֶ֜יךָ שֶׁ֤מֶן זַ֣יִת זָ֛ךְ כָּתִ֖ית לַמָּא֑וֹר לְהַעֲלֹ֥ת נֵ֖ר תָּמִֽיד׃

5 וְלָקַחְתָּ֣ סֹ֔לֶת וְאָפִיתָ֣ אֹתָ֔הּ שְׁתֵּ֥ים עֶשְׂרֵ֖ה חַלּ֑וֹת שְׁנֵי֙
6 עֶשְׂרֹנִ֔ים יִהְיֶ֖ה הַֽחַלָּ֥ה הָאֶחָֽת׃ וְשַׂמְתָּ֥ אוֹתָ֛ם שְׁתַּ֥יִם
מַֽעֲרָכ֖וֹת שֵׁ֣שׁ הַֽמַּעֲרָ֑כֶת עַ֛ל הַשֻּׁלְחָ֥ן הַטָּהֹ֖ר לִפְנֵ֥י יְהוָֽה׃
7 וְנָתַתָּ֥ עַל־הַֽמַּעֲרֶ֖כֶת לְבֹנָ֣ה זַכָּ֑ה וְהָיְתָ֤ה לַלֶּ֙חֶם֙ לְאַזְכָּרָ֔ה
8 אִשֶּׁ֖ה לַֽיהוָֽה׃ בְּי֨וֹם הַשַּׁבָּ֜ת בְּי֣וֹם הַשַּׁבָּ֗ת יַֽעַרְכֶ֛נּוּ לִפְנֵ֥י
9 יְהוָ֖ה תָּמִ֑יד מֵאֵ֥ת בְּנֵֽי־יִשְׂרָאֵ֖ל בְּרִ֥ית עוֹלָֽם׃ וְהָֽיְתָה֙ לְאַֽהֲרֹ֣ן
וּלְבָנָ֔יו וַאֲכָלֻ֖הוּ בְּמָק֣וֹם קָדֹ֑שׁ כִּ֡י קֹדֶשׁ֩ קָֽדָשִׁ֨ים ה֤וּא ל֙וֹ
מֵאִשֵּׁ֥י יְהוָ֖ה חָק־עוֹלָֽם׃

Right column annotations:

Uitti (3b)

Gemser (22b)

Gemser, *NJV*, *NAB*, *NEB* (28b);
Uitti, *RSV* (28b-29)

Uitti (36c)

Gemser, Uitti, *NJV* (43);
NAB, *NEB* (43a); *RSV*
(43a,b?)

NJV, *NAB*, *RSV* (20aβ,b)

Uitti (9c); *NJV*, *NAB*, *RSV*
(9b); *NEB* (9bα)

Leviticus 25

יוֹבֵל הִוא שְׁנַת הַחֲמִשִּׁים 11
שָׁנָה תִּהְיֶה לָכֶם לֹא תִזְרָעוּ וְלֹא תִקְצְרוּ אֶת־סְפִיחֶיהָ
וְלֹא תִבְצְרוּ אֶת־נְזִרֶיהָ: כִּי יוֹבֵל הִוא קֹדֶשׁ תִּהְיֶה לָכֶם 12
מִן־הַשָּׂדֶה תֹּאכְלוּ אֶת־תְּבוּאָתָהּ: בִּשְׁנַת הַיּוֹבֵל הַזֹּאת 13
תָּשֻׁבוּ אִישׁ אֶל־אֲחֻזָּתוֹ: וְכִי־תִמְכְּרוּ מִמְכָּר לַעֲמִיתֶךָ 14
אוֹ קָנֹה מִיַּד עֲמִיתֶךָ אַל־תּוֹנוּ אִישׁ אֶת־אָחִיו: בְּמִסְפַּר 15
שָׁנִים אַחַר הַיּוֹבֵל תִּקְנֶה מֵאֵת עֲמִיתֶךָ בְּמִסְפַּר שְׁנֵי־
תְבוּאֹת יִמְכָּר־לָךְ: לְפִי רֹב הַשָּׁנִים תַּרְבֶּה מִקְנָתוֹ וּלְפִי 16
מְעֹט הַשָּׁנִים תַּמְעִיט מִקְנָתוֹ כִּי מִסְפַּר תְּבוּאֹת הוּא
מֹכֵר לָךְ:

וְהָאָרֶץ לֹא תִמָּכֵר לִצְמִתֻת כִּי־לִי הָאָרֶץ כִּי־גֵרִים 23
וְתוֹשָׁבִים אַתֶּם עִמָּדִי:

וְעָרֵי הַלְוִיִּם בָּתֵּי עָרֵי אֲחֻזָּתָם גְּאֻלַּת עוֹלָם תִּהְיֶה 32
לַלְוִיִּם: וַאֲשֶׁר יִגְאַל מִן־הַלְוִיִּם וְיָצָא מִמְכַּר־בַּיִת וְעִיר 33
אֲחֻזָּתוֹ בַּיֹּבֵל כִּי בָתֵּי עָרֵי הַלְוִיִּם הִוא אֲחֻזָּתָם בְּתוֹךְ
בְּנֵי יִשְׂרָאֵל: וּשְׂדֵה מִגְרַשׁ עָרֵיהֶם לֹא יִמָּכֵר כִּי־אֲחֻזַּת 34
עוֹלָם הוּא לָהֶם: וְכִי־יָמוּךְ אָחִיךָ וּמָטָה יָדוֹ עִמָּךְ 35
וְהֶחֱזַקְתָּ בּוֹ גֵּר וְתוֹשָׁב וָחַי עִמָּךְ: אַל־תִּקַּח מֵאִתּוֹ נֶשֶׁךְ 36
וְתַרְבִּית וְיָרֵאתָ מֵאֱלֹהֶיךָ וְחֵי אָחִיךָ עִמָּךְ: אֶת־כַּסְפְּךָ 37
לֹא־תִתֵּן לוֹ בְּנֶשֶׁךְ וּבְמַרְבִּית לֹא־תִתֵּן אָכְלֶךָ: אֲנִי יְהוָה 38
אֱלֹהֵיכֶם אֲשֶׁר־הוֹצֵאתִי אֶתְכֶם מֵאֶרֶץ מִצְרָיִם לָתֵת לָכֶם
אֶת־אֶרֶץ כְּנַעַן לִהְיוֹת לָכֶם לֵאלֹהִים: וְכִי־יָמוּךְ 39
אָחִיךָ עִמָּךְ וְנִמְכַּר־לָךְ לֹא־תַעֲבֹד בּוֹ עֲבֹדַת עָבֶד:
כְּשָׂכִיר כְּתוֹשָׁב יִהְיֶה עִמָּךְ עַד־שְׁנַת הַיֹּבֵל יַעֲבֹד עִמָּךְ: 40
וְיָצָא מֵעִמָּךְ הוּא וּבָנָיו עִמּוֹ וְשָׁב אֶל־מִשְׁפַּחְתּוֹ וְאֶל־ 41
אֲחֻזַּת אֲבֹתָיו יָשׁוּב: כִּי־עֲבָדַי הֵם אֲשֶׁר־הוֹצֵאתִי אֹתָם 42
מֵאֶרֶץ מִצְרָיִם לֹא יִמָּכְרוּ מִמְכֶּרֶת עָבֶד:

וְכִי תַשִּׂיג יַד גֵּר וְתוֹשָׁב עִמָּךְ
וּמָךְ אָחִיךָ עִמּוֹ וְנִמְכַּר לְגֵר תּוֹשָׁב עִמָּךְ אוֹ לְעֵקֶר
מִשְׁפַּחַת גֵּר: אַחֲרֵי נִמְכַּר גְּאֻלָּה תִּהְיֶה־לּוֹ אֶחָד מֵאֶחָיו 48
יִגְאָלֶנּוּ: אוֹ־דֹדוֹ אוֹ בֶן־דֹּדוֹ יִגְאָלֶנּוּ אוֹ־מִשְּׁאֵר בְּשָׂרוֹ 49
מִמִּשְׁפַּחְתּוֹ יִגְאָלֶנּוּ אוֹ־הִשִּׂיגָה יָדוֹ וְנִגְאָל: וְחִשַּׁב עִם־ 50
קֹנֵהוּ מִשְּׁנַת הִמָּכְרוֹ לוֹ עַד שְׁנַת הַיֹּבֵל וְהָיָה כֶּסֶף מִמְכָּרוֹ
בְּמִסְפַּר שָׁנִים כִּימֵי שָׂכִיר יִהְיֶה עִמּוֹ: אִם־עוֹד רַבּוֹת 51
בַּשָּׁנִים לְפִיהֶן יָשִׁיב גְּאֻלָּתוֹ מִכֶּסֶף מִקְנָתוֹ: וְאִם־מְעַט 52
נִשְׁאַר בַּשָּׁנִים עַד־שְׁנַת הַיֹּבֵל וְחִשַּׁב־לוֹ כְּפִי שָׁנָיו יָשִׁיב
אֶת־גְּאֻלָּתוֹ: כִּשְׂכִיר שָׁנָה בְּשָׁנָה יִהְיֶה עִמּוֹ לֹא־יִרְדֶּנּוּ 53
בְּפֶרֶךְ לְעֵינֶיךָ: וְאִם־לֹא יִגָּאֵל בְּאֵלֶּה וְיָצָא בִּשְׁנַת הַיֹּבֵל 54
הוּא וּבָנָיו עִמּוֹ: כִּי־לִי בְנֵי־יִשְׂרָאֵל עֲבָדִים עֲבָדַי הֵם 55
אֲשֶׁר־הוֹצֵאתִי אוֹתָם מֵאֶרֶץ מִצְרָיִם אֲנִי יְהוָה אֱלֹהֵיכֶם:

Gemser (8-12); Uitti (12a);
NJV, NAB, NEB, RSV (12aα)

Gemser, *NJV, NAB, NEB, RSV*
(16b); Uitti (16c)

Gemser, Uitti, *NAB, NEB,
RSV* (23aβ,b); *NJV* (23aβ)

Uitti, *NJV, NAB, NEB, RSV*
(33b)

Uitti, *NJV, NEB, RSV* (34b)

Gemser, Uitti (38)

Gemser, *NJV, NEB, RSV* (42);
Uitti, *NAB* (42a)

Gemser, Uitti, *NJV, NAB,
RSV* (55); *NEB* (55a)

Leviticus 26

לֹא־תַעֲשׂוּ לָכֶם אֱלִילִם וּפֶסֶל וּמַצֵּבָה לֹא־תָקִימוּ לָכֶם א
וְאֶבֶן מַשְׂכִּית לֹא תִתְּנוּ בְּאַרְצְכֶם לְהִשְׁתַּחֲוֹת עָלֶיהָ כִּי
אֲנִי יְהוָה אֱלֹהֵיכֶם: אֶת־שַׁבְּתֹתַי תִּשְׁמֹרוּ וּמִקְדָּשִׁי תִּירָאוּ 2
אֲנִי יְהוָה:

Gemser, Uitti, *NJV*, *NAB*,
NEB, *RSV* (1b)

Uitti (2b)

(c)   *Notes*

1. (17:3-7a) The law in vv. 3-4 is triply motivated: by the clause
דָּם שָׁפָךְ that precedes the legal consequence (in v. 4bβ) and by two consecutive
phrases that follow it (vv. 5-6, 7a).

2. (18:6) The law in v. 6a is predicated upon God's will: "(for) I am
the Lord." This clause often appears as asyndetic. However, in its extended
form it is sometimes introduced by כִּי, e.g., Lev 20:7, 21:15,23, 22:16, 24:22,
25:17, 26:1.

3. (18:7) The clause in v. 7bα could be taken as motivating the
prescription in v. 7a. However, because of v. 7bβ, it is most likely that it
motivates the injunction that follows it, i.e., "(since) she is your mother,
do not uncover her nakedness." Cf. Uitti, *NAB*.

4. (18:8) Verse 8b is an asyndetic clause and motivates the prescription in v. 8a; cf. 18:10b, 13 (each mc introduced by כִּי).

5. (18:17) The mc is זִמָּה הִוא ([for] it is depravity) and characterizes
the act. The expression שַׁאֲרָה הֵנָּה ("they are kindred"), referring to the actors,
is the mc of the mc.

6. (18:21) In v. 21b, there are two consecutive motive clauses:
v. 21bα is to be understood as: "so that you may not profane...." For v. 21bβ,
see n. 2.

7. (18:22) Verse 22b motivates the law in v. 22a, i.e., "(for) it is
an abomination."

8. (18:23) The clause תֶּבֶל הוּא seems to motivate the legal prescriptions in v. 23a and v. 23bα; cf. *NAB*: "such things are abhorrent."

9. (19:7) In v. 7b, the legal consequence is motivated by פִּגּוּל הוּא,
i.e., "being an offensive thing, it shall not be acceptable."

10. (19:12) Verse 12a seems to be motivated by two consecutive
clauses, v. 12bα,bβ: i.e., "for you would be profaning the name of your God...."
For v. 12bβ, see n. 2.

11. (19:22) This verse constitutes a concluding sentence; cf. Noth,
Leviticus, 41.

12. (19:34) The instruction to love one's neighbor is parenetic (cf.
v. 18); the two motive clauses in v. 34aβ,b motivate the prescription in vv.
33-34aα.

13. (20:9) Verse 9bα motivates the prescription in v. 9a. The "blood formula" (cf. Noth, *Leviticus*, 149-50) is related to the penalty clause (ibid., 150); cf. v. 11b.

14. (20:11) The clause in v. 11aβ is the underlying reason for the death penalty in v. 11b, i.e., "(since) he has uncovered his father's nakedness, both of them shall be put to death...."

15. (20:13) Verse 13aβ is the underlying reason for the death penalty in v. 13b, i.e., "(since) the two of them have done an abhorrent thing, they shall be put to death...."

16. (20:14) The legal consequence in v. 14bα is motivated by two clauses, one before (v. 14aβ) and one after (v. 14bβ).

17. (20:17) The legal consequence in v. 17aβ is motivated by two clauses, one before (v. 17aα, end) and one after (v. 17bα). The "guilt formula" in v. 17 is related to the penalty clause.

18. (20:18) The legal consequence in v. 18b is motivated by an asyndetic clause that precedes it.

19. (20:20) The clause in v. 20aβ is the motive for the legal consequence in v. 20b; cf. v. 11.

20. (20:21) The legal consequence (end of v. 21) is motivated by two consecutive asyndetic clauses that precede it.

21. (20:6) This verse motivates the prescriptions in vv. 1-5. See Noth, *Leviticus*, 155.

22. (21:9) The clause in v. 9bβ constitutes the motive for the death penalty in v. 19bβ.

23. (21:12) Verse 12aβ-b is the primary motive clause for the prohibitive in v. 12aα; v. 12bα is the mc of the mc.

24. (21:17b-21) These verses constitute one legal prescription, and the motivations in v. 18a and v. 21b are repetition of the same idea.

25. (22:15-16) These verses constitute a parenetic conclusion; see Noth, *Leviticus*, 162.

26. (23:3) Verse 3b is an asyndetic mc, understood as "(for) it is sabbath to the Lord...," and motivates v. 3a.

27. (23:36) The clause עֲצֶרֶת הִוא may be taken as motivating v. 36bβ, i.e., "(since) it is a solemn assembly, you shall not work...." However, it is also possible that it is meant to constitute a motivation for the legal consequence in v. 36bα, i.e., "you shall bring an offering by fire to the Lord, (for) it is a solemn assembly." The verse division favors this second interpretation. The exact meaning of the word עֲצֶרֶת is unknown. See Noth, *Leviticus*, 174-75; *NJV*, note to Lev 23:36.

28. (25:2aβ-5) See Chapter II, p. 81.

5.   THE DEUTERONOMIC LAW CORPUS (Deuteronomy 12-26)

(a)   *The Legal Prescriptions*

Deuteronomy 12		Verses		Deut. 14 cont.		Verses
-	intro	(1)		-	intro	(3)
1.	mc	2-3		30.		4-6
2.		4-5		31.	mc	7
3.		6-7aα		32.	mc	8aα
-	par	(7aβ-b)		-	sum	(8bβ)
4.	mc	8-9		33.		8b
5.		10-11		34.		9
-	par	(12)	(n. 2)	35.	mc	10
-	par sum	(13-14)		36.		11-18
6.		15	(n. 3)	37.	mc	19
7.		16a		38.		20
8.		16b	(n. 4)	39.	mc	21aαא
9.		17-18a			v.21aβ	
-	par	(18b,19)		40.		21aαב
10.	intrn mc	20		41.		21b
11.		21-22		42.	mc	22-23
12.	mc(2)	23-25		43.	intrn mc	24-26bα
	v.23aβ-b,25b			-	par	(26bβ)
13.		26		44.	mc	27
14.		27a		45.		28
15.		27bα		46.	mc	29
16.		27bβ			(intrn mc in	
-	par	(28)			v.29a)	
-	par	(29-31)				

Deuteronomy 13				Deuteronomy 15		
				47.	mc	1-2
-	par	(1)		48.		3
17.	mc	2-4		-	par	(4-6)
-	par	(5)	(n. 5)	49.	mc(2)	7-11
18.	mc(2)	6			v.10b,11	
	v.6aαא-aγ			50.		⎡12
19.		⎡7-9a		51.		⎣13-14
20.		9b-10aα			mc v.15	
21.		10aβ		52.	intrn mc	16-17a
22.		10b		53.		17b
	mc(2)	(11a)		-	par	(18)
	v.11b,12			54.		19
23.		13-16a		55.		20
24.		16b		56.		21
25.		17a		57.		22
26.		17b		58.		23a
27.	mc	18-19		59.		23b

Deuteronomy 14				Deuteronomy 16		
28.		⎡1bα		60.	mc	1
29.		⎣1bβ		61.		2
(n. 1)	mc(2)			62.		⎡3aα
	v.1a,2			63.		⎣3aβ
					mc(2)	
					v.3bα,bβ-bγ	

Deut. 16 cont.		Verses		Deuteronomy 19		Verses
	64.	4a			99.	1-2
	65.	4b			100. mc	3
	66.	5-6			- intro	(4a)
	67.	7			101. mc	⎡4b-7
	68.	8 .			102.	⎣8-9
	69.	9			mc v.10	
	70.	10			103.	11-12
	- par	(11-12)			- par	(13)
(n. 6)	71. mc	13-15			104.	14
	72.	16a			105.	15
	73.	16b-17			106. mc(2)	16-20
	74.	18			v.19b,20	
	- intro	(19aα)			- par	(21)
	75.	19aβ				
	76. mc	19b			Deuteronomy 20	
	- par	20				
	77.	⎡21			- par intro	(1)
	78.	⎣22a			107.	2-4
	mc v.22b			(n. 9)	108.	5-8
					109.	9
	Deuteronomy 17				110.	10
					111.	11
	79.	1			112.	12
	80.	⎡2-5			113.	13
	81.	6			114.	14
	82.	7aα			- intro	(15)
	83.	⎣7aβ			115. mc	16-18
	mc v.7b				116. mc	19
	84.	8-11			117.	20
	85. mc(2)	12-13				
	v.12bβ,13				Deuteronomy 21	
	86.	14-15				
	87.	16aαאּ			118.	1-2
	88. mc	16aαﬡ-b			119.	3-4
	89. mc	17a			120. mc(2)	5
	90.	17b			v.5aαﬡ-aβ,b	
	91.	18			121.	6
	92. mc(4)	19-20			122. mc(2)	7-9
	v.19b,20aα,				v.8b,9	
	20aβ,b				123.	10-13
					124. mc	14
	Deuteronomy 18				125. mc	15-17
					126.	⎡18-20
(n. 7)	93. mc	1-2			127.	⎣21aα
	94. mc	3-5			mc(2)	
	95.	6-7			v.21aβ,b	
	96.	8			128. mc	22-23a
	- par	(9)			- par	(23b)
(n. 8)	97. mc(2)	10-12				
	v.12a,b				Deuteronomy 22	
	- par	(13-19)				
	98.	20			129.	1
	- par concl	(21-22)			130.	2
					131.	3

Deut. 22 cont.	Verses
132.	4
133.	⌈5aα
134.	⌊5aβ
mc v.5b	
135. mc(2)	6-7
v.7bα,bβ	
136. mc	8
137. mc	9
138.	10
139.	11
140.	12
141.	⌈13-15
142.	16-17
143.	18
144.	⌊19aα
mc v.19aβ	
145.	19bα
146.	19bβ
147. mc(2)	20-21
v.21aβ-γ,b	
148. mc	22
149. mc(3)	23-24
v.24aγ,aδ,b	
150.	25
(n.10) 151. mc(3)	26-27
v.26aβ,b,27	
152.	28-29a
(n.11) 153. mc	29bα
154.	29bβ

Deuteronomy 23

	Verses
(n.12) 155. mc	1
156.	2
157.	3
(n.13) 158. mc(2)	4-5
v.5a,b	
— nl	(6)
— par	(7)
159. mc	8a
160. mc	8b
161.	9
— intro	(10)
162.	⌈11
163.	12
164.	13
165.	14a-bα
166.	⌊14bβ
mc(2)	
v.15a,b	
167.	16
168.	17a
— par	(17b)
169.	18a

Deut. 23 cont.	Verses
170.	18b
171. mc	19
172. mc	20-21
173. mc	22
— nl	(23)
— par	(24)
174.	25
175.	26

Deuteronomy 24

	Verses
176. mc(2)	1-4a
v.4aβ,aγ	
(intrn mc in	
v.1)	
— par	(4b)
177. mc	5
178. mc	6
179. mc	7
180. mc	8-9
181.	10-11
182. mc(2)	12-13
v.13aβ,b	
183. mc(2)	14-15
v.15aβ,b	
184.	16
185.	⌈17a
186.	⌊17b
mc v.18	
187.	⌈19aα
188.	⌊19aβ
mc v.19b	
189.	⌈20a
190.	20b
191.	21a
192.	⌊21b
mc v.22	

Deuteronomy 25

	Verses
193.	1-2
194. mc	3
195.	4
196.	5
197. mc	6
198.	7
199.	8a
200.	8b-9aα
201.	9aβ
202.	9b
203.	10
204.	11-12a
— par	(12b)

Deut. 25 cont.	Verses
205.	⌐13
206.	│14
- sum	⌊(15)
mc(2)	
v.15b,16	
(n.14) 207. mc	17-19a
- par	(19b)

Deuteronomy 26

208.	1-2
209.	3
210.	4
211.	5-10a
212.	10b
- par	(11)
213. intrn mc	12-15
- par concl	(16-19)

Elsewhere in D

Deuteronomy 1

- intro	(16)
214.	⌐17aα
215.	⌊17aβ
mc v.17aγ	
216.	17b

Deuteronomy 7

217.	1-2
218. mc	3-4
- intro	(5aα)
219.	⌐5aβ
220.	│5aγ
221.	│5bα
222.	⌊5bβ
mc v.6	
- nl	(7-24)
223.	25a
224. mc(2)	25b
v.25bβ,bγ	
225. mc	26a
- par	(26b)

(b)   *The Motive Clauses*

Deuteronomy 12

2 אַבֵּד תְּאַבְּדוּן אֶת־כָּל־
הַמְּקֹמוֹת אֲשֶׁר עָבְדוּ־שָׁם הַגּוֹיִם אֲשֶׁר אַתֶּם יֹרְשִׁים אֹתָם
אֶת־אֱלֹהֵיהֶם עַל־הֶהָרִים הָרָמִים וְעַל־הַגְּבָעוֹת וְתַחַת כָּל־
3 עֵץ רַעֲנָן: וְנִתַּצְתֶּם אֶת־מִזְבְּחֹתָם וְשִׁבַּרְתֶּם אֶת־מַצֵּבֹתָם
וַאֲשֵׁרֵיהֶם תִּשְׂרְפוּן בָּאֵשׁ וּפְסִילֵי אֱלֹהֵיהֶם תְּגַדֵּעוּן וְאִבַּדְתֶּם
4 אֶת־שְׁמָם מִן־הַמָּקוֹם הַהוּא: לֹא־תַעֲשׂוּן כֵּן לַיהוָה
5 אֱלֹהֵיכֶם: כִּי אִם־אֶל־הַמָּקוֹם אֲשֶׁר־יִבְחַר יְהוָה אֱלֹהֵיכֶם
מִכָּל־שִׁבְטֵיכֶם לָשׂוּם אֶת־שְׁמוֹ שָׁם לְשִׁכְנוֹ תִדְרְשׁוּ
6 וּבָאתָ שָׁמָּה: וַהֲבֵאתֶם שָׁמָּה עֹלֹתֵיכֶם וְזִבְחֵיכֶם וְאֵת
מַעְשְׂרֹתֵיכֶם וְאֵת תְּרוּמַת יֶדְכֶם וְנִדְרֵיכֶם וְנִדְבֹתֵיכֶם
7 וּבְכֹרֹת בְּקַרְכֶם וְצֹאנְכֶם: וַאֲכַלְתֶּם־שָׁם לִפְנֵי יְהוָה
אֱלֹהֵיכֶם וּשְׂמַחְתֶּם בְּכֹל מִשְׁלַח יֶדְכֶם אַתֶּם וּבָתֵּיכֶם אֲשֶׁר
8 בֵּרַכְךָ יְהוָה אֱלֹהֶיךָ: לֹא תַעֲשׂוּן כְּכֹל אֲשֶׁר אֲנַחְנוּ עֹשִׂים
9 פֹּה הַיּוֹם אִישׁ כָּל־הַיָּשָׁר בְּעֵינָיו: כִּי לֹא־בָאתֶם עַד־
עָתָּה אֶל־הַמְּנוּחָה וְאֶל־הַנַּחֲלָה אֲשֶׁר־יְהוָה אֱלֹהֶיךָ נֹתֵן
לָךְ:

כ כִּי־יַרְחִיב יְהוָה
אֱלֹהֶיךָ אֶת־גְּבֻלְךָ כַּאֲשֶׁר דִּבֶּר־לָךְ וְאָמַרְתָּ אֹכְלָה בָשָׂר
כִּי־תְאַוֶּה נַפְשְׁךָ לֶאֱכֹל בָּשָׂר בְּכָל־אַוַּת נַפְשְׁךָ תֹּאכַל
21 בָּשָׂר: כִּי־יִרְחַק מִמְּךָ הַמָּקוֹם אֲשֶׁר יִבְחַר יְהוָה אֱלֹהֶיךָ
לָשׂוּם שְׁמוֹ שָׁם וְזָבַחְתָּ מִבְּקָרְךָ וּמִצֹּאנְךָ אֲשֶׁר נָתַן
יְהוָה לְךָ כַּאֲשֶׁר צִוִּיתִךָ וְאָכַלְתָּ בִּשְׁעָרֶיךָ בְּכֹל אַוַּת
22 נַפְשֶׁךָ: אַךְ כַּאֲשֶׁר יֵאָכֵל אֶת־הַצְּבִי וְאֶת־הָאַיָּל כֵּן תֹּאכְלֶנּוּ
23 הַטָּמֵא וְהַטָּהוֹר יַחְדָּו יֹאכְלֶנּוּ: רַק חֲזַק לְבִלְתִּי אֲכֹל
הַדָּם כִּי הַדָּם הוּא הַנָּפֶשׁ וְלֹא־תֹאכַל הַנֶּפֶשׁ עִם־הַבָּשָׂר:
24 לֹא תֹּאכְלֶנּוּ עַל־הָאָרֶץ תִּשְׁפְּכֶנּוּ כַּמָּיִם: לֹא תֹּאכְלֶנּוּ לְמַעַן
יִיטַב לְךָ וּלְבָנֶיךָ אַחֲרֶיךָ כִּי־תַעֲשֶׂה הַיָּשָׁר בְּעֵינֵי יְהוָה:

Uitti (3c); *NAB* (3b)

Uitti, *NJV, NAB, NEB, RSV*
(9)

NJV, NEB, RSV (20aβ)

Uitti (23bα); *NJV, NAB,
RSV* (23aβ-b); *NEB* (23aβ)

Uitti, *NAB, NEB, RSV* (25b);
NJV (25bα,b)

Deuteronomy 13

2 בְּקִרְבְּךָ נָבִיא אוֹ חֹלֵם חֲלוֹם וְנָתַן אֵלֶיךָ אוֹת

3 אוֹ מוֹפֵת: וּבָא הָאוֹת וְהַמּוֹפֵת אֲשֶׁר־דִּבֶּר אֵלֶיךָ לֵאמֹר

נֵלְכָה אַחֲרֵי אֱלֹהִים אֲחֵרִים אֲשֶׁר לֹא־יְדַעְתָּם וְנָעָבְדֵם:

4 לֹא תִשְׁמַע אֶל־דִּבְרֵי הַנָּבִיא הַהוּא אוֹ אֶל־חוֹלֵם הַחֲלוֹם

הַהוּא כִּי מְנַסֶּה יְהוָה אֱלֹהֵיכֶם אֶתְכֶם לָדַעַת הֲיֶשְׁכֶם

אֹהֲבִים אֶת־יְהוָה אֱלֹהֵיכֶם בְּכָל־לְבַבְכֶם וּבְכָל־נַפְשְׁכֶם:

5 אַחֲרֵי יְהוָה אֱלֹהֵיכֶם תֵּלֵכוּ וְאֹתוֹ תִירָאוּ וְאֶת־מִצְוֹתָיו

תִּשְׁמֹרוּ וּבְקֹלוֹ תִשְׁמָעוּ וְאֹתוֹ תַעֲבֹדוּ וּבוֹ תִדְבָּקוּן:

6 וְהַנָּבִיא הַהוּא אוֹ חֹלֵם הַחֲלוֹם הַהוּא יוּמָת כִּי דִבֶּר־סָרָה עַל־

יְהוָה אֱלֹהֵיכֶם הַמּוֹצִיא אֶתְכֶם ׀ מֵאֶרֶץ מִצְרַיִם וְהַפֹּדְךָ

מִבֵּית עֲבָדִים לְהַדִּיחֲךָ מִן־הַדֶּרֶךְ אֲשֶׁר צִוְּךָ יְהוָה אֱלֹהֶיךָ

7 לָלֶכֶת בָּהּ וּבִעַרְתָּ הָרָע מִקִּרְבֶּךָ: ס כִּי יְסִיתְךָ אָחִיךָ

בֶן־אִמֶּךָ אוֹ־בִנְךָ אוֹ־בִתְּךָ אוֹ ׀ אֵשֶׁת חֵיקֶךָ אוֹ רֵעֲךָ אֲשֶׁר

כְּנַפְשְׁךָ בַּסֵּתֶר לֵאמֹר נֵלְכָה וְנַעַבְדָה אֱלֹהִים אֲחֵרִים

8 אֲשֶׁר לֹא יָדַעְתָּ אַתָּה וַאֲבֹתֶיךָ: מֵאֱלֹהֵי הָעַמִּים אֲשֶׁר

סְבִיבֹתֵיכֶם הַקְּרֹבִים אֵלֶיךָ אוֹ הָרְחֹקִים מִמֶּךָּ מִקְצֵה

9 הָאָרֶץ וְעַד־קְצֵה הָאָרֶץ: לֹא־תֹאבֶה לוֹ וְלֹא תִשְׁמַע אֵלָיו

וְלֹא־תָחוֹס עֵינְךָ עָלָיו וְלֹא־תַחְמֹל וְלֹא־תְכַסֶּה עָלָיו: כִּי

הָרֹג תַּהַרְגֶנּוּ יָדְךָ תִּהְיֶה־בּוֹ בָרִאשׁוֹנָה לַהֲמִיתוֹ וְיַד כָּל־

11 הָעָם בָּאַחֲרֹנָה: וּסְקַלְתּוֹ בָאֲבָנִים וָמֵת כִּי בִקֵּשׁ לְהַדִּיחֲךָ

מֵעַל יְהוָה אֱלֹהֶיךָ הַמּוֹצִיאֲךָ מֵאֶרֶץ מִצְרַיִם מִבֵּית עֲבָדִים:

12 וְכָל־יִשְׂרָאֵל יִשְׁמְעוּ וְיִרָאוּן וְלֹא־יוֹסִפוּ לַעֲשׂוֹת כַּדָּבָר

13 הָרָע הַזֶּה בְּקִרְבֶּךָ: ס כִּי־תִשְׁמַע בְּאַחַת עָרֶיךָ אֲשֶׁר

יְהוָה אֱלֹהֶיךָ נֹתֵן לְךָ לָשֶׁבֶת שָׁם לֵאמֹר: יָצְאוּ אֲנָשִׁים

14 בְּנֵי־בְלִיַּעַל מִקִּרְבֶּךָ וַיַּדִּיחוּ אֶת־יֹשְׁבֵי עִירָם לֵאמֹר נֵלְכָה

15 וְנַעַבְדָה אֱלֹהִים אֲחֵרִים אֲשֶׁר לֹא־יְדַעְתֶּם: וְדָרַשְׁתָּ

וְחָקַרְתָּ וְשָׁאַלְתָּ הֵיטֵב וְהִנֵּה אֱמֶת נָכוֹן הַדָּבָר נֶעֶשְׂתָה

16 הַתּוֹעֵבָה הַזֹּאת בְּקִרְבֶּךָ: הַכֵּה תַכֶּה אֶת־יֹשְׁבֵי הָעִיר

הַהִוא לְפִי־חָרֶב הַחֲרֵם אֹתָהּ וְאֶת־כָּל־אֲשֶׁר־בָּהּ וְאֶת־

17 בְּהֶמְתָּהּ לְפִי־חָרֶב: וְאֶת־כָּל־שְׁלָלָהּ תִּקְבֹּץ אֶל־תּוֹךְ

רְחֹבָהּ וְשָׂרַפְתָּ בָאֵשׁ אֶת־הָעִיר וְאֶת־כָּל־שְׁלָלָהּ כָּלִיל

18 לַיהוָה אֱלֹהֶיךָ וְהָיְתָה תֵּל עוֹלָם לֹא תִבָּנֶה עוֹד: וְלֹא־

יִדְבַּק בְּיָדְךָ מְאוּמָה מִן־הַחֵרֶם לְמַעַן יָשׁוּב יְהוָה מֵחֲרוֹן

אַפּוֹ וְנָתַן־לְךָ רַחֲמִים וְרִחַמְךָ וְהִרְבֶּךָ כַּאֲשֶׁר נִשְׁבַּע

19 לַאֲבֹתֶיךָ: כִּי תִשְׁמַע בְּקוֹל יְהוָה אֱלֹהֶיךָ לִשְׁמֹר אֶת־

כָּל־מִצְוֹתָיו אֲשֶׁר אָנֹכִי מְצַוְּךָ הַיּוֹם לַעֲשׂוֹת הַיָּשָׁר בְּעֵינֵי

יְהוָה אֱלֹהֶיךָ:

Uitti, *NJV*, *NAB* (4b);
RSV (3b=4bH)

Uitti (6bff.); *NJV*, *NAB*
(6aβ); *NEB*, *RSV* (5aβ=6aβH)

Uitti (11b-12); *NJV*, *NAB*
(11b); *NEB*, *RSV* (10b=11bH)

Uitti, *NJV*, *NAB* (18b,19);
NEB (17-18=18-19H); *RSV*
(17=18H)

Deuteronomy 14

(n. 1)	א בָּנִים אַתֶּם לַיהוָה אֱלֹהֵיכֶם לֹא תִתְגֹּדְדוּ וְלֹא־תָשִׂימוּ
	2 קָרְחָה בֵּין עֵינֵיכֶם לָמֵת: כִּי עַם קָדוֹשׁ אַתָּה לַיהוָה
	אֱלֹהֶיךָ וּבְךָ בָּחַר יְהוָה לִהְיוֹת לוֹ לְעַם סְגֻלָּה מִכֹּל
	3 הָעַמִּים אֲשֶׁר עַל־פְּנֵי הָאֲדָמָה: ס לֹא תֹאכַל כָּל־
	4 תּוֹעֵבָה: זֹאת הַבְּהֵמָה אֲשֶׁר תֹּאכֵלוּ שׁוֹר שֵׂה כְשָׂבִים
	5,6 וְשֵׂה עִזִּים: אַיָּל וּצְבִי וְיַחְמוּר וְאַקּוֹ וְדִישֹׁן וּתְאוֹ וָזָמֶר: וְכָל־
	בְּהֵמָה מַפְרֶסֶת פַּרְסָה וְשֹׁסַעַת שֶׁסַע שְׁתֵּי פְרָסוֹת מַעֲלַת
	7 גֵּרָה בַּבְּהֵמָה אֹתָהּ תֹּאכֵלוּ: אַךְ אֶת־זֶה לֹא תֹאכְלוּ
	מִמַּעֲלֵי הַגֵּרָה וּמִמַּפְרִיסֵי הַפַּרְסָה הַשְּׁסוּעָה אֶת־הַגָּמָל
	וְאֶת־הָאַרְנֶבֶת וְאֶת־הַשָּׁפָן כִּי־מַעֲלֵה גֵרָה הֵמָּה וּפַרְסָה
	8 לֹא הִפְרִיסוּ טְמֵאִים הֵם לָכֶם: וְאֶת־הַחֲזִיר כִּי־מַפְרִיס
	פַּרְסָה הוּא וְלֹא גֵרָה טָמֵא הוּא לָכֶם מִבְּשָׂרָם לֹא תֹאכֵלוּ
	9 וּבְנִבְלָתָם לֹא תִגָּעוּ: ס אֶת־זֶה תֹּאכְלוּ מִכֹּל אֲשֶׁר
	10 בַּמָּיִם כֹּל אֲשֶׁר־לוֹ סְנַפִּיר וְקַשְׂקֶשֶׂת תֹּאכֵלוּ: וְכֹל אֲשֶׁר
(n. 2)	אֵין־לוֹ סְנַפִּיר וְקַשְׂקֶשֶׂת לֹא תֹאכֵלוּ טָמֵא הוּא לָכֶם: ס
	11,12 כָּל־צִפּוֹר טְהֹרָה תֹּאכֵלוּ: וְזֶה אֲשֶׁר לֹא־תֹאכְלוּ מֵהֶם
	13 הַנֶּשֶׁר וְהַפֶּרֶס וְהָעָזְנִיָּה: וְהָרָאָה וְאֶת־הָאַיָּה וְהַדַּיָּה לְמִינָהּ:
	14,15 וְאֵת כָּל־עֹרֵב לְמִינוֹ: וְאֵת בַּת הַיַּעֲנָה וְאֶת־הַתַּחְמָס וְאֶת־
	16 הַשַּׁחַף וְאֶת־הַנֵּץ לְמִינֵהוּ: אֶת־הַכּוֹס וְאֶת־הַיַּנְשׁוּף
	17,18 וְהַתִּנְשָׁמֶת: וְהַקָּאָת וְאֶת־הָרָחָמָה וְאֶת־הַשָּׁלָךְ: וְהַחֲסִידָה
(n. 3)	19 וְהָאֲנָפָה לְמִינָהּ וְהַדּוּכִיפַת וְהָעֲטַלֵּף: וְכֹל שֶׁרֶץ הָעוֹף טָמֵא
	20,21 הוּא לָכֶם לֹא יֵאָכֵלוּ: כָּל־עוֹף טָהוֹר תֹּאכֵלוּ: לֹא תֹאכְלוּ
	כָל־נְבֵלָה לַגֵּר אֲשֶׁר־בִּשְׁעָרֶיךָ תִּתְּנֶנָּה וַאֲכָלָהּ אוֹ מָכֹר
(n. 4)	לְנָכְרִי כִּי עַם קָדוֹשׁ אַתָּה לַיהוָה אֱלֹהֶיךָ לֹא־תְבַשֵּׁל גְּדִי
	בַּחֲלֵב אִמּוֹ:
	פ
	22 עַשֵּׂר תְּעַשֵּׂר אֵת כָּל־תְּבוּאַת זַרְעֶךָ הַיֹּצֵא הַשָּׂדֶה שָׁנָה
	23 שָׁנָה: וְאָכַלְתָּ לִפְנֵי	יְהוָה אֱלֹהֶיךָ בַּמָּקוֹם אֲשֶׁר־יִבְחַר
	לְשַׁכֵּן שְׁמוֹ שָׁם מַעְשַׂר דְּגָנְךָ תִּירֹשְׁךָ וְיִצְהָרֶךָ וּבְכֹרֹת
	בְּקָרְךָ וְצֹאנֶךָ לְמַעַן תִּלְמַד לְיִרְאָה אֶת־יְהוָה אֱלֹהֶיךָ כָּל־
	24 הַיָּמִים: וְכִי־יִרְבֶּה מִמְּךָ הַדֶּרֶךְ כִּי לֹא תוּכַל שְׂאֵתוֹ
	כִּי־יִרְחַק מִמְּךָ הַמָּקוֹם אֲשֶׁר יִבְחַר יְהוָה אֱלֹהֶיךָ לָשׂוּם
	25 שְׁמוֹ שָׁם כִּי יְבָרֶכְךָ יְהוָה אֱלֹהֶיךָ: וְנָתַתָּה בַּכָּסֶף וְצַרְתָּ
	הַכֶּסֶף בְּיָדְךָ וְהָלַכְתָּ אֶל־הַמָּקוֹם אֲשֶׁר יִבְחַר יְהוָה
	26 אֱלֹהֶיךָ בּוֹ: וְנָתַתָּה הַכֶּסֶף בְּכֹל אֲשֶׁר־תְּאַוֶּה נַפְשְׁךָ בַּבָּקָר
	וּבַצֹּאן וּבַיַּיִן וּבַשֵּׁכָר וּבְכֹל אֲשֶׁר תִּשְׁאָלְךָ נַפְשֶׁךָ וְאָכַלְתָּ
	27 שָּׁם לִפְנֵי יְהוָה אֱלֹהֶיךָ וְשָׂמַחְתָּ אַתָּה וּבֵיתֶךָ: וְהַלֵּוִי
	אֲשֶׁר־בִּשְׁעָרֶיךָ לֹא תַעַזְבֶנּוּ כִּי אֵין לוֹ חֵלֶק וְנַחֲלָה עִמָּךְ:
	28 ס מִקְצֵה	שָׁלֹשׁ שָׁנִים תּוֹצִיא אֶת־כָּל־מַעְשַׂר תְּבוּאָתְךָ
	29 בַּשָּׁנָה הַהִוא וְהִנַּחְתָּ בִּשְׁעָרֶיךָ: וּבָא הַלֵּוִי כִּי אֵין־לוֹ חֵלֶק
	וְנַחֲלָה עִמָּךְ וְהַגֵּר וְהַיָּתוֹם וְהָאַלְמָנָה אֲשֶׁר בִּשְׁעָרֶיךָ וְאָכְלוּ
	וְשָׂבֵעוּ לְמַעַן יְבָרֶכְךָ יְהוָה אֱלֹהֶיךָ בְּכָל־מַעֲשֵׂה יָדְךָ אֲשֶׁר
	תַּעֲשֶׂה:

Uitti (1a,2)

NJV, NAB, RSV (2)

Uitti (7c); *NJV, NEB, RSV*
(7bβ)

Uitti (8b); *NJV, NEB, RSV*
(8aβ)

Uitti (21c); *NJV, NAB, NEB,
RSV* (21aβ)

Uitti, *NJV, NAB, NEB, RSV*
(23b)

NJV (24aγ,b); *NAB* (24aγ);
RSV (24aβ,aγ)

Uitti, *NJV, NAB, NEB, RSV*
(27b)

Uitti (29); *NJV, NAB, RSV*
(29b)

Deuteronomy 15

מִקֵּץ שֶׁבַע־שָׁנִים תַּעֲשֶׂה שְׁמִטָּה: וְזֶה דְּבַר הַשְּׁמִטָּה א ²
שָׁמוֹט כָּל־בַּעַל מַשֵּׁה יָדוֹ אֲשֶׁר יַשֶּׁה בְּרֵעֵהוּ לֹא־יִגֹּשׂ
אֶת־רֵעֵהוּ וְאֶת־אָחִיו כִּי־קָרָא שְׁמִטָּה לַיהֹוָה:

כִּי־יִהְיֶה ⁷
בְךָ אֶבְיוֹן מֵאַחַד אַחֶיךָ בְּאַחַד שְׁעָרֶיךָ בְּאַרְצְךָ אֲשֶׁר
יְהֹוָה אֱלֹהֶיךָ נֹתֵן לָךְ לֹא תְאַמֵּץ אֶת־לְבָבְךָ וְלֹא תִקְפֹּץ
אֶת־יָדְךָ מֵאָחִיךָ הָאֶבְיוֹן: כִּי־פָתֹחַ תִּפְתַּח אֶת־יָדְךָ לוֹ ⁸
וְהַעֲבֵט תַּעֲבִיטֶנּוּ דֵּי מַחְסֹרוֹ אֲשֶׁר יֶחְסַר לוֹ: הִשָּׁמֶר לְךָ ⁹
פֶּן־יִהְיֶה דָבָר עִם־לְבָבְךָ בְלִיַּעַל לֵאמֹר קָרְבָה שְׁנַת־
הַשֶּׁבַע שְׁנַת הַשְּׁמִטָּה וְרָעָה עֵינְךָ בְּאָחִיךָ הָאֶבְיוֹן וְלֹא
תִתֵּן לוֹ וְקָרָא עָלֶיךָ אֶל־יְהֹוָה וְהָיָה בְךָ חֵטְא: נָתוֹן תִּתֵּן ¹⁰
לוֹ וְלֹא־יֵרַע לְבָבְךָ בְּתִתְּךָ לוֹ כִּי בִּגְלַל ׀ הַדָּבָר הַזֶּה
יְבָרֶכְךָ יְהֹוָה אֱלֹהֶיךָ בְּכָל־מַעֲשֶׂךָ וּבְכֹל מִשְׁלַח יָדֶךָ: כִּי ¹¹
לֹא־יֶחְדַּל אֶבְיוֹן מִקֶּרֶב הָאָרֶץ עַל־כֵּן אָנֹכִי מְצַוְּךָ לֵאמֹר
פָּתֹחַ תִּפְתַּח אֶת־יָדְךָ לְאָחִיךָ לַעֲנִיֶּךָ וּלְאֶבְיֹנְךָ בְּאַרְצֶךָ: ס
כִּי־יִמָּכֵר לְךָ אָחִיךָ הָעִבְרִי אוֹ הָעִבְרִיָּה וַעֲבָדְךָ שֵׁשׁ שָׁנִים ¹²
וּבַשָּׁנָה הַשְּׁבִיעִת תְּשַׁלְּחֶנּוּ חָפְשִׁי מֵעִמָּךְ: וְכִי־תְשַׁלְּחֶנּוּ ¹³
חָפְשִׁי מֵעִמָּךְ לֹא תְשַׁלְּחֶנּוּ רֵיקָם: הַעֲנֵיק תַּעֲנִיק לוֹ ¹⁴
מִצֹּאנְךָ וּמִגָּרְנְךָ וּמִיִּקְבֶךָ אֲשֶׁר בֵּרַכְךָ יְהֹוָה אֱלֹהֶיךָ תִּתֶּן
לוֹ: וְזָכַרְתָּ כִּי עֶבֶד הָיִיתָ בְּאֶרֶץ מִצְרַיִם וַיִּפְדְּךָ יְהֹוָה טו
אֱלֹהֶיךָ עַל־כֵּן אָנֹכִי מְצַוְּךָ אֶת־הַדָּבָר הַזֶּה הַיּוֹם: וְהָיָה ¹⁶
כִּי־יֹאמַר אֵלֶיךָ לֹא אֵצֵא מֵעִמָּךְ כִּי אֲהֵבְךָ וְאֶת־בֵּיתֶךָ
כִּי־טוֹב לוֹ עִמָּךְ:

(n. 5)

Uitti, *NJV*, *NAB*, *NEB*, *RSV*
(2bβ)

Uitti, *NJV*, *RSV* (10b,11);
NAB, *NEB* (10b)

Uitti, *NAB* (15)

NJV (16b); *NAB*, *RSV*
(16bα,bβ)

Deuteronomy 16

א שָׁמוֹר֙ אֶת־חֹ֣דֶשׁ הָאָבִ֔יב וְעָשִׂ֣יתָ פֶּ֔סַח לַיהוָ֖ה אֱלֹהֶ֑יךָ כִּ֞י
בְּחֹ֣דֶשׁ הָֽאָבִ֗יב הוֹצִֽיאֲךָ֛ יְהוָ֥ה אֱלֹהֶ֖יךָ מִמִּצְרַ֖יִם לָֽיְלָה׃
2 וְזָבַ֥חְתָּ פֶּ֛סַח לַיהוָ֥ה אֱלֹהֶ֖יךָ צֹ֣אן וּבָקָ֑ר בַּמָּקוֹם֙ אֲשֶׁר־יִבְחַ֣ר
3 יְהוָ֔ה לְשַׁכֵּ֥ן שְׁמ֖וֹ שָֽׁם׃ לֹא־תֹאכַ֤ל עָלָיו֙ חָמֵ֔ץ שִׁבְעַ֥ת יָמִ֛ים
תֹּֽאכַל־עָלָ֥יו מַצּ֖וֹת לֶ֣חֶם עֹ֑נִי כִּ֣י בְחִפָּז֗וֹן יָצָ֙אתָ֙ מֵאֶ֣רֶץ
מִצְרַ֔יִם לְמַ֣עַן תִּזְכֹּר֩ אֶת־י֨וֹם צֵֽאתְךָ֜ מֵאֶ֣רֶץ מִצְרַ֔יִם כֹּ֖ל
יְמֵ֥י חַיֶּֽיךָ׃
13 חַ֧ג הַסֻּכֹּ֛ת תַּעֲשֶׂ֥ה לְךָ֖ שִׁבְעַ֣ת יָמִ֑ים בְּאָ֨סְפְּךָ֔ מִֽגָּרְנְךָ֖
14 וּמִיִּקְבֶֽךָ׃ וְשָׂמַחְתָּ֖ בְּחַגֶּ֑ךָ אַתָּ֨ה וּבִנְךָ֤ וּבִתֶּ֙ךָ֙ וְעַבְדְּךָ֣ וַאֲמָתֶ֔ךָ
טו וְהַלֵּוִ֗י וְהַגֵּ֛ר וְהַיָּת֥וֹם וְהָאַלְמָנָ֖ה אֲשֶׁ֥ר בִּשְׁעָרֶֽיךָ׃ שִׁבְעַ֣ת
יָמִ֗ים תָּחֹג֙ לַיהוָ֣ה אֱלֹהֶ֔יךָ בַּמָּק֖וֹם אֲשֶׁר־יִבְחַ֣ר יְהוָ֑ה כִּ֣י
יְבָרֶכְךָ֞ יְהוָ֣ה אֱלֹהֶ֗יךָ בְּכֹ֤ל תְּבוּאָֽתְךָ֙ וּבְכֹל֙ מַעֲשֵׂ֣ה יָדֶ֔יךָ
16 וְהָיִ֖יתָ אַ֥ךְ שָׂמֵֽחַ׃ שָׁל֣וֹשׁ פְּעָמִ֣ים ׀ בַּשָּׁנָ֡ה יֵרָאֶ֨ה כָל־זְכוּרְךָ֜
אֶת־פְּנֵ֣י ׀ יְהוָ֣ה אֱלֹהֶ֗יךָ בַּמָּקוֹם֙ אֲשֶׁ֣ר יִבְחָ֔ר בְּחַ֧ג הַמַּצּ֛וֹת
וּבְחַ֥ג הַשָּׁבֻע֖וֹת וּבְחַ֣ג הַסֻּכּ֑וֹת וְלֹ֧א יֵרָאֶ֛ה אֶת־פְּנֵ֥י יְהוָ֖ה
17 רֵיקָֽם׃ אִ֖ישׁ כְּמַתְּנַ֣ת יָד֑וֹ כְּבִרְכַּ֛ת יְהוָ֥ה אֱלֹהֶ֖יךָ אֲשֶׁ֥ר נָֽתַן־לָֽךְ׃
18 שֹׁפְטִ֣ים וְשֹֽׁטְרִ֗ים תִּֽתֶּן־לְךָ֙ בְּכָל־שְׁעָרֶ֔יךָ אֲשֶׁ֨ר יְהוָ֧ה אֱלֹהֶ֛יךָ
19 נֹתֵ֥ן לְךָ֖ לִשְׁבָטֶ֑יךָ וְשָׁפְט֥וּ אֶת־הָעָ֖ם מִשְׁפַּט־צֶֽדֶק׃ לֹא־
תַטֶּ֣ה מִשְׁפָּ֔ט לֹ֥א תַכִּ֖יר פָּנִ֑ים וְלֹא־תִקַּ֣ח שֹׁ֔חַד כִּ֣י הַשֹּׁ֗חַד
כ יְעַוֵּר֙ עֵינֵ֣י חֲכָמִ֔ים וִֽיסַלֵּ֖ף דִּבְרֵ֣י צַדִּיקִֽם׃ צֶ֥דֶק צֶ֖דֶק
תִּרְדֹּ֑ף לְמַ֤עַן תִּֽחְיֶה֙ וְיָרַשְׁתָּ֣ אֶת־הָאָ֔רֶץ אֲשֶׁר־יְהוָ֥ה אֱלֹהֶ֖יךָ
21 נֹתֵ֥ן לָֽךְ׃   לֹֽא־תִטַּ֥ע לְךָ֛ אֲשֵׁרָ֖ה כָּל־עֵ֑ץ אֵ֗צֶל מִזְבַּ֛ח
22 יְהוָ֥ה אֱלֹהֶ֖יךָ אֲשֶׁ֥ר תַּעֲשֶׂה־לָּֽךְ׃ וְלֹֽא־תָקִ֥ים לְךָ֖ מַצֵּבָ֑ה
אֲשֶׁ֥ר שָׂנֵ֖א יְהוָ֥ה אֱלֹהֶֽיךָ׃

Uitti, *NJV*, *NAB*, *NEB*, *RSV*
(1b)

Uitti (3bβ,c); *NJV*, *NAB*,
RSV (3bα,bβ)

Uitti (14-15); *NJV*, *NAB*
(15b); *RSV* (15bα,bβ)

Uitti (19cb-20); *NJV*, *NAB*,
NEB, *RSV* (19bβ-c)

NJV, *NAB*, *NEB*, *RSV* (20b)

Uitti, *NJV*, *NEB* (22b)

(n.6)

Deuteronomy 17

א לֹא־תִזְבַּח לַיהוָה אֱלֹהֶיךָ שׁוֹר וָשֶׂה אֲשֶׁר יִהְיֶה בוֹ מוּם

2 כֹּל דָּבָר רָע כִּי תוֹעֲבַת יְהוָה אֱלֹהֶיךָ הוּא: ס כִּי־יִמָּצֵא בְקִרְבְּךָ בְּאַחַד שְׁעָרֶיךָ אֲשֶׁר־יְהוָה אֱלֹהֶיךָ נֹתֵן לָךְ אִישׁ אוֹ־אִשָּׁה אֲשֶׁר יַעֲשֶׂה אֶת־הָרַע בְּעֵינֵי יְהוָה־אֱלֹהֶיךָ לַעֲבֹר בְּרִיתוֹ:

3 אוֹ וַיֵּלֶךְ וַיַּעֲבֹד אֱלֹהִים אֲחֵרִים וַיִּשְׁתַּחוּ לָהֶם וְלַשֶּׁמֶשׁ

4 אוֹ לַיָּרֵחַ אוֹ לְכָל־צְבָא הַשָּׁמַיִם אֲשֶׁר לֹא־צִוִּיתִי: וְהֻגַּד־לְךָ וְשָׁמַעְתָּ וְדָרַשְׁתָּ הֵיטֵב וְהִנֵּה אֱמֶת נָכוֹן הַדָּבָר נֶעֶשְׂתָה

5 הַתּוֹעֵבָה הַזֹּאת בְּיִשְׂרָאֵל: וְהוֹצֵאתָ אֶת־הָאִישׁ הַהוּא אוֹ אֶת־הָאִשָּׁה הַהִוא אֲשֶׁר עָשׂוּ אֶת־הַדָּבָר הָרַע הַזֶּה אֶל־שְׁעָרֶיךָ אֶת־הָאִישׁ אוֹ אֶת־הָאִשָּׁה וּסְקַלְתָּם בָּאֲבָנִים וָמֵתוּ:

6 עַל־פִּי שְׁנַיִם עֵדִים אוֹ שְׁלֹשָׁה עֵדִים יוּמַת הַמֵּת לֹא יוּמַת

7 עַל־פִּי עֵד אֶחָד: יַד הָעֵדִים תִּהְיֶה־בּוֹ בָרִאשֹׁנָה לַהֲמִיתוֹ וְיַד כָּל־הָעָם בָּאַחֲרֹנָה וּבִעַרְתָּ הָרָע מִקִּרְבֶּךָ: פ

8 כִּי יִפָּלֵא מִמְּךָ דָבָר לַמִּשְׁפָּט בֵּין־דָּם ׀ לְדָם וּבֵין נֶגַע לָנֶגַע דִּבְרֵי רִיבֹת בִּשְׁעָרֶיךָ וְקַמְתָּ וְעָלִיתָ אֶל־

9 הַמָּקוֹם אֲשֶׁר יִבְחַר יְהוָה אֱלֹהֶיךָ בּוֹ: וּבָאתָ אֶל־הַכֹּהֲנִים הַלְוִיִּם וְאֶל־הַשֹּׁפֵט אֲשֶׁר יִהְיֶה בַּיָּמִים הָהֵם וְדָרַשְׁתָּ

י וְהִגִּידוּ לְךָ אֵת דְּבַר הַמִּשְׁפָּט: וְעָשִׂיתָ עַל־פִּי הַדָּבָר אֲשֶׁר יַגִּידוּ לְךָ מִן־הַמָּקוֹם הַהוּא אֲשֶׁר יִבְחַר יְהוָה וְשָׁמַרְתָּ

11 לַעֲשׂוֹת כְּכֹל אֲשֶׁר יוֹרוּךָ: עַל־פִּי הַתּוֹרָה אֲשֶׁר יוֹרוּךָ וְעַל־הַמִּשְׁפָּט אֲשֶׁר־יֹאמְרוּ לְךָ תַּעֲשֶׂה לֹא תָסוּר מִן־הַדָּבָר

12 אֲשֶׁר־יַגִּידוּ לְךָ יָמִין וּשְׂמֹאל: וְהָאִישׁ אֲשֶׁר־יַעֲשֶׂה בְזָדוֹן לְבִלְתִּי שְׁמֹעַ אֶל־הַכֹּהֵן הָעֹמֵד לְשָׁרֶת שָׁם אֶת־יְהוָה אֱלֹהֶיךָ אוֹ אֶל־הַשֹּׁפֵט וּמֵת הָאִישׁ הַהוּא וּבִעַרְתָּ הָרָע

13 מִיִּשְׂרָאֵל: וְכָל־הָעָם יִשְׁמְעוּ וְיִרָאוּ וְלֹא יְזִידוּן עוֹד: כִּי־

14 תָבֹא אֶל־הָאָרֶץ אֲשֶׁר יְהוָה אֱלֹהֶיךָ נֹתֵן לָךְ וִירִשְׁתָּהּ וְיָשַׁבְתָּה בָּהּ וְאָמַרְתָּ אָשִׂימָה עָלַי מֶלֶךְ כְּכָל־הַגּוֹיִם אֲשֶׁר

15 סְבִיבֹתָי: שׂוֹם תָּשִׂים עָלֶיךָ מֶלֶךְ אֲשֶׁר יִבְחַר יְהוָה אֱלֹהֶיךָ בּוֹ מִקֶּרֶב אַחֶיךָ תָּשִׂים עָלֶיךָ מֶלֶךְ לֹא תוּכַל לָתֵת עָלֶיךָ

16 אִישׁ נָכְרִי אֲשֶׁר לֹא־אָחִיךָ הוּא: רַק לֹא־יַרְבֶּה־לּוֹ סוּסִים וְלֹא־יָשִׁיב אֶת־הָעָם מִצְרַיְמָה לְמַעַן הַרְבּוֹת סוּס וַיהוָה

17 אָמַר לָכֶם לֹא תֹסִפוּן לָשׁוּב בַּדֶּרֶךְ הַזֶּה עוֹד: וְלֹא יַרְבֶּה־לּוֹ נָשִׁים וְלֹא יָסוּר לְבָבוֹ וְכֶסֶף וְזָהָב לֹא יַרְבֶּה־לּוֹ מְאֹד:

18 וְהָיָה כְשִׁבְתּוֹ עַל כִּסֵּא מַמְלַכְתּוֹ וְכָתַב לוֹ אֶת־מִשְׁנֵה

19 הַתּוֹרָה הַזֹּאת עַל־סֵפֶר מִלִּפְנֵי הַכֹּהֲנִים הַלְוִיִּם: וְהָיְתָה עִמּוֹ וְקָרָא בוֹ כָּל־יְמֵי חַיָּיו לְמַעַן יִלְמַד לְיִרְאָה אֶת־יְהוָה אֱלֹהָיו לִשְׁמֹר אֶת־כָּל־דִּבְרֵי הַתּוֹרָה הַזֹּאת וְאֶת־הַחֻקִּים

כ הָאֵלֶּה לַעֲשֹׂתָם: לְבִלְתִּי רוּם־לְבָבוֹ מֵאֶחָיו וּלְבִלְתִּי סוּר מִן־הַמִּצְוָה יָמִין וּשְׂמֹאול לְמַעַן יַאֲרִיךְ יָמִים עַל־מַמְלַכְתּוֹ הוּא וּבָנָיו בְּקֶרֶב יִשְׂרָאֵל:

Uitti, *NJV*, *NEB*, *RSV* (1b)

Uitti (7b)

Uitti (12b-13)

Uitti (16c); *NJV*, *NEB*, *RSV* (16b)

Uitti, *NJV*, *NAB*, *RSV* (17aβ)

Uitti (19bff.-20); *NJV* (19b,20b); *NAB*, *NEB* (19b); *RSV* (19b,20aα,aβ,b)

Deuteronomy 18

א לֹא־יִהְיֶה לַכֹּהֲנִים הַלְוִיִּם כָּל־שֵׁבֶט לֵוִי חֵלֶק וְנַחֲלָה עִם־

2 יִשְׂרָאֵל אִשֵּׁי יְהוָה וְנַחֲלָתוֹ יֹאכֵלוּן: וְנַחֲלָה לֹא־יִהְיֶה־לּוֹ

3 בְּקֶרֶב אֶחָיו יְהוָה הוּא נַחֲלָתוֹ כַּאֲשֶׁר דִּבֶּר־לוֹ: ס וְזֶה

יִהְיֶה מִשְׁפַּט הַכֹּהֲנִים מֵאֵת הָעָם מֵאֵת זֹבְחֵי הַזֶּבַח אִם־

4 שׁוֹר אִם־שֶׂה וְנָתַן לַכֹּהֵן הַזְּרֹעַ וְהַלְּחָיַיִם וְהַקֵּבָה: רֵאשִׁית

5 דְּגָנְךָ תִּירֹשְׁךָ וְיִצְהָרֶךָ וְרֵאשִׁית גֵּז צֹאנְךָ תִּתֶּן־לּוֹ: כִּי בוֹ

בָּחַר יְהוָה אֱלֹהֶיךָ מִכָּל־שְׁבָטֶיךָ לַעֲמֹד לְשָׁרֵת בְּשֵׁם־

6 יְהוָה הוּא וּבָנָיו כָּל־הַיָּמִים: וְכִי־יָבֹא הַלֵּוִי מֵאַחַד

שְׁעָרֶיךָ מִכָּל־יִשְׂרָאֵל אֲשֶׁר־הוּא גָּר שָׁם וּבָא בְּכָל־אַוַּת

7 נַפְשׁוֹ אֶל־הַמָּקוֹם אֲשֶׁר־יִבְחַר יְהוָה: וְשֵׁרֵת בְּשֵׁם יְהוָה

8 אֱלֹהָיו כְּכָל־אֶחָיו הַלְוִיִּם הָעֹמְדִים שָׁם לִפְנֵי יְהוָה: חֵלֶק

9 כְּחֵלֶק יֹאכֵלוּ לְבַד מִמְכָּרָיו עַל־הָאָבוֹת: ס כִּי אַתָּה בָּא

אֶל־הָאָרֶץ אֲשֶׁר־יְהוָה אֱלֹהֶיךָ נֹתֵן לָךְ לֹא־תִלְמַד לַעֲשׂוֹת

10 כְּתוֹעֲבֹת הַגּוֹיִם הָהֵם: לֹא־יִמָּצֵא בְךָ מַעֲבִיר בְּנוֹ־וּבִתּוֹ בָּאֵשׁ

11 קֹסֵם קְסָמִים מְעוֹנֵן וּמְנַחֵשׁ וּמְכַשֵּׁף: וְחֹבֵר חָבֶר וְשֹׁאֵל

12 אוֹב וְיִדְּעֹנִי וְדֹרֵשׁ אֶל־הַמֵּתִים: כִּי־תוֹעֲבַת יְהוָה כָּל־עֹשֵׂה

אֵלֶּה וּבִגְלַל הַתּוֹעֵבֹת הָאֵלֶּה יְהוָה אֱלֹהֶיךָ מוֹרִישׁ אוֹתָם

מִפָּנֶיךָ:

Uitti (2b)

Uitti, *NJV*, *NAB*, *NEB*, *RSV* (5)

Uitti (12-22); *NJV*, *RSV* (12a,b); *NAB*, *NEB* (12b)

(n. 7)

(n. 8)

Deuteronomy 19

א כִּי־יַכְרִית יְהוָה אֱלֹהֶיךָ אֶת־הַגּוֹיִם אֲשֶׁר יְהוָה אֱלֹהֶיךָ

נֹתֵן לְךָ אֶת־אַרְצָם וִירִשְׁתָּם וְיָשַׁבְתָּ בְעָרֵיהֶם וּבְבָתֵּיהֶם:

2 שָׁלוֹשׁ עָרִים תַּבְדִּיל לָךְ בְּתוֹךְ אַרְצְךָ אֲשֶׁר יְהוָה אֱלֹהֶיךָ

3 נֹתֵן לְךָ לְרִשְׁתָּהּ: תָּכִין לְךָ הַדֶּרֶךְ וְשִׁלַּשְׁתָּ אֶת־גְּבוּל

אַרְצְךָ אֲשֶׁר יַנְחִילְךָ יְהוָה אֱלֹהֶיךָ וְהָיָה לָנוּס שָׁמָּה כָּל־

4 רֹצֵחַ: וְזֶה דְּבַר הָרֹצֵחַ אֲשֶׁר־יָנוּס שָׁמָּה וָחָי אֲשֶׁר יַכֶּה

אֶת־רֵעֵהוּ בִּבְלִי־דַעַת וְהוּא לֹא־שֹׂנֵא לוֹ מִתְּמֹל שִׁלְשֹׁם:

5 וַאֲשֶׁר יָבֹא אֶת־רֵעֵהוּ בַיַּעַר לַחְטֹב עֵצִים וְנִדְּחָה יָדוֹ

בַגַּרְזֶן לִכְרֹת הָעֵץ וְנָשַׁל הַבַּרְזֶל מִן־הָעֵץ וּמָצָא אֶת־

6 רֵעֵהוּ וָמֵת הוּא יָנוּס אֶל־אַחַת הֶעָרִים־הָאֵלֶּה וָחָי: פֶּן־

יִרְדֹּף גֹּאֵל הַדָּם אַחֲרֵי הָרֹצֵחַ כִּי יֵחַם לְבָבוֹ וְהִשִּׂיגוֹ

כִּי־יִרְבֶּה הַדֶּרֶךְ וְהִכָּהוּ נָפֶשׁ וְלוֹ אֵין מִשְׁפַּט־מָוֶת כִּי

7 לֹא שֹׂנֵא הוּא לוֹ מִתְּמוֹל שִׁלְשׁוֹם: עַל־כֵּן אָנֹכִי מְצַוְּךָ

8 לֵאמֹר שָׁלֹשׁ עָרִים תַּבְדִּיל לָךְ: וְאִם־יַרְחִיב יְהוָה

אֱלֹהֶיךָ אֶת־גְּבֻלְךָ כַּאֲשֶׁר נִשְׁבַּע לַאֲבֹתֶיךָ וְנָתַן לְךָ אֶת־

9 כָּל־הָאָרֶץ אֲשֶׁר דִּבֶּר לָתֵת לַאֲבֹתֶיךָ: כִּי־תִשְׁמֹר אֶת־

כָּל־הַמִּצְוָה הַזֹּאת לַעֲשֹׂתָהּ אֲשֶׁר אָנֹכִי מְצַוְּךָ הַיּוֹם לְאַהֲבָה

אֶת־יְהוָה אֱלֹהֶיךָ וְלָלֶכֶת בִּדְרָכָיו כָּל־הַיָּמִים וְיָסַפְתָּ לְךָ

10 עוֹד שָׁלֹשׁ עָרִים עַל הַשָּׁלֹשׁ הָאֵלֶּה: וְלֹא יִשָּׁפֵךְ דָּם נָקִי

בְּקֶרֶב אַרְצְךָ אֲשֶׁר יְהוָה אֱלֹהֶיךָ נֹתֵן לְךָ נַחֲלָה וְהָיָה

עָלֶיךָ דָּמִים:

Uitti (3c); *NJV*, *RSV* (3b); *NAB* (3b?)

Uitti (6-7); *NJV*, *NAB* (6bβ); *NEB* (6-7?); *RSV* (6)

Uitti, *RSV* (10)

Deuteronomy 19 cont.

מו לֹא־יָקוּם עֵד אֶחָד בְּאִישׁ לְכָל־עָוֹן וּלְכָל־חַטָּאת   Uitti (19b-21)
בְּכָל־חֵטְא אֲשֶׁר יֶחֱטָא עַל־פִּי ׀ שְׁנֵי עֵדִים אוֹ עַל־פִּי
16 שְׁלֹשָׁה־עֵדִים יָקוּם דָּבָר: כִּי־יָקוּם עֵד־חָמָס בְּאִישׁ לַעֲנוֹת
17 בּוֹ סָרָה: וְעָמְדוּ שְׁנֵי־הָאֲנָשִׁים אֲשֶׁר־לָהֶם הָרִיב לִפְנֵי
יְהוָה לִפְנֵי הַכֹּהֲנִים וְהַשֹּׁפְטִים אֲשֶׁר יִהְיוּ בַּיָּמִים הָהֵם:
18 וְדָרְשׁוּ הַשֹּׁפְטִים הֵיטֵב וְהִנֵּה עֵד־שֶׁקֶר הָעֵד שֶׁקֶר עָנָה
19 בְאָחִיו: וַעֲשִׂיתֶם לוֹ כַּאֲשֶׁר זָמַם לַעֲשׂוֹת לְאָחִיו וּבִעַרְתָּ
כ הָרָע מִקִּרְבֶּךָ: וְהַנִּשְׁאָרִים יִשְׁמְעוּ וְיִרָאוּ וְלֹא־יֹסִפוּ לַעֲשׂוֹת
21 עוֹד כַּדָּבָר הָרָע הַזֶּה בְּקִרְבֶּךָ:

Deuteronomy 20

2 וְהָיָה כְּקָרָבְכֶם אֶל־הַמִּלְחָמָה וְנִגַּשׁ   Uitti (5bβ); *NJV, NAB, RSV*
3 הַכֹּהֵן וְדִבֶּר אֶל־הָעָם: וְאָמַר אֲלֵהֶם שְׁמַע יִשְׂרָאֵל אַתֶּם   (5b)
קְרֵבִים הַיּוֹם לַמִּלְחָמָה עַל־אֹיְבֵיכֶם אַל־יֵרַךְ לְבַבְכֶם   Uitti (6bβ); *NJV, NAB, RSV*
4 אַל־תִּירְאוּ וְאַל־תַּחְפְּזוּ וְאַל־תַּעַרְצוּ מִפְּנֵיהֶם: כִּי יְהוָה   (6b)
אֱלֹהֵיכֶם הַהֹלֵךְ עִמָּכֶם לְהִלָּחֵם לָכֶם עִם־אֹיְבֵיכֶם לְהוֹשִׁיעַ   Uitti (7bβ); *NJV, NAB, RSV*
5 אֶתְכֶם: וְדִבְּרוּ הַשֹּׁטְרִים אֶל־הָעָם לֵאמֹר מִי־הָאִישׁ אֲשֶׁר   (7b)
בָּנָה בַיִת־חָדָשׁ וְלֹא חֲנָכוֹ יֵלֵךְ וְיָשֹׁב לְבֵיתוֹ פֶּן־יָמוּת   Uitti (8bβ); *NJV, NAB, RSV*
6 בַּמִּלְחָמָה וְאִישׁ אַחֵר יַחְנְכֶנּוּ: וּמִי־הָאִישׁ אֲשֶׁר נָטַע   (8b)
כֶּרֶם וְלֹא חִלְּלוֹ יֵלֵךְ וְיָשֹׁב לְבֵיתוֹ פֶּן־יָמוּת בַּמִּלְחָמָה   Uitti (17b-18); *NJV, NAB,*
7 וְאִישׁ אַחֵר יְחַלְּלֶנּוּ: וּמִי־הָאִישׁ אֲשֶׁר אֵרַשׂ אִשָּׁה וְלֹא   *NEB, RSV* (18)
לְקָחָהּ יֵלֵךְ וְיָשֹׁב לְבֵיתוֹ פֶּן־יָמוּת בַּמִּלְחָמָה וְאִישׁ אַחֵר   Uitti (19b-20); *NAB* (19b?)
8 יִקָּחֶנָּה: וְיָסְפוּ הַשֹּׁטְרִים לְדַבֵּר אֶל־הָעָם וְאָמְרוּ מִי־
הָאִישׁ הַיָּרֵא וְרַךְ הַלֵּבָב יֵלֵךְ וְיָשֹׁב לְבֵיתוֹ וְלֹא יִמַּס אֶת־
9 לְבַב אֶחָיו כִּלְבָבוֹ: וְהָיָה כְּכַלֹּת הַשֹּׁטְרִים לְדַבֵּר אֶל־
הָעָם וּפָקְדוּ שָׂרֵי צְבָאוֹת בְּרֹאשׁ הָעָם:

16 רַק מֵעָרֵי הָעַמִּים הָאֵלֶּה אֲשֶׁר יְהוָה
17 אֱלֹהֶיךָ נֹתֵן לְךָ נַחֲלָה לֹא תְחַיֶּה כָּל־נְשָׁמָה: כִּי־הַחֲרֵם
תַּחֲרִימֵם הַחִתִּי וְהָאֱמֹרִי הַכְּנַעֲנִי וְהַפְּרִזִּי הַחִוִּי וְהַיְבוּסִי
18 כַּאֲשֶׁר צִוְּךָ יְהוָה אֱלֹהֶיךָ: לְמַעַן אֲשֶׁר לֹא־יְלַמְּדוּ אֶתְכֶם
לַעֲשׂוֹת כְּכֹל תּוֹעֲבֹתָם אֲשֶׁר עָשׂוּ לֵאלֹהֵיהֶם וַחֲטָאתֶם
19 לַיהוָה אֱלֹהֵיכֶם: ס כִּי־תָצוּר אֶל־עִיר יָמִים רַבִּים
לְהִלָּחֵם עָלֶיהָ לְתָפְשָׂהּ לֹא־תַשְׁחִית אֶת־עֵצָהּ לִנְדֹּחַ עָלָיו
גַּרְזֶן כִּי מִמֶּנּוּ תֹאכֵל וְאֹתוֹ לֹא תִכְרֹת כִּי הָאָדָם עֵץ הַשָּׂדֶה
לָבֹא מִפָּנֶיךָ בַּמָּצוֹר:

(n. 9)

Deuteronomy 21

כִּי־יִמָּצֵא חָלָל בָּאֲדָמָה אֲשֶׁר יְהוָה אֱלֹהֶיךָ נֹתֵן לְךָ ‪a‬
לְרִשְׁתָּהּ נֹפֵל בַּשָּׂדֶה לֹא נוֹדַע מִי הִכָּהוּ: וְיָצְאוּ זְקֵנֶיךָ ‪2‬
וְשֹׁפְטֶיךָ וּמָדְדוּ אֶל־הֶעָרִים אֲשֶׁר סְבִיבֹת הֶחָלָל: וְהָיָה ‪3‬
הָעִיר הַקְּרֹבָה אֶל־הֶחָלָל וְלָקְחוּ זִקְנֵי הָעִיר הַהִוא עֶגְלַת
בָּקָר אֲשֶׁר לֹא־עֻבַּד בָּהּ אֲשֶׁר לֹא־מָשְׁכָה בְּעֹל: וְהוֹרִדוּ ‪4‬
זִקְנֵי הָעִיר הַהִוא אֶת־הָעֶגְלָה אֶל־נַחַל אֵיתָן אֲשֶׁר לֹא־
יֵעָבֵד בּוֹ וְלֹא יִזָּרֵעַ וְעָרְפוּ־שָׁם אֶת־הָעֶגְלָה בַּנָּחַל: וְנִגְּשׁוּ ‪5‬
הַכֹּהֲנִים בְּנֵי לֵוִי כִּי בָם בָּחַר יְהוָה אֱלֹהֶיךָ לְשָׁרְתוֹ וּלְבָרֵךְ
בְּשֵׁם יְהוָה וְעַל־פִּיהֶם יִהְיֶה כָּל־רִיב וְכָל־נָגַע: וְכֹל זִקְנֵי ‪6‬
הָעִיר הַהִוא הַקְּרֹבִים אֶל־הֶחָלָל יִרְחֲצוּ אֶת־יְדֵיהֶם עַל־
הָעֶגְלָה הָעֲרוּפָה בַנָּחַל: וְעָנוּ וְאָמְרוּ יָדֵינוּ לֹא שָׁפְכוּ ‪7‬
אֶת־הַדָּם הַזֶּה וְעֵינֵינוּ לֹא רָאוּ: כַּפֵּר לְעַמְּךָ יִשְׂרָאֵל ‪8‬
אֲשֶׁר־פָּדִיתָ יְהוָה וְאַל־תִּתֵּן דָּם נָקִי בְּקֶרֶב עַמְּךָ יִשְׂרָאֵל
וְנִכַּפֵּר לָהֶם הַדָּם: וְאַתָּה תְּבַעֵר הַדָּם הַנָּקִי מִקִּרְבֶּךָ ‪9‬
כִּי־תַעֲשֶׂה הַיָּשָׁר בְּעֵינֵי יְהוָה:

כִּי־תֵצֵא לַמִּלְחָמָה עַל־אֹיְבֶיךָ וּנְתָנוֹ יְהוָה אֱלֹהֶיךָ בְּיָדֶךָ ‪i‬
וְשָׁבִיתָ שִׁבְיוֹ: וְרָאִיתָ בַּשִּׁבְיָה אֵשֶׁת יְפַת־תֹּאַר וְחָשַׁקְתָּ ‪11‬
בָהּ וְלָקַחְתָּ לְךָ לְאִשָּׁה: וַהֲבֵאתָהּ אֶל־תּוֹךְ בֵּיתֶךָ וְגִלְּחָה ‪12‬
אֶת־רֹאשָׁהּ וְעָשְׂתָה אֶת־צִפָּרְנֶיהָ: וְהֵסִירָה אֶת־שִׂמְלַת ‪13‬
שִׁבְיָהּ מֵעָלֶיהָ וְיָשְׁבָה בְּבֵיתֶךָ וּבָכְתָה אֶת־אָבִיהָ וְאֶת־
אִמָּהּ יֶרַח יָמִים וְאַחַר כֵּן תָּבוֹא אֵלֶיהָ וּבְעַלְתָּהּ וְהָיְתָה
לְךָ לְאִשָּׁה: וְהָיָה אִם־לֹא חָפַצְתָּ בָּהּ וְשִׁלַּחְתָּהּ לְנַפְשָׁהּ ‪14‬
וּמָכֹר לֹא־תִמְכְּרֶנָּה בַּכָּסֶף לֹא־תִתְעַמֵּר בָּהּ תַּחַת אֲשֶׁר
עִנִּיתָהּ:   כִּי־תִהְיֶיןָ לְאִישׁ שְׁתֵּי נָשִׁים הָאַחַת ‪o‬
אֲהוּבָה וְהָאַחַת שְׂנוּאָה וְיָלְדוּ־לוֹ בָנִים הָאֲהוּבָה וְהַשְּׂנוּאָה
וְהָיָה הַבֵּן הַבְּכוֹר לַשְּׂנִיאָה: וְהָיָה בְּיוֹם הַנְחִילוֹ אֶת־בָּנָיו ‪16‬
אֵת אֲשֶׁר־יִהְיֶה לוֹ לֹא יוּכַל לְבַכֵּר אֶת־בֶּן־הָאֲהוּבָה עַל־
פְּנֵי בֶן־הַשְּׂנוּאָה הַבְּכֹר: כִּי אֶת־הַבְּכֹר בֶּן־הַשְּׂנוּאָה יַכִּיר ‪17‬
לָתֶת לוֹ פִּי שְׁנַיִם בְּכֹל אֲשֶׁר־יִמָּצֵא לוֹ כִּי־הוּא רֵאשִׁית
אֹנוֹ לוֹ מִשְׁפַּט הַבְּכֹרָה: כִּי־יִהְיֶה לְאִישׁ בֵּן סוֹרֵר ‪18‬
וּמוֹרֶה אֵינֶנּוּ שֹׁמֵעַ בְּקוֹל אָבִיו וּבְקוֹל אִמּוֹ וְיִסְּרוּ אֹתוֹ וְלֹא
יִשְׁמַע אֲלֵיהֶם: וְתָפְשׂוּ בוֹ אָבִיו וְאִמּוֹ וְהוֹצִיאוּ אֹתוֹ אֶל־ ‪19‬
זִקְנֵי עִירוֹ וְאֶל־שַׁעַר מְקֹמוֹ: וְאָמְרוּ אֶל־זִקְנֵי עִירוֹ בְּנֵנוּ ‪o‬
זֶה סוֹרֵר וּמֹרֶה אֵינֶנּוּ שֹׁמֵעַ בְּקֹלֵנוּ זוֹלֵל וְסֹבֵא: וּרְגָמֻהוּ ‪21‬
כָל־אַנְשֵׁי עִירוֹ בָאֲבָנִים וָמֵת וּבִעַרְתָּ הָרָע מִקִּרְבֶּךָ וְכָל־
יִשְׂרָאֵל יִשְׁמְעוּ וְיִרָאוּ: ‪s‬ וְכִי־יִהְיֶה בְאִישׁ חֵטְא ‪22‬
מִשְׁפַּט־מָוֶת וְהוּמָת וְתָלִיתָ אֹתוֹ עַל־עֵץ: לֹא־תָלִין ‪23‬
נִבְלָתוֹ עַל־הָעֵץ כִּי־קָבוֹר תִּקְבְּרֶנּוּ בַּיּוֹם הַהוּא כִּי־קִלְלַת
אֱלֹהִים תָּלוּי וְלֹא תְטַמֵּא אֶת־אַדְמָתְךָ אֲשֶׁר יְהוָה אֱלֹהֶיךָ
נֹתֵן לְךָ נַחֲלָה:

Uitti (5bff.); *NJV*, *NAB*,
NEB, *RSV* (5aβ–b)

Uitti (9); *NJV*, *NAB* (9b)

Uitti (14bγ); *NJV*, *NAB*,
NEB, *RSV* (14bβ)

Uitti (17aγ,b); *NJV*, *NAB*,
NEB (17b); *RSV* (17bα)

Uitti (21b,c)

Uitti (23aγ,b); *NJV*, *NEB*,
RSV (23aβ); *NAB* (23aβ=mc of
23b)

Deuteronomy 22

ה

לֹא־יִהְיֶה כְלִי־גֶבֶר עַל־אִשָּׁה
וְלֹא־יִלְבַּשׁ גֶּבֶר שִׂמְלַת אִשָּׁה כִּי תוֹעֲבַת יְהוָה אֱלֹהֶיךָ
כָּל־עֹשֵׂה אֵלֶּה׃
פ

6 כִּי יִקָּרֵא קַן־צִפּוֹר ׀ לְפָנֶיךָ בַּדֶּרֶךְ בְּכָל־עֵץ ׀ אוֹ עַל־
הָאָרֶץ אֶפְרֹחִים אוֹ בֵיצִים וְהָאֵם רֹבֶצֶת עַל־הָאֶפְרֹחִים
7 אוֹ עַל־הַבֵּיצִים לֹא־תִקַּח הָאֵם עַל־הַבָּנִים׃ שַׁלֵּחַ תְּשַׁלַּח
אֶת־הָאֵם וְאֶת־הַבָּנִים תִּקַּח־לָךְ לְמַעַן יִיטַב לָךְ וְהַאֲרַכְתָּ
8 יָמִים׃ כִּי תִבְנֶה בַּיִת חָדָשׁ וְעָשִׂיתָ מַעֲקֶה לְגַגֶּךָ
9 וְלֹא־תָשִׂים דָּמִים בְּבֵיתֶךָ כִּי־יִפֹּל הַנֹּפֵל מִמֶּנּוּ׃ לֹא־
תִזְרַע כַּרְמְךָ כִּלְאָיִם פֶּן־תִּקְדַּשׁ הַמְלֵאָה הַזֶּרַע אֲשֶׁר תִּזְרָע
וּתְבוּאַת הַכָּרֶם׃

13 14 כִּי־יִקַּח אִישׁ אִשָּׁה וּבָא אֵלֶיהָ וּשְׂנֵאָהּ׃ וְשָׂם לָהּ
עֲלִילֹת דְּבָרִים וְהוֹצִיא עָלֶיהָ שֵׁם רָע וְאָמַר אֶת־הָאִשָּׁה
הַזֹּאת לָקַחְתִּי וָאֶקְרַב אֵלֶיהָ וְלֹא־מָצָאתִי לָהּ בְּתוּלִים׃
טו וְלָקַח אֲבִי הַנַּעֲרָ וְאִמָּהּ וְהוֹצִיאוּ אֶת־בְּתוּלֵי הַנַּעֲרָ אֶל־
16 זִקְנֵי הָעִיר הַשָּׁעְרָה׃ וְאָמַר אֲבִי הַנַּעֲרָ אֶל־הַזְּקֵנִים אֶת־
17 בִּתִּי נָתַתִּי לָאִישׁ הַזֶּה לְאִשָּׁה וַיִּשְׂנָאֶהָ׃ וְהִנֵּה־הוּא
שָׂם עֲלִילֹת דְּבָרִים לֵאמֹר לֹא־מָצָאתִי לְבִתְּךָ בְּתוּלִים
וְאֵלֶּה בְּתוּלֵי בִתִּי וּפָרְשׂוּ הַשִּׂמְלָה לִפְנֵי זִקְנֵי הָעִיר׃
18 וְלָקְחוּ זִקְנֵי הָעִיר־הַהִוא אֶת־הָאִישׁ וְיִסְּרוּ אֹתוֹ׃ וְעָנְשׁוּ
19 אֹתוֹ מֵאָה כֶסֶף וְנָתְנוּ לַאֲבִי הַנַּעֲרָ כִּי הוֹצִיא שֵׁם רָע
עַל בְּתוּלַת יִשְׂרָאֵל וְלוֹ־תִהְיֶה לְאִשָּׁה לֹא־יוּכַל לְשַׁלְּחָהּ
כ כָּל־יָמָיו׃ ס וְאִם־אֱמֶת הָיָה הַדָּבָר הַזֶּה לֹא־נִמְצְאוּ
21 בְתוּלִים לַנַּעֲרָ׃ וְהוֹצִיאוּ אֶת־הַנַּעֲרָ אֶל־פֶּתַח בֵּית־אָבִיהָ
וּסְקָלוּהָ אַנְשֵׁי עִירָהּ בָּאֲבָנִים וָמֵתָה כִּי־עָשְׂתָה נְבָלָה
בְּיִשְׂרָאֵל לִזְנוֹת בֵּית אָבִיהָ וּבִעַרְתָּ הָרָע מִקִּרְבֶּךָ׃ ס
22 כִּי־יִמָּצֵא אִישׁ שֹׁכֵב ׀ עִם־אִשָּׁה בְעֻלַת־בַּעַל וּמֵתוּ גַּם־
שְׁנֵיהֶם הָאִישׁ הַשֹּׁכֵב עִם־הָאִשָּׁה וְהָאִשָּׁה וּבִעַרְתָּ הָרָע
23 מִיִּשְׂרָאֵל׃ ס כִּי יִהְיֶה נַעֲרָ בְתוּלָה מְאֹרָשָׂה לְאִישׁ
24 וּמְצָאָהּ אִישׁ בָּעִיר וְשָׁכַב עִמָּהּ׃ וְהוֹצֵאתֶם אֶת־שְׁנֵיהֶם
אֶל־שַׁעַר ׀ הָעִיר הַהִוא וּסְקַלְתֶּם אֹתָם בָּאֲבָנִים וָמֵתוּ אֶת־
הַנַּעֲרָ עַל־דְּבַר אֲשֶׁר לֹא־צָעֲקָה בָעִיר וְאֶת־הָאִישׁ עַל־
דְּבַר אֲשֶׁר־עִנָּה אֶת־אֵשֶׁת רֵעֵהוּ וּבִעַרְתָּ הָרָע מִקִּרְבֶּךָ׃
כה ס וְאִם־בַּשָּׂדֶה יִמְצָא הָאִישׁ אֶת־הַנַּעֲרָ הַמְאֹרָשָׂה
וְהֶחֱזִיק־בָּהּ הָאִישׁ וְשָׁכַב עִמָּהּ וּמֵת הָאִישׁ אֲשֶׁר־שָׁכַב
26 עִמָּהּ לְבַדּוֹ׃ וְלַנַּעֲרָ לֹא־תַעֲשֶׂה דָבָר אֵין לַנַּעֲרָ חֵטְא מָוֶת
כִּי כַּאֲשֶׁר יָקוּם אִישׁ עַל־רֵעֵהוּ וּרְצָחוֹ נֶפֶשׁ כֵּן הַדָּבָר
27 הַזֶּה׃ כִּי בַשָּׂדֶה מְצָאָהּ צָעֲקָה הַנַּעֲרָ הַמְאֹרָשָׂה וְאֵין
28 מוֹשִׁיעַ לָהּ׃ ס כִּי־יִמְצָא אִישׁ נַעֲרָ בְתוּלָה אֲשֶׁר לֹא־
29 אֹרָשָׂה וּתְפָשָׂהּ וְשָׁכַב עִמָּהּ וְנִמְצָאוּ׃ וְנָתַן הָאִישׁ הַשֹּׁכֵב
עִמָּהּ לַאֲבִי הַנַּעֲרָ חֲמִשִּׁים כָּסֶף וְלוֹ־תִהְיֶה לְאִשָּׁה תַּחַת
אֲשֶׁר עִנָּהּ לֹא־יוּכַל שַׁלְּחָהּ כָּל־יָמָיו׃

(n.10)

(n.11)

Uitti, *NJV*, *NAB*, *NEB*, *RSV* (5b)

Uitti, *NJV* (7b); *RSV* (7bα,bβ)

Uitti, *NJV*, *RSV* (8b)

Uitti (9b,c); *NJV*, *RSV* (9b)

Uitti (19aγ); *NJV*, *NAB*, *NEB*, *RSV* (19aβ)

Uitti (21aγ,b); *NJV*, *NAB*, *RSV* (21aβ)

Uitti (22b)

Uitti (24aγ-δ,b); *NJV*, *NAB*, *NEB*, *RSV* (24aβ-γ)

Uitti, *RSV* (26b-27); *NJV* (26b); *NAB* (26aβ); *NEB* (26aβ?); *NEB* (27)

Uitti (29aγ); *NJV*, *NAB*, *NEB*, *RSV* (29baב)

Deuteronomy 23

לֹא־יִקַּח אִישׁ אֶת־אֵשֶׁת אָבִיו וְלֹא יְגַלֶּה כְּנַף אָבִיו: ס א (n.12)
לֹא־יָבֹא פְצוּעַ־דַּכָּה וּכְרוּת שָׁפְכָה בִּקְהַל יְהוָה: ס 2
לֹא־יָבֹא מַמְזֵר בִּקְהַל יְהוָה גַּם דּוֹר עֲשִׂירִי לֹא־יָבֹא לוֹ 3
בִּקְהַל יְהוָה: ס   לֹא־יָבֹא עַמּוֹנִי וּמוֹאָבִי בִּקְהַל 4
יְהוָה גַּם דּוֹר עֲשִׂירִי לֹא־יָבֹא לָהֶם בִּקְהַל יְהוָה עַד־
עוֹלָם: עַל־דְּבַר אֲשֶׁר לֹא־קִדְּמוּ אֶתְכֶם בַּלֶּחֶם וּבַמַּיִם ה
בַּדֶּרֶךְ בְּצֵאתְכֶם מִמִּצְרָיִם וַאֲשֶׁר שָׂכַר עָלֶיךָ אֶת־בִּלְעָם (n.13)
בֶּן־בְּעוֹר מִפְּתוֹר אֲרַם נַהֲרַיִם לְקַלְלֶךָּ וְלֹא־אָבָה יְהוָה 6
אֱלֹהֶיךָ לִשְׁמֹעַ אֶל־בִּלְעָם וַיַּהֲפֹךְ יְהוָה אֱלֹהֶיךָ לְּךָ אֶת־
הַקְּלָלָה לִבְרָכָה כִּי אֲהֵבְךָ יְהוָה אֱלֹהֶיךָ: לֹא־תִדְרֹשׁ 7
שְׁלֹמָם וְטֹבָתָם כָּל־יָמֶיךָ לְעוֹלָם: לֹא־תְתַעֵב 8
אֲדֹמִי כִּי אָחִיךָ הוּא לֹא־תְתַעֵב מִצְרִי כִּי־גֵר הָיִיתָ
בְאַרְצוֹ: בָּנִים אֲשֶׁר־יִוָּלְדוּ לָהֶם דּוֹר שְׁלִישִׁי יָבֹא לָהֶם 9
בִּקְהַל יְהוָה: ס   כִּי־תֵצֵא מַחֲנֶה עַל־אֹיְבֶיךָ וְנִשְׁמַרְתָּ י
מִכֹּל דָּבָר רָע: כִּי־יִהְיֶה בְךָ אִישׁ אֲשֶׁר לֹא־יִהְיֶה 11
טָהוֹר מִקְּרֵה־לָיְלָה וְיָצָא אֶל־מִחוּץ לַמַּחֲנֶה לֹא יָבֹא
אֶל־תּוֹךְ הַמַּחֲנֶה: וְהָיָה לִפְנוֹת־עֶרֶב יִרְחַץ בַּמָּיִם 12
וּכְבֹא הַשֶּׁמֶשׁ יָבֹא אֶל־תּוֹךְ הַמַּחֲנֶה: וְיָד תִּהְיֶה לְךָ 13
מִחוּץ לַמַּחֲנֶה וְיָצָאתָ שָׁמָּה חוּץ: וְיָתֵד תִּהְיֶה לְךָ עַל־ 14
אֲזֵנֶךָ וְהָיָה בְּשִׁבְתְּךָ חוּץ וְחָפַרְתָּה בָהּ וְשַׁבְתָּ וְכִסִּיתָ
אֶת־צֵאָתֶךָ: כִּי יְהוָה אֱלֹהֶיךָ מִתְהַלֵּךְ ׀ בְּקֶרֶב מַחֲנֶךָ טו
לְהַצִּילְךָ וְלָתֵת אֹיְבֶיךָ לְפָנֶיךָ וְהָיָה מַחֲנֶיךָ קָדוֹשׁ וְלֹא־
יִרְאֶה בְךָ עֶרְוַת דָּבָר וְשָׁב מֵאַחֲרֶיךָ: ס   לֹא־ 16
תַסְגִּיר עֶבֶד אֶל־אֲדֹנָיו אֲשֶׁר־יִנָּצֵל אֵלֶיךָ מֵעִם אֲדֹנָיו:
עִמְּךָ יֵשֵׁב בְּקִרְבְּךָ בַּמָּקוֹם אֲשֶׁר־יִבְחַר בְּאַחַד שְׁעָרֶיךָ 17
בַּטּוֹב לוֹ לֹא תּוֹנֶנּוּ: ס   לֹא־תִהְיֶה קְדֵשָׁה מִבְּנוֹת 18
יִשְׂרָאֵל וְלֹא־יִהְיֶה קָדֵשׁ מִבְּנֵי יִשְׂרָאֵל: לֹא־תָבִיא אֶתְנַן 19
זוֹנָה וּמְחִיר כֶּלֶב בֵּית יְהוָה אֱלֹהֶיךָ לְכָל־נֶדֶר כִּי תוֹעֲבַת
יְהוָה אֱלֹהֶיךָ גַּם־שְׁנֵיהֶם: ס   לֹא־תַשִּׁיךְ לְאָחִיךָ כ
נֶשֶׁךְ כֶּסֶף נֶשֶׁךְ אֹכֶל נֶשֶׁךְ כָּל־דָּבָר אֲשֶׁר יִשָּׁךְ: לַנָּכְרִי 21
תַשִּׁיךְ וּלְאָחִיךָ לֹא תַשִּׁיךְ לְמַעַן יְבָרֶכְךָ יְהוָה אֱלֹהֶיךָ בְּכֹל
מִשְׁלַח יָדֶךָ עַל־הָאָרֶץ אֲשֶׁר־אַתָּה בָא־שָׁמָּה לְרִשְׁתָּהּ:
ס כִּי־תִדֹּר נֶדֶר לַיהוָה אֱלֹהֶיךָ לֹא תְאַחֵר לְשַׁלְּמוֹ כִּי־ 22
דָרֹשׁ יִדְרְשֶׁנּוּ יְהוָה אֱלֹהֶיךָ מֵעִמָּךְ וְהָיָה בְךָ חֵטְא:

Uitti, *NAB* (5-6); *NJV* (5a,b); *NEB* (4[=5H],5b[=6bH]); *RSV* (4a,b[=5H],5b[=6bH])

Uitti, *NJV*, *NAB* (8aβ); *NEB*, *RSV* (7aβ=8aβH)

Uitti, *NJV*, *NAB* (8bβ); *NEB*, *RSV* (7bβ=8bβH)

Uitti (15); *NJV*, *NAB* (15aα=mc of 15aβ); *NEB*, *RSV* (14-15H)

Uitti, *NJV* (19b); *NEB*, *RSV* (18b=19bH)

Uitti, *NJV*, *NAB* (21b); *NEB*, *RSV* (20b-21bH)

Uitti, *NJV*, *NAB*, *RSV* (22b)

Deuteronomy 24

א כִּי־יִקַּח אִישׁ אִשָּׁה וּבְעָלָהּ וְהָיָה אִם־לֹא תִמְצָא־חֵן בְּעֵינָיו כִּי־מָצָא בָהּ עֶרְוַת דָּבָר וְכָתַב לָהּ סֵפֶר כְּרִיתֻת 2 וְנָתַן בְּיָדָהּ וְשִׁלְּחָהּ מִבֵּיתוֹ: וְיָצְאָה מִבֵּיתוֹ וְהָלְכָה וְהָיְתָה 3 לְאִישׁ־אַחֵר: וּשְׂנֵאָהּ הָאִישׁ הָאַחֲרוֹן וְכָתַב לָהּ סֵפֶר כְּרִיתֻת וְנָתַן בְּיָדָהּ וְשִׁלְּחָהּ מִבֵּיתוֹ אוֹ כִי יָמוּת הָאִישׁ הָאַחֲרוֹן אֲשֶׁר־ לְקָחָהּ לוֹ לְאִשָּׁה: לֹא־יוּכַל בַּעְלָהּ הָרִאשׁוֹן אֲשֶׁר־שִׁלְּחָהּ 4 לָשׁוּב לְקַחְתָּהּ לִהְיוֹת לוֹ לְאִשָּׁה אַחֲרֵי אֲשֶׁר הֻטַּמָּאָה כִּי־תוֹעֵבָה הִוא לִפְנֵי יְהוָה וְלֹא תַחֲטִיא אֶת־הָאָרֶץ אֲשֶׁר יְהוָה אֱלֹהֶיךָ נֹתֵן לְךָ נַחֲלָה: כִּי־יִקַּח אִישׁ אִשָּׁה ה חֲדָשָׁה לֹא יֵצֵא בַּצָּבָא וְלֹא־יַעֲבֹר עָלָיו לְכָל־דָּבָר נָקִי יִהְיֶה לְבֵיתוֹ שָׁנָה אֶחָת וְשִׂמַּח אֶת־אִשְׁתּוֹ אֲשֶׁר־לָקָח: 6 לֹא־יַחֲבֹל רֵחַיִם וָרָכֶב כִּי־נֶפֶשׁ הוּא חֹבֵל: ס כִּי־ 7 יִמָּצֵא אִישׁ גֹּנֵב נֶפֶשׁ מֵאֶחָיו מִבְּנֵי יִשְׂרָאֵל וְהִתְעַמֶּר־בּוֹ וּמְכָרוֹ וּמֵת הַגַּנָּב הַהוּא וּבִעַרְתָּ הָרָע מִקִּרְבֶּךָ: ס הִשָּׁמֶר 8 בְּנֶגַע־הַצָּרַעַת לִשְׁמֹר מְאֹד וְלַעֲשׂוֹת כְּכֹל אֲשֶׁר־יוֹרוּ אֶתְכֶם הַכֹּהֲנִים הַלְוִיִּם כַּאֲשֶׁר צִוִּיתִם תִּשְׁמְרוּ לַעֲשׂוֹת: זָכוֹר אֵת 9 אֲשֶׁר־עָשָׂה יְהוָה אֱלֹהֶיךָ לְמִרְיָם בַּדֶּרֶךְ בְּצֵאתְכֶם מִמִּצְרָיִם: ס כִּי־תַשֶּׁה בְרֵעֲךָ מַשַּׁאת מְאוּמָה לֹא־תָבֹא י אֶל־בֵּיתוֹ לַעֲבֹט עֲבֹטוֹ: בַּחוּץ תַּעֲמֹד וְהָאִישׁ אֲשֶׁר אַתָּה 11 נֹשֶׁה בוֹ יוֹצִיא אֵלֶיךָ אֶת־הַעֲבוֹט הַחוּצָה: וְאִם־אִישׁ עָנִי 12 הוּא לֹא תִשְׁכַּב בַּעֲבֹטוֹ: הָשֵׁב תָּשִׁיב לוֹ אֶת־הַעֲבוֹט 13 כְּבֹא הַשֶּׁמֶשׁ וְשָׁכַב בְּשַׂלְמָתוֹ וּבֵרֲכֶךָּ וּלְךָ תִּהְיֶה צְדָקָה לִפְנֵי יְהוָה אֱלֹהֶיךָ: לֹא־תַעֲשֹׁק שָׂכִיר עָנִי וְאֶבְיוֹן 14 מֵאַחֶיךָ אוֹ מִגֵּרְךָ אֲשֶׁר בְּאַרְצְךָ בִּשְׁעָרֶיךָ: בְּיוֹמוֹ תִתֵּן טו שְׂכָרוֹ וְלֹא־תָבוֹא עָלָיו הַשֶּׁמֶשׁ כִּי עָנִי הוּא וְאֵלָיו הוּא נֹשֵׂא אֶת־נַפְשׁוֹ וְלֹא־יִקְרָא עָלֶיךָ אֶל־יְהוָה וְהָיָה בְךָ חֵטְא: ס לֹא־יוּמְתוּ אָבוֹת עַל־בָּנִים וּבָנִים לֹא־יוּמְתוּ עַל־אָבוֹת אִישׁ 16 בְּחֶטְאוֹ יוּמָתוּ: ס לֹא תַטֶּה מִשְׁפַּט גֵּר יָתוֹם וְלֹא תַחֲבֹל 17 בֶּגֶד אַלְמָנָה: וְזָכַרְתָּ כִּי עֶבֶד הָיִיתָ בְּמִצְרַיִם וַיִּפְדְּךָ יְהוָה 18 אֱלֹהֶיךָ מִשָּׁם עַל־כֵּן אָנֹכִי מְצַוְּךָ לַעֲשׂוֹת אֶת־הַדָּבָר הַזֶּה: ס כִּי תִקְצֹר קְצִירְךָ בְשָׂדֶךָ וְשָׁכַחְתָּ עֹמֶר בַּשָּׂדֶה לֹא־ 19 תָשׁוּב לְקַחְתּוֹ לַגֵּר לַיָּתוֹם וְלָאַלְמָנָה יִהְיֶה לְמַעַן יְבָרֶכְךָ יְהוָה אֱלֹהֶיךָ בְּכֹל מַעֲשֵׂה יָדֶיךָ: ס כִּי תַחְבֹּט זֵיתְךָ לֹא כ תְפַאֵר אַחֲרֶיךָ לַגֵּר לַיָּתוֹם וְלָאַלְמָנָה יִהְיֶה: כִּי תִבְצֹר 21 כַּרְמְךָ לֹא תְעוֹלֵל אַחֲרֶיךָ לַגֵּר לַיָּתוֹם וְלָאַלְמָנָה יִהְיֶה: וְזָכַרְתָּ כִּי־עֶבֶד הָיִיתָ בְּאֶרֶץ מִצְרָיִם עַל־כֵּן אָנֹכִי מְצַוְּךָ 22 לַעֲשׂוֹת אֶת־הַדָּבָר הַזֶּה:	NJV, NAB, NEB, RSV (1bα) Uitti (4b); NJV (4aβ,aβ); RSV (4aβ-b) Uitti (5b); NJV, NAB, RSV (5bβ?) Uitti, NJV, NAB, RSV (6b) Uitti (7b) Uitti (9) Uitti (13aγ,b); NJV (13aβ,b); NAB, NEB, RSV (13aβ) Uitti (15aγ,b); NJV, NEB, RSV (15aβ,b); NAB (15aβ) Uitti, NAB (18) Uitti, NJV, NAB, NEB, RSV (19b) Uitti (21b-22) NAB (22)

Deuteronomy 25

א כִּי־יִהְיֶה רִיב בֵּין אֲנָשִׁים וְנִגְּשׁוּ אֶל־הַמִּשְׁפָּט וּשְׁפָטוּם

2 וְהִצְדִּיקוּ אֶת־הַצַּדִּיק וְהִרְשִׁיעוּ אֶת־הָרָשָׁע: וְהָיָה אִם־

בִּן הַכּוֹת הָרָשָׁע וְהִפִּילוֹ הַשֹּׁפֵט וְהִכָּהוּ לְפָנָיו כְּדֵי רִשְׁעָתוֹ

3 בְּמִסְפָּר: אַרְבָּעִים יַכֶּנּוּ לֹא יֹסִיף פֶּן־יֹסִיף לְהַכֹּתוֹ עַל־

4 אֵלֶּה מַכָּה רַבָּה וְנִקְלָה אָחִיךָ לְעֵינֶיךָ: לֹא־תַחְסֹם שׁוֹר

5 בְּדִישׁוֹ: ס כִּי־יֵשְׁבוּ אַחִים יַחְדָּו וּמֵת אַחַד מֵהֶם וּבֵן

אֵין־לוֹ לֹא־תִהְיֶה אֵשֶׁת־הַמֵּת הַחוּצָה לְאִישׁ זָר יְבָמָהּ יָבֹא

6 עָלֶיהָ וּלְקָחָהּ לוֹ לְאִשָּׁה וְיִבְּמָהּ: וְהָיָה הַבְּכוֹר אֲשֶׁר תֵּלֵד

7 יָקוּם עַל־שֵׁם אָחִיו הַמֵּת וְלֹא־יִמָּחֶה שְׁמוֹ מִיִּשְׂרָאֵל: וְאִם־

לֹא יַחְפֹּץ הָאִישׁ לָקַחַת אֶת־יְבִמְתּוֹ וְעָלְתָה יְבִמְתּוֹ הַשַּׁעְרָה

אֶל־הַזְּקֵנִים וְאָמְרָה מֵאֵן יְבָמִי לְהָקִים לְאָחִיו שֵׁם בְּיִשְׂרָאֵל

8 לֹא אָבָה יַבְּמִי: וְקָרְאוּ־לוֹ זִקְנֵי־עִירוֹ וְדִבְּרוּ אֵלָיו וְעָמַד

9 וְאָמַר לֹא חָפַצְתִּי לְקַחְתָּהּ: וְנִגְּשָׁה יְבִמְתּוֹ אֵלָיו לְעֵינֵי

הַזְּקֵנִים וְחָלְצָה נַעֲלוֹ מֵעַל רַגְלוֹ וְיָרְקָה בְּפָנָיו וְעָנְתָה

וְאָמְרָה כָּכָה יֵעָשֶׂה לָאִישׁ אֲשֶׁר לֹא־יִבְנֶה אֶת־בֵּית אָחִיו:

10 וְנִקְרָא שְׁמוֹ בְּיִשְׂרָאֵל בֵּית חֲלוּץ הַנָּעַל: ס כִּי־יִנָּצוּ

11 אֲנָשִׁים יַחְדָּו אִישׁ וְאָחִיו וְקָרְבָה אֵשֶׁת הָאֶחָד לְהַצִּיל אֶת־

12 אִישָׁהּ מִיַּד מַכֵּהוּ וְשָׁלְחָה יָדָהּ וְהֶחֱזִיקָה בִּמְבֻשָׁיו: וְקַצֹּתָה

13 אֶת־כַּפָּהּ לֹא תָחוֹס עֵינֶךָ: ס לֹא־יִהְיֶה לְךָ בְּכִיסְךָ אֶבֶן

14 וָאָבֶן גְּדוֹלָה וּקְטַנָּה: לֹא־יִהְיֶה לְךָ בְּבֵיתְךָ אֵיפָה וְאֵיפָה

15 גְּדוֹלָה וּקְטַנָּה: אֶבֶן שְׁלֵמָה וָצֶדֶק יִהְיֶה־לָּךְ אֵיפָה שְׁלֵמָה

וָצֶדֶק יִהְיֶה־לָּךְ לְמַעַן יַאֲרִיכוּ יָמֶיךָ עַל הָאֲדָמָה אֲשֶׁר־

16 יְהוָה אֱלֹהֶיךָ נֹתֵן לָךְ: כִּי תוֹעֲבַת יְהוָה אֱלֹהֶיךָ כָּל־עֹשֵׂה

אֵלֶּה כֹּל עֹשֵׂה עָוֶל:

פ

17 זָכוֹר אֵת אֲשֶׁר־עָשָׂה לְךָ עֲמָלֵק בַּדֶּרֶךְ בְּצֵאתְכֶם מִמִּצְרָיִם:

18 אֲשֶׁר קָרְךָ בַּדֶּרֶךְ וַיְזַנֵּב בְּךָ כָּל־הַנֶּחֱשָׁלִים אַחֲרֶיךָ וְאַתָּה

19 עָיֵף וְיָגֵעַ וְלֹא יָרֵא אֱלֹהִים: וְהָיָה בְּהָנִיחַ יְהוָה אֱלֹהֶיךָ |

לְךָ מִכָּל־אֹיְבֶיךָ מִסָּבִיב בָּאָרֶץ אֲשֶׁר יְהוָה־אֱלֹהֶיךָ נֹתֵן

לְךָ נַחֲלָה לְרִשְׁתָּהּ תִּמְחֶה אֶת־זֵכֶר עֲמָלֵק מִתַּחַת הַשָּׁמָיִם

לֹא תִּשְׁכָּח:

(n.14)

Uitti, *NJV*, *NAB*, *RSV* (3b)

Uitti, *NJV*, *NAB*, *NEB*, *RSV* (6b)

Uitti, *RSV* (15b,16); *NJV* (15); *NAB*, *NEB* (15b)

Deuteronomy 1:16-17

17 לֹא־תַכִּירוּ

פָנִים בַּמִּשְׁפָּט כַּקָּטֹן כַּגָּדֹל תִּשְׁמָעוּן לֹא תָגוּרוּ מִפְּנֵי־אִישׁ

כִּי הַמִּשְׁפָּט לֵאלֹהִים הוּא וְהַדָּבָר אֲשֶׁר יִקְשֶׁה מִכֶּם

תַּקְרִבוּן אֵלַי וּשְׁמַעְתִּיו:

NJV, *NAB*, *NEB*, *RSV* (17aγ)

Deuteronomy 7

3 וְלֹא

תִתְחַתֵּן בָּם בִּתְּךָ לֹא־תִתֵּן לִבְנוֹ וּבִתּוֹ לֹא־תִקַּח לִבְנֶךָ:
4 כִּי־יָסִיר אֶת־בִּנְךָ מֵאַחֲרַי וְעָבְדוּ אֱלֹהִים אֲחֵרִים וְחָרָה
5 אַף־יְהוָה בָּכֶם וְהִשְׁמִידְךָ מַהֵר: כִּי־אִם־כֹּה תַעֲשׂוּ לָהֶם
מִזְבְּחֹתֵיהֶם תִּתֹּצוּ וּמַצֵּבֹתָם תְּשַׁבֵּרוּ וַאֲשֵׁירֵהֶם תְּגַדֵּעוּן
6 וּפְסִילֵיהֶם תִּשְׂרְפוּן בָּאֵשׁ: כִּי עַם קָדוֹשׁ אַתָּה לַיהוָה
אֱלֹהֶיךָ בְּךָ בָּחַר ׀ יְהוָה אֱלֹהֶיךָ לִהְיוֹת לוֹ לְעַם סְגֻלָּה
מִכֹּל הָעַמִּים אֲשֶׁר עַל־פְּנֵי הָאֲדָמָה:

כה   פְּסִילֵי
אֱלֹהֵיהֶם תִּשְׂרְפוּן בָּאֵשׁ לֹא־תַחְמֹד כֶּסֶף וְזָהָב עֲלֵיהֶם
וְלָקַחְתָּ לָךְ פֶּן תִּוָּקֵשׁ בּוֹ כִּי תוֹעֲבַת יְהוָה אֱלֹהֶיךָ הוּא:
26 וְלֹא־תָבִיא תוֹעֵבָה אֶל־בֵּיתֶךָ וְהָיִיתָ חֵרֶם כָּמֹהוּ

NJV, NAB, RSV (4)

NJV, RSV (6?); NAB, NEB (6)

NJV, NAB, RSV (25bβ,bγ);
NEB (25bβ?,bγ)

NJV (26aβ?); NAB (26aβ)

(c)   *Notes*

1. (14:1-2) See Chapter II, p. 75.

2. (14:10b) An asyndetic mc, understood as "(for) it is unclean for
you."

3. (14:19) Verse 19aβ motivates the legal consequence in v. 19b.

4. (14:21a) The clause in v. 21aβ appears to motivate the prescription
in v. 21aα. Cf. *NAB*.

5. (15:10b-11) These verses motivate the law in vv. 7-8; vv. 9-10a
are parenetic.

6. (16:14) This verse embodies a parenetic statement.

7. (18:2b) This half verse seems to constitute the underlying reason
for the prohibition in v. 2a, i.e., the Levites shall have no portion, because
the Lord is their portion.

8. (18:12b) This second motivation, beginning with וּבִגְלַל, really provides a justification for the Lord's driving out the nations before Israel; cf.
Chapter II, n. 56.

9. (20:5-8) In vv. 5-8 it is not the legal prescription which is motivated, but the statements of the שֹׁטְרִים ("the officials," *NJV*) in vv. 5b, 6b, 7b,
8b; therefore they are not counted.

10. (22:26) The injunction in v. 26a is motivated by three consecutive
clauses. Verse 26a is understood as: "since she is not guilty of a capital
offense." Cf. *NAB*.

11. (22:29) In most translations, the clause אֲשֶׁר עִנָּהּ תַּחַת is taken as
motivating what precedes it, e.g., *RSV, NEB, NAB*. The verse division favors this
interpretation. However, it is also possible to understand it as motivating the
prohibition against divorce that follows it, as in *NJV*.

12. (23:1) Verse 1b is usually understood as a separate prescription,
e.g., *RSV, NAB, NEB*(?). Yet, וְלֹא ("so that not, lest") can be understood as
introducing a motive clause, i.e., "lest he removes his father's garment (namely,

lays claim to what his father possessed). Cf. *NJV*. In fact, in Deut 27:20, uncovering the garment is clearly taken as a motive clause (with כִּי) attached to the curse against lying with the father's wife.

13. (23:5b) וַאֲשֶׁר is carried over from עַל דְּבַר אֲשֶׁר of v. 5a.

14. (25:17-19a) Verses 17-18 constitute the motivation for the command in v. 19a.

6.   THE PRIESTLY CODE

(a)   *The Legal Prescriptions*

Genesis 9		Verses		Exod. 12 cont.		Verses
	– intro	(1-2)		15.		43b
(n. 1)	1.	3		16.		44
	2.	4		17.		45
	– intro	(5)		18.		46a
	3. mc	6		19.		46b
	– concl	(7)		20.		47
				21.		48
Genesis 17				– par		(49)
				– nl		(50-51)
	– intro	(10)				
(n. 2)	4. mc	⌐11		**Exodus 13**		
(n. 3)	5. mc	⌐12-13				
(n. 4)	mc v.14			– intro		(1)
			(n. 8)	22. mc		2
Exodus 12			(n. 9)	– intro		(3-5)
				23.		⌐6a,(7a)
	– intro	(1)		24.		6b
	6.	2		25.		7bα
(n. 5)	– com	(3-13)		26.		7bβ
	– intro	(14)		27.		8
	7.	⌐15aα	(n.10)	mc v.9		
	8.	⌐15aβ		– par concl		(10)
	mc v.15b			28.		11-12
	9.	16		29.		13aα
	– par intro	(17)		30.		13aβ
	10.	⌐18		31.		13b
	11.	⌐19a		32.		14-16
	mc v.19b					
	– sum	(20)		**Exodus 27**		
(n. 6)	– intro	(21a)				
	12.	21b		– intro		(20aα)
	13.	⌐22a		33. mc(2)		20aβ-b
	14.	⌐22b		v.20aβ,b		
	mc v.23			34.		21a
	– par	(24-27)		– par		(21b)
	– concl	(28)				
	– nl	(29-42)				
(n. 7)	– intro	(43a)				

Exodus 29		Verses		Lev. 1 cont.		Verses
(n.11)	35. mc	27-28		62.		9a
	36. mc(2)	29	(n.19)	63. mc		9b
	v.29bα,bβ			64.		10
	37.	30		65.		11a
	- com	(31-37)		66.		11b
	38.	38-40		67.		12a
	39.	41		68.		12b
	- concl	(42-46)		69.		13a
			(n.20)	70. mc		13b
Exodus 30				71.		14
				72.		15aα,aβ
(n.12)	- com	(1-6)		73.		15aγ
	40.	7-8		74.		15b
	41.	9a		75.		16
	42.	9b		76.		17aα
	43. mc	10	(n.21)	77. mc		17aβ-b
(n.13)	- intro	(11)				
	44. mc	12-15	**Leviticus 2**			
(n.14)	45. mc	16				
(n.15)	- com	(17-18)		78.		1a
	46. mc	19-21a		79.		1bα
	- par	(21b)		80.		1bβ-2aαא
(n.16)	- com	(22-25)		81.		2aαℸ-b
	47.	26-29		82.		3
	48.	30		83.		4
	- intro	(31)		84.		5
	49.	⌐32aα		85.		6aα
	50.	⌊32aβ		86.		6aβ
(n.17)	mc(2)v.32b,33		(n.22)		mc v.6b	
(n.18)	- com	(34-36)		87.		7
	51. mc	37-38		88.		8
				89.		9aα
Exodus 31				90.		9aβ-b
				91.		10
	- par intro	(12-14)		92. mc		11-12
	52.	15		93.		13
	- concl	(16-17)		94.		14
				95.		15aα
Exodus 35				96.		15aβ
			(n.23)		mc v.15b	
	- intro	(1)		97.		16
	53.	2a				
	54.	2b	**Leviticus 3**			
	55.	3				
				- intro		(1a)
Leviticus 1				98.		1b
				99.		2aα
	- intro	(1-2)		100.		2aβ
	56.	3		101.		2b
	57. mc	4		102.		3-4
	58.	5a		103.		5
	59.	5b		- intro		(6)
	60.	6		104.		7
	61.	7-8				

Lev. 3 cont.		Verses		Lev. 4 cont.		Verses
105.		8aα		149.		35aα
106.		8aβ		150.		35aβ
107.		8b		–	concl	(35b)
108.		9-10				
109.		11		**Leviticus 5**		
110.		12				
111.		13aα		151.		1-5
112.		13aβ		152.		6a
113.		13b		–	concl	(6b)
114.		14-15		153.		7
115.		16a-bα		154.		⌈8
–	sum	(16bβ)		155.		9a
–	par	(17a)	(n.27)		mc v.9b	
116.		17b		156.		10a
				–	concl	(10b)
Leviticus 4				157.		⌈11a
				158.		11bα
–	intro	(1-2)		159.		11bβ
117.		3			mc v.11b	
118.		4a		160.		12aαא
119.		4bα		161.		12aβב
120.		4bβ	(n.28)		mc v.12b	
121.		5-7		–	concl	(13)
122.		8-10a		–	intro	(14)
123.		10b		162.		15
124.		11-12		163.		16a
125.		13-14aα		–	concl	(16b)
126.		14bβ		164.		17-18a
127.		15a	(n.29)	–	concl	(18b-19)
128.		15b		–	intro	(20)
129.		16-18		165.		21-24
130.		19a				25
131.		19b		–	concl	(26)
132.		20a				
(n.24)	– concl	(20b)		**Leviticus 6**		
(n.25)	133. mc	21				
134.		22-23		–	intro	(1-2a)
135.		24aα		166.		2b
(n.26)	136.	24aβ-b		167.		3aα
137.		25		168.		3aβ-b
138.		26a		169.		4a
–	concl	(26b)		170.		4b
139.		27-28		–	intro	(5aα)
140.		29a		171.		5aβ
141.		29b		172.		5bα
142.		30		173.		5bβ
143.		31aαא		–	sum	(6)
144.		31aβב		–	intro	(7)
–	concl	(31b)		174.		8a
145.		32		175.		8b
146.		33a	(n.30)	176.	mc(2)	9-10
147.		33b			v.10aβ,b	
148.		34		–	concl	(11)

	Lev. 6 cont.		Verses
	–	intro	(12)
	177.		13-14
	178.		15a
	179.		15b
	–	concl	(16)
	–	intro	(17-18a)
(n.31)	180.	mc	18b
	181.		19
	182.		20a
	183.		20b
	184.		21a
	185.		21b
(n.32)	186.	mc	22
	187.		23a
	188.		23b

Leviticus 7

			Verses
	–	intro	(1)
	189.		2a
	190.		2b
	191.		3-4
(n.33)	192.	mc	5
(n.34)	193.	mc	6
	–	intro	(7a)
	194.		7b
	195.		8
	196.		9
	197.		10
	–	intro	(11)
	198.		12
	199.		13
	200.		14a
	201.		14b
	202.		15
	203.		16a
	204.		16b
	205.		17
(n.35)	206.	mc	18a
	207.		18b
	208.		19aα
	209.		19aβ
(n.36)	210.	mc	19b-20
	211.		21
	–	intro	(22-23a)
	212.	mc	23b-25
(n.37)	213.	mc	26-27
	–	intro	(28-29a)
	214.		29b-30
	215.		31a
	216.		31b
	217.		32
	218.		33
		mc v.34	
	–	concl	(35-38)

	Leviticus 10		Verses
	–	intro	(8)
	219.	mc(3)	9-11
		v.9aβ,10,11	
	–	intro	(12aα‏א)
	220.	mc	12aꓸ-b
	221.	mc(2)	13
		v.13aβ,b	
	222.	mc	14
	223.		15a
	–	par concl	(15b)

Leviticus 11

			Verses
	–	intro	(1-2a)
	224.		2b-3
(n.38)	225.	mc	4-6
	226.	mc	7
	–	sum	(8aα)
(n.39)	227.	mc	8aβ-b
	228.		9
	229.		⌈10-11bα
	230.		⌊11bβ
(n.40)		mc v.10b-11a	
	–	sum	(12)
(n.41)	231.	mc	13-19
	232.		20
	233.		21-22
	–	sum	(23)
	–	intro	(24-25)
(n.42)	234.	mc	26
(n.43)	235.	mc	27
(n.44)	236.	mc	28
	237.		29-31
	238.		32
	239.		33a-bα
	240.		33bβ
	241.		34a
	242.		34b
(n.45)	243.	mc	35
	244.		36a
	245.		36b
	246.		37
	247.		38
	248.		39
	249.		40a
	250.		40b
(n.46)	251.	mc	41
	252.	mc	42
	–	par concl	(43-47)

Leviticus 12

			Verses
	–	intro	(1-2aα)
	253.		2aβ-b
	254.		3

Lev. 12 cont.		Verses		Lev. 13 cont.		Verses
255.		4		302.		47–49
256.		5a		303.		50
257.		5b		304.		51
258.		6		305.	mc	52
259.		7aαא		306.		53–54a
–	concl	(7aαב–aβ)		307.		54b
–	concl	(7b)	(n.59)	308.	mc	55
260.		8a		309.		56
–	concl	(8b)		310.		57
				311.		58
Leviticus 13				–	concl	(59)
–	intro	(1)		**Leviticus 14**		
261.		2				
262.		3		–	intro	(1–2a)
263.		4		312.		2b–4
264.		5		313.		5–6
(n.47) 265.	mc	6a–bα		314.		7a–bα
266.		6bβ		315.		7bβ
267.		7		316.		8
(n.48) 268.	mc	8		317.		9
269.		9		318.		10–11
270.		10–11a		319.		12
271.	mc	11b		320.	mc	13
(n.49) 272.	mc	12–13		321.		14
(n.50) 273.	mc	14–15		322.		15–18a
274.		16		–	concl	(18b)
(n.51) 275.		17		323.		19a
276.		18–19		324.		19b–20aα
(n.52) 277.	mc	20		325.		20aβ
278.		21		–	concl	(20b)
(n.53) 279.	mc	22	(n.60)	326.	mc	21a
280.		23		327.		21b
(n.54) 281.	mc	24–25		328.		22
282.		26		329.		23
(n.55) 283.	mc	27		330.		24
284.	mc	28		331.		25aαא
(n.56) 285.	mc	29–30		332.		25aαב–b
286.		31	(n.61)	333.	mc	26–29
287.		32–33		334.		30–31a
288.		34a–bα		–	concl	(31b)
289.		34bβ		–	concl	(32)
(n.57) 290.	mc	35–36		–	intro	(33)
291.		37		335.		34–35
292.		38–39		336.	mc	36a
293.		40		337.		36b
294.		41		338.		37–38
(n.58) 295.	mc	42–44		339.		39–40
296.		45aα		340.		41
297.		45aβ		341.		42
298.		45aγ		342.		43–44
299.		45b		343.		45
300.		46a		344.		46
301.		46b		345.		47a
				346.		47b

Lev. 14 cont.		Verses		Lev. 16 cont.		Verses
347.	mc	48		386.		5
348.		49		387.		6
349.		50		388.		7-8
350.		51		389.		9
351.		52-53a	(n.62)	390.	mc(2)	10
-	concl	(53b)			v.10aβⴲ,b	
-	concl	(54-57)		391.	mc(2)	11-13
					v.13bα,bβ	
Leviticus 15				392.		14
				393.		15aα
-	intro	(1-3)		394.		15aβ-b
352.		4a		-	concl	(16a)
353.		4b		395.		16b
354.		5		396.		17a
355.		6		397.		17b-18
356.		7		398.		19a
357.		8		-	concl	(19b)
358.		9		399.		20
359.		10a		400.		21a-bα
360.		10b		401.		21bβ-22
361.		11		402.		23
362.		12a		403.		24a
363.		12b		404.		24b
364.		13		405.		25
365.		14		406.		26
366.		15a		407.		27
-	concl	(15b)		408.		28
367.		16		-	par intro	(29a)
368.		17		409.		⌐29bα
369.		18		410.		⌊29bβ
370.		19			mc v.30	
371.		20a		-	sum	(31)
372.		20b		411.		32a
373.		21		412.		32b
374.		22		413.		33a
375.		23		414.		33b
376.		24a		-	par concl	(34)
377.		24b				
-	intro	(25)		**Leviticus 27**		
378.		26a				
379.		26b		-	intro	(1-2)
380.		27		415.		3
381.		28		416.		4
382.		29		417.		5a
383.		30a		418.		5b
-	concl	(30b)		419.		6a
-	concl	(31-33)		420.		6b
				421.		7a
Leviticus 16				422.		7b
				423.		8
-	intro	(1-2aα)		424.		9
384.	mc(2)	2aβ-b		425.		10a
	v.2bαⴲ,bβ			426.		10b
385.		3-4		427.		11-12

Lev. 27 cont.		Verses
428.		13
429.		14
430.		15
431.		16
432.		17
433.		18
434.		19
435.		20
436.		21
437.		22-23
438.		24
439.		25
440.		26
441.		27a
442.		27b
443.		28
444.		29
445.		30
446.		31
447.		32
448.		32a
449.		32b
–	concl	(34)

Numbers 3

(n.63)	– intro	(5)
450.	mc	6
451.		7
452.		8
453.		9
454.		10

Numbers 5

–	intro	(5-6aαא)
455.		6aⵡ-7
456.		8
457.		9
458.		10
–	intro	(11-12a)
459.		12b-15aαא
460.		15aⵡ-aβ
461.		15bα
462.		15bβ
	mc v.15bγ-bδ	
463.		16
464.		17
465.		18aα
466.		18aβ
467.		18b
468.		19-22
469.		23a
470.		23b

Num. 5 cont.		Verses
471.	mc	24
472.		25
473.		26a
474.		26b
–	nl	(27-28)
–	concl	(29-31)

Numbers 6

–	intro	(1-2a)
475.		2b-3bα
476.		3bβ
477.		4
478.		5
479.	mc	6-7
–	sum	(8)
480.		9
481.		10
482.		11a
483.		11b-12aα
484.		12aβ
485.	mc	12b
–	intro	(13a)
486.		13b
487.		14-15
488.		16-17
489.		18a
490.		18b
491.		19-20aαא
492.		20aⵡ-aβ
493.		20b
–	concl	(21)
–	intro	(22-23aα)
494.		23aβ-26
–	par concl	(27)

Numbers 8

(n.64)	– intro	(23-24a)
495.		24b
496.		25
497.		26a
–	concl	(26b)

Numbers 9

–	intro	(9-10a)
498.		10b-11a
499.		11b
500.		12aα
501.		12aβ
502.		12b
503.	mc	13
504.		14a
–	par	(14b)

	Numbers 10		Verses
	–	intro	(1)
(n.65)	505.	mc	2
	506.		3
	507.		4
	508.		5
	509.		6a
	–	sum	(6b)
	510.		7
	511.		8a
	–	par intro	(8b)
	512.	mc	9
	513.	mc(2)	10
		v.10bα,bβ	

	Numbers 15		
	–	intro	(1-3)
	514.		4-5
	515.		6-7
	516.		8-10
	–	sum	(11-13)
	517.		14
	–	par	(15-16)
	–	intro	(17-18a)
	518.		18b-20
	519.		21
	–	intro	(22-23)
	520.		24a
	521.		24b
	–	concl	(25-26)
	522.		27
	–	concl	(28)
	–	par	(29)
(n.66)	523.	mc	30-31
	–	nl	(32-36)
	–	intro	(37-38aα)
	524.		38aβ
	525.		38b-39aαℵ
	526.		39aαℶ-aβ
		mc(3)	
		v.39b,40,41	

	Numbers 18		
	–	intro	(1aα)
(n.67)	527.		1aβ-aγ
	528.		1b
	529.		2-3a
	530.	mc	3b
	–	sum	(4-5)
	–	concl	(6-7)
	–	intro	(8-9a)
	531.		9b
	532.		10
	533.		11a
	534.		11b
	535.		12a

	Num. 18 cont.		Verses
	536.		13a
	537.		13b
	538.		14
	539.		15a
	540.		15bα
	541.		15bβ
	542.		16
(n.68)	543.	mc	17a
	544.		17bαℵ
	545.		17bαℶ-bβ
	546.		18
	–	sum	(19)
	–	intro	(20aαℵ)
(n.69)	547.	mc	20aαℶ-b
	548.		21
	549.		22-23a
	–	par concl	(23b-24)
	–	intro	(25-26aα)
	550.		26aβ-b
	551.		27-28a
	552.		28b
	553.		29
	–	intro	(30a)
	554.		30b
	555.	mc	31
	–	concl	(32)

	Numbers 19		
	–	intro	(1-2bαℵ)
	556.		2bαℶ-3a
	557.		3b
	558.		4
	559.		5
	560.		6
	561.		7
	562.		8
(n.70)	563.	mc	9
	564.		10a
	–	par	(10b)
	565.		11
	566.		12
(n.71)	567.	mc(2)	13(cf.20)
		v.13aαℶ,b	
	568.		14aβ-b
	569.		15
	570.		16
	571.		17
	572.		18
	573.		19a-bα
	574.		19bβ
	–	par	(21a)
	575.		21bα
	576.		21bβ
	577.		22a
	578.		22b

			Num. 29 cont.	Verses
	Numbers 27	Verses	623.	25a
	− intro	(8a)	624.	25b
	579.	8b	625.	26-27
	580.	9	626.	28a
	581.	10	627.	28b
	582.	11a	628.	29-30
	− par	(11b)	629.	31a
			630.	31b
	Numbers 28		631.	32-33
			632.	34a
	− intro	(1-3aα)	633.	34b
	583.	3aβ-4	634.	35
	584.	5-7	635.	36-37
	585.	8	636.	38a
	586.	9-10	637.	38b
	587.	11-14a	− concl	(39)
	− concl	(14b)	− concl	(30:1)
	588.	15		
	589.	16	Numbers 30	
	590.	17a		
	591.	18	− intro	(2)
	592.	19-21	638.	3
(n.72)	593. mc	22	639.	4-5
	594.	23	640. mc	6
	595.	24	641.	7-8
	596.	25	642.	9
	597.	26	643.	10
	598.	27-29	644.	11-12
(n.73)	599. mc	30	(n.75) 645. mc	13
	600.	31	− sum	(14-16)
			− concl	(17)
	Numbers 29			
			Numbers 33	
	601.	1a		
	602.	1b	− intro	(50-51a)
	603.	2-4	646.	51b-52aα
(n.74)	604. mc	5	647.	52aβ
	605.	6	648.	52bα
	606.	7a	649.	52bβ
	607.	7b	650. mc	53
	608.	8-10	651.	54
	609.	11a	− nl	(55-56)
	610.	11b		
	611.	12a	Numbers 35	
	612.	12b		
	613.	13-15	(n.76) − com	(1-8)
	614.	16a	− intro	(9-10a)
	615.	16b	652. mc	10b-12
	616.	17-18	653.	13-14
	617.	19a	654. mc	15
	618.	19b	(n.77) 655. mc	16
	619.	20-21	656. mc	17
	620.	22a	657. mc	18
	621.	22b	658.	19
	622.	23-24		

Num. 35 cont.		Verses
659.		20-21a
660.	mc	21b
661.		22-24
662.		25a
663.		25b
664.	mc	26-28
-	concl	(29)
665.		30a
666.		30b
667.		31
668.		32
-	par concl	(33-34)

Numbers 36

669.	mc(2)	8
	v.8b,9	

(b)   *The Motive Clauses*

Genesis 9:6

שֹׁפֵךְ֙ דַּ֣ם הָֽאָדָ֔ם בָּֽאָדָ֖ם דָּמ֣וֹ
יִשָּׁפֵ֑ךְ כִּ֚י בְּצֶ֣לֶם אֱלֹהִ֔ים עָשָׂ֖ה אֶת־הָאָדָֽם׃

Uitti, *NJV*, *NAB*, *NEB*, *RSV*
(6b)

Genesis 17

זֹ֣את בְּרִיתִ֞י

אֲשֶׁ֣ר תִּשְׁמְר֗וּ בֵּינִי֙ וּבֵ֣ינֵיכֶ֔ם וּבֵ֥ין זַרְעֲךָ֖ אַחֲרֶ֑יךָ הִמּ֣וֹל
לָכֶ֖ם כָּל־זָכָֽר׃ וּנְמַלְתֶּ֕ם אֵ֖ת בְּשַׂ֣ר עָרְלַתְכֶ֑ם וְהָיָה֙ לְא֔וֹת ¹¹
בְּרִ֖ית בֵּינִ֥י וּבֵינֵיכֶֽם׃ וּבֶן־שְׁמֹנַ֣ת יָמִ֗ים יִמּ֥וֹל לָכֶ֛ם כָּל־זָכָ֖ר ¹²
לְדֹרֹתֵיכֶ֑ם יְלִ֣יד בָּ֔יִת וּמִקְנַת־כֶּ֨סֶף֙ מִכֹּ֣ל בֶּן־נֵכָ֔ר אֲשֶׁ֛ר לֹ֥א
מִֽזַּרְעֲךָ֖ הֽוּא׃ הִמּ֧וֹל ׀ יִמּ֛וֹל יְלִ֥יד בֵּֽיתְךָ֖ וּמִקְנַ֣ת כַּסְפֶּ֑ךָ ¹³
וְהָיְתָ֧ה בְרִיתִ֛י בִּבְשַׂרְכֶ֖ם לִבְרִ֥ית עוֹלָֽם׃ וְעָרֵ֣ל ׀ זָכָ֗ר אֲשֶׁר֙ ¹⁴
לֹֽא־יִמּ֜וֹל אֶת־בְּשַׂ֣ר עָרְלָת֗וֹ וְנִכְרְתָ֛ה הַנֶּ֥פֶשׁ הַהִ֖וא מֵעַמֶּ֑יהָ
אֶת־בְּרִיתִ֖י הֵפַֽר׃

Uitti (13b)

Uitti (14b)

(n. 2)

(n. 3)

(n. 4)

Exodus 12

שִׁבְעַת יָמִים מַצּוֹת תֹּאכֵלוּ אַךְ בַּיּוֹם טו   *NJV, RSV* (15b)
הָרִאשׁוֹן תַּשְׁבִּיתוּ שְּׂאֹר מִבָּתֵּיכֶם כִּי ׀ כָּל־אֹכֵל חָמֵץ   *NJV, NEB, RSV* (19b)
וְנִכְרְתָה הַנֶּפֶשׁ הַהִוא מִיִּשְׂרָאֵל מִיּוֹם הָרִאשֹׁן עַד־יוֹם   *NJV, RSV* (23); *NAB* (23aאα)
הַשְּׁבִעִי: וּבַיּוֹם הָרִאשׁוֹן מִקְרָא־קֹדֶשׁ וּבַיּוֹם הַשְּׁבִיעִי 16
מִקְרָא־קֹדֶשׁ יִהְיֶה לָכֶם כָּל־מְלָאכָה לֹא־יֵעָשֶׂה בָהֶם
אַךְ אֲשֶׁר יֵאָכֵל לְכָל־נֶפֶשׁ הוּא לְבַדּוֹ יֵעָשֶׂה לָכֶם:
וּשְׁמַרְתֶּם אֶת־הַמַּצּוֹת כִּי בְּעֶצֶם הַיּוֹם הַזֶּה הוֹצֵאתִי אֶת־ 17
צִבְאוֹתֵיכֶם מֵאֶרֶץ מִצְרָיִם וּשְׁמַרְתֶּם אֶת־הַיּוֹם הַזֶּה
לְדֹרֹתֵיכֶם חֻקַּת עוֹלָם: בָּרִאשֹׁן בְּאַרְבָּעָה עָשָׂר יוֹם לַחֹדֶשׁ 18
בָּעֶרֶב תֹּאכְלוּ מַצֹּת עַד יוֹם הָאֶחָד וְעֶשְׂרִים לַחֹדֶשׁ
בָּעָרֶב: שִׁבְעַת יָמִים שְׂאֹר לֹא יִמָּצֵא בְּבָתֵּיכֶם כִּי ׀ כָּל־ 19
אֹכֵל מַחְמֶצֶת וְנִכְרְתָה הַנֶּפֶשׁ הַהִוא מֵעֲדַת יִשְׂרָאֵל בַּגֵּר
וּבְאֶזְרַח הָאָרֶץ: כָּל־מַחְמֶצֶת לֹא תֹאכֵלוּ בְּכֹל מוֹשְׁבֹתֵיכֶם כ
תֹּאכְלוּ מַצּוֹת: פ

(n. 6)   וַיִּקְרָא מֹשֶׁה לְכָל־זִקְנֵי יִשְׂרָאֵל וַיֹּאמֶר אֲלֵהֶם מִשְׁכוּ וּקְחוּ 21
לָכֶם צֹאן לְמִשְׁפְּחֹתֵיכֶם וְשַׁחֲטוּ הַפָּסַח: וּלְקַחְתֶּם אֲגֻדַּת 22
אֵזוֹב וּטְבַלְתֶּם בַּדָּם אֲשֶׁר־בַּסַּף וְהִגַּעְתֶּם אֶל־הַמַּשְׁקוֹף
וְאֶל־שְׁתֵּי הַמְּזוּזֹת מִן־הַדָּם אֲשֶׁר בַּסָּף וְאַתֶּם לֹא תֵצְאוּ
אִישׁ מִפֶּתַח־בֵּיתוֹ עַד־בֹּקֶר: וְעָבַר יְהוָה לִנְגֹּף אֶת־מִצְרַיִם 23
וְרָאָה אֶת־הַדָּם עַל־הַמַּשְׁקוֹף וְעַל שְׁתֵּי הַמְּזוּזֹת וּפָסַח
יְהוָה עַל־הַפֶּתַח וְלֹא יִתֵּן הַמַּשְׁחִית לָבֹא אֶל־בָּתֵּיכֶם לִנְגֹּף:

Exodus 13

(n. 8)   וַיְדַבֵּר יְהוָה אֶל־מֹשֶׁה לֵּאמֹר: קַדֶּשׁ־לִי כָל־בְּכוֹר פֶּטֶר 2   *NAB* (2b)
(n. 9)   כָּל־רֶחֶם בִּבְנֵי יִשְׂרָאֵל בָּאָדָם וּבַבְּהֵמָה לִי הוּא: וַיֹּאמֶר 3   *NJV* (9); *NAB, NEB, RSV* (9b)
מֹשֶׁה אֶל־הָעָם זָכוֹר אֶת־הַיּוֹם הַזֶּה אֲשֶׁר יְצָאתֶם מִמִּצְרַיִם
מִבֵּית עֲבָדִים כִּי בְּחֹזֶק יָד הוֹצִיא יְהוָה אֶתְכֶם מִזֶּה וְלֹא
יֵאָכֵל חָמֵץ: הַיּוֹם אַתֶּם יֹצְאִים בְּחֹדֶשׁ הָאָבִיב: וְהָיָה
כִי־יְבִיאֲךָ יְהוָה אֶל־אֶרֶץ הַכְּנַעֲנִי וְהַחִתִּי וְהָאֱמֹרִי וְהַחִוִּי
וְהַיְבוּסִי אֲשֶׁר נִשְׁבַּע לַאֲבֹתֶיךָ לָתֶת לָךְ אֶרֶץ זָבַת חָלָב
וּדְבָשׁ וְעָבַדְתָּ אֶת־הָעֲבֹדָה הַזֹּאת בַּחֹדֶשׁ הַזֶּה: שִׁבְעַת 6
יָמִים תֹּאכַל מַצֹּת וּבַיּוֹם הַשְּׁבִיעִי חַג לַיהוָה: מַצּוֹת 7
יֵאָכֵל אֵת שִׁבְעַת הַיָּמִים וְלֹא־יֵרָאֶה לְךָ חָמֵץ וְלֹא־יֵרָאֶה
לְךָ שְׂאֹר בְּכָל־גְּבֻלֶךָ: וְהִגַּדְתָּ לְבִנְךָ בַּיּוֹם הַהוּא לֵאמֹר 8
(n.10)   בַּעֲבוּר זֶה עָשָׂה יְהוָה לִי בְּצֵאתִי מִמִּצְרָיִם: וְהָיָה לְךָ 9
לְאוֹת עַל־יָדְךָ וּלְזִכָּרוֹן בֵּין עֵינֶיךָ לְמַעַן תִּהְיֶה תּוֹרַת יְהוָה
בְּפִיךָ כִּי בְּיָד חֲזָקָה הוֹצִאֲךָ יְהוָה מִמִּצְרָיִם:

Exodus 27:20

וְאַתָּה תְּצַוֶּה ׀ אֶת־בְּנֵי יִשְׂרָאֵל וְיִקְחוּ אֵלֶיךָ שֶׁמֶן זַיִת זָךְ   NJV, RSV (20aβ,b); NAB
כָּתִית לַמָּאוֹר לְהַעֲלֹת נֵר תָּמִיד: (20aβ?,b); NEB (20b)

Exodus 29

(n.11)   וְקִדַּשְׁתָּ אֵת ׀ חֲזֵה הַתְּנוּפָה וְאֵת שׁוֹק הַתְּרוּמָה   27   Uitti (28); NJV, NEB, RSV
         אֲשֶׁר הוּנַף וַאֲשֶׁר הוּרָם מֵאֵיל הַמִּלֻּאִים מֵאֲשֶׁר לְאַהֲרֹן   (28aβ-b)
         וּמֵאֲשֶׁר לְבָנָיו: וְהָיָה לְאַהֲרֹן וּלְבָנָיו לְחָק־עוֹלָם מֵאֵת   28   NJV, NAB, NEB, RSV (29b)
         בְּנֵי יִשְׂרָאֵל כִּי תְרוּמָה הוּא וּתְרוּמָה יִהְיֶה מֵאֵת בְּנֵי
         יִשְׂרָאֵל מִזִּבְחֵי שַׁלְמֵיהֶם תְּרוּמָתָם לַיהוָה: וּבִגְדֵי הַקֹּדֶשׁ   29
         אֲשֶׁר לְאַהֲרֹן יִהְיוּ לְבָנָיו אַחֲרָיו לְמָשְׁחָה בָהֶם וּלְמַלֵּא
         בָם אֶת־יָדָם:

Exodus 30

         וְהִקְטִיר   7   Uitti (10b,c)
         עָלָיו אַהֲרֹן קְטֹרֶת סַמִּים בַּבֹּקֶר בַּבֹּקֶר בְּהֵיטִיבוֹ אֶת־הַנֵּרֹת   NJV, NAB, RSV (12b)
         יַקְטִירֶנָּה: וּבְהַעֲלֹת אַהֲרֹן אֶת־הַנֵּרֹת בֵּין הָעַרְבַּיִם יַקְטִירֶנָּה   8   Uitti, NJV, NAB, RSV (16b)
         קְטֹרֶת תָּמִיד לִפְנֵי יְהוָה לְדֹרֹתֵיכֶם: לֹא־תַעֲלוּ עָלָיו קְטֹרֶת   9   NJV, NAB, NEB, RSV (20aβ)
         זָרָה וְעֹלָה וּמִנְחָה וְנֵסֶךְ לֹא תִסְּכוּ עָלָיו: וְכִפֶּר אַהֲרֹן עַל   י   Uitti (21aβ,b); NJV, NAB,
         קַרְנֹתָיו אַחַת בַּשָּׁנָה מִדַּם חַטַּאת הַכִּפֻּרִים אַחַת בַּשָּׁנָה   NEB, RSV (21aβ)
         יְכַפֵּר עָלָיו לְדֹרֹתֵיכֶם קֹדֶשׁ־קָדָשִׁים הוּא לַיהוָה:
(n.13)   וַיְדַבֵּר יְהוָה אֶל־מֹשֶׁה לֵּאמֹר: כִּי תִשָּׂא אֶת־רֹאשׁ בְּנֵי   11
                                                                          12
         יִשְׂרָאֵל לִפְקֻדֵיהֶם וְנָתְנוּ אִישׁ כֹּפֶר נַפְשׁוֹ לַיהוָה בִּפְקֹד
         אֹתָם וְלֹא־יִהְיֶה בָהֶם נֶגֶף בִּפְקֹד אֹתָם: זֶה ׀ יִתְּנוּ כָּל־   13
         הָעֹבֵר עַל־הַפְּקֻדִים מַחֲצִית הַשֶּׁקֶל בְּשֶׁקֶל הַקֹּדֶשׁ עֶשְׂרִים
         גֵּרָה הַשֶּׁקֶל מַחֲצִית הַשֶּׁקֶל תְּרוּמָה לַיהוָה: כֹּל הָעֹבֵר   14
         עַל־הַפְּקֻדִים מִבֶּן עֶשְׂרִים שָׁנָה וָמָעְלָה יִתֵּן תְּרוּמַת יְהוָה:
         הֶעָשִׁיר לֹא־יַרְבֶּה וְהַדַּל לֹא יַמְעִיט מִמַּחֲצִית הַשָּׁקֶל   15
         לָתֵת אֶת־תְּרוּמַת יְהוָה לְכַפֵּר עַל־נַפְשֹׁתֵיכֶם: וְלָקַחְתָּ אֶת־   16
         כֶּסֶף הַכִּפֻּרִים מֵאֵת בְּנֵי יִשְׂרָאֵל וְנָתַתָּ אֹתוֹ עַל־עֲבֹדַת
         אֹהֶל מוֹעֵד וְהָיָה לִבְנֵי יִשְׂרָאֵל לְזִכָּרוֹן לִפְנֵי יְהוָה לְכַפֵּר
(n.14)   עַל־נַפְשֹׁתֵיכֶם: פ
(n.15)   וַיְדַבֵּר יְהוָה אֶל־מֹשֶׁה לֵּאמֹר: וְעָשִׂיתָ כִּיּוֹר נְחֹשֶׁת וְכַנּוֹ   17
                                                                          18
         נְחֹשֶׁת לְרָחְצָה וְנָתַתָּ אֹתוֹ בֵּין־אֹהֶל מוֹעֵד וּבֵין הַמִּזְבֵּחַ
         וְנָתַתָּ שָׁמָּה מָיִם: וְרָחֲצוּ אַהֲרֹן וּבָנָיו מִמֶּנּוּ אֶת־יְדֵיהֶם   19
         וְאֶת־רַגְלֵיהֶם: בְּבֹאָם אֶל־אֹהֶל מוֹעֵד יִרְחֲצוּ־מַיִם וְלֹא   כ
         יָמֻתוּ אוֹ בְגִשְׁתָּם אֶל־הַמִּזְבֵּחַ לְשָׁרֵת לְהַקְטִיר אִשֶּׁה
         לַיהוָה: וְרָחֲצוּ יְדֵיהֶם וְרַגְלֵיהֶם וְלֹא יָמֻתוּ   21

Exod. 30 cont.

	31	Uitti (32b)
	32	
(n.17)	33	
(n.18)	34	
	36	
	37	
	38	

וְאֶל־בְּנֵי יִשְׂרָאֵל תְּדַבֵּר לֵאמֹר שֶׁמֶן

מִשְׁחַת־קֹדֶשׁ יִהְיֶה זֶה לִי לְדֹרֹתֵיכֶם׃ עַל־בְּשַׂר אָדָם

לֹא יִיסָךְ וּבְמַתְכֻּנְתּוֹ לֹא תַעֲשׂוּ כָּמֹהוּ קֹדֶשׁ הוּא קֹדֶשׁ

יִהְיֶה לָכֶם׃ אִישׁ אֲשֶׁר יִרְקַח כָּמֹהוּ וַאֲשֶׁר יִתֵּן מִמֶּנּוּ עַל־

זָר וְנִכְרַת מֵעַמָּיו׃ וַיֹּאמֶר יְהוָה אֶל־מֹשֶׁה קַח־לְךָ

סַמִּים נָטָף ׀ וּשְׁחֵלֶת וְחֶלְבְּנָה סַמִּים וּלְבֹנָה זַכָּה בַּד בְּבַד

יִהְיֶה׃ וְעָשִׂיתָ אֹתָהּ קְטֹרֶת רֹקַח מַעֲשֵׂה רוֹקֵחַ מְמֻלָּח לה

טָהוֹר קֹדֶשׁ׃ וְשָׁחַקְתָּ מִמֶּנָּה הָדֵק וְנָתַתָּה מִמֶּנָּה לִפְנֵי

הָעֵדֻת בְּאֹהֶל מוֹעֵד אֲשֶׁר אִוָּעֵד לְךָ שָׁמָּה קֹדֶשׁ קָדָשִׁים

תִּהְיֶה לָכֶם׃ וְהַקְּטֹרֶת אֲשֶׁר תַּעֲשֶׂה בְּמַתְכֻּנְתָּהּ לֹא

תַעֲשׂוּ לָכֶם קֹדֶשׁ תִּהְיֶה לְךָ לַיהוָה׃ אִישׁ אֲשֶׁר־יַעֲשֶׂה

כָמוֹהָ לְהָרִיחַ בָּהּ וְנִכְרַת מֵעַמָּיו׃

Leviticus 1

	3	NJV, NAB, RSV (4b)
		Uitti (9bβ,γ,δ)
	4	Uitti (13c)
	5	Uitti (17c)
	6	
	7	
	8	
	9	
(n.19)		
	י	
	11	
	12	
	13	
(n.20)	14	
	טו	
	16	
	17	
(n.21)		

אִם־עֹלָה קָרְבָּנוֹ מִן־הַבָּקָר זָכָר תָּמִים

יַקְרִיבֶנּוּ אֶל־פֶּתַח אֹהֶל מוֹעֵד יַקְרִיב אֹתוֹ לִרְצֹנוֹ לִפְנֵי

יְהוָה׃ וְסָמַךְ יָדוֹ עַל רֹאשׁ הָעֹלָה וְנִרְצָה לוֹ לְכַפֵּר עָלָיו׃

וְשָׁחַט אֶת־בֶּן הַבָּקָר לִפְנֵי יְהוָה וְהִקְרִיבוּ בְּנֵי אַהֲרֹן

הַכֹּהֲנִים אֶת־הַדָּם וְזָרְקוּ אֶת־הַדָּם עַל־הַמִּזְבֵּחַ סָבִיב

אֲשֶׁר־פֶּתַח אֹהֶל מוֹעֵד׃ וְהִפְשִׁיט אֶת־הָעֹלָה וְנִתַּח אֹתָהּ

לִנְתָחֶיהָ׃ וְנָתְנוּ בְּנֵי אַהֲרֹן הַכֹּהֵן אֵשׁ עַל־הַמִּזְבֵּחַ וְעָרְכוּ

עֵצִים עַל־הָאֵשׁ׃ וְעָרְכוּ בְּנֵי אַהֲרֹן הַכֹּהֲנִים אֵת הַנְּתָחִים

אֶת־הָרֹאשׁ וְאֶת־הַפָּדֶר עַל־הָעֵצִים אֲשֶׁר עַל־הָאֵשׁ אֲשֶׁר

עַל־הַמִּזְבֵּחַ׃ וְקִרְבּוֹ וּכְרָעָיו יִרְחַץ בַּמָּיִם וְהִקְטִיר הַכֹּהֵן

אֶת־הַכֹּל הַמִּזְבֵּחָה עֹלָה אִשֵּׁה רֵיחַ־נִיחוֹחַ לַיהוָה׃

וְאִם־מִן־הַצֹּאן קָרְבָּנוֹ מִן הַכְּשָׂבִים אוֹ מִן־הָעִזִּים לְעֹלָה

זָכָר תָּמִים יַקְרִיבֶנּוּ׃ וְשָׁחַט אֹתוֹ עַל יֶרֶךְ הַמִּזְבֵּחַ צָפֹנָה

לִפְנֵי יְהוָה וְזָרְקוּ בְּנֵי אַהֲרֹן הַכֹּהֲנִים אֶת־דָּמוֹ עַל־הַמִּזְבֵּחַ

סָבִיב׃ וְנִתַּח אֹתוֹ לִנְתָחָיו וְאֶת־רֹאשׁוֹ וְאֶת־פִּדְרוֹ וְעָרַךְ

הַכֹּהֵן אֹתָם עַל־הָעֵצִים אֲשֶׁר עַל־הָאֵשׁ אֲשֶׁר עַל־הַמִּזְבֵּחַ׃

וְהַקֶּרֶב וְהַכְּרָעַיִם יִרְחַץ בַּמָּיִם וְהִקְרִיב הַכֹּהֵן אֶת־הַכֹּל

וְהִקְטִיר הַמִּזְבֵּחָה עֹלָה הוּא אִשֵּׁה רֵיחַ נִיחֹחַ לַיהוָה׃

וְאִם מִן־הָעוֹף עֹלָה קָרְבָּנוֹ לַיהוָה וְהִקְרִיב מִן־הַתֹּרִים

אוֹ מִן־בְּנֵי הַיּוֹנָה אֶת־קָרְבָּנוֹ׃ וְהִקְרִיבוֹ הַכֹּהֵן אֶל־הַמִּזְבֵּחַ

וּמָלַק אֶת־רֹאשׁוֹ וְהִקְטִיר הַמִּזְבֵּחָה וְנִמְצָה דָמוֹ עַל קִיר

הַמִּזְבֵּחַ׃ וְהֵסִיר אֶת־מֻרְאָתוֹ בְּנֹצָתָהּ וְהִשְׁלִיךְ אֹתָהּ אֵצֶל

הַמִּזְבֵּחַ קֵדְמָה אֶל־מְקוֹם הַדָּשֶׁן׃ וְשִׁסַּע אֹתוֹ בִכְנָפָיו לֹא

יַבְדִּיל וְהִקְטִיר אֹתוֹ הַכֹּהֵן הַמִּזְבֵּחָה עַל־הָעֵצִים אֲשֶׁר

עַל־הָאֵשׁ עֹלָה הוּא אִשֵּׁה רֵיחַ נִיחֹחַ לַיהוָה׃

Leviticus 2

וְאִם־מִנְחָה עַל־ ה   Uitti (6b)

6 הַמַּחֲבַת קָרְבָּנֶךָ סֹלֶת בְּלוּלָה בַשֶּׁמֶן מַצָּה תִהְיֶה: פָּתוֹת   Uitti, *NJV, NAB, RSV* (11b)

7 אֹתָהּ פִּתִּים וְיָצַקְתָּ עָלֶיהָ שָׁמֶן מִנְחָה הִוא: וְאִם־   Uitti (15b)

(n.22) 8 מִנְחַת מַרְחֶשֶׁת קָרְבָּנֶךָ סֹלֶת בַּשֶּׁמֶן תֵּעָשֶׂה: וְהֵבֵאתָ

אֶת־הַמִּנְחָה אֲשֶׁר יֵעָשֶׂה מֵאֵלֶּה לַיהוָה וְהִקְרִיבָהּ אֶל־

9 הַכֹּהֵן וְהִגִּישָׁהּ אֶל־הַמִּזְבֵּחַ: וְהֵרִים הַכֹּהֵן מִן־הַמִּנְחָה

אֶת־אַזְכָּרָתָהּ וְהִקְטִיר הַמִּזְבֵּחָה אִשֵּׁה רֵיחַ נִיחֹחַ לַיהוָה:

10 וְהַנּוֹתֶרֶת מִן־הַמִּנְחָה לְאַהֲרֹן וּלְבָנָיו קֹדֶשׁ קָדָשִׁים מֵאִשֵּׁי

11 יְהוָה: כָּל־הַמִּנְחָה אֲשֶׁר תַּקְרִיבוּ לַיהוָה לֹא תֵעָשֶׂה

חָמֵץ כִּי כָל־שְׂאֹר וְכָל־דְּבַשׁ לֹא־תַקְטִירוּ מִמֶּנּוּ אִשֶּׁה

12 לַיהוָה: קָרְבַּן רֵאשִׁית תַּקְרִיבוּ אֹתָם לַיהוָה וְאֶל־הַמִּזְבֵּחַ

13 לֹא־יַעֲלוּ לְרֵיחַ נִיחֹחַ: וְכָל־קָרְבַּן מִנְחָתְךָ בַּמֶּלַח תִּמְלָח

וְלֹא תַשְׁבִּית מֶלַח בְּרִית אֱלֹהֶיךָ מֵעַל מִנְחָתֶךָ עַל כָּל־

14 קָרְבָּנְךָ תַּקְרִיב מֶלַח: וְאִם־תַּקְרִיב מִנְחַת בִּכּוּרִים

לַיהוָה אָבִיב קָלוּי בָּאֵשׁ גֶּרֶשׂ כַּרְמֶל תַּקְרִיב אֵת מִנְחַת

(n.23) 15 בִּכּוּרֶיךָ: וְנָתַתָּ עָלֶיהָ שֶׁמֶן וְשַׂמְתָּ עָלֶיהָ לְבֹנָה מִנְחָה

הִוא:

Leviticus 4

21 וְהוֹצִיא אֶת־   Uitti (21b)

הַפָּר אֶל־מִחוּץ לַמַּחֲנֶה וְשָׂרַף אֹתוֹ כַּאֲשֶׁר שָׂרַף אֵת הַפָּר   Uitti (24b)

(n.25) הָרִאשׁוֹן חַטַּאת הַקָּהָל הוּא: פ

22 אֲשֶׁר נָשִׂיא יֶחֱטָא וְעָשָׂה אַחַת מִכָּל־מִצְוֹת יְהוָה אֱלֹהָיו

23 אֲשֶׁר לֹא־תֵעָשֶׂינָה בִּשְׁגָגָה וְאָשֵׁם: אוֹ־הוֹדַע אֵלָיו חַטָּאתוֹ

אֲשֶׁר חָטָא בָּהּ וְהֵבִיא אֶת־קָרְבָּנוֹ שְׂעִיר עִזִּים זָכָר תָּמִים:

(n.26) 24 וְסָמַךְ יָדוֹ עַל־רֹאשׁ הַשָּׂעִיר וְשָׁחַט אֹתוֹ בִּמְקוֹם אֲשֶׁר־

יִשְׁחַט אֶת־הָעֹלָה לִפְנֵי יְהוָה חַטָּאת הוּא:

Leviticus 5

וְהִקְרִיב אֶת־אֲשֶׁר לַחַטָּאת רִאשׁוֹנָה וּמָלַק אֶת־   Uitti (9b)

9 רֹאשׁוֹ מִמּוּל עָרְפּוֹ וְלֹא יַבְדִּיל: וְהִזָּה מִדַּם הַחַטָּאת עַל־   Uitti, *NJV, NAB, NEB, RSV*

(n.27) קִיר הַמִּזְבֵּחַ וְהַנִּשְׁאָר בַּדָּם יִמָּצֵה אֶל־יְסוֹד הַמִּזְבֵּחַ חַטָּאת   (11bβ)

10 הוּא: וְאֶת־הַשֵּׁנִי יַעֲשֶׂה עֹלָה כַּמִּשְׁפָּט וְכִפֶּר עָלָיו הַכֹּהֵן   Uitti (12b)

11 מֵחַטָּאתוֹ אֲשֶׁר־חָטָא וְנִסְלַח לוֹ: וְאִם־לֹא תַשִּׂיג

יָדוֹ לִשְׁתֵּי תֹרִים אוֹ לִשְׁנֵי בְנֵי־יוֹנָה וְהֵבִיא אֶת־קָרְבָּנוֹ

אֲשֶׁר חָטָא עֲשִׂירִת הָאֵפָה סֹלֶת לְחַטָּאת לֹא־יָשִׂים עָלֶיהָ

12 שֶׁמֶן וְלֹא־יִתֵּן עָלֶיהָ לְבֹנָה כִּי חַטָּאת הִוא: וֶהֱבִיאָהּ אֶל־

הַכֹּהֵן וְקָמַץ הַכֹּהֵן מִמֶּנָּה מְלוֹא קֻמְצוֹ אֶת־אַזְכָּרָתָהּ

(n.28) וְהִקְטִיר הַמִּזְבֵּחָה עַל אִשֵּׁי יְהוָה חַטָּאת הִוא:

Leviticus 6

9 וְהַנּוֹתֶרֶת מִמֶּנָּה יֹאכְלוּ אַהֲרֹן וּבָנָיו מַצּוֹת תֵּאָכֵל   Uitti (10aβ,b)

בְּמָקוֹם קָדֹשׁ בַּחֲצַר אֹהֶל־מוֹעֵד יֹאכְלוּהָ: לֹא תֵאָפֶה   Uitti (18c)

(n.30)   חָמֵץ חֶלְקָם נָתַתִּי אֹתָהּ מֵאִשָּׁי קֹדֶשׁ קָדָשִׁים הִוא כַּחַטָּאת   Uitti, *NAB* (22b)

__וְכָאָשָׁם:__

17
18 וַיְדַבֵּר יְהוָה אֶל־מֹשֶׁה לֵּאמֹר: דַּבֵּר אֶל־אַהֲרֹן וְאֶל־

בָּנָיו לֵאמֹר זֹאת תּוֹרַת הַחַטָּאת בִּמְקוֹם אֲשֶׁר תִּשָּׁחֵט

הָעֹלָה תִּשָּׁחֵט הַחַטָּאת לִפְנֵי יְהוָה קֹדֶשׁ קָדָשִׁים הִוא:

(n.31)   19 הַכֹּהֵן הַמְחַטֵּא אֹתָהּ יֹאכְלֶנָּה בְּמָקוֹם קָדֹשׁ תֵּאָכֵל

כ בַּחֲצַר אֹהֶל מוֹעֵד: כֹּל אֲשֶׁר־יִגַּע בִּבְשָׂרָהּ יִקְדָּשׁ

וַאֲשֶׁר יִזֶּה מִדָּמָהּ עַל־הַבֶּגֶד אֲשֶׁר יִזֶּה עָלֶיהָ תְּכַבֵּס בְּמָקוֹם

21 קָדֹשׁ: וּכְלִי־חֶרֶשׂ אֲשֶׁר תְּבֻשַּׁל־בּוֹ יִשָּׁבֵר וְאִם־בִּכְלִי

22 נְחֹשֶׁת בֻּשָּׁלָה וּמֹרַק וְשֻׁטַּף בַּמָּיִם: כָּל־זָכָר בַּכֹּהֲנִים

(n.32)   יֹאכַל אֹתָהּ קֹדֶשׁ קָדָשִׁים הִוא:

Leviticus 7

4 וְאֵת שְׁתֵּי   Uitti (5b)

הַכְּלָיֹת וְאֶת־הַחֵלֶב אֲשֶׁר עֲלֵיהֶן אֲשֶׁר עַל־הַכְּסָלִים וְאֶת־   Uitti (6c); *NAB* (6bβ)

(n.33)   ה הַיֹּתֶרֶת עַל־הַכָּבֵד עַל־הַכְּלָיֹת יְסִירֶנָּה: וְהִקְטִיר אֹתָם   *RSV* (25)

(n.34)   6 הַכֹּהֵן הַמִּזְבֵּחָה אִשֶּׁה לַיהוָה אָשָׁם הוּא: כָּל־זָכָר

בַּכֹּהֲנִים יֹאכְלֶנּוּ בְּמָקוֹם קָדוֹשׁ יֵאָכֵל קֹדֶשׁ קָדָשִׁים הוּא:

17
18 וְהַנּוֹתָר מִבְּשַׂר הַזָּבַח בַּיּוֹם הַשְּׁלִישִׁי בָּאֵשׁ יִשָּׂרֵף: וְאִם

הֵאָכֹל יֵאָכֵל מִבְּשַׂר־זֶבַח שְׁלָמָיו בַּיּוֹם הַשְּׁלִישִׁי לֹא

(n.35)   יֵרָצֶה הַמַּקְרִיב אֹתוֹ לֹא יֵחָשֵׁב לוֹ פִּגּוּל יִהְיֶה וְהַנֶּפֶשׁ

19 הָאֹכֶלֶת מִמֶּנּוּ עֲוֹנָהּ תִּשָּׂא: וְהַבָּשָׂר אֲשֶׁר־יִגַּע בְּכָל־טָמֵא

לֹא יֵאָכֵל בָּאֵשׁ יִשָּׂרֵף וְהַבָּשָׂר כָּל־טָהוֹר יֹאכַל בָּשָׂר:

(n.36)   כ וְהַנֶּפֶשׁ אֲשֶׁר־תֹּאכַל בָּשָׂר מִזֶּבַח הַשְּׁלָמִים אֲשֶׁר לַיהוָה

21 וְטֻמְאָתוֹ עָלָיו וְנִכְרְתָה הַנֶּפֶשׁ הַהִוא מֵעַמֶּיהָ: וְנֶפֶשׁ כִּי־

תִגַּע בְּכָל־טָמֵא בְּטֻמְאַת אָדָם אוֹ בִּבְהֵמָה טְמֵאָה אוֹ

בְּכָל־שֶׁקֶץ טָמֵא וְאָכַל מִבְּשַׂר־זֶבַח הַשְּׁלָמִים אֲשֶׁר לַיהוָה

22 וְנִכְרְתָה הַנֶּפֶשׁ הַהִוא מֵעַמֶּיהָ: וַיְדַבֵּר יְהוָה אֶל־מֹשֶׁה

23 לֵּאמֹר: דַּבֵּר אֶל־בְּנֵי יִשְׂרָאֵל לֵאמֹר כָּל־חֵלֶב שׁוֹר וְכֶשֶׂב

24 וָעֵז לֹא תֹאכֵלוּ: וְחֵלֶב נְבֵלָה וְחֵלֶב טְרֵפָה יֵעָשֶׂה לְכָל־

כה מְלָאכָה וְאָכֹל לֹא תֹאכְלֻהוּ: כִּי כָּל־אֹכֵל חֵלֶב מִן

__הַבְּהֵמָה אֲשֶׁר יַקְרִיב מִמֶּנָּה אִשֶּׁה לַיהוָה וְנִכְרְתָה הַנֶּפֶשׁ__

26 הָאֹכֶלֶת מֵעַמֶּיהָ: וְכָל־דָּם לֹא תֹאכְלוּ בְּכֹל מוֹשְׁבֹתֵיכֶם

27 לָעוֹף וְלַבְּהֵמָה: כָּל־נֶפֶשׁ אֲשֶׁר־תֹּאכַל כָּל־דָּם וְנִכְרְתָה

(n.37)   __הַנֶּפֶשׁ הַהִוא מֵעַמֶּיהָ:__

Lev. 7 cont.

²⁸ וַיְדַבֵּ֥ר יְהוָ֖ה אֶל־מֹשֶׁ֥ה לֵּאמֹֽר׃ דַּבֵּ֞ר אֶל־בְּנֵ֤י יִשְׂרָאֵל֙
²⁹ לֵאמֹ֔ר הַמַּקְרִ֞יב אֶת־זֶ֤בַח שְׁלָמָיו֙ לַֽיהוָ֔ה יָבִ֧יא אֶת־קָרְבָּנ֛וֹ
לַֽיהוָ֖ה מִזֶּ֥בַח שְׁלָמָֽיו׃ יָדָ֣יו תְּבִיאֶ֔ינָה אֵ֖ת אִשֵּׁ֣י יְהוָ֑ה אֶת־
הַחֵ֤לֶב עַל־הֶֽחָזֶה֙ יְבִיאֶ֔נּוּ אֵ֣ת הֶחָזֶ֗ה לְהָנִ֥יף אֹת֛וֹ תְּנוּפָ֖ה
לִפְנֵ֥י יְהוָֽה׃ וְהִקְטִ֧יר הַכֹּהֵ֛ן אֶת־הַחֵ֖לֶב הַמִּזְבֵּ֑חָה וְהָיָה֙
³¹ הֶֽחָזֶ֔ה לְאַהֲרֹ֖ן וּלְבָנָֽיו׃ וְאֵת֙ שׁ֣וֹק הַיָּמִ֔ין תִּתְּנ֥וּ תְרוּמָ֖ה
³² לַכֹּהֵ֑ן מִזִּבְחֵ֖י שַׁלְמֵיכֶֽם׃ הַמַּקְרִ֞יב אֶת־דַּ֧ם הַשְּׁלָמִ֛ים וְאֶת־
³³ הַחֵ֖לֶב מִבְּנֵ֣י אַהֲרֹ֑ן ל֧וֹ תִהְיֶ֛ה שׁ֥וֹק הַיָּמִ֖ין לְמָנָֽה׃ כִּי֩
³⁴ אֶת־חֲזֵ֨ה הַתְּנוּפָ֜ה וְאֵ֣ת ׀ שׁ֣וֹק הַתְּרוּמָ֗ה לָקַ֙חְתִּי֙ מֵאֵ֣ת
בְּנֵֽי־יִשְׂרָאֵ֔ל מִזִּבְחֵ֖י שַׁלְמֵיהֶ֑ם וָאֶתֵּ֣ן אֹתָ֡ם לְאַהֲרֹ֣ן הַכֹּהֵ֡ן
וּלְבָנָ֜יו לְחָק־עוֹלָ֖ם מֵאֵ֥ת בְּנֵ֥י יִשְׂרָאֵֽל׃

Uitti (34-36); *NJV, NAB,
RSV* (34)

Leviticus 10

⁸
⁹ וַיְדַבֵּ֣ר יְהוָ֔ה אֶֽל־אַהֲרֹ֖ן לֵאמֹֽר׃ יַ֣יִן וְשֵׁכָ֞ר אַל־תֵּ֣שְׁתְּ ׀
אַתָּ֣ה ׀ וּבָנֶ֣יךָ אִתָּ֗ךְ בְּבֹאֲכֶ֛ם אֶל־אֹ֥הֶל מוֹעֵ֖ד וְלֹ֣א תָמֻ֑תוּ
חֻקַּ֥ת עוֹלָ֖ם לְדֹרֹתֵיכֶֽם׃ וּֽלֲהַבְדִּ֔יל בֵּ֥ין הַקֹּ֖דֶשׁ וּבֵ֣ין הַחֹ֑ל
¹¹ וּבֵ֥ין הַטָּמֵ֖א וּבֵ֣ין הַטָּהֽוֹר׃ וּלְהוֹרֹ֖ת אֶת־בְּנֵ֣י יִשְׂרָאֵ֑ל אֵ֚ת
כָּל־הַ֣חֻקִּ֔ים אֲשֶׁ֨ר דִּבֶּ֧ר יְהוָ֛ה אֲלֵיהֶ֖ם בְּיַד־מֹשֶֽׁה׃
¹² וַיְדַבֵּ֣ר מֹשֶׁ֣ה אֶֽל־אַהֲרֹ֡ן וְאֶ֣ל אֶלְעָזָר֩ וְאֶל־אִ֨יתָמָ֜ר ׀ בָּנָ֣יו
הַנּֽוֹתָרִ֗ים קְח֣וּ אֶת־הַמִּנְחָ֗ה הַנּוֹתֶ֙רֶת֙ מֵאִשֵּׁ֣י יְהוָ֔ה וְאִכְל֥וּהָ
¹³ מַצּ֖וֹת אֵ֣צֶל הַמִּזְבֵּ֑חַ כִּ֛י קֹ֥דֶשׁ קָֽדָשִׁ֖ים הִֽוא׃ וַאֲכַלְתֶּ֤ם
אֹתָהּ֙ בְּמָק֣וֹם קָדֹ֔שׁ כִּ֣י חָקְךָ֤ וְחָק־בָּנֶ֙יךָ֙ הִ֔וא מֵאִשֵּׁ֖י יְהוָ֑ה
¹⁴ כִּי־כֵ֖ן צֻוֵּֽיתִי׃ וְאֵת֩ חֲזֵ֨ה הַתְּנוּפָ֜ה וְאֵ֣ת ׀ שׁ֣וֹק הַתְּרוּמָ֗ה
תֹּֽאכְלוּ֙ בְּמָק֣וֹם טָה֔וֹר אַתָּ֕ה וּבָנֶ֥יךָ וּבְנֹתֶ֖יךָ אִתָּ֑ךְ כִּֽי־חָקְךָ֤
וְחָק־בָּנֶ֙יךָ֙ נִתְּנ֔וּ מִזִּבְחֵ֖י שַׁלְמֵ֥י בְּנֵ֥י יִשְׂרָאֵֽל׃

NJV (9aβ,10,11); *NEB, RSV*
(9aβ)

NJV., RSV (12b); *NAB* (13b
on 14a)

NJV, RSV (13aβ,b); *NEB* (13b)

NJV, NAB, NEB, RSV (14b)

Leviticus 11

	אַךְ אֶת־ 4	Uitti (4bβ); *NEB*, *RSV* (4bα)
(n.38)	זֶה לֹא תֹאכְלוּ מִמַּעֲלֵי הַגֵּרָה וּמִמַּפְרִסֵי הַפַּרְסָה אֶת־	Uitti (5b); *NEB*, *RSV* (5aβ)
	הַגָּמָל כִּי־מַעֲלֵה גֵרָה הוּא וּפַרְסָה אֵינֶנּוּ מַפְרִיס טָמֵא הוּא	Uitti (6b); *NEB*, *RSV* (6aβ,γ)
	לָכֶם: וְאֶת־הַשָּׁפָן כִּי־מַעֲלֵה גֵרָה הוּא וּפַרְסָה לֹא יַפְרִיס ה	Uitti (7b); *NEB*, *RSV* (7aβ,γ)
	טָמֵא הוּא לָכֶם: וְאֶת־הָאַרְנֶבֶת כִּי־מַעֲלַת גֵּרָה הִוא 6	*NEB* (13aβ)
	וּפַרְסָה לֹא הִפְרִיסָה טְמֵאָה הִוא לָכֶם: וְאֶת־הַחֲזִיר כִּי־ 7	*NEB* (35aβ–b)
	מַפְרִיס פַּרְסָה הוּא וְשֹׁסַע שֶׁסַע פַּרְסָה וְהוּא גֵּרָה לֹא־	Uitti (42b); *NJV*, *NEB*, *RSV*
(n.39)	יִגָּר טָמֵא הוּא לָכֶם: מִבְּשָׂרָם לֹא תֹאכֵלוּ וּבְנִבְלָתָם לֹא 8	(42bβ)
	תִגָּעוּ טְמֵאִים הֵם לָכֶם: אֶת־זֶה תֹּאכְלוּ מִכֹּל אֲשֶׁר בַּמָּיִם 9	
	כֹּל אֲשֶׁר־לוֹ סְנַפִּיר וְקַשְׂקֶשֶׂת בַּמַּיִם בַּיַּמִּים וּבַנְּחָלִים	
	אֹתָם תֹּאכֵלוּ: וְכֹל אֲשֶׁר אֵין־לוֹ סְנַפִּיר וְקַשְׂקֶשֶׂת בַּיַּמִּים י	
	וּבַנְּחָלִים מִכֹּל שֶׁרֶץ הַמַּיִם וּמִכֹּל נֶפֶשׁ הַחַיָּה אֲשֶׁר בַּמָּיִם	
(n.40)	שֶׁקֶץ הֵם לָכֶם: וְשֶׁקֶץ יִהְיוּ לָכֶם מִבְּשָׂרָם לֹא תֹאכֵלוּ 11	
	וְאֶת־נִבְלָתָם תְּשַׁקֵּצוּ: כֹּל אֲשֶׁר אֵין־לוֹ סְנַפִּיר וְקַשְׂקֶשֶׂת 12	
(n.41)	בַּמַּיִם שֶׁקֶץ הוּא לָכֶם: וְאֶת־אֵלֶּה תְּשַׁקְּצוּ מִן־הָעוֹף לֹא 13	
	יֵאָכְלוּ שֶׁקֶץ הֵם אֶת־הַנֶּשֶׁר וְאֶת־הַפֶּרֶס וְאֵת הָעָזְנִיָּה:	
	וְאֶת־הַדָּאָה וְאֶת־הָאַיָּה לְמִינָהּ: אֵת כָּל־עֹרֵב לְמִינוֹ: 14 טו	
	וְאֵת בַּת הַיַּעֲנָה וְאֶת־הַתַּחְמָס וְאֶת־הַשָּׁחַף וְאֶת־הַנֵּץ 16	
	לְמִינֵהוּ: וְאֶת־הַכּוֹס וְאֶת־הַשָּׁלָךְ וְאֶת־הַיַּנְשׁוּף: וְאֶת־ 17 18	
	הַתִּנְשֶׁמֶת וְאֶת־הַקָּאָת וְאֶת־הָרָחָם: וְאֵת הַחֲסִידָה הָאֲנָפָה 19	
	לְמִינָהּ וְאֶת־הַדּוּכִיפַת וְאֶת־הָעֲטַלֵּף:	
(n.42)	לְכָל־הַבְּהֵמָה אֲשֶׁר הִוא 26	
	מַפְרֶסֶת פַּרְסָה וְשֶׁסַע אֵינֶנָּה שֹׁסַעַת וְגֵרָה אֵינֶנָּה מַעֲלָה	
(n.43)	טְמֵאִים הֵם לָכֶם כָּל־הַנֹּגֵעַ בָּהֶם יִטְמָא: וְכֹל הוֹלֵךְ עַל־ 27	
(n.44)	כַּפָּיו בְּכָל־הַחַיָּה הַהֹלֶכֶת עַל־אַרְבַּע טְמֵאִים הֵם לָכֶם	
	כָּל־הַנֹּגֵעַ בְּנִבְלָתָם יִטְמָא עַד־הָעָרֶב: וְהַנֹּשֵׂא אֶת־נִבְלָתָם 28	
	יְכַבֵּס בְּגָדָיו וְטָמֵא עַד־הָעָרֶב טְמֵאִים הֵמָּה לָכֶם: ס	

	וְכֹל אֲשֶׁר־יִפֹּל מִנִּבְלָתָם עָלָיו יִטְמָא לה
(n.45)	תַּנּוּר וְכִירַיִם יֻתָּץ טְמֵאִים הֵם וּטְמֵאִים יִהְיוּ לָכֶם: אַךְ 36
	מַעְיָן וּבוֹר מִקְוֵה־מַיִם יִהְיֶה טָהוֹר וְנֹגֵעַ בְּנִבְלָתָם יִטְמָא:
	וְכִי יִפֹּל מִנִּבְלָתָם עַל־כָּל־זֶרַע זֵרוּעַ אֲשֶׁר יִזָּרֵעַ טָהוֹר 37
	הוּא: וְכִי יֻתַּן־מַיִם עַל־זֶרַע וְנָפַל מִנִּבְלָתָם עָלָיו טָמֵא 38
	הוּא לָכֶם: ס וְכִי יָמוּת מִן־הַבְּהֵמָה אֲשֶׁר־הִיא לָכֶם 39
	לְאָכְלָה הַנֹּגֵעַ בְּנִבְלָתָהּ יִטְמָא עַד־הָעָרֶב: וְהָאֹכֵל מִנִּבְלָתָהּ מ
	יְכַבֵּס בְּגָדָיו וְטָמֵא עַד־הָעָרֶב וְהַנֹּשֵׂא אֶת־נִבְלָתָהּ יְכַבֵּס
	בְּגָדָיו וְטָמֵא עַד־הָעָרֶב: וְכָל־הַשֶּׁרֶץ הַשֹּׁרֵץ עַל־הָאָרֶץ 41
(n.46)	שֶׁקֶץ הוּא לֹא יֵאָכֵל: כֹּל הוֹלֵךְ עַל־גָּחוֹן וְכֹל הוֹלֵךְ 42
	עַל־אַרְבַּע עַד כָּל־מַרְבֵּה רַגְלַיִם לְכָל־הַשֶּׁרֶץ הַשֹּׁרֵץ עַל־
	הָאָרֶץ לֹא תֹאכְלוּם כִּי־שֶׁקֶץ הֵם:

Leviticus 13

4 וְאִם־בַּהֶרֶת לְבָנָה הִוא
בְּעוֹר בְּשָׂרוֹ וְעָמֹק אֵין־מַרְאֶהָ מִן־הָעוֹר וּשְׂעָרָה לֹא־הָפַךְ
לָבָן וְהִסְגִּיר הַכֹּהֵן אֶת־הַנֶּגַע שִׁבְעַת יָמִים׃ וְרָאָהוּ הַכֹּהֵן ה
בַּיּוֹם הַשְּׁבִיעִי וְהִנֵּה הַנֶּגַע עָמַד בְּעֵינָיו לֹא־פָשָׂה הַנֶּגַע
6 בָּעוֹר וְהִסְגִּירוֹ הַכֹּהֵן שִׁבְעַת יָמִים שֵׁנִית׃ וְרָאָה הַכֹּהֵן
אֹתוֹ בַּיּוֹם הַשְּׁבִיעִי שֵׁנִית וְהִנֵּה כֵּהָה הַנֶּגַע וְלֹא־פָשָׂה
הַנֶּגַע בָּעוֹר וְטִהֲרוֹ הַכֹּהֵן מִסְפַּחַת הִוא וְכִבֶּס בְּגָדָיו וְטָהֵר׃ (n.47)
7 וְאִם־פָּשֹׂה תִפְשֶׂה הַמִּסְפַּחַת בָּעוֹר אַחֲרֵי הֵרָאֹתוֹ אֶל־
8 הַכֹּהֵן לְטָהֳרָתוֹ וְנִרְאָה שֵׁנִית אֶל־הַכֹּהֵן׃ וְרָאָה הַכֹּהֵן (n.48)
וְהִנֵּה פָּשְׂתָה הַמִּסְפַּחַת בָּעוֹר וְטִמְּאוֹ הַכֹּהֵן צָרַעַת הִוא׃ פ
9 נֶגַע צָרַעַת כִּי תִהְיֶה בְּאָדָם וְהוּבָא אֶל־הַכֹּהֵן׃ וְרָאָה הַכֹּהֵן י
וְהִנֵּה שְׂאֵת־לְבָנָה בָּעוֹר וְהִיא הָפְכָה שֵׂעָר לָבָן וּמִחְיַת
11 בָּשָׂר חַי בַּשְׂאֵת׃ צָרַעַת נוֹשֶׁנֶת הִוא בְּעוֹר בְּשָׂרוֹ וְטִמְּאוֹ
12 הַכֹּהֵן לֹא יַסְגִּרֶנּוּ כִּי טָמֵא הוּא׃ וְאִם־פָּרוֹחַ תִּפְרַח הַצָּרַעַת
בָּעוֹר וְכִסְּתָה הַצָּרַעַת אֵת כָּל־עוֹר הַנֶּגַע מֵרֹאשׁוֹ וְעַד־
13 רַגְלָיו לְכָל־מַרְאֵה עֵינֵי הַכֹּהֵן׃ וְרָאָה הַכֹּהֵן וְהִנֵּה כִסְּתָה
הַצָּרַעַת אֶת־כָּל־בְּשָׂרוֹ וְטִהַר אֶת־הַנָּגַע כֻּלּוֹ הָפַךְ לָבָן (n.49)
14 טָהוֹר הוּא׃ וּבְיוֹם הֵרָאוֹת בּוֹ בָּשָׂר חַי יִטְמָא׃ וְרָאָה טו
הַכֹּהֵן אֶת־הַבָּשָׂר הַחַי וְטִמְּאוֹ הַבָּשָׂר הַחַי טָמֵא הוּא (n.50)
צָרַעַת הוּא׃

18 19 וּבָשָׂר כִּי־יִהְיֶה בוֹ־בְעֹרוֹ שְׁחִין וְנִרְפָּא׃ וְהָיָה בִּמְקוֹם
הַשְּׁחִין שְׂאֵת לְבָנָה אוֹ בַהֶרֶת לְבָנָה אֲדַמְדָּמֶת וְנִרְאָה
אֶל־הַכֹּהֵן׃ וְרָאָה הַכֹּהֵן וְהִנֵּה מַרְאֶהָ שָׁפָל מִן־הָעוֹר כ
וּשְׂעָרָהּ הָפַךְ לָבָן וְטִמְּאוֹ הַכֹּהֵן נֶגַע־צָרַעַת הִוא בַּשְּׁחִין (n.52)
21 פָּרָחָה׃ וְאִם ׀ יִרְאֶנָּה הַכֹּהֵן וְהִנֵּה אֵין־בָּהּ שֵׂעָר לָבָן וּשְׁפָלָה
אֵינֶנָּה מִן־הָעוֹר וְהִיא כֵהָה וְהִסְגִּירוֹ הַכֹּהֵן שִׁבְעַת יָמִים׃
22 23 וְאִם־פָּשֹׂה תִפְשֶׂה בָּעוֹר וְטִמֵּא הַכֹּהֵן אֹתוֹ נֶגַע הִוא׃ וְאִם־ (n.53)
תַּחְתֶּיהָ תַּעֲמֹד הַבַּהֶרֶת לֹא פָשָׂתָה צָרֶבֶת הַשְּׁחִין הִוא
24 וְטִהֲרוֹ הַכֹּהֵן׃ אוֹ בָשָׂר כִּי־יִהְיֶה בְעֹרוֹ מִכְוַת־אֵשׁ
וְהָיְתָה מִחְיַת הַמִּכְוָה בַּהֶרֶת לְבָנָה אֲדַמְדֶּמֶת אוֹ לְבָנָה׃
וְרָאָה אֹתָהּ הַכֹּהֵן וְהִנֵּה נֶהְפַּךְ שֵׂעָר לָבָן בַּבַּהֶרֶת וּמַרְאֶהָ כה
עָמֹק מִן־הָעוֹר צָרַעַת הִוא בַּמִּכְוָה פָּרָחָה וְטִמֵּא אֹתוֹ הַכֹּהֵן
26 נֶגַע צָרַעַת הִוא׃ וְאִם ׀ יִרְאֶנָּה הַכֹּהֵן וְהִנֵּה אֵין־בַּבַּהֶרֶת (n.54)
שֵׂעָר לָבָן וּשְׁפָלָה אֵינֶנָּה מִן־הָעוֹר וְהִוא כֵהָה וְהִסְגִּירוֹ
27 הַכֹּהֵן שִׁבְעַת יָמִים׃ וְרָאָהוּ הַכֹּהֵן בַּיּוֹם הַשְּׁבִיעִי אִם־
פָּשֹׂה תִפְשֶׂה בָּעוֹר וְטִמֵּא הַכֹּהֵן אֹתוֹ נֶגַע צָרַעַת הִוא׃ (n.55)
28 וְאִם־תַּחְתֶּיהָ תַעֲמֹד הַבַּהֶרֶת לֹא־פָשְׂתָה בָעוֹר וְהִוא כֵהָה
שְׂאֵת הַמִּכְוָה הִוא וְטִהֲרוֹ הַכֹּהֵן כִּי־צָרֶבֶת הַמִּכְוָה הִוא׃ פ
29 וְאִישׁ אוֹ אִשָּׁה כִּי־יִהְיֶה בוֹ נָגַע בְּרֹאשׁ אוֹ בְזָקָן׃ וְרָאָה ל
הַכֹּהֵן אֶת־הַנֶּגַע וְהִנֵּה מַרְאֵהוּ עָמֹק מִן־הָעוֹר וּבוֹ שֵׂעָר
צָהֹב דָּק וְטִמֵּא אֹתוֹ הַכֹּהֵן נֶתֶק הוּא צָרַעַת הָרֹאשׁ אוֹ (n.56)
הַזָּקָן הוּא׃

Uitti (6b)
Uitti (8b)
Uitti, *NJV*, *NAB*, *NEB*, *RSV* (11bβ)
Uitti (13b); *NJV*, *NAB* (13bα)
Uitti, *NAB* (15b); *RSV* (15bβ)
Uitti (20b)
Uitti (22b)
Uitti (25bα,c)
Uitti (27c)
Uitti (28b); *NJV*, *NAB*, *RSV* (28bβ)
Uitti (30c); *NAB* (30bαב,bβ)

Lev. 13 cont.

Hebrew	Refs
וְאִם־פָּשֹׂה יִפְשֶׂה הַנֶּתֶק בָּעוֹר לה	Uitti (36b)
36 אַחֲרֵי טָהֳרָתוֹ׃ וְרָאָהוּ הַכֹּהֵן וְהִנֵּה פָּשָׂה הַנֶּתֶק בָּעוֹר	Uitti (44c); *NAB* (44bβ)
לֹא־יְבַקֵּר הַכֹּהֵן לַשֵּׂעָר הַצָּהֹב טָמֵא הוּא׃	Uitti (52aε); *NJV, NAB,*
	NEB, RSV (52bα)
וְכִי־יִהְיֶה בְקָרַחַת 12	Uitti (55cβ)
אוֹ בְנַבַּחַת נֶגַע לָבָן אֲדַמְדָּם צָרַעַת פֹּרַחַת הִוא בְּקָרַחְתּוֹ	
אוֹ בְנַבַּחְתּוֹ׃ וְרָאָה אֹתוֹ הַכֹּהֵן וְהִנֵּה שְׂאֵת־הַנֶּגַע לְבָנָה 43	
אֲדַמְדֶּמֶת בְּקָרַחְתּוֹ אוֹ בְנַבַּחְתּוֹ כְּמַרְאֵה צָרַעַת עוֹר בָּשָׂר׃	
אִישׁ־צָרוּעַ הוּא טָמֵא הוּא טַמֵּא יְטַמְּאֶנּוּ הַכֹּהֵן בְּרֹאשׁוֹ 44	
נִגְעוֹ׃	

וְשָׂרַף אֶת־הַבֶּגֶד אוֹ אֶת־הַשְּׁתִי אוֹ אֶת־ 52	
הָעֵרֶב בַּצֶּמֶר אוֹ בַפִּשְׁתִּים אוֹ אֶת־כָּל־כְּלִי הָעוֹר אֲשֶׁר־	
יִהְיֶה בוֹ הַנָּגַע כִּי־צָרַעַת מַמְאֶרֶת הִוא בָּאֵשׁ תִּשָּׂרֵף׃ וְאִם 53	
יִרְאֶה הַכֹּהֵן וְהִנֵּה לֹא־פָשָׂה הַנֶּגַע בַּבֶּגֶד אוֹ בַשְּׁתִי אוֹ	
בָעֵרֶב אוֹ בְּכָל־כְּלִי־עוֹר׃ וְצִוָּה הַכֹּהֵן וְכִבְּסוּ אֵת אֲשֶׁר־ 54	
בּוֹ הַנָּגַע וְהִסְגִּירוֹ שִׁבְעַת־יָמִים שֵׁנִית׃ וְרָאָה הַכֹּהֵן אַחֲרֵי נה	
הֻכַּבֵּס אֶת־הַנֶּגַע וְהִנֵּה לֹא־הָפַךְ הַנֶּגַע אֶת־עֵינוֹ וְהַנֶּגַע לֹא־	
פָשָׂה טָמֵא הוּא בָּאֵשׁ תִּשְׂרְפֶנּוּ פְּחֶתֶת הִוא בְּקָרַחְתּוֹ אוֹ	
בְנַבַּחְתּוֹ׃	

(n.57)

(n.58)

(n.59)

Leviticus 14

Hebrew	Refs
וְשָׁחַט אֶת־הַכֶּבֶשׂ בִּמְקוֹם אֲשֶׁר 13	Uitti (13bc); *NJV, NAB, RSV*
יִשְׁחַט אֶת־הַחַטָּאת וְאֶת־הָעֹלָה בִּמְקוֹם הַקֹּדֶשׁ כִּי כַּחַטָּאת	(13b); *NEB* (13bα)
הָאָשָׁם הוּא לַכֹּהֵן קֹדֶשׁ קָדָשִׁים הוּא׃	*NAB, RSV* (21a)
וְאִם־דַּל הוּא וְאֵין יָדוֹ 21	*NJV, NAB, RSV* (36aα)
מַשֶּׂגֶת וְלָקַח כֶּבֶשׂ אֶחָד אָשָׁם לִתְנוּפָה לְכַפֵּר עָלָיו׃	

וּמִן־הַשֶּׁמֶן יִצֹק הַכֹּהֵן עַל־כַּף 26	
הַכֹּהֵן הַשְּׂמָאלִית׃ וְהִזָּה הַכֹּהֵן בְּאֶצְבָּעוֹ הַיְמָנִית מִן־הַשֶּׁמֶן 27	
אֲשֶׁר עַל־כַּפּוֹ הַשְּׂמָאלִית שֶׁבַע פְּעָמִים לִפְנֵי יְהוָה׃ וְנָתַן 28	
הַכֹּהֵן מִן־הַשֶּׁמֶן אֲשֶׁר עַל־כַּפּוֹ עַל־תְּנוּךְ אֹזֶן הַמִּטַּהֵר	
הַיְמָנִית וְעַל־בֹּהֶן יָדוֹ הַיְמָנִית וְעַל־בֹּהֶן רַגְלוֹ הַיְמָנִית עַל־	
מְקוֹם דַּם הָאָשָׁם׃ וְהַנּוֹתָר מִן־הַשֶּׁמֶן אֲשֶׁר עַל־כַּף הַכֹּהֵן 29	
יִתֵּן עַל־רֹאשׁ הַמִּטַּהֵר לְכַפֵּר עָלָיו לִפְנֵי יְהוָה׃	

(n.60)

(n.61)

וַיְדַבֵּר יְהוָה אֶל־מֹשֶׁה וְאֶל־אַהֲרֹן לֵאמֹר׃ כִּי תָבֹאוּ אֶל־ 33 34	
אֶרֶץ כְּנַעַן אֲשֶׁר אֲנִי נֹתֵן לָכֶם לַאֲחֻזָּה וְנָתַתִּי נֶגַע צָרַעַת	
בְּבֵית אֶרֶץ אֲחֻזַּתְכֶם׃ וּבָא אֲשֶׁר־לוֹ הַבַּיִת וְהִגִּיד לַכֹּהֵן לה	
לֵאמֹר כְּנֶגַע נִרְאָה לִי בַּבָּיִת׃ וְצִוָּה הַכֹּהֵן וּפִנּוּ אֶת־הַבַּיִת 36	
בְּטֶרֶם יָבֹא הַכֹּהֵן לִרְאוֹת אֶת־הַנֶּגַע וְלֹא יִטְמָא כָּל־אֲשֶׁר	
בַּבָּיִת	

Lev. 14 cont.

וְאִם־בֹּא ⁴⁸

יָבֹא הַכֹּהֵן וְרָאָה וְהִנֵּה לֹא־פָשָׂה הַנֶּגַע בַּבָּיִת אַחֲרֵי הִטֹּחַ
אֶת־הַבָּיִת וְטִהַר הַכֹּהֵן אֶת־הַבַּיִת כִּי נִרְפָּא הַנָּגַע:

Uitti (48d); *NJV*, *NAB*, *NEB*,
RSV (48bβ)

Leviticus 16

וַיֹּאמֶר יְהוָה אֶל־מֹשֶׁה דַּבֵּר אֶל־אַהֲרֹן ²
אָחִיךָ וְאַל־יָבֹא בְכָל־עֵת אֶל־הַקֹּדֶשׁ מִבֵּית לַפָּרֹכֶת אֶל־
פְּנֵי הַכַּפֹּרֶת אֲשֶׁר עַל־הָאָרֹן וְלֹא יָמוּת כִּי בֶּעָנָן אֵרָאֶה
עַל־הַכַּפֹּרֶת:

NJV, *RSV* (2bβ,γ); *NEB*
(2bγ)

NAB, *RSV* (10b)

וְהִקְרִיב אַהֲרֹן אֶת־הַשָּׂעִיר אֲשֶׁר עָלָה עָלָיו הַגּוֹרָל לַיהוָה ⁹
וְעָשָׂהוּ חַטָּאת: וְהַשָּׂעִיר אֲשֶׁר עָלָה עָלָיו הַגּוֹרָל לַעֲזָאזֵל י
יָעֳמַד־חַי לִפְנֵי יְהוָה לְכַפֵּר עָלָיו לְשַׁלַּח אֹתוֹ לַעֲזָאזֵל
הַמִּדְבָּרָה: וְהִקְרִיב אַהֲרֹן אֶת־פַּר הַחַטָּאת אֲשֶׁר־לוֹ ¹¹
וְכִפֶּר בַּעֲדוֹ וּבְעַד בֵּיתוֹ וְשָׁחַט אֶת־פַּר הַחַטָּאת אֲשֶׁר־לוֹ:
וְלָקַח מְלֹא־הַמַּחְתָּה גַּחֲלֵי־אֵשׁ מֵעַל הַמִּזְבֵּחַ מִלִּפְנֵי יְהוָה ¹²
וּמְלֹא חָפְנָיו קְטֹרֶת סַמִּים דַּקָּה וְהֵבִיא מִבֵּית לַפָּרֹכֶת:
וְנָתַן אֶת־הַקְּטֹרֶת עַל־הָאֵשׁ לִפְנֵי יְהוָה וְכִסָּה ׀ עֲנַן הַקְּטֹרֶת ¹³
אֶת־הַכַּפֹּרֶת אֲשֶׁר עַל־הָעֵדוּת וְלֹא יָמוּת:

Uitti (13b,c); *NJV*, *NAB*,
RSV (13bα,β); *NEB* (13bβ)

Uitti (29-34a); *NJV*, *NEB*,
RSV (30); *NAB* (30 on 31)

וְהָיְתָה לָכֶם לְחֻקַּת ²⁹
עוֹלָם בַּחֹדֶשׁ הַשְּׁבִיעִי בֶּעָשׂוֹר לַחֹדֶשׁ תְּעַנּוּ אֶת־נַפְשֹׁתֵיכֶם
וְכָל־מְלָאכָה לֹא תַעֲשׂוּ הָאֶזְרָח וְהַגֵּר הַגָּר בְּתוֹכְכֶם:
כִּי־בַיּוֹם הַזֶּה יְכַפֵּר עֲלֵיכֶם לְטַהֵר אֶתְכֶם מִכֹּל חַטֹּאתֵיכֶם ל
לִפְנֵי יְהוָה תִּטְהָרוּ:

Numbers 3

וַיְדַבֵּר יְהוָה אֶל־מֹשֶׁה לֵּאמֹר: הַקְרֵב אֶת־מַטֵּה לֵוִי ⁶
וְהַעֲמַדְתָּ אֹתוֹ לִפְנֵי אַהֲרֹן הַכֹּהֵן וְשֵׁרְתוּ אֹתוֹ:

(n.62)

(n.63)

Numbers 5

11 וַיְדַבֵּר יְהוָה אֶל־מֹשֶׁה לֵּאמֹר: דַּבֵּר אֶל־בְּנֵי יִשְׂרָאֵל
12 וְאָמַרְתָּ אֲלֵהֶם אִישׁ אִישׁ כִּי־תִשְׂטֶה אִשְׁתּוֹ וּמָעֲלָה בוֹ
13 מָעַל: וְשָׁכַב אִישׁ אֹתָהּ שִׁכְבַת־זֶרַע וְנֶעְלַם מֵעֵינֵי אִישָׁהּ
וְנִסְתְּרָה וְהִיא נִטְמָאָה וְעֵד אֵין בָּהּ וְהִוא לֹא נִתְפָּשָׂה:
14 וְעָבַר עָלָיו רוּחַ־קִנְאָה וְקִנֵּא אֶת־אִשְׁתּוֹ וְהִוא נִטְמָאָה אוֹ־
עָבַר עָלָיו רוּחַ־קִנְאָה וְקִנֵּא אֶת־אִשְׁתּוֹ וְהִיא לֹא נִטְמָאָה:
15 וְהֵבִיא הָאִישׁ אֶת־אִשְׁתּוֹ אֶל־הַכֹּהֵן וְהֵבִיא אֶת־קָרְבָּנָהּ
עָלֶיהָ עֲשִׂירִת הָאֵיפָה קֶמַח שְׂעֹרִים לֹא־יִצֹק עָלָיו שֶׁמֶן
וְלֹא־יִתֵּן עָלָיו לְבֹנָה כִּי־מִנְחַת קְנָאֹת הוּא מִנְחַת זִכָּרוֹן
<u>מַזְכֶּרֶת עָוֹן</u>:

23 וְכָתַב אֶת־
24 הָאָלֹת הָאֵלֶּה הַכֹּהֵן בַּסֵּפֶר וּמָחָה אֶל־מֵי הַמָּרִים: וְהִשְׁקָה
אֶת־הָאִשָּׁה אֶת־מֵי הַמָּרִים הַמְאָרֲרִים וּבָאוּ בָהּ הַמַּיִם
<u>הַמְאָרֲרִים לְמָרִים</u>:

Uitti, *NJV, NAB, NEB, RSV*
(15bβ)

NJV, NAB (24b)

Numbers 6

6 כָּל־יְמֵי הַזִּירוֹ לַיהוָה עַל־
7 נֶפֶשׁ מֵת לֹא יָבֹא: לְאָבִיו וּלְאִמּוֹ לְאָחִיו וּלְאַחֹתוֹ לֹא־
8 יִטַּמָּא לָהֶם בְּמֹתָם כִּי נֵזֶר אֱלֹהָיו עַל־רֹאשׁוֹ: כֹּל יְמֵי
9 נִזְרוֹ קָדֹשׁ הוּא לַיהוָה: וְכִי־יָמוּת מֵת עָלָיו בְּפֶתַע פִּתְאֹם
וְטִמֵּא רֹאשׁ נִזְרוֹ וְגִלַּח רֹאשׁוֹ בְּיוֹם טָהֳרָתוֹ בַּיּוֹם הַשְּׁבִיעִי
10 יְגַלְּחֶנּוּ: וּבַיּוֹם הַשְּׁמִינִי יָבִא שְׁתֵּי תֹרִים אוֹ שְׁנֵי בְּנֵי יוֹנָה
11 אֶל־הַכֹּהֵן אֶל־פֶּתַח אֹהֶל מוֹעֵד: וְעָשָׂה הַכֹּהֵן אֶחָד
לְחַטָּאת וְאֶחָד לְעֹלָה וְכִפֶּר עָלָיו מֵאֲשֶׁר חָטָא עַל־הַנָּפֶשׁ
12 וְקִדַּשׁ אֶת־רֹאשׁוֹ בַּיּוֹם הַהוּא: וְהִזִּיר לַיהוָה אֶת־יְמֵי נִזְרוֹ
וְהֵבִיא כֶּבֶשׂ בֶּן־שְׁנָתוֹ לְאָשָׁם וְהַיָּמִים הָרִאשֹׁנִים יִפְּלוּ כִּי
<u>טָמֵא נִזְרוֹ</u>:

Uitti (7b-8); *NJV, NAB,
NEB, RSV* (7b)

Uitti, *NJV, NAB, NEB, RSV*
(12bβ)

Numbers 9

9 וַיְדַבֵּר יְהוָה אֶל־מֹשֶׁה לֵּאמֹר: דַּבֵּר אֶל־בְּנֵי יִשְׂרָאֵל
לֵאמֹר אִישׁ אִישׁ כִּי־יִהְיֶה טָמֵא לָנֶפֶשׁ אוֹ בְדֶרֶךְ רְחֹקָה
11 לָכֶם אוֹ לְדֹרֹתֵיכֶם וְעָשָׂה פֶסַח לַיהוָה: בַּחֹדֶשׁ הַשֵּׁנִי
בְּאַרְבָּעָה עָשָׂר יוֹם בֵּין הָעַרְבַּיִם יַעֲשׂוּ אֹתוֹ עַל־מַצּוֹת
12 וּמְרֹרִים יֹאכְלֻהוּ: לֹא־יַשְׁאִירוּ מִמֶּנּוּ עַד־בֹּקֶר וְעֶצֶם לֹא
13 יִשְׁבְּרוּ־בוֹ בְּכָל־חֻקַּת הַפֶּסַח יַעֲשׂוּ אֹתוֹ: וְהָאִישׁ אֲשֶׁר־
הוּא טָהוֹר וּבְדֶרֶךְ לֹא־הָיָה וְחָדַל לַעֲשׂוֹת הַפֶּסַח וְנִכְרְתָה
הַנֶּפֶשׁ הַהִוא מֵעַמֶּיהָ כִּי קָרְבַּן יְהוָה לֹא הִקְרִיב בְּמֹעֲדוֹ
<u>חֶטְאוֹ יִשָּׂא הָאִישׁ הַהוּא</u>:

Uitti (13aδ); *NJV, RSV*
(13b); *NAB, NEB* (13bα)

Numbers 10

(n.65)

עֲשֵׂה לְךָ שְׁתֵּי חֲצוֹצְרֹת   2   Uitti, *NJV*, *RSV* (9b)
כֶּסֶף מִקְשָׁה תַּעֲשֶׂה אֹתָם וְהָיוּ לְךָ לְמִקְרָא הָעֵדָה וּלְמַסַּע   Uitti (10b)
אֶת־הַמַּחֲנוֹת׃

וְכִי־תָבֹאוּ מִלְחָמָה בְּאַרְצְכֶם עַל־הַצַּר הַצֹּרֵר   9
אֶתְכֶם וַהֲרֵעֹתֶם בַּחֲצֹצְרֹת וְנִזְכַּרְתֶּם לִפְנֵי יְהוָה אֱלֹהֵיכֶם
וְנוֹשַׁעְתֶּם מֵאֹיְבֵיכֶם׃ וּבְיוֹם שִׂמְחַתְכֶם וּבְמוֹעֲדֵיכֶם   ·
וּבְרָאשֵׁי חָדְשֵׁכֶם וּתְקַעְתֶּם בַּחֲצֹצְרֹת עַל עֹלֹתֵיכֶם וְעַל
זִבְחֵי שַׁלְמֵיכֶם וְהָיוּ לָכֶם לְזִכָּרוֹן לִפְנֵי אֱלֹהֵיכֶם אֲנִי
יְהוָה אֱלֹהֵיכֶם׃

Numbers 15

אֲם־נֶפֶשׁ אַחַת תֶּחֱטָא בִשְׁגָגָה וְהִקְרִיבָה עֵז בַּת־שְׁנָתָהּ   27   Uitti (31); *NJV*, *NAB*, *RSV*
לְחַטָּאת׃ וְכִפֶּר הַכֹּהֵן עַל־הַנֶּפֶשׁ הַשֹּׁגֶגֶת בְּחֶטְאָה בִשְׁגָגָה   28   (31a on 31bα)
לִפְנֵי יְהוָה לְכַפֵּר עָלָיו וְנִסְלַח לוֹ׃ הָאֶזְרָח בִּבְנֵי יִשְׂרָאֵל   29   *NJV* (39b)
וְלַגֵּר הַגָּר בְּתוֹכָם תּוֹרָה אַחַת יִהְיֶה לָכֶם לָעֹשֶׂה בִּשְׁגָגָה׃   Uitti (41)
הַנֶּפֶשׁ אֲשֶׁר־תַּעֲשֶׂה בְּיָד רָמָה מִן־הָאֶזְרָח וּמִן־הַגֵּר אֶת־   ל
יְהוָה הוּא מְגַדֵּף וְנִכְרְתָה הַנֶּפֶשׁ הַהִוא מִקֶּרֶב עַמָּהּ׃
(n.66)   כִּי דְבַר־יְהוָה בָּזָה וְאֶת־מִצְוָתוֹ הֵפַר הִכָּרֵת וּ תִּכָּרֵת הַנֶּפֶשׁ   31
הַהִוא עֲוֹנָה בָהּ׃

וַיֹּאמֶר יְהוָה אֶל־מֹשֶׁה לֵּאמֹר׃ דַּבֵּר אֶל־בְּנֵי יִשְׂרָאֵל   37 38
וְאָמַרְתָּ אֲלֵהֶם וְעָשׂוּ לָהֶם צִיצִת עַל־כַּנְפֵי בִגְדֵיהֶם לְדֹרֹתָם
וְנָתְנוּ עַל־צִיצִת הַכָּנָף פְּתִיל תְּכֵלֶת׃ וְהָיָה לָכֶם לְצִיצִת   39
וּרְאִיתֶם אֹתוֹ וּזְכַרְתֶּם אֶת־כָּל־מִצְוֹת יְהוָה וַעֲשִׂיתֶם אֹתָם
וְלֹא־תָתוּרוּ אַחֲרֵי לְבַבְכֶם וְאַחֲרֵי עֵינֵיכֶם אֲשֶׁר־אַתֶּם
זֹנִים אַחֲרֵיהֶם׃ לְמַעַן תִּזְכְּרוּ וַעֲשִׂיתֶם אֶת־כָּל־מִצְוֹתָי   מ
וִהְיִיתֶם קְדֹשִׁים לֵאלֹהֵיכֶם׃ אֲנִי יְהוָה אֱלֹהֵיכֶם אֲשֶׁר   41
הוֹצֵאתִי אֶתְכֶם מֵאֶרֶץ מִצְרַיִם לִהְיוֹת לָכֶם לֵאלֹהִים אֲנִי
יְהוָה אֱלֹהֵיכֶם׃

Numbers 18

(n.67)

א וַיֹּאמֶר יְהוָה אֶל־אַהֲרֹן אַתָּה וּבָנֶיךָ וּבֵית־אָבִיךָ אִתָּךְ תִּשְׂאוּ
אֶת־עֲוֹן הַמִּקְדָּשׁ וְאַתָּה וּבָנֶיךָ אִתָּךְ תִּשְׂאוּ אֶת־עֲוֹן כְּהֻנַּתְכֶם׃
2 וְגַם אֶת־אַחֶיךָ מַטֵּה לֵוִי שֵׁבֶט אָבִיךָ הַקְרֵב אִתָּךְ וְיִלָּווּ
עָלֶיךָ וִישָׁרְתוּךָ וְאַתָּה וּבָנֶיךָ אִתָּךְ לִפְנֵי אֹהֶל הָעֵדֻת׃
3 וְשָׁמְרוּ מִשְׁמַרְתְּךָ וּמִשְׁמֶרֶת כָּל־הָאֹהֶל אַךְ אֶל־כְּלֵי הַקֹּדֶשׁ
וְאֶל־הַמִּזְבֵּחַ לֹא יִקְרָבוּ וְלֹא־יָמֻתוּ גַם־הֵם גַם־אַתֶּם׃

16 וּפְדוּיָו מִבֶּן־חֹדֶשׁ תִּפְדֶּה
בְּעֶרְכְּךָ כֶּסֶף חֲמֵשֶׁת שְׁקָלִים בְּשֶׁקֶל הַקֹּדֶשׁ עֶשְׂרִים

(n.68)

17 גֵּרָה הוּא׃ אַךְ בְּכוֹר־שׁוֹר אוֹ בְכוֹר כֶּשֶׂב אוֹ־בְכוֹר עֵז
לֹא תִפְדֶּה קֹדֶשׁ הֵם אֶת־דָּמָם תִּזְרֹק עַל־הַמִּזְבֵּחַ וְאֶת־
18 חֶלְבָּם תַּקְטִיר אִשֶּׁה לְרֵיחַ נִיחֹחַ לַיהוָה׃ וּבְשָׂרָם יִהְיֶה־
19 לָּךְ כַּחֲזֵה הַתְּנוּפָה וּכְשׁוֹק הַיָּמִין לְךָ יִהְיֶה׃ כֹּל תְּרוּמֹת
הַקֳּדָשִׁים אֲשֶׁר יָרִימוּ בְנֵי־יִשְׂרָאֵל לַיהוָה נָתַתִּי לְךָ וּלְבָנֶיךָ
וְלִבְנֹתֶיךָ אִתְּךָ לְחָק־עוֹלָם בְּרִית מֶלַח עוֹלָם הִוא לִפְנֵי
20 יְהוָה לְךָ וּלְזַרְעֲךָ אִתָּךְ׃ וַיֹּאמֶר יְהוָה אֶל־אַהֲרֹן בְּאַרְצָם

(n.69)

לֹא תִנְחָל וְחֵלֶק לֹא־יִהְיֶה לְךָ בְּתוֹכָם אֲנִי חֶלְקְךָ
וְנַחֲלָתְךָ בְּתוֹךְ בְּנֵי יִשְׂרָאֵל׃

ל וַאֲמַרְתָּ אֲלֵהֶם בַּהֲרִימְכֶם אֶת־חֶלְבּוֹ
מִמֶּנּוּ וְנֶחְשַׁב לַלְוִיִּם כִּתְבוּאַת גֹּרֶן וְכִתְבוּאַת יָקֶב׃
31 וַאֲכַלְתֶּם אֹתוֹ בְּכָל־מָקוֹם אַתֶּם וּבֵיתְכֶם כִּי־שָׂכָר הוּא
לָכֶם חֵלֶף עֲבֹדַתְכֶם בְּאֹהֶל מוֹעֵד׃

NJV, NAB, RSV (3bβ)

Uitti (17b)

Uitti (20b–24)

Uitti, NJV, NAB, RSV (31b)

Numbers 19

9 וְאָסַף אִישׁ טָהוֹר אֵת אֵפֶר הַפָּרָה וְהִנִּיחַ
מִחוּץ לַמַּחֲנֶה בְּמָקוֹם טָהוֹר וְהָיְתָה לַעֲדַת בְּנֵי־יִשְׂרָאֵל

(n.70)

י לְמִשְׁמֶרֶת לְמֵי נִדָּה חַטָּאת הִוא׃ וְכִבֶּס הָאֹסֵף אֶת־אֵפֶר
הַפָּרָה אֶת־בְּגָדָיו וְטָמֵא עַד־הָעָרֶב וְהָיְתָה לִבְנֵי יִשְׂרָאֵל
11 וְלַגֵּר הַגָּר בְּתוֹכָם לְחֻקַּת עוֹלָם׃ הַנֹּגֵעַ בְּמֵת לְכָל־נֶפֶשׁ
12 אָדָם וְטָמֵא שִׁבְעַת יָמִים׃ הוּא יִתְחַטָּא־בוֹ בַּיּוֹם הַשְּׁלִישִׁי
וּבַיּוֹם הַשְּׁבִיעִי יִטְהָר וְאִם־לֹא יִתְחַטָּא בַּיּוֹם הַשְּׁלִישִׁי
13 וּבַיּוֹם הַשְּׁבִיעִי לֹא יִטְהָר׃ כָּל־הַנֹּגֵעַ בְּמֵת בְּנֶפֶשׁ הָאָדָם
אֲשֶׁר־יָמוּת וְלֹא יִתְחַטָּא אֶת־מִשְׁכַּן יְהוָה טִמֵּא וְנִכְרְתָה

(n.71)

הַנֶּפֶשׁ הַהִוא מִיִּשְׂרָאֵל כִּי מֵי נִדָּה לֹא־זֹרַק עָלָיו טָמֵא
יִהְיֶה עוֹד טֻמְאָתוֹ בוֹ׃

Uitti (9c); NEB (9bβ)

Uitti (13b,c); NJV, NAB, RSV (13bα)

Numbers 28

17 וּבַחֲמִשָּׁה עָשָׂר יוֹם לַחֹדֶשׁ הַזֶּה חָג שִׁבְעַת יָמִים מַצּוֹת
18 יֵאָכֵל: בַּיּוֹם הָרִאשׁוֹן מִקְרָא־קֹדֶשׁ כָּל־מְלֶאכֶת עֲבֹדָה לֹא
19 תַעֲשׂוּ: וְהִקְרַבְתֶּם אִשֶּׁה עֹלָה לַיהוָה פָּרִים בְּנֵי־בָקָר
שְׁנַיִם וְאַיִל אֶחָד וְשִׁבְעָה כְבָשִׂים בְּנֵי שָׁנָה תְּמִימִם יִהְיוּ
20 לָכֶם: וּמִנְחָתָם סֹלֶת בְּלוּלָה בַשָּׁמֶן שְׁלֹשָׁה עֶשְׂרֹנִים
לַפָּר וּשְׁנֵי עֶשְׂרֹנִים לָאַיִל תַּעֲשׂוּ: 21 עִשָּׂרוֹן עִשָּׂרוֹן תַּעֲשֶׂה
22 לַכֶּבֶשׂ הָאֶחָד לְשִׁבְעַת הַכְּבָשִׂים: וּשְׂעִיר חַטָּאת אֶחָד
לְכַפֵּר עֲלֵיכֶם:

(n.72)

26 וּבְיוֹם הַבִּכּוּרִים בְּהַקְרִיבְכֶם מִנְחָה
חֲדָשָׁה לַיהוָה בְּשָׁבֻעֹתֵיכֶם מִקְרָא־קֹדֶשׁ יִהְיֶה לָכֶם כָּל־
27 מְלֶאכֶת עֲבֹדָה לֹא תַעֲשׂוּ: וְהִקְרַבְתֶּם עוֹלָה לְרֵיחַ נִיחֹחַ
לַיהוָה פָּרִים בְּנֵי־בָקָר שְׁנַיִם אַיִל אֶחָד שִׁבְעָה כְבָשִׂים בְּנֵי
28 שָׁנָה: וּמִנְחָתָם סֹלֶת בְּלוּלָה בַשָּׁמֶן שְׁלֹשָׁה עֶשְׂרֹנִים לַפָּר
29 הָאֶחָד שְׁנֵי עֶשְׂרֹנִים לָאַיִל הָאֶחָד: עִשָּׂרוֹן עִשָּׂרוֹן לַכֶּבֶשׂ
30 הָאֶחָד לְשִׁבְעַת הַכְּבָשִׂים: שְׂעִיר עִזִּים אֶחָד לְכַפֵּר עֲלֵיכֶם:

(n.73)

Numbers 29

א וּבַחֹדֶשׁ הַשְּׁבִיעִי בְּאֶחָד לַחֹדֶשׁ מִקְרָא־קֹדֶשׁ יִהְיֶה לָכֶם
כָּל־מְלֶאכֶת עֲבֹדָה לֹא תַעֲשׂוּ יוֹם תְּרוּעָה יִהְיֶה לָכֶם:
2 וַעֲשִׂיתֶם עֹלָה לְרֵיחַ נִיחֹחַ לַיהוָה פַּר בֶּן־בָּקָר אֶחָד אַיִל
3 אֶחָד כְּבָשִׂים בְּנֵי־שָׁנָה שִׁבְעָה תְּמִימִם: וּמִנְחָתָם סֹלֶת
בְּלוּלָה בַשָּׁמֶן שְׁלֹשָׁה עֶשְׂרֹנִים לַפָּר שְׁנֵי עֶשְׂרֹנִים לָאָיִל:
4 וְעִשָּׂרוֹן אֶחָד לַכֶּבֶשׂ הָאֶחָד לְשִׁבְעַת הַכְּבָשִׂים: וּשְׂעִיר־
עִזִּים אֶחָד חַטָּאת לְכַפֵּר עֲלֵיכֶם:

(n.74)

Numbers 30

6 וְאִם־
הֵנִיא אָבִיהָ אֹתָהּ בְּיוֹם שָׁמְעוֹ כָּל־נְדָרֶיהָ וֶאֱסָרֶיהָ אֲשֶׁר
אָסְרָה עַל־נַפְשָׁהּ לֹא יָקוּם וַיהוָה יִסְלַח־לָהּ כִּי־הֵנִיא אָבִיהָ
אֹתָהּ:

Uitti (6b); *NJV*, *NAB* (6bβ);
NEB, *RSV* (5bβ=6bβH)

Uitti (13b); *NAB* (13bα)

13 וְאִם־הָפֵר יָפֵר אֹתָם ׀ אִישָׁהּ בְּיוֹם שָׁמְעוֹ
כָּל־מוֹצָא שְׂפָתֶיהָ לִנְדָרֶיהָ וּלְאִסַּר נַפְשָׁהּ לֹא יָקוּם אִישָׁהּ
הֲפֵרָם וַיהוָה יִסְלַח־לָהּ:

(n.75)

Numbers 33

51 דַּבֵּר אֶל־בְּנֵי   NJV, NAB, NEB, RSV (53b)
יִשְׂרָאֵל וְאָמַרְתָּ אֲלֵהֶם כִּי אַתֶּם עֹבְרִים אֶת־הַיַּרְדֵּן אֶל־
אֶרֶץ כְּנָעַן: 52 וְהוֹרַשְׁתֶּם אֶת־כָּל־יֹשְׁבֵי הָאָרֶץ מִפְּנֵיכֶם
וְאִבַּדְתֶּם אֵת כָּל־מַשְׂכִּיֹּתָם וְאֵת כָּל־צַלְמֵי מַסֵּכֹתָם תְּאַבֵּדוּ
וְאֵת כָּל־בָּמוֹתָם תַּשְׁמִידוּ: 53 וְהוֹרַשְׁתֶּם אֶת־הָאָרֶץ וִישַׁבְתֶּם־
בָּהּ כִּי לָכֶם נָתַתִּי אֶת־הָאָרֶץ לָרֶשֶׁת אֹתָהּ:

Numbers 35

9 וַיְדַבֵּר יְהֹוָה אֶל־מֹשֶׁה לֵּאמֹר: דַּבֵּר אֶל־בְּנֵי יִשְׂרָאֵל   Uitti, NJV, NAB, NEB, RSV
וְאָמַרְתָּ אֲלֵהֶם כִּי אַתֶּם עֹבְרִים אֶת־הַיַּרְדֵּן אַרְצָה כְּנָעַן: (12b)
11 וְהִקְרִיתֶם לָכֶם עָרִים עָרֵי מִקְלָט תִּהְיֶינָה לָכֶם וְנָס שָׁמָּה   Uitti (15c); NJV, NAB, NEB,
רֹצֵחַ מַכֵּה־נֶפֶשׁ בִּשְׁגָגָה: 12 וְהָיוּ לָכֶם הֶעָרִים לְמִקְלָט   RSV (15b)
מִגֹּאֵל וְלֹא יָמוּת הָרֹצֵחַ עַד־עָמְדוֹ לִפְנֵי הָעֵדָה לַמִּשְׁפָּט: Uitti (28a); NJV, RSV (28)
13 וְהֶעָרִים אֲשֶׁר תִּתֵּנוּ שֵׁשׁ־עָרֵי מִקְלָט תִּהְיֶינָה לָכֶם:
אֵת שְׁלֹשׁ הֶעָרִים תִּתְּנוּ מֵעֵבֶר לַיַּרְדֵּן וְאֵת שְׁלֹשׁ הֶעָרִים 14
תִּתְּנוּ בְּאֶרֶץ כְּנָעַן עָרֵי מִקְלָט תִּהְיֶינָה: 15 לִבְנֵי יִשְׂרָאֵל
וְלַגֵּר וְלַתּוֹשָׁב בְּתוֹכָם תִּהְיֶינָה שֵׁשׁ־הֶעָרִים הָאֵלֶּה לְמִקְלָט
(n.77)   לָנוּס שָׁמָּה כָּל־מַכֵּה־נֶפֶשׁ בִּשְׁגָגָה: 16 וְאִם־בִּכְלִי בַרְזֶל
הִכָּהוּ וַיָּמֹת רֹצֵחַ הוּא מוֹת יוּמַת הָרֹצֵחַ: 17 וְאִם בְּאֶבֶן יָד
אֲשֶׁר־יָמוּת בָּהּ הִכָּהוּ וַיָּמֹת רֹצֵחַ הוּא מוֹת יוּמַת הָרֹצֵחַ:
18 אוֹ בִּכְלִי עֵץ־יָד אֲשֶׁר־יָמוּת בּוֹ הִכָּהוּ וַיָּמֹת רֹצֵחַ הוּא
מוֹת יוּמַת הָרֹצֵחַ: 19 גֹּאֵל הַדָּם הוּא יָמִית אֶת־הָרֹצֵחַ
בְּפִגְעוֹ־בוֹ הוּא יְמִיתֶנּוּ: וְאִם־בְּשִׂנְאָה יֶהְדָּפֶנּוּ אוֹ־הִשְׁלִיךְ כ
עָלָיו בִּצְדִיָּה וַיָּמֹת: אוֹ בְאֵיבָה הִכָּהוּ בְיָדוֹ וַיָּמֹת מוֹת־ 21
יוּמַת הַמַּכֶּה רֹצֵחַ הוּא

26 וְאִם־
יָצֹא יֵצֵא הָרֹצֵחַ אֶת־גְּבוּל עִיר מִקְלָטוֹ אֲשֶׁר יָנוּס שָׁמָּה:
27 וּמָצָא אֹתוֹ גֹּאֵל הַדָּם מִחוּץ לִגְבוּל עִיר מִקְלָטוֹ וְרָצַח
28 גֹּאֵל הַדָּם אֶת־הָרֹצֵחַ אֵין לוֹ דָּם: כִּי בְעִיר מִקְלָטוֹ יֵשֵׁב
עַד־מוֹת הַכֹּהֵן הַגָּדֹל וְאַחֲרֵי מוֹת הַכֹּהֵן הַגָּדֹל יָשׁוּב הָרֹצֵחַ
אֶל־אֶרֶץ אֲחֻזָּתוֹ:

Numbers 36

7 וְלֹא־תִסֹּב נַחֲלָה לִבְנֵי   Uitti (8b-9); NJV, NAB, RSV
יִשְׂרָאֵל מִמַּטֶּה אֶל־מַטֶּה כִּי אִישׁ בְּנַחֲלַת מַטֵּה אֲבֹתָיו   (8b)
8 יִדְבְּקוּ בְּנֵי יִשְׂרָאֵל: וְכָל־בַּת יֹרֶשֶׁת נַחֲלָה מִמַּטּוֹת בְּנֵי
יִשְׂרָאֵל לְאֶחָד מִמִּשְׁפַּחַת מַטֵּה אָבִיהָ תִּהְיֶה לְאִשָּׁה לְמַעַן
9 יִירְשׁוּ בְּנֵי יִשְׂרָאֵל אִישׁ נַחֲלַת אֲבֹתָיו: וְלֹא־תִסֹּב נַחֲלָה
מִמַּטֶּה לְמַטֶּה אַחֵר כִּי־אִישׁ בְּנַחֲלָתוֹ יִדְבְּקוּ מַטּוֹת בְּנֵי
יִשְׂרָאֵל:

(c) *Notes*

1. (Gen 9:3) With this instruction, man is given permission to eat animal flesh as part of his regular diet (cf. Gen 1:29). On the question of whether or not "permissions" are to be counted as legal prescriptions, see the discussion in Chapter II, pp. 82-83.

2. (Gen 17:11) Verse 11b can be taken as an mc indicating purpose: "so that it may be the sign of the covenant...." On -ל וְהָיָה, meaning "to fulfill the function of," "serve as," see BDB (226).

3. (Gen 17:13) Verse 13b (cf. v. 11b) can be taken as an mc indicating purpose: "so that my covenant may be...." Uitti takes it as an mc.

4. (Gen 17:14) This verse does not seem to constitute a separate legal prescription; it indicates the adverse consequence in case of noncompliance, much in the same vein as the motive clauses in Exod 12:15, 19; Lev 7:25; 23:29, etc. (all introduced by כִּי), and therefore can be considered an mc for the legal prescriptions in vv. 11 and 12-13, i.e., "for if any male who is uncircumcised (עָרֵל) fails to circumcise the flesh of his foreskin, that person shall be cut off...." Gen 17:14b is an asyndetic mc to the mc in v. 14a (cf. GKC, #158a; Joüon, #170b).

5. (Exod 12:3-13) These verses appear to embody ad hoc commands, rather than legal prescriptions. The motivation in v. 12ff. indicates that the reference is to the Passover of Egypt; cf. Noth, *Exodus*, 96; Ibn Ezra on Exod 12:3. On the Rabbinic distinction between the Passover of Egypt and the Passover of the subsequent generations, see *Mishna Pes.* 9:5 (*TB*, *Pes.* 96a,b); *Mekilta, Bo.*

6. (Exod 12:21-27) These verses are attributed to J or to the compiler of JE. See Driver, *Introduction*, 28-29. However, vv. 24-27a seem to be a Deuteronomic supplement, with v. 27b referring back to vv. 21-23; cf. Noth, *Exodus*, 97.

7. (Exod 12:43-49) These instructions, introduced by "this is the law of the passover (offering)," seem to presuppose an agricultural community, mentioning as they do "natives of the land," "sojourners," "strangers," "day laborers," etc. (Noth, *Exodus*, 100), and therefore are to be viewed as legal prescriptions rather than ad hoc commands of the desert period. Verse 50 probably refers to vv. 21-28.

8. (Exod 13:2) *NAB* considers v. 2b an mc ("for it belongs to me"). However, it is possible to start the motivation with the word פֶּטֶר, "(for) the first issue of every womb among the Israelites, be it man or beast, is mine."

9. (Exod 13:3-16) These verses are attributed to J or to the compiler of JE. See Driver, *Introduction*, 28-29. However, as Noth argues, vv. 1-16 appear as "Deuteronomistic" (cf. *Exodus*, 101).

10. (Exod 13:9) This verse indicates the purpose behind the legal prescription in vv. 6-8; cf. Noth, *Exodus*, 101; *NJV*, ad loc.

11. (Exod 29:27-30) The instructions of Exod 29:1-35 were carried out according to Leviticus 8. Yet, vv. 27-30 contain directives that are regarded as valid for future times as well.

12. (Exod 30:1-6) This is an ad hoc command and was carried out according to Exod 37:25-28. Verses 7-10 constitute legal prescriptions (cf. vv. 8, 10).

13.   (Exod 30:11f.)   The instructions in Exod 30:11-16 most probably
refer to any time a poll tax is to be levied.   Verses 13-15 are illustrations.
See Noth, *Exodus*, 236.

14.   (Exod 30:16)   Cf. n. 10 above.

15.   (Exod 30:17-18)   This is an ad hoc command (cf. Exod 38:8; 40:30,
32); vv. 19-21b constitute legal prescriptions (cf. v. 21b).

16.   (Exod 30:22-25)   This is an ad hoc command (cf. Exod 37:29); vv.
26-33 constitute legal prescriptions (cf. v. 31).

17.   (Exod 30:32b-33)   Verse 32b is the primary motivation; v. 33 is not
a separate legal prescription but a secondary motivation indicating the adverse
consequence in case of noncompliance (cf. n. 4 above).

18.   (Exod 30:34-36)   This is an ad hoc command (cf. Exod 37:29); vv.
37-38 are laws.   See Noth, *Exodus*, 239.   For the mc in v. 38, see above, nn.
4 and 17.

19.   (Lev 1:9bβ)   This clause seems to constitute the underlying reason
for v. 9b and can be rendered as: "(for) it (is) a burnt offering, an offering
of fire..." (cf. vv. 13, 17).

20.   (Lev 1:13b)   Cf. n. 19 above.   Here we have the full formulation of
the asyndetic mc.

21.   (Lev 1:17)   Cf. n. 20.

22.   (Lev 2:6b)   This can be understood as: "(for) it is a meal
offering."

23.   (Lev 2:15b)   Cf. n. 22.

24.   (Lev 4:20b)   The פֶר formula constitutes a concluding sentence;
cf. vv. 26b, 31b, 35b.   See Noth, *Leviticus*, 41.

25.   (Lev 4:21b)   This can be understood as: "(for) it is the sin offering of the congregation."

26.   (Lev 4:24b)   Cf. n. 25.

27.   (Lev 5:9b)   Cf. n. 25; cf. v. 11bγ.

28.   (Lev 5:12b)   Cf. n. 25; cf. v. 11bγ.

29.   (Lev 5:18b-19)   This constitutes a concluding formula; cf. *NAB*.

30.   (Lev 6:9-10)   Verses 10aβ and 10b appear to indicate the reason
behind the law in vv. 9-10aα.

31.   (Lev 6:18b)   Verse 18bβ can be understood as: "(for) it is most
holy."

32.   (Lev 6:22b)   Cf. n. 31.

33.   (Lev 7:5b)   Verse 5b can be understood as: "(for) it is a guilt
offering."

34.   (Lev 7:6b)   Cf. n. 31.

35. (Lev 7:18a) Verse 18aβ can be understood as: "(for) it is an offensive thing"; cf. Lev 19:7.

36. (Lev 7:19b-20) Verse 20 does not constitute a separate legal prescription; it simply indicates the adverse consequence in case of noncompliance and, therefore, can be taken as an mc; cf. v. 25.

37. (Lev 7:26-27) Verse 27 is related to v. 26, in the same way that v. 25 is related to v. 24; and therefore, as in v. 25, v. 27, too, can be considered a motivating sentence.

38. (Lev 11:4-6) Here the same mc is repeated for three different animals, whereas in Deut 14:7, one mc applies to the same three animals. Lev 11:4-6 will be considered one motivated prescription.

39. (Lev 11:8b) Verse 8b is understood as: "(for) they are unclean for you."

40. (Lev 11:10b-11a) This constitutes the motivation behind the prohibitions in vv. 11bα, 11bβ.

41. (Lev 11:13-14) Verse 13aβב is the motivation for the prohibition in v. 13aα-aβא; vv. 13b-19 are examples.

42. (Lev 11:26) Verse 26aβ is the motivation behind the command in v. 26b.

43. (Lev 11:27) Verse 27aβ is the motivation behind the command in v. 27b.

44. (Lev 11:28) Verse 28b is the motivation behind the command in v. 28a.

45. (Lev 11:35) Verse 35aβ-b is the motivation behind the law in v. 35aα and can be understood as in *NEB*: "for they are unclean and you shall treat them as such."

46. (Lev 11:41b) Verse 41bα is the motivation behind the prohibition in v. 41bβ and can be understood as: "(since) they are loathsome."

47. (Lev 13:6b) Verse 6bαב is the motivation behind v. 6bα and can be understood as: "(for) it is merely a rash."

48. (Lev 13:8b) Verse 8bβ is the motivation behind v. 8bα and can be understood as: "(for) it is leprosy"; cf. v. 28. On the term "leprosy," see Chapter II, n. 155.

49. (Lev 13:13) Verse 13bα is the motivation behind v. 13bβ (which refers to v. 13a) and can be understood as in *NJV*: "for he has turned all white."

50. (Lev 13:14-15) Verse 15bβ motivates v. 15bα (which refers to vv. 14-15a).

51. (Lev 13:17b) Verse 17bβ does not seem to constitute an mc. It rather indicates the consequence of the priest's action. Thus *NAB* has: "and thus he will be clean."

52. (Lev 13:20b) Verse 20bβ motivates v. 20bα.

53. (Lev 13:22b) Verse 22bβ motivates v. 22bα.

54. (Lev 13:25b) Verse 25bβ motivates v. 25bα.

55. (Lev 13:27b) Verse 27bγ motivates v. 27bβ.

56. (Lev 13:30b) Verse 30bβ-bγ motivates v. 30bα.

57. (Lev 13:36) The last two words, טמא הוא, motivate v. 36bα and can be understood as: "(for) he is unclean."

58. (Lev 13:44b) Verse 44bβ motivates v. 44bα.

59. (Lev 13:55) Verse 55b motivates v. 55a. The clause, טמא הוא, in v. 55a is diagnostic and not an mc.

60. (Lev 14:21a) Here the purpose of the guilt offering is stated (cf. *NAB*, *RSV*), thus constituting an mc.

61. (Lev 14:29b) This indicates the purpose behind the instruction in vv. 26-29a, thus constituting an mc.

62. (Lev 16:10) Here the instruction to keep alive the goat that was set aside for Azazel is accompanied by two statements of purpose.

63. (Num 3:5-10) This section seems to contain legislation rather than ad hoc commands, since it is expected that the structure of the priesthood and the responsibilities of the priests will continue in the future as well., Verses 11-13 do not embody law imposing obligations upon others but a statement of God to Moses in which he states that he is setting aside the Levites from among the Israelites for his service.

64. (Num 8:23-26) This most probably represents a later modification of an earlier command regarding the age at which the Levites were permitted to enter the cultic service. The present text places the entry at the age of twenty-five in contrast to thirty in 4:3, 23, 30. See Noth, *Numbers*, 69.

65. (Num 10:2) Verse 2b expresses the purpose behind the prescription in v. 2a; i.e., "so that they may serve you to summon the community...."

66. (Num 15:30-31) Verse 31a constitutes the motivation for v. 31b which refers to v. 30.

67. (Num 18:1) The reference in v. 1 is probably both to Aaron and his descendants (Noth, *Numbers*, 134); vv. 1-7 can be considered legislation, rather than ad hoc commands.

68. (Num 18:17a) The last two words in v. 17a constitute an asyndetic mc, i.e., "(for) they are holy."

69. (Num 18:20) Verse 20b seems to indicate the reason behind the law in v. 20a and can be rendered as: "(for) I am your portion...."

70. (Num 19:9) Verse 9b indicates the purpose behind v. 9a, thus functioning as an mc; v. 9b (חטאת הוא) is an mc of the mc.

71. (Num 19:13) Verse 20 repeats, partly with altered wording, v. 13; cf. Noth, *Numbers*, 143. In Num 19:13, v. 13aα constitutes the primary motivation behind the command in v. 13aβ (cf. v. 20 with פי); v. 13b constitutes the secondary motivation of the same command.

72. (Num 28:22b) Verse 22b indicates the purpose behind the instruction in v. 22a, thus functioning as an mc.

73. (Num 28:30) Cf. n. 72.

74. (Num 29:5) Cf. n. 72.

75. (Num 30:13) Verse 13bα constitutes the motivation behind the law in v. 13a.

76. (Num 35:1-8) As in Num 34:1-15, 35:1-8, too, appears to be an ad hoc command given once and for all and therefore will be treated as such.

77. (Num 35:16) The death penalty in this verse is justified (as in vv. 17, 18, 21) on account of the fact that the accused is a murderer.

BIBLIOGRAPHY

Ackroyd, P. R. *Exile and Restoration*. The Old Testament
  Library. Philadelphia: Westminster, 1968.

Albright, W. F. "Canaanite-Phoenician Sources of Hebrew
  Wisdom." VTSup 3 (1955) 1-15.

_____. *From the Stone Age to Christianity*. New York:
  Doubleday Anchor, 1957.

_____. "The Judicial Reform of Jehoshaphat." Pp. 61-82 in
  Alexander Marx Jubilee Volume. Ed. S. Lieberman. New
  York: J.P.S., 1950.

_____. Review of "Die Ursprünge" by A. Alt. *JBL* 55 (1936)
  164-69.

_____. "Some Oriental Glosses on the Homeric Problem."
  AJA 54 (1950) 162-76.

_____. "A Teacher to a Man of Shechem About 1400 B.C."
  BASOR 86 (1942) 28-31.

_____. "The Gezer Calendar." *BASOR* 92 (1943) 16-26.

Alp, S. "Military Instructions of the Hittite King Tuthaliya
  IV. (?)." *Belleten* 11 (1947) 384-402, 403-414.

Alster, B. *The Instructions of Suruppak: A Sumerian Proverb
  Collection*. Mesopotamia-Copenhagen Studies in
  Assyriology 2. Copenhagen: Akademisk Forlag, 1974.

Alt, A. "The Origins of Israelite Law." Pp. 103-71 in *Essays
  on Old Testament History and Religion*. New York:
  Doubleday Anchor, 1968.

Audet, J. P. "Origines comparées de la double tradition de la
  loi et de la sagesse dans le Proche-Orient ancien."
  International Congress of Orientalists 25 (1960) 1. 352-57.

Baltzer, K. *The Covenant Formulary in Old Testament, Jewish
  and Early Christian Writings*. Philadelphia: Fortress,
  1971.

Beattie, D. R. G. "The Book of Ruth as Evidence for Israelite
  Legal Practice." *VT* 24 (1974) 251-67.

Bentzen, A. *Introduction to the Old Testament*. 2 vols. in 1.
  2nd ed. Copenhagen: G. E. C. Gad, 1952.

Beyerlin, W. *Origins and History of the Oldest Sinaitic
  Traditions*. Oxford: Blackwell, 1965.

Beyerlin, W. "Die Paränese im Bundesbuch und ihre Herkunft."
    Pp. 9-29 in *Gottes Wort und Gottes Land* [H.-W. Herzberg
    Festschrift]. Ed. H. G. Reventlow. Göttingen: Vanden-
    hoeck und Ruprecht, 1965.

Bezold, C. *Babylonisch-assyrisches Glossar*. Heidelberg: Carl
    Winter's Universitäts Buchhandlung, 1926.

Blackman, A. M., and Peet, T. E. "Papyrus Lansing: A Transla-
    tion with Notes." *JEA* 11 (1925) 284-98.

Borger, R. *Babylonisch-assyrische Lesestücke*. Heft I. Rome:
    Pontificum Institutum Biblicum, 1963.

Brichto, H. C. "Blessing and Cursing." *EncJud* 4, 1084-86.

_____. *The Problem of "Curse" in the Hebrew Bible*. JBL
    Monograph Series 13. Philadelphia: Society of Biblical
    Literature, 1968.

Bright, J. *Jeremiah*. AB 21. New York: Doubleday, 1965.

_____. "The Apodictic Prohibition: Some Observations."
    JBL 92 (1973) 185-204.

Brown, F.; Driver, S. R.; and Briggs, C. A. *A Hebrew and
    English Lexicon of the Old Testament*. Oxford: Clarendon,
    1968.

Budd, P. J. "Priestly Instruction in Pre-Exilic Israel."
    VT 23 (1973) 1-14.

Burrows, M. (ed.). *The Dead Sea Scrolls of St. Mark's Monastery*.
    Vol. 1. New Haven: American Schools of Oriental Research,
    1950.

_____. "Levirate Marriage in Israel." *JBL* 59 (1940) 23-33.

_____. "The Marriage of Boaz and Ruth." *JBL* 59 (1940)
    445-54.

Buss, M. J. "The Study of Forms." Pp. 1-56 in *Old Testament
    Form Criticism*. Ed. J. H. Hayes. San Antonio: Trinity
    University, 1974.

Cardascia, G. *Les lois assyriennes*. Paris: Les Editions du
    Cerf, 1969.

Carmichael, C. M. *The Laws of Deuteronomy*. Ithaca: Cornell
    University, 1974.

Cassuto, U. *A Commentary on the Book of Exodus*. Jerusalem:
    Magnes, 1967.

Cazelles, H. *Etudes sur le code de l'alliance*. Paris:
    Letouzey et Ané, 1946.

Cazelles, H. "Les origines du décalogue." *Eretz-Israel* 9
(1969) 14-19.

_____, and Grelot, P. *Introduction à la Bible*. Vol. 1.
Ed. A. Robert and A. Feuillet. Tournai: Desclée, 1957.

Chiera, E., and Lacheman, E. *Joint Expedition with Iraq Museum
at Nuzi*. Paris: American Schools of Oriental Research,
1923-.

Childs, B. S. Review of *Jahve, Jerusalem und die Völker* by
H. M. Lutz. *JBL* 87 (1968) 461-62.

Chomsky, W. "The Dawn of Jewish Education." Pp. 19-27 in
Gratz College Annual of Jewish Studies 3. Ed. S. T. Lachs
and I. D. Passow. Philadelphia, 1974.

Civil, M. "New Sumerian Law Fragments." Pp. 1-12 in *Studies
in Honor of Benno Landsberger on his Seventy-Fifth
Birthday*. AS 16. Chicago: University of Chicago, 1965.

Clark, W. M. "Law." Pp. 99-139 in *Old Testament Form
Criticism*. Ed. J. H. Hayes. San Antonio: Trinity
University, 1974.

Cody, A. *A History of the Old Testament Priesthood*. AnBib 35.
Rome: Pontifical Biblical Institute, 1969.

Cowley, A. *Aramaic Papyri of the Fifth Century B.C.*
Oxford: Clarendon, 1923.

Crenshaw, J. L. "Method in Determining Wisdom Influence upon
'Historical' Literature." *JBL* 88 (1969) 129-42.

_____. "Wisdom." Pp. 225-64 in *Old Testament Form
Criticism*. Ed. J. H. Hayes. San Antonio: Trinity
University, 1974.

Daube, D. *Studies in Biblical Law*. New York: KTAV, 1969.

Dawson, W. R. "New Literary Works from Ancient Egypt."
Asian Review 21 (1925) 305-12.

Dentan, R. C. "The Literary Affinities of Exodus XXXIV 6ff."
VT 13 (1963) 34-51.

Diakonoff, I. M. "Some Remarks on the Reforms of Urukagina."
RA 52 (1958) 1-15.

van Dijk, J. J. A. *La sagesse sumero-accadienne*. Leiden:
Brill, 1953.

Donner, H., and Röllig, W. *Kanaanäische und aramäische
Inschriften*. Vols. I-III. Wiesbaden: Harrassowitz,
1962-64.

Dossin, G. "L'article 142/143 du Code de Hammurabi." *RA* 42
     (1948) 113-24.

Driver, G. R. *Semitic Writing*. London: Oxford University,
     1948.

_____, and Miles, J. C. *The Assyrian Laws*. Oxford:
     Clarendon, 1935.

_____. *The Babylonian Laws*. Oxford: Clarendon, 1956 (Vol.
     1), 1955 (Vol. 2).

Driver, S. R. *The Book of Exodus*. Cambridge Bible for
     Schools and Colleges. Cambridge: University Press, 1953.

_____. *Deuteronomy*. International Critical Commentary.
     Vol. 5. New York: Scribner's, 1909.

_____. *An Introduction to the Literature of the Old
     Testament*. Meridian Books. 9th ed. Cleveland/New York:
     World Publishing, 1967.

Dumas, F. *La civilisation de l'Egypte pharaonique*. Paris:
     Arthaud, 1965.

Ebeling, E. *Die akkadische Gebetsserie "Handerhebung."*
     Berlin: Akademie Verlag, 1953.

Edgerton, W. F. "Nauri Decree of Seti I." *JNES* 6 (1967)
     219-30.

Eichrodt, W. *Theology of the Old Testament*. Vols. 1-2.
     Philadelphia: Westminster, 1961, 1967.

Eissfeldt, O. *The Old Testament: An Introduction*. New York:
     Harper and Row, 1965.

Eitan, I. "Hebrew and Semitic Particles." *AJSL* 44 (1927/28)
     177-205, 254-60.

Ellis, M. de J. "*simdatu* in the Old Babylonian Sources."
     JCS 24 (1972) 79-82.

Erman, A. *Neuaegyptische Grammatik*. Leipzig: Engelmann, 1933.

Ewald, H. *The History of Israel*. 8 vols. London: Longmans,
     Green, 1869-86.

Falk, Z. W. *Hebrew Law in Biblical Times*. Jerusalem:
     Wahrmann, 1964.

Falkenstein, A. Review of *Cuneiform Texts from Babylonian
     Tablets in the British Museum*, Part 42, by H. H. Figulla.
     OLZ 56 (1961) 368-74.

Fensham, F. C. "The Possibility of the Presence of Casuistic Legal Material at the Making of the Covenant at Sinai." *PEQ* 93 (1961) 143-46.

Feucht, C. *Untersuchungen zum Heiligkeitsgesetz.* Berlin: Evangelische Verlagsanstalt, 1964.

Figula, H. H. "Lawsuit Concerning a Sacrilegious Theft at Erech." *Iraq* 13 (1951) 95-101.

Finet, A. *L'accadien des lettres de Mari.* Bruxelles: Palais des Académies, 1956.

Finkelstein, J. J. "Ammiṣaduqa's Edict and the Babylonian 'Law Codes.'" *JCS* 15 (1961) 91-104.

_____. "The Edict of Ammiṣaduqa: A New Text." *RA* 63 (1969) 45-64.

_____. "The Edict of Ammisaduqa." *ANET*, 526-28.

_____. "The Laws of Ur-Nammu." *JCS* 22 (1968/69) 66-82.

_____. "The Laws of Ur-Nammu." *ANET*, 523-25.

_____, and Greenberg, M. (eds.). *Oriental and Biblical Studies: Collected Writings of E. A. Speiser.* Philadelphia: University of Pennsylvania, 1967.

Fitzmyer, J. A. *The Aramaic Inscriptions of Sefîre.* BibOr 19. Rome: Pontifical Biblical Institute, 1967.

Fohrer, G. *Introduction to the Old Testament.* Nashville/New York: Abingdon, 1968.

_____. "Das sogenannte apodiktisch formulierte Recht und der Dekalog." *Kerygma und Dogma* 11 (1965) 49-74.

Frankena, R. "The Vassal Treaties of Esarhaddon and the Dating of Deuteronomy." *OTS* 14 (1965) 122-54.

Friedrich, J. *Die hethitischen Gesetze.* Documenta et Monumenta Orientis Antiqui 7. Leiden: Brill, 1959.

Gadd, C. J. *Ideas of Divine Rule in the Ancient East.* London: Oxford, 1948.

_____. *Teachers and Students in the Oldest Schools.* London: School of Oriental and African Studies, University of London, 1956.

Gardiner, A. H. *Egyptian Grammar.* London: Oxford University, 1957.

_____. "A New Moralizing Text." Festschrift Hermann zum 80. Geburtstag. *WZKM* 54 (1957) 43-45.

Gelb, I. J., et al. (eds.). *The Assyrian Dictionary of the Oriental Institute of the University of Chicago.* Chicago: Oriental Institute, 1956-.

Gemser, B. "The Importance of the Motive Clause in Old Testament Law." VTSup 1 (1953) 50-66. Reprinted, pp. 96-115 in *Adhuc loquitur--Collected Essays by Dr. B. Gemser.* Ed. A. van Selms and A. S. van der Woude. Pretoria Oriental Series 7. Leiden: Brill, 1968.

_____. "The Instructions of Onchsheshonqy and Biblical Wisdom Literature." VTSup 7 (1960) 102-28.

Gerstenberger, E. "Covenant and Commandment." *JBL* 84 (1965) 38-51.

_____. *Wesen und Herkunft des "Apodiktischen Rechts."* WMANT 20. Neukirchen: Neukirchen Verlag, 1965.

Gesenius, W. *Gesenius' Hebrew and Chaldee Lexicon to the Old Testament Scriptures.* Grand Rapids: Eerdmans, 1957.

_____. *Gesenius' Hebrew Grammar.* Ed. E. Kautzsch. Tr. A. Cowley. Oxford: Clarendon, 1910.

Gevirtz, S. "West Semitic Curses and the Problem of the Origins of Hebrew Law." *VT* 11 (1961) 137-58.

Gilmer, H. W. *The If-You Form in Israelite Law.* SBLDS 15. Missoula: Scholars Press, 1975.

Ginsberg, H. L. "The Words of Ahiqar." *ANET*, 427-30.

Glanville, S. R. K. The Instructions of Onchsheshonqy. *Catalogue of Demotic Papyri in the British Museum* (1955)

Goetze, A. *The Laws of Eshnunna.* AASOR 31 (1956).

_____. "The Laws of Eshnunna." *ANET*, 161-63.

_____. *Kizzuwatna.* YOS Researches 22. New Haven: Yale University, 1940.

Gordis, R. *Koheleth: The Man and His World.* 3rd augmented ed. New York: Schocken, 1971.

_____. "Quotations as Literary Usage in Biblical, Oriental, and Rabbinic Literature." *HUCA* 22 (1949) 157-219.

Gordon, E. I. "A New Look at the Wisdom of Sumer and Akkad." *BiOr* 17 (1960) 122-50.

Gottwald, N. K. *A Light to the Nations.* New York: Harper and Brothers, 1959.

Greenberg, M. "Bribery." *IDB* 1, 465.

_____. "Crimes and Punishments." *IDB* 1, 733-44.

_____. "Decalogue." *EncJud* 5, 1435-46.

_____. *The Ḫab/piru*. AOS 39. New Haven: American
Oriental Society, 1955.

_____. "Ḫab/piru and Hebrews." Pp. 188-200 in *The World
History of the Jewish People*, Vol. 2: *Patriarchs*. Ed. B.
Mazar. New Brunswick: Rutgers University, 1970.

_____. "Some Postulates of Biblical Criminal Law." Pp. 5-
28 in *Yehezkel Kaufmann Jubilee Volume*. Ed. M. Haran.
Jerusalem: Magnes, 1960. Reprinted, pp. 18-37 in *The
Jewish Expression*. Ed. I. Goldin. Toronto: Bantam, 1970.

Greengus, S. "The Old Babylonian Marriage Contract." *JAOS* 89
(1969) 505-32.

Greenwood, D. "Rhetorical Criticism and Formgeschichte: Some
Methodological Considerations." *JBL* 89 (1970) 418-26.

Gressmann, H. *Die älteste Geschichtsschreibung und Prophetie
Israels*. SAT 2/1. Göttingen: Vandenhoeck & Ruprecht,
1910.

Gunkel, H. "Fundamental Problems of Hebrew Literary History."
Pp. 57-68 in *What Remains of the Old Testament, and Other
Essays*. New York: Macmillan, 1928.

_____. *The Legends of Genesis*. New York: Schocken, 1964.

Hahn, H. F. *The Old Testament in Modern Research*.
Philadelphia: Fortress, 1966.

Hallo, W. W. "Individual Prayer in Sumerian: The Continuity
of a Tradition." *JAOS* 88 (1968) 71-89.

_____, and Simpson, W. K. *The Ancient Near East: A History*.
New York: Harcourt Brace Jovanovich, 1971.

Hals, R. M. "Is There a Genre of Preached Law?" Pp. 1-12 in
Society of Biblical Literature 1973 Seminar Papers 1.
Ed. G. MacRae. Cambridge: Society of Biblical Literature,
1973.

Haran, M. "Holiness Code." *EncJud* 8, 820-25.

Harper, R. F. *Assyrian and Babylonian Letters Belonging to the
Kouyunjik Collection of the British Museum*. 14 vols.
Chicago/London: University of Chicago, 1892-1914.

Harrelson, W. J. "Law in the OT." *IDB* 3, 77-89.

Harris, J. R.; Conybeare, F. C.; and Lewis, S. A. *Aḥiḳar*.
London: C. J. Clay, 1898.

Harrison, R. K. "Leprosy." *IDB* 3, 111-13.

_____. "Ten Commandments." *IDB* 4, 569-73.

Hayes, A. D. H. "Israel before the Monarchy." *Bulletin of the*
    Society for Old Testament Study. Summer Meeting, 1973,
    p. 7.

Hayes, J. H. (ed.). *Old Testament Form Criticism*. San
    Antonio: Trinity University, 1974.

Heinemann, J. *Ta'amei ha-mitsvot be-sifrut Yisrael*. 2 vols.
    5th ed. Jerusalem: Magnes, 1966.

Herrmann, S. "Das 'apodiktische Recht'--Erwägungen zur
    Klärung dieses Begriffs." *MIO* 15 (1969) 249-61.

Hillers, D. R. *Covenant: The History of a Biblical Idea*.
    Baltimore: Johns Hopkins University, 1970.

_____. *Treaty-Curses and the Old Testament Prophets*.
    BibOr 16. Rome: Pontifical Biblical Institute, 1964.

Hilprecht, H. V. (ed.). *The Babylonian Expedition of the*
    University of Pennsylvania. Series A: *Cuneiform Texts*.
    Philadelphia: University of Pennsylvania, 1893-1911.

Hoffner, H. A. "The Laws of the Hittites." Ph.D. disserta-
    tion. Waltham: Brandeis University, 1963.

Horton, F. L. "A Reassessment of the Legal Forms in the
    Pentateuch and their Functions." Pp. 347-96 in *Society of*
    Biblical Literature 1971 Seminar Papers 2. Cambridge:
    Society of Biblical Literature, 1971.

_____. "Form and Structure in Laws Relating to Women:
    Leviticus 18:6-18." Pp. 20-33 in *Society of Biblical*
    Literature 1973 Seminar Papers 1. Ed. G. MacRae.
    Cambridge: Society of Biblical Literature, 1973.

Hurvitz, A. "The Evidence of Language in Dating the Priestly
    Code." *RB* 81 (1974) 24-56.

Hyatt, J. P. *Commentary on Exodus*. New Century Bible.
    London: Oliphants, 1971.

Ishida, T. "The Leaders of the Tribal Leagues 'Israel' in the
    Pre-Monarchic Period." *RB* 80 (1973) 514-30.

Jacob, E. *Theology of the Old Testament*. New York: Harper
    and Brothers, 1958.

Jepsen, A. *Untersuchungen zum Bundesbuch*. BWANT 3/5.
    Stuttgart: W. Kohlhammer, 1927.

Jirku, A. *Das weltliche Recht im Alten Testament*. Gütersloh:
    Bortelsmann, 1927.

Joüon, P. *Grammaire de l'Hebreu Biblique*. Rome: Institut
    Biblique Pontifical, 1923.

Kaster, J. "Education, O.T." *IDB* 2, 27-34.

Kaufmann, Y. "The Biblical Age." Pp. 1-92 in *Great Ages and
    Ideas of the Jewish People*. Ed. L. W. Schwartz. New
    York: Random House, 1956.

_____. *The Religion of Israel*. Trans. and abridged by M.
    Greenberg. Chicago: University of Chicago, 1960.

_____. *Sepher Shopheṭim*. Jerusalem: Kiryat Sepher, 1964.

_____. *Toledot ha-emunah ha-Yisraelit*. 8 vols. Jerusalem/
    Tel-Aviv: Bialik Institute-Dvir, 1937-69.

Kilian, R. "Apodiktisches und kasuistisches Recht im Licht
    ägyptischer Analogien." *BZ* 7 (1963) 185-202.

_____. *Literarkritische und formgeschichtliche Unter-
    suchung des Heiligkeitsgesetzes*. Bonn: Peter Hanstein,
    1963.

King, L. W. *Babylonian Magic and Sorcery*. London: Luzac, 1896.

Kitchen, K. A. *Ancient Orient and Old Testament*. Chicago:
    Inner-Varsity, 1968.

Knight, D. A. "The Understanding of 'Sitz im Leben' in Form
    Criticism." Pp. 105-25 in *Society of Biblical Literature
    1974 Seminar Papers* 1. Ed. G. MacRae. Cambridge: Society
    of Biblical Literature, 1974.

Knudtzon, J. A., et al. *Die El-Amarna Tafeln*. 2 vols. Vorder-
    asiatische Bibliothek 2. Aalen: Otto Zeller, 1964 (reprint
    of 1915 edition).

Koch, K. *The Growth of the Biblical Tradition*. New York:
    Scribner's, 1969.

Koenig, J. "L'activité hermeneutique des scribes dans la
    transmission du texte de l'Ancien Testament." *RHR* 161
    (1962) 141-74, 162 (1962) 1-43.

Köhler, L. "Justice in the Gate." Pp. 127-50 in *Hebrew Man*.
    Nashville: Abingdon, 1956.

Kornfeld, W. *Studien zum Heiligkeitsgesetz*. Wien: Herder,
    1952.

Koschaker, P., and Ungnad, A. *Hammurabi's Gesetz*. Leipzig:
    Edward Pfeiffer, 1923.

Kramer, S. N. *The Sumerians: Their History, Culture and
    Character*. Chicago: University of Chicago, 1970.

Kramer, S. N. "Sumerian Literary Texts from Nippur." *AASOR* 23
    (1944) 11-40.

Kraus, F. R. *Ein Edikt des Königs Ammi-Ṣaduqa von Babylon*.
    Studia et Documenta 5. Leiden: Brill, 1958.

_____. "Ein zentrales Problem des altmesopotamischen
    Rechtes: Was ist der Codex Hammu-rabi?" *Genava* 8 (1960)
    283-96.

Kraus, H.-J. *Worship in Israel*. Richmond: John Knox, 1966.

Kutscher, E. Y. *The Language and Linguistic Background of the
    Isaiah Scroll* (Hebrew). Jerusalem: Magnes, 1959.

Lambert, M. "La literature Sumerienne." *RA* 55 (1961) 177-96,
    56 (1962) 81-90.

_____. "Les reformes d'Urukagina." *RA* 50 (1956) 169-84.

Lambert, W. G. *Babylonian Wisdom Literature*. Oxford:
    Clarendon, 1960.

Landsberger, B. "Die babylonischen Termini für Gesetz und
    Recht." Pp. 219-34 in *Symbolae ad iura orientis antiqui
    pertinentes Paulo Koschaker dedicatae*. Ed. T. Folkers.
    Studia et Documenta 2. Leiden: Brill, 1939.

_____. "Jungfräulichkeit: Ein Beitrag zum Thema 'Beilager
    und Eheschliessung' (mit einem Anhang: Neue Lesungen und
    Deutungen im Gesetzbuch von Ešnunna)." Pp. 41-105 in
    Symbolae juridicae et historicae Martino David dedicatae.
    Vol. 2. Ed. J. A. Ankum, R. Feenstra and W. F. Leemans.
    Leiden: Brill, 1968.

Langlamet, F. "Israel et l'habitant du pays." *RB* 76 (1969)
    321-51, 481-507.

Leemans, W. F. *The Old Babylonian Merchant: His Business and
    His Social Position*. Leiden: Brill, 1950.

_____. "Some Aspects of Theft and Robbery in Old Babylonian
    Documents." *RSO* 32 (1957) 661-66.

Leichty, E. *The Omen Series Šumma Izbu*. Texts from Cuneiform
    Sources 4. New York: Augustin, 1970.

Lestienne, M. "Les dix 'paroles' et le décalogue." *RB* 79
    (1972) 484-510.

Lewy, H. "Gleanings from a New Volume of Nuzi Texts." *OrNS* 10
    (1941) 201-22.

Lewy, I. "Dating of Covenant Code Sections on Humaneness and
    Righteousness." *VT* 7 (1957) 322-36.

L'Hour, J.   "Une legislation criminelle dans le Deutéronome."
     Biblica 44 (1963) 1-28.

_____.   "Les interdits *to'eba* dans le Deutéronome."   *RB* 71
     (1964) 481-503.

Liedke, G.   *Gestalt und Bezeichnung alttestamentlicher Rechts-
     sätze.*   WMANT 39.   Neukirchen: Neukirchener Verlag, 1971.

Lohfink, N.   *Das Hauptgebot.*   AnBib 20.   Rome: Pontifical
     Biblical Institute, 1963.

Loewenstamm, S.   "משפט המקרא, משפט."   (Hebrew).   Pp. 625-28 in
     Encyclopaedia Biblica 5.   Jerusalem: Bialik Institute,
     1968.

Luckenbill, D. D.   *Ancient Records of Assyria and Babylonia.*
     2 vols.   Chicago: University of Chicago, 1927.

MacKenzie, R. A. F.   "The Formal Aspect of Ancient Near Eastern
     Law."   Pp. 31-44 in *The Seed of Wisdom: Essays in Honour
     of T. J. Meek.*   Ed. W. S. McCullough.   Toronto: University
     of Toronto, 1964.

_____.   "The Forms of Israelite Law."   Ph.D. dissertation.
     Rome: Pontifical Biblical Institute, 1949.

_____.   Review of *Wesen und Herkunft* by E. Gerstenberger.
     CBQ 28 (1966) 500-501.

Malamat, A.   "The Period of the Judges."   Pp. 129-63 in *The
     World History of the Jewish People*, III: *Judges*.   Ed. B.
     Mazar.   New Brunswick: Rutgers University, 1971.

Malfroy, J.   "Sagesse et loi dans le Deutéronome."   *VT* 15
     (1965) 49-65.

Marzal, A.   "Mari Clauses in 'Casuistic' and 'Apodictic'
     Styles."   *CBQ* 33 (1971) 333-64, 492-509.

McCarthy, D. J.   *Treaty and Covenant.*   AnBib 21.   Rome:
     Pontifical Biblical Institute, 1963.

McKane, W.   *Prophets and Wise Men.*   SBT 44.   London: SCM, 1965.

_____.   *Proverbs.*   The Old Testament Library.   Philadelphia:
     Westminster, 1970.

Meek, T. J.   "The Asyndeton Clause in the Code of Hammurabi."
     JNES 5 (1946) 64-72.

_____.   "The Code of Hammurabi."   *ANET*, 163-80.

_____.   "The Co-ordinate Adverbial Clause in Hebrew."
     JAOS 49 (1929) 156-59.

_____.   *Hebrew Origins.*   New York: Harper & Brothers, 1960.

Meek, T. J.   "Lapses of Old Testament Translators." *JAOS* 58
    (1938) 122-29.

_____.   "The Middle Assyrian Laws." *ANET*, 180-88.

_____.   "The Syntax of the Sentence in Hebrew." *JBL* 64
    (1945) 1-13.

Mendenhall, G. E.   "Ancient Oriental and Biblical Law." *BA* 17
    (1954) 49-76. Reprinted, pp. 3-21 in his *Law and Covenant
    in Israel and the Ancient Near East*. Pittsburgh: The
    Presbyterian Board of Colportage of Western Pennsylvania,
    1955. Also in *BAR* 3, 3-24.

Merendino, R.   *Das deuteronomische Gesetz*. BBB 31. Bonn:
    Hanstein, 1969.

Michaeli, F.   *Les livres des Chroniques, d'Esdras et de Néhémie*.
    Neuchâtel: Delachaux, 1967.

Michaud, H.   *Sur la pierre et l'argile*. Neuchâtel: Delachaux,
    1958.

Montet, P.   *Egypt and the Bible*. Philadelphia: Fortress, 1968.

Morgenstern, J.   "The Book of the Covenant." *HUCA* 5 (1928)
    1-151; 7 (1930) 19-258; 8/9 (1931/32) 1-150, 741-46;
    33 (1962) 59-105.

Mowinckel, S.   *Le Décalogue*. Paris: L. Alcan, 1927.

Muilenburg, J.   "Form Criticism and Beyond." *JBL* 88 (1969)
    1-18.

_____.   "The Linguistic and Rhetorical Usages of the
    Particle כי in the Old Testament." *HUCA* 32 (1961) 135-61.

_____.   *The Way of Israel: Biblical Faith and Ethics*.
    New York: Harper Torch Books, 1965.

Müller, D. H.   *Die Gesetze Hammurabis*. Wien: Alfred Holder,
    1903.

Murphy, R. E.   "Form Criticism and Wisdom Literature." *CBQ* 31
    (1969) 475-83.

Myers, J. M.   *Ezra-Nehemiah*. AB 14. New York: Doubleday,
    1965.

_____.   *I and II Chronicles*. AB 12,13. New York: Double-
    day, 1965.

Neufeld, E.   *The Hittite Laws*. London: Luzac, 1951.

Nicholson, E. W.   *Deuteronomy and Tradition*. Philadelphia:
    Fortress, 1967.

Nielsen, E. *The Ten Commandments in New Perspective*. SBT 2/7.
    London: SCM, 1968.

Noth, M. "Das Amt des 'Richters Israels.'" Pp. 404-17 in
    A. Bertholet Festschrift. Ed. W. Baumgartner, et al.
    Tübingen: J. C. B. Mohr, 1950.

_____. *Exodus*. The Old Testament Library. Philadelphia:
    Westminster, 1962.

_____. *The History of Israel*. New York: Harper and Row,
    1960.

_____. *The Laws in the Pentateuch and Other Studies*.
    Philadelphia: Fortress, 1967.

_____. *Leviticus*. The Old Testament Library. Philadelphia:
    Westminster, 1965.

_____. *Numbers*. The Old Testament Library. Philadelphia:
    Westminster, 1968.

_____. *Überlieferungsgeschichtliche Studien*. Tübingen:
    Max Niemeyer, 1957.

Nougayrol, J. "Sagesse (R.S. 22.439)." *Ugaritica* 5 (1968)
    273-90.

Oppenheim, A. L. *Ancient Mesopotamia*. Chicago: University of
    Chicago, 1968.

Orlinsky, H. J. (ed.). *Notes on the New Translation of the
    Torah*. Philadelphia: Jewish Publications Society of
    America, 1969.

_____. "The Tribal System of Israel and Related Groups in
    the Period of the Judges." Pp. 375-87 in *Studies and
    Essays in Honor of A. A. Neuman*. Ed. M. Ben-Horin.
    Leiden: Brill, 1962. Also in *Oriens Antiquus* 1 (1962)
    11-20. Reprinted, pp. 66-77 in his *Essays in Biblical
    Culture and Bible Translation*. New York: KTAV, 1974.

Östborn, G. *Tora in the Old Testament*. Lund: H. Ohlssons,
    1945.

Paul, S. *Studies in the Book of the Covenant in Light of
    Cuneiform and Biblical Law*. VTSup 18. Leiden: Brill,
    1970.

Pedersen, J. *Israel: Its Life and Culture*. Vols. 1-4.
    London: Oxford University, 1959.

Perdue, L. G. *Wisdom and Cult*. SBLDS 30. Missoula: Scholars
    Press, 1977.

Perrin, N. *What is Redaction Criticism?* Guides to Biblical
    Scholarship. Philadelphia: Fortress, 1973.

Petschow, H. "Stilformen antiker Gesetze und Rechtssamlungen."
     ZSS 82 (1965) 24-38.

Pettinato, G. *Die Ölwahrsagung bei den Babyloniern*. Studi
     Semitici 22. Rome: Istituto di Studi del Vicino Oriente,
     1966.

Pfeiffer, R. H. *Introduction to the Old Testament*. New York:
     Harper and Brothers, 1948.

_____, and Speiser, E. A. *One Hundred New Selected Nuzi
     Tablets*. AASOR 16. New Haven: American Schools of
     Oriental Research, 1936.

Phillips, A. *Ancient Israel's Criminal Law*. Oxford: Basil
     Blackwell, 1970.

van der Ploeg, J. "Studies in Hebrew Law." *CBQ* 12 (1950)
     248-59, 416-27; 13 (1951) 28-43, 164-71, 296-307.

Poebel, A. *Das appositionell bestimmte Pronomen der 1. Pers.
     Sing. in den westsemitischen Inschriften und im Alten
     Testament*. AS 3. Chicago: University of Chicago, 1932.

Posener, G. "Literature." Pp. 220-55 in *The Legacy of Egypt*.
     Ed. J. R. Harris. Oxford: Clarendon, 1971.

Pritchard, J. B. (ed.). *Ancient Near Eastern Texts Relating
     to the Old Testament*. 3rd ed. Princeton: Princeton
     University, 1969.

Puech, E., and Rofé, A. "L'inscription de la citadelle
     d'Amman." *RB* 80 (1973) 531-46.

von Rad, G. *Deuteronomy*. The Old Testament Library.
     Philadelphia: Westminster, 1966.

_____. "Deuteronomy." *IDB* 1, 831-38.

_____. "The Form-Critical Problem of the Hexateuch." Pp.
     1-78 in his *The Problem of the Hexateuch and Other Essays*.
     Edinburgh: Oliver & Boyd, 1965.

_____. *Old Testament Theology*. Vols. 1-2. Edinburgh/
     London: Oliver & Boyd, 1962, 1965.

_____. *Studies in Deuteronomy*. SBT 9. Chicago: Regnery,
     1953.

_____. *Wisdom in Israel*. London: SCM, 1972.

Rankin, O. S. *Israel's Wisdom Literature*. New York:
     Schocken, 1969.

Rapaport, I. "The Origins of Hebrew Law." *PEQ* 73 (1941)
     158-67.

Rast, W. E. *Tradition History and the Old Testament*. Guides
     to Biblical Scholarship. Philadelphia: Fortress, 1972.

Rendtorff, R. *Die Gesetze in der Priesterschrift*. Göttingen: Vandenhoeck & Ruprecht, 1954.

Reventlow, H. G. *Gebot und Predigt im Dekalog*. Gütersloh: Gerd Mohn, 1962.

_____. *Das Heiligkeitsgesetz*. WMANT 6. Neukirchen: Neukirchener Verlag, 1961.

Richter, W. *Recht und Ethos*. SANT 15. Munich: Kösel Verlag, 1966.

Ringgren, H. *Israelite Religion*. Philadelphia: Fortress, 1966.

Rofé, A. "The Strata of the Law about the Centralization of Worship in Deuteronomy and the History of the Deuteronomic Movement." VTSup 22 (1971) 221-26.

Rosenthal, F. "Canaanite and Aramaic Inscriptions." *ANET*, 653-662.

Rowley, H. H. "The Marriage of Ruth." Pp. 171-94 in *The Servant of the Lord and Other Essays on the Old Testament*. Oxford: Blackwell, 1965.

Rozenberg, M. S. "The Stem *SPṬ*: An Investigation of Biblical and Extra-Biblical Sources." Ph.D. dissertation. Philadelphia: University of Pennsylvania, 1963.

Ryle, H. E. *The Books of Ezra and Nehemiah*. Cambridge Bible for Schools and Colleges. Cambridge: University Press, 1907.

Sadaqa, A., and R. (eds.). *Jewish and Samaritan Version of the Pentateuch*. Jerusalem: Rubin Mass, 1961-64.

Sanders, J. A. *The Dead Sea Psalms Scroll*. Ithaca: Cornell University, 1967.

Sandmel, S. *The Enjoyment of Scripture*. New York: Oxford University, 1972.

_____. *The Hebrew Scriptures*. New York: Knopf, 1963.

Sarna, N. *Understanding Genesis*. New York: Schocken, 1970.

Scheil, V. *Recueil de lois assyriennes*. Paris: Paul Geuthner, 1921.

_____. "Les nourices en Babylonie et le #194 du Code." *RA* 11 (1914) 175-82.

Scholem, G. "Commandments, Reasons for." *EncJud* 5, 783-92.

Schulz, H. *Das Todesrecht im Alten Testament*. BZAW 114. Berlin: A. Topelmann, 1969.

Scott, R. B. Y. *Proverbs-Ecclesiastes*. AB 18. New York: Doubleday, 1965.

Scott, R. B. Y. *The Way of Wisdom in the Old Testament*. New
    York: Macmillan, 1971.

Seeligmann, I. L. "Indications of Editorial Alteration and
    Adaptation in the Massoretic Text and the Septuagint."
    VT 11 (1961) 201-21.

_____. *The Septuagint Version of Isaiah*. Leiden: Brill,
    1948.

Seidl, E. "Law-Egyptian." *The Encyclopaedia of the Social
    Sciences* 9 (1933) 209-11.

Seitz, G. *Redaktionsgeschichtliche Studien zum Deuteronomium*.
    BWANT 13. Stuttgart: Kohlhammer, 1971.

Shaffer, A. "Sumerian Sources of Tablet XII of the Epic of
    Gilgamesh." Ph.D. dissertation. Philadelphia: University
    of Pennsylvania, 1963.

Simpson, W. K. *The Literature of Ancient Egypt*. New Haven:
    Yale University, 1973.

Smith, J. M. P. *The Origin and History of Hebrew Law*.
    Chicago: University of Chicago, 1931.

von Soden, W. *Akkadisches Handwörterbuch*. Wiesbaden:
    Harrassowitz, 1959-.

_____. *Grundriss der akkadischen Grammatik*. AnOr 33.
    Rome: Pontifical Biblical Institute, 1952.

Sommer, D. *Les inscriptions araméennes de Sfirê*. Paris:
    Imprimerie Nationale, 1958.

Speiser, E. A. "Authority and Law in Mesopotamia." *JAOS*
    Supp. 17 (1954) 8-15. Reprinted, pp. 313-23 in *Oriental
    and Biblical Studies--Collected Writings of E. A. Speiser*.
    Ed. J. J. Finkelstein and M. Greenberg. Philadelphia:
    University of Pennsylvania, 1967.

_____. "The Case of the Obliging Servant." *JCS* 8 (1954)
    98-105. Reprinted, pp. 344-66 in *Oriental and Biblical
    Studies--Collected Writings of E. A. Speiser*. Ed. J. J.
    Finkelstein and M. Greenberg. Philadelphia: University
    of Pennsylvania, 1967.

_____. "Cuneiform Law and the History of Civilization."
    PAPS 107 (1963) 536-41.

_____. "New Kirkuk Documents Relating to Family Laws."
    AASOR 10 (1930) 1-74.

_____. "The Manner of the King." Pp. 280-87 in *The World
    History of the Jewish People*, III: *Judges*. Ed. B. Mazar.
    New Brunswick: Rutgers University, 1971.

Staerk, W. *Das Deuteronomium, sein Inhalt und seine liter-
    arische Form*. Leipzig: Hinrichs, 1894.

Stamm, J. J., and Andrew, M. E. *The Ten Commandments in Recent Research*. SBT 2/2. London: SCM, 1967.

Steele, F. R. "Lipit-Ishtar Law Code." *AJA* 52 (1948) 425-50.

Stein, H. "What is Redaktionsgeschichte?" *JBL* 88 (1969) 45-56.

Steurnagel, C. *Der Rahmen des Deuteronomiums*. Halle a.S.: Wischan & Wettengel, 1894.

Szlechter, E. "Le code de Lipit-Ishtar." *RA* 51 (1957) 57-82, 177-96; 52 (1958) 74-90.

_____. "Effets de l'absence (volontaire) en droit assyro-babylonien." *OrNS* 34 (1965) 289-311.

_____. "Effets de la captivité en droit assyro-babylonien." *RA* 57 (1963) 181-92; 58 (1964) 23-35.

_____. "Essai d'explication des clauses: *muttatam gullubu, abbuttam šakânu* et *abbuttam gullubu*." *ArOr* 17 (1949) 402-12.

_____. *Les lois d'Ešnunna*. Paris: Sirey, 1954.

_____. *Tablettes juridiques de la 1re dynastie de Babylone*. Paris: Sirey, 1958.

Ta-Shma, I. M. "Karet." *EncJud* 10, 788-89.

Théodoridès, A. "A propos de la loi dans l'Egypte pharaonique." *RIDA* 14 (1967) 107-52.

_____. "La loi dans l'Egypte pharaonique." *RIDA* 12 (1965) 492-93.

Thompson, R. C. *The Epic of Gilgamish*. London: Luzac, 1928.

Thureau-Dangin, F. *Une relation de la huitième campagne de Sargon*. TCL 3. Paris: Geuthner, 1912.

_____. "Textes de Mari." *RA* 33 (1936) 169-79.

_____. *Textes mathématiques babyloniens*. Leiden: Brill, 1938.

Tigay, J. "Literary-Critical Studies in the Gilgamesh Epic: An Assyriological Contribution to Biblical Literary Criticism." Ph.D. dissertation. New Haven: Yale University, 1971.

_____. "An Empirical Basis for the Documentary Hypothesis." *JBL* 94 (1975) 329-42.

de Tillesse, G. M. "Sections 'tu' et sections 'vous' dans le Deuteronome." *VT* 12 (1962) 47-86.

Torralba, J. G. "Decalogo ritual, Ex. 34, 10-26." *EB* 20
    (1961) 407-21.

_____. "Motivación deuteronómica del Precepto del Sabat."
    EB 29 (1970) 73-99.

Tsevat, M. "The Basic Meaning of the Biblical Sabbath."
    ZAW 84 (1972) 447-59.

Tucker, G. M. *Form Criticism of the Old Testament*. Guides to
    Biblical Scholarship. Philadelphia: Fortress, 1971.

Uitti, R. W. "The Motive Clause in Old Testament Law." Ph.D.
    dissertation. Chicago: Lutheran School of Theology, 1973.

de Vaux, R. *Ancient Israel: Its Life and Institutions*. New
    York: McGraw-Hill, 1961.

Vink, J. G. "The Date and Origin of the Priestly Code in the
    Old Testament." *OTS* 15 (1969) 1-144.

Virolleaud, C. *L'astrologie chaldéenne*. Paris: Paul Geuthner,
    1910.

Wagner, V. *Rechtssätze in gebundener Sprache und Rechts-
    satzreihen im israelitischen Recht*. BZAW 127. Berlin:
    de Gruyter, 1972.

von Waldow, H. E. "Some Thoughts on Old Testament Form Criti-
    cism." Pp. 587-600 in *Society of Biblical Literature 1971
    Seminar Papers* 2. Cambridge: Society of Biblical Litera-
    ture, 1971.

Watts, J. D. W. "Infinitive Absolute as Imperative and the
    Interpretation of Exodus 20:8." *ZAW* 74 (1962) 141-45.

Weidner, E. "Hof- und Harems-Erlasse assyrischer Könige aus
    dem 2. Jahrtausend v. Chr." *AfO* 17 (1956) 257-93.

Weidner, E. F. *Politische Dokumente aus Kleinasien*. Boghazköi
    Studien 8-9. Leipzig, 1923.

Weinfeld, M. "The Book of Deuteronomy in its Relation to
    Wisdom" (Hebrew). Pp. 89-111 in *Yehezkel Kaufmann
    Jubilee Volume*. Ed. M. Haran. Jerusalem: Magnes, 1960.

_____. "Covenant." *EncJud* 5, 1012-22.

_____. "Deuteronomy." *EncJud* 5, 1573-82.

_____. *Deuteronomy and the Deuteronomic School*. Oxford:
    Clarendon, 1972.

_____. "God the Creator in Gen. 1 and in the Prophecy of
    Second Isaiah" (Hebrew). *Tarbiz* 37 (1968) 105-32 (Eng.
    summary, pp. I-II).

Weinfeld, M. "The Origin of the Apodictic Law." *VT* 23 (1973)
     63-75.

_____. "The Origin of the Humanism in Deuteronomy." *JBL* 80
     (1961) 241-47.

Weingreen, J. "The Case of the Daughters of Zelophechad."
     VT 16 (1966) 518-22.

_____. "The Case of the Woodgatherer." *VT* 16 (1966) 361-64.

Weippert, M. *The Settlement of the Israelite Tribes in Pales-
     tine.* SBT 2/21. London: SCM, 1971.

Wellhausen, J. *Prolegomena to the History of Ancient Israel.*
     Meridian Books. Cleveland: World Publishing, 1961.

Weiser, A. *The Old Testament: Its Formation and Development.*
     New York: Association, 1963.

_____. *The Psalms.* The Old Testament Library. Phila-
     delphia: Westminster, 1962.

Whybray, R. N. *The Intellectual Tradition in the Old Testament.*
     BZAW 135. Berlin/New York: de Gruyter, 1974.

Wilcoxen, J. "Narrative." Pp. 57-98 in *Old Testament Form
     Criticism.* Ed. J. H. Hayes. San Antonio: Trinity Uni-
     versity, 1974.

Williams, J. G. "Concerning One of the Apodictic Formulas."
     VT 14 (1964) 484-89.

_____. "Addenda." *VT* 15 (1965) 113.

Williams, R. J. "Egypt and Israel." Pp. 257-90 in *The Legacy
     of Egypt.* Ed. J. R. Harris. Oxford: Clarendon, 1971.

_____. "Scribal Training in Ancient Egypt." *JAOS* 92 (1972)
     214-21.

Wilson, J. A. *The Burden of Egypt.* Chicago: University of
     Chicago, 1951.

_____. "Authority and Law in the Ancient Orient." *JAOS*
     Supp. 17 (1954) 1-7.

Wiseman, D. J. *The Alalakh Tablets.* London: British Institute
     of Archaeology of Ankara, 1953.

_____. "The Laws of Hammurabi Again." *JSS* 7 (1962) 161-72.

_____. "The Vassal Treaties of Esarhaddon." *Iraq* 20 (1958)
     1-100.

Wolff, H. W. "Die Begründungen der prophetischen Heils- und
     Unheilssprüche." *ZAW* 52 (1934) 1-21.

Yaron, R. "Forms in the Laws of Eshnunna." *RIDA* 9 (1962)
     137-53.

_____. *The Laws of Eshnunna*. Jerusalem: Magnes, 1969.

Zimmerli, W. "Ich bin Jahwe." Pp. 179-209 in *Geschichte und
     Altes Testament* [A. Alt Festschrift]. BHT 16. Tübingen:
     J. C. B. Mohr, 1953. Reprinted, pp. 11-40 in his *Gottes
     Offenbarung*. TBü 19. München: Chr. Kaiser, 1963.

A

Ad hoc commands, 77-78, 96, 221
Admonitions of an Egyptian Sage, 169
Advice to a Prince, 7
Aḥiqar, 170
Amenemhet, 169
Amenemopet, 38, 169
A New Moralizing Text, 169
Ani, 169
"Apodictic"; see *sub* Legal forms

B

Book of the Covenant, 18-19, 21-22, 35, 68, 87-89, 98-103,
    123-125, 173, 194, 196-197, 204, 221

C

Carthage Tariff, 30
"Casuistic"; see *sub* Legal forms
Counsels of Wisdom, 38, 168
Covenant renewal ceremony, 4, 25-27, 125-126, 220
Cultic Decalogue, 29, 89-90, 98-103, 125-126, 203-204, 221
Cuneiform legal corpora, 29-30
    Eshnunna, 30-32, 34-36, 154, 157
    Hammurabi, 30, 32, 34-35, 37, 154-162, 167, 170-174, 223-224
    Hittite, 30, 32, 34-36, 155
    Lipit-Ishtar, 30, 209
    Middle-Assyrian, 30, 32, 34, 37, 155, 162-167, 170-171,
        173-174, 209, 223
    Neo-Babylonian, 30, 32, 34, 36, 37, 155
    Ur-Nammu, 30
    YBC 2177, 30
    nature of, 173-175

D

Decalogue, 24, 27, 76, 86-87, 98-100, 125, 194-196, 198, 203,
    221
Deuteronomic Code, 18, 21, 24, 29, 35, 92-95, 98-104, 111-112,
    114-116, 123-124, 126, 197-198, 200-204, 221
Duauf, 169

E

Edict of Ammiṣaduqa, 171, 208
Eshmunazar of Sidon, 207
Explicative notes, 66, 224

F

Form criticism, biblical, 5-10
    cuneiform literature, 32

329